# The
# General Strike

May 1926

## CHRISTOPHER FARMAN

Rupert Hart-Davis   London

Granada Publishing Limited
First published 1972 by Rupert Hart-Davis Ltd
3 Upper James Street London W1R 4BP

Copyright © 1972 by Christopher Farman

ISBN 0 246 64071 5
Printed in Great Britain by Willmer Brothers Limited, Birkenhead

'*Our old country can be well proud of itself, as during the last nine days there has been a strike in which four million people have been affected, not a shot has been fired and no one killed, it shows what a wonderful people we are.*'
                    King George V writing in his diary on 12 May 1926.

'*You're the wonder of the world. If this had happened in America there'd have been more than a thousand deaths by now.*'
American comedian Will Rogers quoted in the *Daily Express*, 14 May 1926.

'*Little more than a nine days' wonder, costing Great Britain tens of millions and leaving other nations asking whether it was a baulked revolution or play-acting on a stupendous scale.*'
                    Beatrice Webb writing in her diary on 14 May 1926.

# Contents

| | | |
|---|---|---:|
| *List of Illustrations* | | ix |
| *Acknowledgements* | | xi |
| 1 | The Healer | 1 |
| 2 | Ishmael and The Golden Calf | 13 |
| 3 | Armistice | 28 |
| 4 | The Samuel Report | 51 |
| 5 | 'Not a Penny off the Pay, Not a Second on the Day' | 68 |
| 6 | 'A Case of Bare Fists' | 89 |
| 7 | Battle Orders | 114 |
| 8 | The Fourth Estate | 124 |
| 9 | Stomping at Savoy Hill | 143 |
| 10 | The Rank-and-File | 152 |
| 11 | Reluctant Revolutionaries | 167 |
| 12 | A Struggle of Exhaustion | 183 |
| 13 | Liberals to the Left and Liberals to the Right | 203 |
| 14 | Extrication | 214 |
| 15 | The Surrender | 228 |
| 16 | Spoils of War | 244 |
| *Appendices* | | 263 |
| *References* | | 281 |
| *Bibliography* | | 291 |
| *Index* | | 295 |

# List of Illustrations

*Between pages 132 and 133*

Before the strike: Ramsay MacDonald with A. J. Cook.
Herbert Smith, President of the Miners' Federation.
Volunteers working the railways during the General Strike.
A lady volunteer transport driver.
Undergraduate volunteers operating the signal box at Bletchley station.
Volunteer porter at King's Cross station.
The Civil Constabulary Reserve recruited from Territorial Army units.
The teams in the Police v. Strikers football match at Plymouth, 10 May 1926.
An armoured car in Oxford Street.
A food convoy passing through Canning Town under military escort.
Mounted police with batons clearing the road after an outbreak of violence.
A van overturned by strikers in Blackfriars Road.
The attempt to wreck the 'Flying Scotsman' with 300 passengers aboard.
The First Brigade of Guards returning to Aldershot after the General Strike.
Stanley Baldwin in his hour of triumph at 10 Downing Street.

For my parents.

# *Acknowledgements*

My thanks are due to many people, too numerous to mention, for the help and encouragement they have given me during the preparation of this book. I owe a particularly heavy debt to the following : Mrs Tydfil Bennison, A. J. Cook's daughter; Miss Louise Cook, A. J. Cook's sister; the Rt. Hon. Lord Citrine; Mr. E. Brown, Chief Librarian of the Trades Union Congress; the staff of the British Library of Political & Economic Science. I would also like to thank the following publishers for permission to quote copyright passages : Oxford University Press, Longmans, Hutchinson, Weidenfeld and Nicolson, Constable, Hodder and Stoughton and Macmillan. I should like to express my gratitude, above all, to Miss Mary Hill, who was forced to endure the anxieties and perplexities of the Nine Days for more than two years.

Chapter One

# *The Healer*

'I have but one ambition during my term of office... I want to see that the people of this country have realised the truth of what I have been attempting to express. I want them to realise that we in the Unionist party are as anxious as anyone who speaks in the name of Socialism to do all in our power for the betterment of our people... I want to see in the next year or two the beginning of a better unity between all classes of our people. If there are those who want to fight the class war we will take up the challenge, and we will beat them by the hardness of our heads and the largeness of our hearts. I want to leave this country, when my term ends, in better heart than it has been for years. I want to be a healer and I believe that as these things have to be done through the instrumentality of parties, the Unionist party is the one upon which the country must lean if it desires these ends.'

Stanley Baldwin, speaking at Edinburgh in July 1923. (From the *Manchester Guardian*, 28 July 1923.)

'The new P.M. caught the public imagination...almost immediately that he took office. His placidity, his common sense, his moderation, his modesty and his obvious sincerity caused people to say, "This is the man, a typical Englishman, for whom we have been looking for so long. We are sick of Welshmen and lawyers, the best brains and supermen. We want the old type of English statesman, who is fair-minded, judicious and responsible, rather than the man who is so clever that he thinks ahead of everyone else." The result was that the Syndicate Press (both Carmelite House and Beaverbrook's papers) realised that it would be a commercially bad proposition to embarrass the sort of government which the people wanted, at any rate for the moment. The result has been roses, roses all the way so as to make one quite nervous, remembering the old warning about "beware of him of whom all men speak well".'

Lord Winterton, Under-Secretary at the India Office, in a letter to Lord Lytton, Governor–General of Bengal, 11 September 1923.

At 5.30 p.m. on 4 November 1924, King George V brought the first Labour Government to a formal but gracious end. The King assured his retiring Prime Minister 'that he would always regard him as a friend and that, whether in office or out of office, His Majesty trusted that he could always look to him to do his best for the country and for the Throne'.[1] The doubts and misgivings which the King had felt ten months earlier, when he had been obliged to send for the leader of the Labour party and ask him to form a Government—'dear Grandmama...I wonder what she would have thought'—had been entirely dispelled. James Ramsay MacDonald and his colleagues had proved quite as able to adopt civilised behaviour and knee breeches as any Conservative or Liberal administration. There was the occasional disquieting incident, as when a victory rally at the Royal Albert Hall, presided over by MacDonald himself, broke into the *Marseillaise* and the *Red Flag*. But the leader of the Labour party explained the problem very frankly. If he had attempted to prevent the *Red Flag* being sung on such an occasion, a riot would inevitably have ensued 'They had got into the way of singing this song,' Lord Stamfordham, the King's private secretary recorded, 'and it will be by degrees that he [Mr MacDonald] hopes to break down this habit.'[2]

Certain of MacDonald's colleagues had continued to make intemperate speeches, but in view of the Socialist principles which all members of the Labour party were supposed to proclaim, ten months of Labour Government had been anything but revolutionary. The eminently trustworthy Asquith, holding the balance of power with 158 Liberal votes, had helped MacDonald to make sure of that. It was really rather unfortunate, therefore, that MacDonald had spoiled such a promising experiment with his precipitate handling of the Bolsheviks. First, there had been his insistence on establishing full diplomatic and trade relations with Communist Russia. His Majesty had felt constrained to point out how abhorrent it would be for him to receive any representative who had been connected, directly or indirectly, with the abominable murder of Tsar Nicholas, his own first cousin. Happily, MacDonald had entirely understood the King's feelings and had been content to settle for a Russian minister instead of an ambassador, thus confining His Majesty's own dealings with Bolshevism to the formal minimum. Less amenable to MacDonald's Russian initiative had been the Conservative Opposition and many of the nation's leading newspapers.

Secondly, MacDonald had become gratuitously enmeshed in the affairs of Britain's own miniscule Communist party. In the summer an insolent article in *Workers' Weekly*, the party paper, had urged

2

members of the armed forces to help the workers smash capitalism. With all due propriety and patriotism, the Attorney-General had initiated proceedings under the Incitement to Mutiny Act of 1795 against the paper's editor, J. R. Campbell. Predictably, MacDonald had been assailed by his usual Left-wing critics—James Maxton, the unstable Clydesider, and George Lansbury, the fervent Cockney moralist. The subsequent discovery that, not only had Campbell been wounded and decorated for outstanding gallantry in the Great War, but that he was only *acting* editor of *Workers' Weekly*, had led the Attorney-General to withdraw the prosecution.

Already cool towards the terms of the two treaties which MacDonald had signed with the Russians and singularly unimpressed by the Attorney-General's explanation, the Conservative Opposition charged the Prime Minister with interfering in the course of justice to appease the extremists in his party. Labour's wild men were a problem His Majesty knew all about. Had not MacDonald at the very outset of his premiership spoken 'very openly' to the King of 'the very difficult position he was in vis-à-vis his own extremists'?[3] The King also knew that most members of the Labour Party were just as sceptical and suspicious of Bolshevism as most members of the Tory party. Only a month before, Labour's annual conference had rejected Communist affiliation and resolved that individual Communists were no longer eligible for endorsement as Labour candidates in any election. Such forthrightness against the forces of darkness did not, however, prevent the Conservatives from tabling a motion of censure on the Government for its handling of the Campbell Case. Even the Liberals suspended their benevolent toleration of Labour to the extent of tabling an amendment calling for a Select Committee of inquiry into the affair. Regarding both motion and amendment as personal affronts, MacDonald proclaimed that a majority for either would be regarded by him as a vote of no confidence. The Conservatives dropped their own motion in favour of the Liberal amendment, which was inevitably carried against Labour's voting minority. The following day MacDonald asked the King for a dissolution and the third General Election in three years was held on 29 October 1924.

By a curious—and for MacDonald, unfortunate—chance, just four days before polling the newspapers published a letter purportedly from Gregory Zinoviev, President of the Communist International, to the central committee of the British Communist party. This stressed the importance of the Anglo-Russian Treaties and went on to urge the formation of a British Red Army directorate and the creation of revolutionary cells in the armed forces as the necessary prelude to a Bolshevik insurrection in Britain. As if to underline its

3

authenticity, published alongside it was a letter of protest from the Foreign Office to the Russian chargé d'affaires in London. It came as no great surprise, therefore, to the King, or to those less exalted, to find, when the election results were published, that the Conservatives had a vast majority: 415 seats compared with Labour's 152 and the Liberals' 42. The Conservatives had gained 157 new seats; Labour had lost 42, and the Liberals, decimated beyond revival, had lost 116, with the redoubtable Asquith himself going down to humiliating defeat at the hands of his Labour opponent at Paisley. Thus MacDonald's melancholy attendance on His Majesty on the eve of Guy Fawkes Day. Elegant, courtly, grave—one might almost say a member of the nobility if one did not know better—the leader of the Labour party bade his farewell. 'I like him,' noted the King in his diary that evening, 'and have always found him quite straight.'

One hour later the King sent for Stanley Baldwin and entrusted him with the formation of a new Government. Noticeably absent from this meeting were the subtle constraints apparent when His Majesty had first offered Baldwin the premiership, in the summer of 1924. Then their interview had been overshadowed by two regrettable circumstances: the ill health and retirement of Andrew Bonar Law, Baldwin's predecessor; and the frantic disappointment of the Foreign Secretary, Lord Curzon, in being passed over in favour of Baldwin, merely Chancellor of the Exchequer and 'a person of the utmost insignificance'.* Now Bonar Law had gone to his Maker and Lord Curzon was reconciled as well as he could be to the nation's ingratitude. He had even been persuaded by the modest, tactful and persuasive Baldwin to stay on as Foreign Secretary and had retained his imperious tenure of Carlton Terrace until—very much against His Majesty's advice—Baldwin had insisted on going to the country at the end of 1923.

Determined to secure work for the million-and-a-half unemployed, Baldwin had appealed specifically for a mandate for Protection: only import duties, he argued, could protect British industry and British workers from the effects of cut-throat foreign competitors. The King had emphasised the disadvantages of fighting an election on such an issue.[4] All the bitterness of the ancient conflict between

*Nicolson quotes this outburst in his *Curzon: The Last Phase*, p. 355, published in 1937. But in his *King George the Fifth*, published in 1952, he implies that his earlier account of Curzon's reaction may have been exaggerated. He quotes Stamfordham's memorandum describing the interview with Curzon. 'While Lord Curzon naturally felt his supersession by a comparatively inexperienced and unknown man, he spoke in the warmest and most friendly terms of Mr. Baldwin.' (*King George the Fifth*, pp. 377-378.) It is possible that Curzon's outburst occurred later and in less formal company.

Protection and Free Trade would be revived; with most of the world in a chaotic and dangerous state, a contentious electoral battle in Britain could only add to the general turmoil; it was quite possible that Baldwin would be unable to win a majority with such a policy; finally, had the Prime Minister not realised that, by fighting for Protection, he would allow the two shattered wings of the Liberal party, led respectively by Asquith and Lloyd George, to reunite under the old Liberal war banner of Free Trade? Baldwin's answer was that a dissolution was now expected and the subsequent election had, indeed, fulfilled the King's prophecies. The Liberals had reunited under Asquith's leadership; the Labour party had joined the Liberals in denouncing a policy which would mean higher prices for the consumer; and the aroused passions of Free Traders in all classes and parties had swept out of existence the comfortable majority which Bonar Law had won for the Tories in November 1922.

Although Baldwin, with 258 seats in the new House, still commanded the largest single party, the Liberals, with 158, and Labour, with 191, immediately combined to defeat him. It was then that the King, with some trepidation, had sent for MacDonald, as leader of the second largest party, and asked him to form an administration. Now, with a sound Tory Government once more in office and backed by one of the largest parliamentary majorities of the century, His Majesty could surely look forward at last to the economic prosperity and social harmony which had eluded his realm since the end of the Great War. David Lloyd George, the Welshman, had presented him with venality at Westminster and Whitehall and violence in Ireland, and much of Wales, Scotland and England, too. Bonar Law, the Irishman, had managed to unseat the unscrupulous Welshman by detaching the bulk of the Tory party from his Coalition, but had been forced to retire through ill health before achieving much else. MacDonald, the Scotsman, had been allowed to pursue his moderate though basically undesirable experiment in Socialism for a few months. Now Baldwin, the Englishman from the Shires, with Protection firmly re-interred, had a further chance of redeeming the fallow harvest of the post-war years.

The King spoke frankly and urgently to his Prime Minister of a new conflict which seemed to be threatening the country.[5] It was essential, His Majesty declared, to combat anything like class warfare, which the extremists in the Labour party were inclined to make a sort of war-cry. The Opposition would come back to Westminster disappointed and embittered and it was the King's earnest hope that Mr Baldwin would restrain his own followers from doing anything to increase their irritation. Otherwise, it was to be feared that disagreeable and unruly disorder would occur in the House. Mr Baldwin was, equally aware of the dangers and assured His Majesty that he would do his best to avoid any action likely to stir up class antagonism. The King was well satisfied. Mr Baldwin, it seemed, was going to provide sane, sensible and above all, peaceful government.

If Stanley Baldwin had been a less modest man he might have indulged in some justifiable self-congratulation in November 1924. First elected to Parliament in 1908 at the age of thirty-nine for his father's old constituency of Bewdley, in Worcestershire, he had spent the early years of his political life as a painstaking but obscure backbencher. At one time he had seriously contemplated retiring from politics altogether and devoting himself exclusively to the family steel business. But in 1917 Bonar Law, the Tory leader, had secured his appointment as Financial Secretary of the Board of Trade. This had not been a happy period for Baldwin. The subservience of the Tory party to the capricious Coalition premiership of Lloyd George had distressed him; the ruthless ambition of 'the hardfaced men', as he called them, who had climbed on to the irresistible Lloyd George bandwagon in 1918, had pervaded public life and had allowed Lloyd George to corrupt it to an appalling degree. The sale of honours, the prostitution of judicial office, the casual revelation of Cabinet business to Press Lords, had forced Baldwin to recognise 'the morally disintegrating effect of Lloyd George on all whom he had to deal with'.[6]

In October 1922, Baldwin and other Tory critics of the Lloyd George regime had gathered at the Carlton Club and finally prevailed on Bonar Law and a majority of Tory M.P.s to repudiate the Coalition. Though cast out, Lloyd George had been joined in the wilderness, out of loyalty, by the brightest stars in the Tory firmament: Austen Chamberlain, Lord Birkenhead, Lord Balfour, and the Tory-turned-Liberal-turned-anti-Socialist Constitutionalist, Winston Churchill. Bonar Law had won a comfortable majority at the election of November 1922, and had turned to making the best use of the Tory talent available to him: out of this he had formed what Churchill disparagingly called a Cabinet of 'the Second Eleven'. Birkenhead believed it to be a Cabinet of 'second-class intellects', but as Lord Robert Cecil aptly remarked, second-class intellects were preferable to second-class characters.

It had been Bonar Law's intention to allow passions to cool between his own supporters and the Coalition Tories and then to retire and hand over leadership of a united party to Austen Chamberlain. But there had been no time for this. Cancer of the throat had

6

compelled his retirement after only seven months in office and it had been necessary for the King to choose his successor from the ranks of 'the Second Eleven'. Bonar Law had declined to recommend his successor and it had fallen to the King to make a final choice which, in the absence of Chamberlain and the Tory 'All Stars', had fallen between Curzon and Baldwin, now Chancellor of the Exchequer. Advised of Curzon's widespread unpopularity within the Tory party and reluctant to appoint a peer as premier, the King had sent for Baldwin virtually by default.* Those who knew the new Prime Minister at all were aware of his enthusiasm for cricket and his taste for romantic poetry—Rudyard Kipling was his first cousin. What was not known of him was his anonymous gift in 1919 of £120,000—a fifth of his personal fortune—to the Treasury as a means of matching in some way the sacrifice of the war generation. The example was not followed.

Baldwin had set himself two primary tactical objectives: the continuing political isolation of Lloyd George—'a real corrupter of public life'[7]—and the return to the Tory fold of Austen Chamberlain and the other members of 'the First Eleven'. The Tariff Election of 1923 had done much to win the Tory Coalitionists over to Baldwin; the Red Letter Election of 1924 set the seal on this reunion and ruined the Liberal party by panicking most anti-Labour voters into the arms of the Tories. Baldwin was not, as Neville Chamberlain, Austen's half-brother, observed, 'so simple as he makes out'.[8] In a broader sense, Baldwin had set himself the far harder task of binding up the wounds inflicted by the violent social and political antagonisms of the years since the war. Despite the steady constitutional advance of the Labour party since 1918 and the gradual ebb of the insurrectionary tide which had threatened to engulf the industrial centres in 1919 and 1920, Baldwin did not need the King to remind him of the dangers of class war. A significant minority in the Labour movement had never been weaned away from the doctrine of 'industrial action'. At the root of this doctrine was a contempt for the whole Parliamentary system, a belief that, however well Labour played by the rules of the game, it would always be denied the fruits of victory. To this minority it was self-evident that the working-class would win reforms—and ultimate power—only by exercising the one real sanction it possessed : the withdrawal of its labour.

The idea of a general strike was far older than the idea of a

* Although the retiring Prime Minister made no recommendation, the King was told that an unsigned memorandum by J. C. C. Davidson, Law's Parliamentary Private Secretary, arguing in favour of Baldwin, 'practically expressed the views of Mr Bonar Law.' Law, in fact, knew nothing of the memo.[9]

working class majority capturing power in Parliament. In 1831 William Benbow published a pamphlet called *The Grand National Holiday and Congress of the Productive Classes,* in which he argued that if all the wage-earners simply stayed at home, or took a 'Grand National Holiday', the Government and ruling classes would be forced to submit to their demands. The Chartists took up the idea, but were unable to convince the conservative and craft-conscious trade unions. An updated version of the doctrine appeared at the turn of the century when Daniel de Leon, founder of the American Socialist Labour party, began preaching the necessity of revolution through industrial action. De Leon rejected the existing trade unions as being too corrupted by reformism to provide suitable bases for revolutionary activity and urged, instead, the formation of one vast, all-embracing international body, the Industrial Workers of the World, which would not be weakened by the craft divisions and national rivalries of the existing unions. In 1910 Tom Mann, a leader of the London dock strike of 1889, returned to England after eight years in the Dominions, and put forward a tactical variation of De Leonism. Mann accepted that the existing unions were unfitted to perform a militant role. The answer, however, was not to go outside them but to work within them to break down artificial craft barriers and promote revolutionary consciousness. 'I know it will be a formidable task', he wrote, 'to get the existing unions to unite wholeheartedly and share courageously in the class war. But I believe that it can be done.'

There was intense conflict between the rival tacticians of revolutionary Syndicalism but the doctrine itself made considerable headway during the years immediately prior to the War. Strikes among miners, dockers, railwaymen, building workers, and engineers all owed their origin to unofficial leaders adhering to some form of Syndicalism. Few of the strikers saw clearly the revolutionary objective they were supposed to be striking for, but a tradition of industrial militancy was established and took particularly firm root on Clydeside and in the South Wales coalfields. In 1915 rank-and-file militancy and a reaction against the limitations of sectional union bargaining brought together the miners, the railwaymen, and the transport workers into what was known as the 'Triple Alliance'. Each union pledged its support to the others on questions of hours and wages. A strike by one was to be a strike by all. Controlling as it did over one-and-a-quarter million workers in the nation's key industries, the Alliance posed a formidable threat to the Government. The threat was suspended during the war, but rose up again immediately after, inflated by economic difficulties in the mines and on the railways and by resentment of British military intervention in Russia. Deception by the Government and hesitation by the leaders of the Alliance prevented a trial of strength in 1919, but neither side doubted that this was a mere postponement.

Before the showdown with the 'Triple Alliance', however, the Government was forced to meet an extraordinary challenge from those who had always firmly repudiated industrial action for political ends. Labour party and T.U.C. leaders had deprecated militant industrial action in 1919. But in the summer of 1920 the overwhelming anger of the Labour movement at the prospect of renewed British intervention in Russia forced the Labour leaders to threaten something which they had always feared as much as the Tory party: a general strike. Lloyd George was warned that any despatch of munitions or troops to help the reactionary Poles in their war against Russia would be opposed by a general down-tools. Britain did not enter a war against Russia and soon after Lloyd George took the first steps in normalising Anglo-Russian relations since the Bolshevik revolution of 1917. What weighed against British intervention quite as much as the prospects of a general strike was the sudden and dramatic improvement of the Polish position. British intervention was simply no longer a military necessity. But to the enthusiasts of industrial action—both inside and outside the 'Triple Alliance'—the end of British military entanglement in Russia was a positive vindication of their doctrine : hot air from the politicians had visibly failed; resolute action by the workers had triumphed.

The euphoria was short-lived. At the beginning of 1921, the Government precipitated its delayed reckoning with the 'Triple Alliance'. During the war the mines had been placed under Government control. This was not due to end until August, but the Government announced that it would cease in March. Immediately, the owners gave notice of drastic wage cuts which were to operate from the date of de-control. The Miners' Federation rejected the terms and a lock-out began on 31 March. Declaring a state of emergency, the Government moved troops into the coalfields and mounted machine guns at the pitheads. The other members of the 'Triple Alliance' promised to withdraw their labour on 15 April and the T.U.C. and the Labour party pledged their support for the miners. The long-delayed trial of strength between unions and Government seemed at last to have come. But on the eve of the strike Frank Hodges, secretary of the Miners' Federation, hinted to M.P.s that, as a temporary compromise, the miners might be prepared to accept district settlements instead of a national wages agreement, provided these were related to the cost of living. A

9

national agreement was one of the miners' vital demands and Hodges was promptly disowned by his own executive. But an opening for escape had been presented to the other members of the Alliance, whose taste for industrial action had diminished with the negotiation of satisfactory settlements in their own industries. Urged on by Jimmy Thomas, secretary of the National Union of Railwaymen, the Alliance accused the miners of intransigence and withdrew the strike notices which were to have become operative on Friday 15 April—Black Friday as it came to be known in the Labour movement. The miners were left to fight their own battle, a battle they lost with disastrous consequences three months later. There was no national settlement and wages in all districts, with the exception of Yorkshire, where there was a slight rise, were cut by between 10 and 40 per cent.

Demoralised by the sudden capitulation of Labour's industrial giant, many other unions, including the engineers, shipyard workers and textile workers, had wage cuts forced on them during the final months of Lloyd George's premiership. Many drew the conclusion that industrial action was bound to fail in the face of inherent organisational difficulties and determined Government action; others, that timidity and treachery alone had turned the 'Triple Alliance' into the 'Cripple Alliance'. Among the miners hatred of the Government and coal-owners was matched only by hatred of the 'Traitor Thomas', an attitude which was to have a profound effect on the events of 1926.

An unexpected boom in the British coal trade early in 1923 following the French occupation of the Ruhr and the protest strike by German miners, and the concession of higher wages helped to reduce some of the bitterness in the coalfields. A steady drop in unemployment during 1923 from 2 million to under $1\frac{1}{2}$ million and the coming to power in 1924 of a Labour Government able to carry out a positive if limited programme of reform helped to shift the emphasis away from industrial to political action. But the Tories' wild exploitation of the Red Letter scare at the end of 1924 brought all the old cynicism and suspicion of Parliamentary methods welling up again. For the militants, and for a good many moderates too, the Red Letter Election was spectacular confirmation that Labour's opponents, while insisting that the workers should play by the rules, had themselves no intention of being bound by the rules when it came to injuring Labour. There was no doubt in any section of the Labour movement that the Zinoviev letter was a forgery, that the Tories knew this even if they had not actually connived at it, and that they had deliberately whipped up an hysterical Red Scare in order to discredit the Labour party. It was apparent, therefore, to Baldwin as well as the King, that there was every danger of renewed class war.

For Labour's defeated champion, Ramsay MacDonald, the dangers were greater and more immediate. He had jilted the ardent partner of a short but peculiarly passionate love affair. Regarding his condemnation of the war and his fervent rhetoric on social justice as signs of true Socialist conviction, the Left-wing in the Parliamentary Labour party had secured MacDonald's re-election as leader in November 1922. He had originally been elected leader in 1909, but had been forced to resign in favour of Arthur Henderson at the outbreak of war because of his uncompromising pacifist views and had actually lost his seat in the election of 1918. On returning to Parliament in 1922, the messianic MacDonald was regarded by the keepers of the Socialist conscience in the Independent Labour party and dour class-fighters of the so-called Clydeside Brigade in the Parliamentary Labour party as their man. It did not take the Left long to discover its mistake. MacDonald's taste for gracious living which isolated him from draughty Labour halls and trade union committee rooms; the patrician pose which excited coy speculation among society *grandes-dames* about the mysterious nobleman who must surely have sired him; his inept handling of the Campbell Case and his tardy reaction to the Zinoviev letter and the Foreign Office machinations which had clearly preceded it; his vigorous repudiation of industrial action, when it was clear that Labour's opponents were not so fastidious about the means they chose to victory : all these dislikes, suspicions, and criticisms came together in the winter of 1924–5 into a great groundswell of disenchantment with the leader of the Labour party. As Beatrice Webb noted in her dyspeptic diary: 'Hot-air propaganda in mean streets and industrial slums combined with chill moderation on the Treasury Bench and courtly phrases at Society functions may be the last word in political efficiency; but it is unsavoury, and leads among the rank-and-file, to deep discouragement. Even Sidney is depressed.'[10]

The Left and the Right in the Parliamentary Labour party were united in wishing to replace MacDonald as leader, but mutual detestation prevented either from fielding a candidate who had the faintest chance of winning support from the other. The only compromise candidate available was once again Arthur Henderson. Immediately after the General Election Philip Snowden, who had been MacDonald's Chancellor of the Exchequer, urged Henderson to put himself forward; representatives of the Clydeside Brigade, the powerful group of Left-wing Scottish M.P.s who had done so much to secure MacDonald's elevation in 1922, also urged Henderson to challenge him for the leadership. Henderson rejected their pleas, arguing that MacDonald was the best leader they had got or were likely to get : he was the only Labour personality with a real following in the country and a change of leadership would only bring even greater disunity in the party. For the present, MacDonald's critics could only nurse their grievances.

A far greater danger to MacDonald—and ultimately to Baldwin—was threatened by the increasing alienation of trade union leaders such as Ernie Bevin, of the Transport Workers. They had not been pleased with their exclusion from the inner circles of the Labour Government and they found MacDonald's undisguised preference for high society and barely-concealed contempt for themselves deeply offensive. Of all the union leaders, only Jimmy Thomas, of the N.U.R., who had been Colonial Secretary, and was himself a prodigious social climber, enjoyed MacDonald's confidence. Even before the Labour Government's fall, the historic links between the party and the trade unions had been seriously weakened. The humiliating defeat of October 1924, deepened the erosion. A feeling began to spread that perhaps, after all, the Labour party was a time-wasting irrelevancy; that it might be possible to by-pass the Westminster charade altogether if the unions went about their own business in their own way. There was little of Syndicalist philosophy behind this new mood, but it gave rise to a dangerous contempt for parliamentary activity and created a new opening for industrial militancy.

## Chapter Two

# *Ishmael and The Golden Calf*

'The world as it is is far too agreeable for all the members of the Labour party who belong, in effect, to the governing class. What the Left propose is frequently neither practicable nor desirable; but the Right is not leading the party forward; it is merely hanging back in the attitude of the "Thoroughly Comfortable". How difficult it is for the well-to-do to lead the very poor towards the promised land!'

Beatrice Webb writing in her diary, 12 February 1925.

'We first visited some slum houses. I never saw such a sight. Oddly enough I have never been in real slum houses, and I as near as two pins sat down and howled: the whole thing came on me with such force. Five and six in one room. Think of the children! We went on to see various housing schemes. They have unlimited room in which to build but they have hardly started on the real problem. The people were very friendly which touched me very much. They seemed to know one would give one's life to help: they can't know how impotent one is.'

Stanley Baldwin, writing to J. C. C. Davidson on 4 June 1925, of his visit to Dundee.

While the tide swelled against MacDonald, the Communist party increased its attempts to penetrate the Labour movement. With an active membership of less than 5,000 and barred from direct affiliation to the Labour party, the Communists concentrated their efforts in the trade unions. They had much greater success than their limited numbers and resources alone would have made possible. Tory and Liberal attacks upon the Anglo-Soviet Treaties revived much of the pro-Soviet sentiment which had gripped the British Labour movement in 1920. In 1924 the annual Congress of the T.U.C. was addressed for the first time by a fraternal delegate from the Soviet trade unions. Congress also accepted an invitation to send a delegation to Russia and two leading Left-wingers—Alonzo Swales, of the Engineers, and Alf Purcell, of the Furnishing Trades

Association—were elected chairman and vice-chairman of the T.U.C. Purcell had moved a resolution approving the Soviet system of workers' councils at the inaugural conference of the British Communist party in 1920 and had then travelled on to Moscow to discuss plans for the launching of the Red International of Labour Unions, which was to rival the 'reformist' International Federation of Trade Unions based in Amsterdam. Though no longer a member of the Communist party, Purcell still embroidered his speeches with Marxist rhetoric and he and Swales were valuable assets to the Communist party in its campaign to swing the unions to the Left after the Red Letter debacle. The party was helped even more by the absence from the General Council of notable Right-wingers such as Jimmy Thomas, who had resigned on their inclusion in MacDonald's Government.

With a cohesion and discipline which had been lacking among the pre-war advocates of Syndicalism, the Communist-controlled National Minority Movement also worked hard in 1924 and 1925 to secure a firm foothold in the unions. Under the vigorous and efficient leadership of Harry Pollitt, a young Lancashire boilermaker who had organised a National Hands off Russia Committee in 1920, and Tom Mann, the venerable elder statesman of revolutionary politics in Britain, the Minority Movement's task was defined as 'not to organise independent revolutionary trade unions, or to split revolutionary elements away from existing organisations affiliated to the T.U.C....but to convert the revolutionary minority within each industry into a revolutionary majority'.[1] Although the Minority Movement succeeded in building up responsive factions among the engineers, transport workers, and railwaymen, it was among the miners that it achieved its most spectacular success.

Early in 1924 Frank Hodges, secretary of the Miners' Federation and no friend of the Communists, was obliged to resign following his appointment as Civil Lord of the Admiralty in the Labour Government. The well-organised Minority Movement faction among the South Wales miners, the largest district in the Federation, decided to back A. J. Cook, miners' agent for central Rhondda, as Hodges' successor. Cook went on to secure the official South Wales nomination and won the national ballot. Also a former member of the Communist party, Cook had resigned in 1921 when he was criticised for backing the disastrous agreement forced on the miners by the collapse of the 'Triple Alliance'. But he was still proud; he claimed to call himself 'a disciple of Karl Marx and a humble follower of Lenin' and supported the Communist party because 'I agree with nine-tenths of its policy'. He had suffered imprisonment in the spring of 1918 for declaiming pacifist views, and again in 1921 for 'intimidation' and 'unlawful assembly'. In 1924 Arthur James Cook became not only the most ardent and forceful protagonist of industrial action for political ends but, as secretary of Britain's biggest trade union, the most powerful.

A wild but hypnotic orator, whose revolutionary fervour was flavoured with the religious revivalism of his days as a Baptist lay preacher, his pithead meetings drew crowds even greater than those which had listened to Keir Hardie. Cook was a mirror-image of every miner's frustrations and yearnings. In private conversation often in tears himself when describing the privations of the miners, Cook was able to produce an astonishing effect on his public audiences. Lord Sankey, a High Court Judge who chaired the Royal Commission on the mining industry in 1919, once stood at the back of a crowded miners' meeting to hear Cook speak. Within fifteen minutes half the audience was in tears and Sankey admitted to having the greatest difficulty in restraining himself from weeping.[2] Still only forty, Cook was the best-loved miners' leader of all time. The son of a soldier, he had been born in the small Somerset mining village of Wookey. After leaving elementary school he had migrated to the South Wales coalfields at the turn of the century and plunged wholeheartedly into the turbulent mining struggles of the pre-war years. A firm advocate of industrial action, he was co-author of a well-known Syndicalist pamphlet, *The Miners' Next Step*. Beatrice Webb, who nicknamed him 'the Billy Sunday of the Labour movement', viewed him with a mixture of middle-class Fabian distaste and fascination:

> He is a loosely built ugly-featured man—looks low-caste—not at all the skilled artisan type, more the agricultural labourer. He is oddly remarkable in appearance because of his excitability of gesture, mobility of expression in his large-lipped mouth, glittering china-blue eyes, set close together in a narrow head with lanky yellow hair—altogether a man you watch with a certain admiring curiosity...it is clear that he has no intellect and not much intelligence—he is a quivering mass of emotions, a mediumistic magnetic sort of creature—not without personal attractiveness—an inspired idiot, drunk with his own words, dominated by his own slogans. I doubt whether he even knows what he is going to say or what he has just said.[3]

Fred Bramley, secretary of the T.U.C., was appalled at Cook's election. As soon as it was announced he went racing into his assistant, Walter Citrine. 'Have you seen who has been elected secretary of the Miners' Federation?' he yelled. 'Cook, a raving, tearing Communist. Now the miners are in for a bad time.'⁴ Just how bad Bramley could not know. But the seeds were sown long before 1924. In 1920 the phenomenal post-war boom in the British coal industry came to an equally phenomenal end. In their wisdom the peacemakers at Versailles issued a *diktat* that Germany was to meet part of its reparations to the coal-producing nations of France, Belgium, and Italy in coal. The world groaned under a flood of black mineral and within a year the export price of British coal slumped by more than half. Forced to balance the coal budget at a cost of £5 million a month, Lloyd George ordered the immediate return of the mines to private ownership and abandoned the miners to wage cuts of up to 40 per cent. The Franco-Belgian occupation of the Ruhr in 1923 and the strike in the Ruhr coalfields had led to a revival of British coal exports and enabled Arthur Cook to secure his first victory. After an independent inquiry set up by the Labour Government, the owners reluctantly conceded higher wages and a modest profit-sharing scheme. But within weeks of the agreement, the French withdrew from the Ruhr and German coal production began once more to disrupt the economies of the vanquisher nations. As British coal exports slumped from 42 million tons in the first half of 1924 to 35 million tons in the first half of 1925, miners and owners began to prepare for the inevitable battle to be fought in the summer of 1925, when their twelve-month agreement came to an end.

Coal mining was by no means the only industry to suffer the effects of cheap foreign competition. Textiles, shipbuilding and engineering were all badly hit and at no time since 1921 had unemployment fallen much below 1½ million. But the distress of the miners excited a unique passion and bitterness. There was a feeling, which extended far beyond the Labour movement, that the unpleasantness and danger of digging into the bowels of the earth deserved better reward than an average weekly wage of 60 shillings. This feeling was reinforced by the inefficiency and arrogance with which the coal-owners managed their affairs and Lloyd George's blatant duplicity in 1919. A series of pre-war Royal Commissions into the mining industry had impugned its management and convinced the miners that only nationalisation would solve the industry's problems. A further Royal Commission was set up in 1919 under Lord Justice Sankey to study the immediate issue of wages and hours and the longer-term question of nationalisation, and the Government undertook to adopt its report 'in spirit and in letter'. But the Commission, which was made up of six miners' nominees—including Sidney Webb—three coal-owners, and three industrialists, was unable to reach total unanimity on anything. In March it produced three separate interim reports on wages and hours: one from Sankey and the three industrialists; one from the coal-owners; and one from the miners' nominees. The contentious issue of nationalisation was deferred, but the report by Sankey and the three industrialists declared that 'Even upon the evidence already given, the present system of ownership and working in the coal industry stands condemned, and some other system must be substituted for it, either nationalisation or a method of unification by national purchase and/or joint control.' The Government accepted this report—including its strictures on ownership—and so, too, did the miners after a national ballot. In June the members of the Commission produced four further reports which dealt specifically with the future ownership of the industry. One from Sankey recommended outright nationalisation; one from the miners' nominees recommended nationalisation and workers' control; the mine-owners and two of the industrialists favoured nationalisation of the coal royalties but not of the colliery companies; the fourth report by Sir Arthur Duckham, one of the industrialists, recommended district amalgamations.

Although a majority of seven out of the thirteen members of the Commission favoured public ownership of the mines, Lloyd George used the excuse of lack of unanimity to reject the proposal and suggested, instead, Duckham's scheme. This the miners were not prepared to accept and Lloyd George was relieved from the embarrassment of having to do anything at all which might offend the 'hard-faced men' who dominated the Coalition. Among the miners this surrender to the coal-owners' lobby created an unassailable conviction that Governments were enemies to be defeated rather than neutral umpires whose advice should be sought. As Baldwin was to complain during the crisis of 1926: 'In this as in so many other things L.G. has left us a legacy of trouble.'[5]

But at the beginning of 1925 the full extent of Lloyd George's legacy was still undisclosed: with the Labour party relegated once more to the Opposition benches and the Liberal party in ruins, Baldwin turned to the task of providing 'sane, commonsense government, not carried away by revolutionary theories or hare-brained schemes'. His comfortable, pipe-smoking image enhanced the pleas he continually made for an end of class bitterness and industrial strife. He summed up his approach to industrial problems in March 1925, in a speech of simple but extraordinarily powerful eloquence. A Bill, introduced by one of his own backbenchers, sought to interfere with the political levy paid by trade unions to the Labour party. Aware that such a Bill had overwhelming support in his own party,

Baldwin rose, nevertheless, to oppose it. 'I want my party today', he told M.P.s, 'to make a gesture to the country…and say to them: "We have our majority; we believe in the justice of this Bill, which has been brought in today, but we are going to withdraw our hand, and we are not going to push our political advantage home at a moment like this. Suspicion which has prevented stability in Europe is the one poison that is preventing stability at home, and we offer the country today this: We, at any rate, are not going to fire the first shot. We stand for peace. We stand for the removal of suspicion in the country." Although I know that there are those who work for different ends from most of us in this House, yet there are many in all ranks and all parties who will re-echo my prayer: "Give us peace in our time, O Lord." ' The effect of this speech, even on veterans of the Clydeside Brigade, was considerable. There was a feeling that evening, one of them later recalled, that 'the antagonism, the bitterness, the class rivalry were unworthy; and that understanding and amity were possible'.[6]

The worthy sentiments of a euphoric spring evening in Westminster were soon negated by the economic and political realities of 1925. The harshest and most immediate economic reality was the progressive decline of the mining industry in the face of resumed German competition and the determination of the owners to maintain profits at the expense of the miners. The most disturbing political reality was the resurgence of trade union militancy since Black Friday. Baldwin's chief preoccupation at the beginning of 1925, however, was with neither of these. At the centre of his attention was Lloyd George and the formidable threat which Baldwin believed he still posed to the newly-restored unity of the Tory party. It was not difficult for the Prime Minister to tempt the Tory Coalitionists he wanted into his Cabinet. The breach caused by the break-up of Lloyd George's Government in 1922 was largely healed after the Tariff Election and Austen Chamberlain now served as Foreign Secretary and Lord Birkenhead as Secretary of State for India. But there was still Lloyd George, leading the Liberal remnant in the House of Commons since Asquith's elevation to the Lords, to act as a powerful fulcrum for the discontented and the ambitious. It was also clear that Lloyd George had no intention of accepting permanently the defeat which Baldwin had played a large part in engineering in 1922; he was determined to make a comeback and was prepared to use for that purpose whatever cause or faction was conveniently to hand. In Baldwin's estimation the most potent weapon to Lloyd George's hand was Winston Churchill. Brought back into the Government by Lloyd George in 1917 after his contentious embroilment in the Dardanelles Campaign and subsequent resignation as First Lord of the Admiralty, Churchill had followed his old chief and mentor into political exile in 1922.

Defeated in the General Elections of 1922 and 1923 and at a by-election early in 1924, Churchill had finally stormed his way back into the House of Commons as 'Constitutionalist' candidate for Epping at the General Election of 1924. Like Lloyd George, he was ambitious. Like Lloyd George, he was frustrated. Together these two represented a far greater menace to the harmony and stability of the Tory party than Baldwin was prepared to countenance. Austen Chamberlain underlined Baldwin's own fears about Churchill. 'If you leave him out he will be leading a Tory rump in six months' time.'[7] The solution, therefore, was to bring him in. Precisely the same considerations had prompted Lloyd George to include him as Minister of Munitions in 1917. The permutation of appointments in 1924 left the Treasury available. Offered the Chancellorship by Baldwin, the honourable member for Epping at first thought that he was meant to become Chancellor of the Duchy of Lancaster, but accepted gratefully anyway. When he realised that Baldwin meant him to be Chancellor of the Exchequer, Churchill's surprise and delight were boundless. The restless, miserable days in the wilderness without office, party, or even constituency were over. With tears in his eyes, the new Chancellor pledged his utmost loyalty to Baldwin, adding, 'You have done more for me than Lloyd George ever did'.[8]

Churchill's appointment was received by all parties with varying degrees of astonishment, anger and dismay. His lack of experience in financial matters entered only fractionally into their calculations. On the Tory benches his desertion into the ranks of the Liberals in 1904 and his description of Bonar Law's Government as 'the Second Eleven' still aroused formidable hostility. He was not even a member of the Tory party when Baldwin appointed him and did not rejoin until the following year. His second desertion did not endear him to Lloyd George and the Liberals, and former colleagues in both parties suspected both his motives and his judgment. A. G. Gardiner, former editor of the Liberal *Daily News*, summed up the new Chancellor's position with brutal but approximate accuracy: 'He is an Ishmael in public life, loathed by the Tories whom he left and has now returned to; distrusted by the Liberals, on whose backs he first mounted to power; hated by Labour, whom he scorns and insults, and who see in him the potential Mussolini of a wave of reaction.'[9] The Tories could be appeased and the Liberals ignored; it was possible to do neither in the case of Labour. None of Baldwin's colleagues was distinguished for his 'softness' towards Socialism; indeed, Austen Chamberlain's first act as Foreign Secretary was to renounce the Anglo-Soviet Treaties already signed by MacDonald. But it was Churchill who appeared as the unrepentant caricature of all those prejudices and passions most detested by the Left.

It was he who, as Home Secretary, had drafted troops into the South Wales coalfields; it was he who, as Secretary for War, had pressed for intervention in Russia to the point when, in 1920, the Labour party and the T.U.C. had intervened themselves with the threat of a general strike; it was he who, in the same year, had publicly defended the Black and Tans, claiming for them the same freedom as the Chicago or New York police in dealing with gangsters. His rancorous verbal assaults on the Labour party were delivered with little regard for the doctrinal niceties of Soviet collectivism and British democratic Socialism. Fenner Brockway, an old electoral rival of Churchill's, expressed Labour's view. 'Of all the politicians, Mr Churchill has shown himself most unfit for the responsibility of Government. His *forte* is to be a disturber of the peace, whether at home or abroad. He is a political adventurer, with a genius for acts of mischievous irresponsibility. He is militant to his fingertips... Mr Churchill's record shows him to be a public danger and a menace to the peace of the world.'[10] A contemporary observer of Churchill's apocalyptic platform manner wrote: 'Indeed, he is such a preposterous little fellow, with his folded arms and tufted forelock and his Lyceum Theatre voice, that if one did not detest him one might love him for his sheer perversity.'[11]

But even the most unflattering assessment of the new Chancellor could not have prepared the nation for what J. M. Keynes was to call 'The Economic Consequences of Mr Churchill'. In his first Budget speech on 28 April 1925, Churchill announced that Britain would be returning to the gold standard at the pre-war parity rate between the dollar and the pound. The pound sterling had been forced off the gold standard in 1914 and ever since the end of hostilities it had been the obsession of bankers and politicians alike to clamber back on to it. For the City, the return to gold meant an increase in the value of sterling in world money markets and the restoration of London as the world's principal money market. For the politicians, the renewed supremacy of sterling at pre-war parity meant a reassuring 'return to normalcy' and enabled the pound 'to look the dollar in the face'. Unfortunately, this irresistible blend of greed and nostalgia obscured the fact that the pound was being over-valued by some 10 per cent. The immediate consequence, therefore, of Mr Churchill was that foreign buyers of British goods had to pay 10 per cent more in their own currency or British exporters had to accept 10 per cent less in sterling. The already desperately hard-pressed British export industries naturally sought for ways of reducing their costs by an equivalent amount and it was soon made clear that wages would bear the burden.

Lacking financial expertise himself and acutely aware of his political vulnerability, Churchill willingly accepted the doctrine preached to him as an article of faith by the Treasury, the Bank of England and his own Cabinet colleagues. He claimed seven years later 'to have gone the whole hog against it' and that it had been 'a vile trap to destroy us'.[12] But it was easy to be wise in the aftermath. In 1925 Churchill's view was that a return to gold and pre-war parity was a return to 'reality'. The Government and the City of London were not alone in believing this. Philip Snowden, Labour Chancellor in 1924, was as firmly convinced as any Tory banker that gold and parity were prescriptions for industrial prosperity as well as financial pre-eminence. There were few who contradicted this. One was the economist J. M. Keynes. In his prophetic pamphlet, *The Economic Consequences of Mr Churchill*, Keynes asserted that the Chancellor had been misled by his advisers. 'In doing what he did in the actual circumstances of last spring, he was just asking for trouble. For he was committing himself to force down money-wages and all money values, without any idea how it was done.' This action, Keynes argued, would mean:

> Engaging in a struggle with each separate group in turn, with no prospect that the final result will be fair, and no guarantee that the stronger groups will not gain at the expense of the weaker. The working-classes cannot be expected to understand, better than Cabinet ministers, what is happening. Those who are attacked first are faced with a depreciation of their standard of life, because the cost of living will not fall until all of the others have been attacked too; and therefore they are justified in defending themselves. Nor can the classes first subjected to a reduction of money-wages be guaranteed that this will be compensated later by a corresponding fall in the cost of living... Therefore they are bound to resist so long as they can; and it must be war until those who are economically weakest are beaten to the ground.

The immediate effects of the return to gold and parity might have been mitigated with generous and imaginative Government help to those forced to bear the burden, but this would have required an assault on financial orthodoxy which Churchill, in 1925, had neither the desire nor the capacity to launch. His Budget, according to

21

Baldwin, followed 'the soundest lines of prudence and Conservative finance'—which was precisely what was wrong with it. It granted surtax relief, it reduced income tax by sixpence, and it imposed an inexplicable duty on artificial silk and lace. It did nothing to relieve the difficulties of those industries shortly to be crippled by a 10 per cent increase in costs. It was attacked by Hubert Henderson, another of the tiny band of dissenting economists, for adding substantially to the difficulties of industry and concentrating favour upon the rentier and salaried man. 'The more Mr Churchill's budget is studied,' he wrote, 'the more incredible does the folly of it seem. When its various aspects have been fully digested, certainly when its consequences have become apparent, it will surely rank, both from the financial and political standpoints, as an ineptitude without parallel in our recent history.'[13]

It did not take long for the economic consequences of Mr Churchill to become apparent, and although the return to gold was the expression of an overwhelming political consensus, it was, of course, Churchill whom the trade unions discovered armed and mounted outside their tents, bearing aloft the banner of usury. The miners were the first to taste the effects of the Chancellor's return to 'reality'. Almost as soon as the improved 1924 agreement had been signed, the artificial boom produced by French occupation of the Ruhr came to an end. As the Ruhr mines resumed production a renewed flood of German coal poured into European markets destroying the virtual monopoly which Britain had enjoyed for eighteen months. Within a year of the 1924 agreement exports fell from an annual rate of 65 million tons to one of 43 million tons and unemployment, which at 2.9 per cent had been the lowest of any industry in 1923, rose to 17.5 per cent. In 1923–4 the industry had made a net profit of £59 million. By June 1925, the industry was running at a loss of £1 million a month and 300,000 miners were out of work. The further difficulties imposed by gold and parity made an attempt to reduce costs inevitable. At the end of June—within two months of Churchill's Budget announcement—the mine-owners announced that the current agreement would end on 31 July. Under the new agreement which they proposed there were to be immediate wage reductions of between 10 and 25 per cent and abolition of the national minimum, establishing the ratio of wages to profits, a principle which the miners had finally obtained in 1921 after a struggle lasting since the turn of the century. The new agreement envisaged a return to local wage bargaining, which would mean vast discrepancies between the comparatively rich areas like West Yorkshire and the very poor ones such as the Forest of Dean. Under the new proposals, a married labourer with three children in the Forest of Dean would receive 4s. 4d. a day—5½d. less than he would get on the dole. But however low wages might fall, the owners' standard profit was to be maintained. As Keynes observed, the miners were the first 'victims of the economic juggernaut'. To him they represented 'in the flesh the "fundamental adjustments" engineered by the Treasury and the Bank of England to satisfy the impatience of the City Fathers to bridge the "moderate gap" between $4.40 and $4.86. They (and others to follow) are the "moderate sacrifice" still necessary to ensure the stability of the gold standard.'

The miners rejected the proposals, refusing even an 'interchange of views' until the notices terminating the current agreement were withdrawn. The onslaught against wages and living standards had not been unforeseen and in March the miners had invited the transport workers, railwaymen, shipbuilders and engineers to discuss with them the possibility of forming a new Industrial Alliance. No one, least of all the miners, had forgotten Black Friday, but despite mutual wariness the various unions agreed to set up a small subcommittee to draft a constitution. It was still in session when the mine-owners posted their notices at the end of June, so the miners turned for help to the General Council of the T.U.C. Under the mandate agreed at the 1924 Congress, the General Council was entitled to be informed of disputes involving large numbers of workers and had the right to organise 'all such moral and material support' as circumstances demanded. The moral support was immediately forthcoming. The General Council placed itself 'without qualification and unreservedly at the disposal of the Miners' Federation' and endorsed the Federation's refusal to negotiate on the basis of reduced wages or increased hours.

An attempt by the Government to bring the miners and owners together failed and the miners refused to appear before a Court of Inquiry which was set up on 13 July under the chairmanship of H. P. MacMillan, a Scottish advocate. The Miners' Federation stated that it was unable to co-operate with any Court of Inquiry 'that has for its object the ascertainment of whether the mine-workers' wages can be reduced or their hours extended, but it repeats its willingness to meet the coal-owners in open conference as soon as they have withdrawn their proposals'. It was in this atmosphere of mounting tension that the executives of unions involved in the Industrial Alliance met again on 17 July, reinforced by the Iron and Steel Trades Confederation, the Electrical Trades Union and the Foundry Workers. There was not the coolness at this meeting which had been apparent at the earlier one. Uppermost now in the minds of delegates was the fear that the wage cuts directed at the miners would shortly be directed at workers in their own industries and that, unless the unions came together for their mutual protection, they would be unable to resist. The constitution presented by Bevin on behalf of the drafting committee was accepted unanimously by the assembled executives for consideration by their respective unions and Cook was able to write: 'Once again, ringing throughout the industrial areas of Britain, in every mine, workshop and factory is that blessed word—unity.'

But the miners had no time to wait for the laborious process of endorsement by each union and the support promised by the T.U.C. could only be as effective as the unions concerned with the movement of coal decided to make it. Bevin provided the lead. On 23 July he moved a resolution at a conference of transport workers pledging full support to the miners and full co-operation with the General Council in carrying out any measures that they might decide to take. This was accepted without dissent. A few days later the railway unions also pledged their support and set up a joint committee with the transport workers to prepare for the embargo on the movement of coal which the General Council had ordered in the event of a lockout. Ironically, Baldwin had asserted his attitude to industrial problems only the previous month: 'The organisations of employees and men, if they take their coats off to it, are far more able to work out the solution of their troubles than the politicians. Let them put the State out of their minds and get down to it.' By the middle of July any hopes the Government still cherished that this was possible in the mining industry were unceremoniously dispelled by Herbert Smith, president of the Miners' Federation. Smith, who had held office since 1922, had been a title-holding prize fighter during his youth in the Yorkshire coalfields. Now aged sixty-three, he had forgotten none of his ringcraft and combined sledgehammer bluntness with remarkable agility in a tight corner. In July 1925, he was in an aggressive mood. 'You are responsible', he told members of the Cabinet, 'for the position we are in—your Government. An inquiry was held in 1919, and certain findings were the result of that inquiry. A Coalition Government was in power at that time, and both pledged themselves; yet you have refused to accept it; or, in other words, you believe in private enterprise, although private enterprise has failed to function. It is your baby, which you must supply with milk.'*

* According to R. H. Tawney, who had been one of the miners' nominees on the Sankey Commission, Smith's trouble was that he 'saw England as a coal-pit with some grass growing on the top.'[14]

Baldwin now took personal charge of the mediation efforts and eventually persuaded the owners to concede the principle of a national minimum wage. 'What have you to give?' he asked the miners. 'Nowt,' replied Smith, 'we have nowt to give.' Meanwhile, another less formal attempt was being made to break the deadlock. On 25 July several members of the T.U.C. General Council attended a Royal Garden Party. One of them was Mary Quaile, women's organiser of the transport workers, who discussed the crisis with Queen Mary. The Queen's distress was considerable and next day A. J. Cook received an invitation to see the King at Buckingham Palace. Cook's reaction was characteristic. 'Why the hell should I go to see the King?' he exclaimed to Walter Citrine. 'I'll show them that they have a different man from Frank Hodges to deal with now... I am going to fight these people. I believe a fight is certain. There is only one way of doing it. That is to fight.' When Citrine urged discretion Cook replied: 'Don't forget I have something to pay back. It is just six years ago since they not only handcuffed me but led me in chains from one end of the train, in Swansea station, to the other, in full view of the public. The same at Cardiff station.'[15]

On 28 July the Court of Inquiry presented its report. Despite the miners' boycott, the Court was largely sympathetic to them, recommending a national minimum wage and emphasising the need for reorganisation of the industry. Attached to the report was a memorandum by Sir Josiah Stamp arguing that the difficulties in the industry could be entirely explained 'by the immediate and necessary effects of the return to gold'. There were certainly other factors leading to coal's decline, but Stamp's observations lent powerful support to the miners' contention that, since the Government had helped to create the problem, it was up to the Government to help solve it. Baldwin, however, strenuously rejected any suggestion of a Government subsidy. On 29 July he told the miners 'that the Government would not grant any subsidy' and that the coal industry 'must stand on its own economic foundations'; on 30 July, with less than thirty-six hours to go before the lock-out and embargo, he again emphatically rejected the idea of a subsidy and urged that wage reductions would have to play their part in lowering industrial costs if heavy unemployment was ever to be conquered. According to the miners, who reported later that day to a special conference of trade union executives, the Prime Minister's actual words were: 'All the workers in this country have got to face a reduction of wages to help put industry on its feet.' This was an exaggeration of what Baldwin had actually said, but hardly an exaggeration of what he meant and it confirmed the fears shared by other trade unionists. The conference of executives not only approved the General Council's plans for an embargo on coal, but also empowered the Council to issue strike orders and give financial assistance.

By now it was clear to Baldwin that the unions were not bluffing and on the evening of 30 July he turned once again to the owners. He warned them that a general strike was about to begin and asked if they understood the gravity of the situation. They replied that they did, but were unable to make any further concessions. One hour later the Cabinet met. Baldwin had made up his mind the previous day that, unless there was a last-minute concession on the part of the miners or the owners, a subsidy would have to be given to the industry while a further inquiry attempted to thrash out its basic problems. Churchill, although unhappy about an apparent submission to trade union pressure, had agreed. Both now urged the Cabinet to accept the realities of the situation. If the miners struck, the railways would be practically certain to be drawn in when their men were dismissed for refusing to move coal; other transport workers would join the dispute, and the seamen and electricians could also become involved. A strike lasting three months would cost £70 million and cause a severe trade setback. There was also a danger of civil strife. In a report to the King, Maurice Hankey, Permanent Secretary to the Cabinet, stated: 'Fascists numbering anything from fifty to a hundred thousand are organised for different reasons.'[16] In fact, membership of Fascist organisations totalled only a few thousands and Hankey may have been applying the term to all militantly anti-Communist bodies such as the British Empire Union and National Citizens' Union. What finally convinced the waverers in the Cabinet that a subsidy was essential was Baldwin's argument that the country was not yet psychologically prepared for a major confrontation with the unions. In his report to the King, Hankey wrote:

Many members of the Cabinet think that the struggle is inevitable and must come sooner or later: the P.M. does not share this view. The majority of the Cabinet regard the present moment as badly chosen for the fight, though the conditions would be more favourable nine months hence. Public opinion is to a considerable extent on the miners' side ... There is a strong feeling amongst some of the House of Commons Unionist members in favour of the miners, though those same members thoroughly dislike the idea of a subsidy. Finally, a majority of the Cabinet decided upon the subsidy proposal—every reasonable man would accept it and a letter from the miners to this effect was received during the Cabinet. It is true the owners will not favour a subsidy. The P.M. will be negotiating through the night.

Neville Chamberlain, the Minister of Health, recorded in his diary: 'The moment I heard S.B. describe this course of action (the subsidy) a load fell away from my heart.'[17] The King, who was informed immediately of the Cabinet's decision, shared Chamberlain's relief and wrote in his own diary that same evening: 'So, thank God! There will be no strike now. I am much relieved.'[18]

First, Baldwin secured an undertaking from the Miners' Federation to co-operate in 'a full investigation into the methods of improving the productive efficiency of the industry for the purpose of increasing its competitive power in world markets'. In return, he guaranteed to subsidise wages at their current level for nine months while the inquiry carried out its work. (Baldwin had estimated the subsidy at £10 million, but adverse trading conditions pushed it up to £23 million.) Baldwin then saw the owners, who accused him of paying 'Danegeld' and refused at first to withdraw their notices. Evan Williams, chairman of the Mining Association, prophesied that the General Strike would begin on the day the subsidy ended. The owners, Chamberlain noted laconically, were 'not a prepossessing crowd'. The next day, Friday 31 July, Baldwin met both sides to confirm their obligations and those of the Government, and at 4.00 p.m. news of the settlement was wired to district associations of the Miners' Federation and to the transport unions, with instructions that members were to remain at work. 'Well, sir,' Cook remarked to Churchill, 'I am glad we have settled it.' 'Yes,' replied Churchill, 'it is a good job it is over, but you have done it over my blood-stained corpse. I have got to find the money for it now.'[19] The Chancellor, according to Citrine, 'did not seem at all affected by the negotiations. He was fresh-faced and very much like the cartoons in the newspapers. He was smoking a long cigar all the time. I noticed that when he was in the room with Baldwin, during the negotiations, he put his tall silk hat on the table in front of him, with his gloves and walking stick alongside it. Possibly some of these actions were characteristic of his journalist days. Purcell told me that Churchill was a decent chap to speak to. Churchill had told Purcell that some of his friends should be in goal, but they didn't matter.'

Chapter Three

# *Armistice*

'It will be the endeavour of the Mining Association, during the
respite purchased by Mr Baldwin, to expose to the public the
ramifications and activities of our English "Reds", the methods
by which they control the Miners' Federation and other unions
and their policy towards industry and the state.'

Statement by the Mining Association of Great Britain, August 1925.

'I know some people are saying we have forced the hands of the
Government and that we are Bolshevists and all that sort of thing.
If it means by Bolshevism the spreading of brotherly love for
each other, and not seeking to put the country into a chaotic
position without going back to slavery, then I do not mind being
called a Bolshevist, as I do not intend going back there.'

Herbert Smith, president of the Miners' Federation of Great Britain,
speaking at a Miners' Delegate Conference, 19 August 1925.

'Thirty-four weeks to go—Thirty-four weeks to go to what? To
the termination of the mining agreement and the opening of the
greatest struggle in the history of the British working class. We
must prepare for the struggle.'

*Workers' Weekly*, 28 August 1925.

'It is only too apparent that the public fails to apprehend two
factors in the situation. The extent to which the "labour" movement
and the Trade Unions, which form the backbone of the movement,
are permeated and controlled by subversive elements and minority
movements is not realised; the reason why the issue is being fought
out in the mining industry is not understood. The red resolutions
passed by the Trade Union Congress at Scarborough are in danger
of being forgotten and no reliance may be placed upon the ability
of the Labour party to carry into effect the anti-Communist resolution passed at Liverpool. Nor is the point grasped that if this attack
against colliery owners were to succeed it would immediately be
transferred to some other industry that was considered "ripe" for
nationalisation.'

A letter from the Mining Association of Great Britain to members of the Iron and Steel Manufacturers' Association on 2 November 1925.

Immediately after Red Friday, the Government set about reassuring its supporters and preparing the ground for a resumption of hostilities the following spring. It achieved both purposes by deliberately raising an issue which had been in the minds of the Cabinet during the July crisis but had not been stated publicly or in private negotiations with the miners and the T.U.C. The issue which Cabinet members now began to emphasise was the threat to constitutional government which would be implicit in any sympathetic strike action on behalf of the miners. By bringing the constitutional challenge to the forefront and emphasising their determination to defeat it, Baldwin and his colleagues sought to appease those who criticised them for giving way on the subsidy and to win the support of public opinion. Appearing as the defenders of parliamentary democracy was a much surer way of rallying the country than by appearing as the allies of the coal-owners. By raising the constitutional issue, the Government was also serving notice on the trade unions that they would not have such an easy victory next time and this helped to widen the rift between militants and moderates. The Home Secretary, Sir William Joynson-Hicks—'Jix' to friends and cartoonists alike—struck the new keynote at a meeting in Northampton as early as 2 August: 'I say to you, coming straight from the Cabinet councils, the thing is not finished. The danger is not over. Sooner or later this question has got to be fought out by the people of the land. Is England to be governed by Parliament and the Cabinet or by a handful of trade union leaders?' On 4 August Baldwin himself assured a Conservative meeting that the Government would deal with the political power of combined unions.

Cabinet spokesmen enlarged on the theme during the Parliamentary debate on the coal subsidy on 6 August. Churchill was frank about the necessity of winning over public opinion:

'In the event of a struggle, whatever its character might be, however ugly the episodes which would mark it, I have no doubt that the State, the national State, would emerge victorious in spite of all the rough and awkward corners it might have to turn. But if you are going to embark on a struggle of this kind, be quite sure that decisive public opinion is behind you . . . As the struggle widened, as it became a test of whether the country was to be ruled by Parliament or by some other organisation not responsible by our elective processes to the people as a whole—as that issue emerged more and more, with every increase in the gravity of the struggle, new sources of strength would have to come to the State or some action, which in ordinary circumstances we should consider quite impossible, would, just as in the case of the Great War, be taken with general assent and as a matter of course.'

Taunted by Lloyd George that he had been 'afraid of facing cold steel', Baldwin admitted that the public had not had time to comprehend the implications of a general strike. He then gave a clear warning that any future battle would be fought upon ground chosen by the Government, not by the unions: 'If the will to strife should overcome the will to peace temporarily—and it would only be temporarily in this country—and if we were again confronted with a challenge of the nature I have described, let me say that no minority in a free country has ever yet coerced the whole community. The community will always protect itself, for the community must be fed and it will see that it gets its food. And let me say this too : I am convinced that, if the time should come when the community has to protect itself with the full strength of the Government behind it, the community will do so and the response of the community will astonish the forces of anarchy throughout the world.'

Despite the Labour movement's jubilation at what seemed an easy and spectacular victory, Herbert Smith had no illusions: 'We have no need to glorify about a victory. It is only an armistice, and it will depend largely how we stand between now and 1 May next year as an organisation in respect of unity as to what will be the ultimate results.'[1] Nor did everyone on the Opposition benches share the *Daily Herald*'s enthusiasm for what it called Red Friday.

At the I.L.P. summer school on 3 August, Ramsay MacDonald spoke as though Baldwin had personally betrayed him: 'The Government has simply handed over—the appearance, at any rate—of victory to the very forces that sane, well-considered Socialism feels to be its greatest enemy. If the Government had fought their policy out, we should have respected it. It just suddenly doubled up. The consequence has been to increase the power and prestige of those who do not believe in political action.'[2] MacDonald's chagrin, if not his indiscretion, is understandable. Since Labour's defeat in 1924, the rift between the political and industrial wings of the movement had been widening. Disillusionment with MacDonald and the Parliamentary Labour leadership rather than genuine revolutionary sentiment dictated the mood of the unions, but it found expression in a revival of enthusiasm for Soviet Russia. In February the T.U.C.

General Council angered the Tory Press and alarmed MacDonald by pressing the Russian application to join the Amsterdam-based International Federation of Trade Unions. This was despite the abuse which had been heaped on it by the Russian-sponsored Red International of Labour Unions. In April an Anglo-Soviet Trade Union Conference met in London and set up a joint advisory council to further the Russian application. By May the tensions within the British Labour movement were so great that to Beatrice Webb it seemed only a matter of time before the unions severed their connection with the party entirely. 'The simple truth is', she wrote, 'that, owing to MacDonald's loss of prestige, the universal distrust and disillusionment of the active workers, the inner circles of the Labour movement are more at cross-purposes than I have ever known them.'[3] In June she observed:

'The plain truth is that J.R.M. has lost all his morale with the P.L.P. as well as with the inner councils of the T.U. movement, and his growing alienation from the I.L.P. is only symbolic of a general "rotting" of his influence. He is also suffering from professed arthritis and looks very ill. He still commands big audiences, but he has no body of ardent friends and is getting more and more isolated . . . Certainly the Liberals must be smiling in very broad smiles over the revolutionary speeches of Smillie, Maxton, Lansbury, and Cook, on the one hand, and, on the other, the vision of J. H. Thomas in frock coat and top hat at Ascot and J.R.M. taking tea with their Majesties at the Air Force pageant!'

But the trade unions did not sever their connection with the Labour party: they simply ignored it. In July the General Council summoned a Special Congress on Unemployment. Both A. J. Cook and Herbert Smith addressed it, but no Labour party representative was invited to participate or even attend. During the mining crisis in July, MacDonald was painstakingly excluded from all discussions and it was not until the evening of 30 July—after the conference of executives had endorsed the General Council's plans for a coal embargo—that the leader of the Labour party and his colleagues were grudgingly informed of what was happening and advised to say as little as possible on the crisis in the House. Even this belated meeting had been arranged only after heated discussion at the conference of executives earlier in the day.

Baldwin's sudden capitulation on 31 July was regarded by MacDonald, therefore, as a direct incitement to further industrial action and a possibly mortal blow at what remained of the links between the Labour party and the unions. A. J. Cook left no one in any doubt as to how he interpreted the situation: 'Next May we shall be faced with the greatest crisis and the greatest struggle we have ever known, and we are preparing for it. We shall prepare a Commissariat department. I am going to get a fund, if I can, that will buy grub so that when the struggle comes we shall have grub distributed in the homes of our people. I don't care a hang for any government, or army, or navy. They can come along with their bayonets. Bayonets don't cut coal. We have already beaten, not only the employers, but the strongest government in modern times.' This kind of speech confirmed MacDonald's worst fears and obligingly provided proof of the Government's contention that any large-scale strike action in 1926 would have to be resisted as a challenge to constitutional freedom. The swing away from parliamentarianism in the Labour movement was graphically reflected in the pages of the *Daily Herald*, which during August ran a debate on the enterprising theme of 'Should the Workers Take up Arms?'

But as significant as the debate itself was the deep division on aims and tactics which it revealed between the various advocates of industrial action. For committed syndicalists like Arthur Cook, industrial action was a prelude to the overthrow of capitalist society. For pragmatists like Ernie Bevin, it was no more than a necessary but strictly limited weapon for defending working-class living standards. The success of the campaign against intervention in 1920, in which he personally had played a leading part, and the victory of Red Friday had convinced Bevin that industrial action, or rather the threat of industrial action, was an effective and legitimate weapon in the working-class armoury. But he scorned the heady romanticism of the revolutionaries as vigorously as MacDonald. A more astute leader of the Labour party would have recognised that Bevin was in the wrong camp and attempted to wean him out of it, for without Bevin's backing the challenge represented by the industrial militants could hardly have materialised. It would have been difficult, perhaps impossible, to have shifted a man of Bevin's massive conviction, but MacDonald did not try. Temperamentally incapable of conciliating those whom he feared or disliked, vanity rather than strategy dictated MacDonald's behaviour, and Bevin had wounded his vanity. Later in the year, W. J. Brown, secretary of the Civil Service Clerical Association, was surprised at the intensity of MacDonald's hatred for Bevin. When Brown told Bevin that the leader of the Labour party had referred to him as 'a swine', Bevin was unperturbed. 'Ah, you've found him out then? We all do sooner or later.'[4]

Throughout the arid and uncomfortable remainder of August,

the Left continued to dismay MacDonald and provide ammunition for the Government. On 22 August Mrs Webb noted that 'Maxton, Wheatley, Lansbury and Cook are the four leaders of this revolutionary Socialism, and judged by their public utterances they have really convinced themselves that the capitalist citadel is falling'. Supporters and opponents of MacDonald had an opportunity of testing their strength during the second week of September when the fifty-seventh annual Trades Union Congress met at Scarborough. Superficially, the Congress was a spectacular triumph for militancy. In his presidential address, Alonzo Swales detected 'clear indications of a world movement rising in revolt and determined to shake off the shackles of wage slavery'. The T.U.C. secretary Fred Bramley, who two years earlier had denounced A. J. Cook as 'a raving, tearing Communist', proclaimed that Russia had established 'the first revolution in all history aiming at and securing the overthrow of economic exploitation', adding, 'We consider it our duty to stand by the working-class movement of Russia'. Michael Tomsky, attending Congress for the second year running as fraternal delegate from the Soviet Trade Unions, was suitably responsive. 'When the Russian unions found that they were alone in the struggle for unity, they turned to the British trade union movement, and their experience has told them they did right . . . We have started the campaign together: let us finish it together.'

Four resolutions sponsored by Communist and Minority Movement delegates were passed by large majorities. These condemned the 'enslavement' of the German workers by the Dawes Plan for reparations, a plan which MacDonald himself had helped to negotiate in 1924; demanded 'the right of all peoples in the British Empire to self-determination', which infuriated Jimmy Thomas, the former Colonial Secretary; urged the formation of factory committees as 'indispensable weapons in the struggle to force the capitalists to relinquish their grip on industry'—a direct incitement to industrial action for political ends; and called on the General Council to continue its efforts to promote the formation of an all-embracing Trade Union International. But on the crucial issue of how the trade union movement was to face up to any further confrontation with the Government, Congress was more cautious. A proposal by Citrine that each union should vest in its own executive the power to declare a strike in collaboration with the General Council had been vetoed by the Council itself even before Scarborough. A further Communist-backed resolution, calling for the General Council to be given powers to levy affiliated unions, order strikes, and make arrangements with the Co-operative movement for feeding strikers, was supported by Arthur Cook, but not by other prominent Left-wing delegates. Their own union autonomy was more important to them than class solidarity and they refused to be moved by Cook's appeal for practical preparations: 'It was because on 31 July there was an organisation ready to act without considering any constitution that the miners received help... Be realists my friends. Realise that it is only power that counts...this resolution gives this power.' The Right was not so silent. Jimmy Thomas of the N.U.R. pointed out that the General Council itself had asked for no further powers— 'they are content, and rightly and wisely content, to rely upon the power they already possess'. J. R. Clynes, secretary of the General and Municipal Workers, and another ex-member of MacDonald's Government, expressed his doubts with considerable candour: 'I do not fear, on this subject, to throw such weight as I have on the side of caution. I am not in fear of the capitalist class. The only class I fear is our own. I think, therefore, it will be better not to divide the Congress by insisting on a vote on this question, but that these proposals should be withdrawn and that we should put our trust in our leaders.' Bevin also urged Congress not to vote on the resolution, and it was referred to the General Council for consideration.

It was a General Council in which the balance of forces was decisively changed as a result of Scarborough. From 1923, Left-wingers had chaired the Council and prominent Right-wingers had been absent serving in MacDonald's Government. But at Scarborough the conservative Arthur Pugh, of the Iron and Steel Trades Confederation, was elected to succeed Swales as chairman and Jimmy Thomas, the most aggressive opponent of industrial action, was voted back on to the Council. Bevin, a rogue elephant to both the Right and Left, also joined the Council for the first time, and it was these three who were to dominate it during the next twelve crucial months. But Purcell, Hicks, and Swales all remained members and it was some months before the new focus of power became clear. Certainly, MacDonald was not optimistic at the immediate outcome. 'The whole Congress', he wrote to Lord Stamfordham, the King's private secretary, 'was dominated by the belief that in a coal dispute non-political industrial action brought the government to its knees and the present state of feverish uncertainty and of widespread ill will was never absent from the minds of delegates... The situation is not good. There is a widespread feeling that strong language and brave resolutions should be adopted; and loyalty to the poor devils who have to bear the burden of action is not very strong.'[5]

MacDonald found the atmosphere at Liverpool, where the Labour party met for its annual conference two weeks later, much more congenial. In contrast to Swales's opening speech at Scarborough, Charlie Cramp, industrial secretary of the N.U.R., and retiring chairman of the Labour party, denounced class war and revolution. 'In our practice as a political party we do actually transcend the conflict of classes; we direct our energies to constructive work and ask for the co-operation of all classes.' Despite the Left-wing agitation which had been fermenting since July, the Liverpool conference not only decided to exclude individual Communists from membership of the Labour party, but went on to urge trade unions to refrain from nominating Communist delegates to Labour party conferences and meetings. Bevin joined MacDonald in denouncing the Communists, but made it clear that, although he rejected the notion of a revolutionary general strike, he upheld the right of the unions to support each other with sympathetic strikes. He also moved a resolution calling on the party not to accept office as a minority government. 'Is there a single resolution that has been carried at this conference', he asked, 'that you could get through the House of Commons with Labour in a minority? If you cannot do that, then you must be prepared to compromise, and if you compromise you will destroy the confidence of the people in sending you to the House to represent them.' An unsympathetic and increasingly restless audience provoked Bevin into making an indiscreet personal attack on MacDonald, in which he referred to the electoral deal MacDonald had made with the Liberals at Leicester before the war. Jimmy Thomas poked gentle ridicule at Bevin and MacDonald emphasised the main weakness of the resolution—that it would tie the party's hands even in a situation when it might be vital for a minority Labour Government to assume office. It was clear that the resolution would be heavily defeated, but Bevin obstinately insisted on forcing a card vote.

Liverpool did nothing to improve relations between Bevin and MacDonald, nor between Bevin and Thomas, but it enabled the leader of the Labour party to reassert his authority to a remarkable degree. After a year in which it had seemed simply a matter of time before he was removed, Beatrice Webb was able to write that MacDonald had done 'brilliantly'.[6] She noted that 'The dramatic change from the neo-Russian Communism of the Trades Union Congress of a few weeks ago to the silent voting down, by a two million majority, of the successive Communist resolutions at the Labour Party Conference, is certainly baffling to the student of British democracy—for practically the two Conferences represent the same membership. It is all a question of platform leadership: in both cases the thousand delegates trooped after the man who sat on the platform and managed the business! Today the question arising is what will be the relation between the Executive that sits at 33 and the Executive that sits at 32 Eccleston Square?' Before Mrs Webb had an opportunity of discovering the answer, both wings of the Labour movement were swept into yet another passionate confrontation with the Government.

On 14 October at the evening performance of an amateur dramatic society the inimitable Jix announced : 'I believe that the greater part of the audience will be pleased to hear that warrants have been issued and in the majority of cases have been executed for the arrest of a certain number of notorious Communists.' That day police had raided offices of the Communist Party, Young Communist League, National Minority Movement, and *Workers' Weekly*, arresting eight leading officials, including Albert Inkpin, the party secretary, and Harry Pollitt, secretary of the Minority Movement. A few days later four more leading Communists were arrested. All twelve were charged with seditious libel and incitement to mutiny on divers days since 1 January 1924. There was an immediate and massive outcry from all sections of the Labour movement and individuals offering to stand bail for the arrested Communists ranged from George Lansbury and A. J. Cook to Bernard Shaw and the Dowager Countess of Warwick. An Old Bailey jury returned a verdict of guilty at the end of November and five of the accused, including Inkpin and Pollitt, were immediately sentenced to twelve months' imprisonment. The judge offered to bind over the remaining seven to be of good behaviour if they promised to renounce all further association with 'an illegal party carrying on illegal work in this country'. All refused and received sentences of six months.

'The Communist party', wrote George Hicks, the bricklayers' leader, in the Left-wing *Sunday Worker*, 'is now in the same position as the trade unions were during the early part of the last century.' A resolution demanding the release of the Communists was adopted at a joint meeting of the General Council of the T.U.C. and the National Executive of the Labour party—Beatrice Webb's 'two Executives'—and even MacDonald felt compelled to move a resolution in the House of Commons condemning the trial. Criticism of the Government was not confined to Labour members. Sir John Simon, a former Liberal Attorney-General and Home Secretary, observed that 'it is only in the very last resort that this sort of prosecution should be adopted and I am bound to say I did expect, when I heard the prosecution was undertaken, that we were going to have proved matters far more immediately significant than seem to have been proved'. The Government was to derive rather more comfort from Simon six months later.

For the Communist party itself the prosecutions occurred at a singularly opportune moment. The Labour Left, which the party had been assiduously cultivating for more than eighteen months, had refused to come to its support at Liverpool and had shown scant sympathy immediately after. In spite of its own disenchantment with MacDonald, the I.L.P. had refused the Communist party's suggestion of an alliance, and George Lansbury, MacDonald's chief scourge in Parliament, declared only four days before the first arrests that, 'the Left-wing is no more prepared than the workers' movement as a whole to be bored or manipulated from King Street, or for that matter from Moscow itself'.[7] The political martyrdom helpfully bestowed by Jix ended the Communist party's growing isolation from the more orthodox Left, and by 24 October Lansbury was asserting that the Communists were part of 'the indivisible movement of the working class'.[8] A furious MacDonald publicly called it a 'disservice' to prosecute the Communist party at such a time and warned that its 'potentialities for sedition' had only been increased. Within days of the Old Bailey verdicts another series of politically emotive trials began in Cardiff and Carmarthen. More than 200 South Wales anthracite miners were sentenced to terms of imprisonment ranging from fourteen days to twelve months for acts of violence during a strike in July. Ben Griffiths, secretary of the Mining Clerks' Guild, wrote that the Carmarthen jury 'was composed of the aristocratic big guns of the county, mainly of the landed proprietor class, and has Colonel F. Dudley Williams-Drummond, estate agent to Lord Cawdor, as its foreman. There are also two colonels, three majors, a captain, a knight, a parson, and an agent for a local lady with a big income from royalties. Those are to try trade union fighters'.[9]

A desire to placate his own extremists for the humiliation of Red Friday undoubtedly played a part in Baldwin's decision to launch the first overtly political trial in England since the days of the Chartists. It was at the annual conference of the Tory party in Brighton, on 8 October, that he promised to consider prosecuting the Communist party and it was only six days later that the first arrests were made. But the decisive factor does appear to have been a genuine fear of Communist activity and influence inside the unions. J. C. C. Davidson, Baldwin's closest political confidant, and a key Government figure before and during the General Strike, has written:

We were at this time particularly worried about revolutionary activities in the country. In January 1924, the Communist International had thrown its full weight behind United Front tactics and was prepared to use them within the factories and the trade unions, which were their natural link between the Communist party and the workers. Their policy was to establish cells within the factories and form factory committees, which could be linked regionally. Opposition to the moderate trade union leaders was to be fostered, particularly in certain industries. Communists were to take the lead in all disputes. The Communist party in this country was small. It had only 5,000 members, but we thought it could gain a secure hold on certain parts of the trade union movement in the mining industry and by the attempts to organise the unemployed. Committees of action had been set up in many factories and trade unions, factory newspapers were used to influence workers, and demands were made for more nationalisation and increased unemployment pay. MacDonald's failure to act, and the mounting unemployment figures while the Labour party had been in office, made for a growing disillusion in the labour movement that was dangerous... The T.U.C. Conference at Scarborough in 1925 seemed to show the growing influence of the [Communist] movement... The growing industrial crisis in the mines would clearly give them a good chance of success, as we were told that strike committees were being organised in the trade unions and in the services.[10]

But in launching what was so clearly a political trial, Baldwin seriously compromised his own concept of 'Peace in Our Time' and hastened rather than halted the developments noted by Davidson. Baldwin showed more finesse in his handling of other measures to meet the threat of industrial militancy. A rather ramshackle emergency Supply and Transport Committee was already in existence when Baldwin assumed the premiership in 1923. Originally set up by Lloyd George during the dangerous months of 1919, it had been ready to go into action on the eve of Black Friday in 1921. Maintained thereafter on a skeleton basis by two civil servants and a clerk, it was revived by Baldwin, and handed over to Davidson, who was also appointed Chancellor of the Duchy of Lancaster. Davidson remained Chancellor, but assumed the newly-created title and functions of Chief Civil Commissioner. He undertook these further duties in strict secrecy, receiving his salary as Commissioner not from the Treasury but direct from Tory party funds. Between May 1923, and the General Election at the end of the year, Davidson, assisted by John Anderson, the outstandingly able Permanent Under-

Secretary to the Home Office, created the nucleus of a new and much more effective emergency organisation. Ten regional commissioners were appointed in England and Wales to be responsible for maintaining transport, food supplies and essential services such as light and power in their own areas in the event of serious industrial disruption. The Lord Advocate assumed responsibility for Scotland. Arrangements were also made to take over the British Broadcasting Company and possibly to produce a Government news sheet if the newspapers ceased publication. According to Davidson, 'Work continued unremittingly until the fall of the Government in 1923'.

With Labour's accession to power, a potentially embarrassing situation arose. As a secret memorandum to Davidson from one of his assistants pointed out, 'It is possible that, if the Labour Government decided that the present organisation, designed to meet industrial crisis, should be continued, the Chief Civil Commissioner appointed under that Government, might well be a prominent trade unionist, like Mr Smillie or Mr Frank Hodges. In this event, whoever was appointed would at once become acquainted with all the machinery for quelling that very crisis which he himself, when in opposition, may have done his best to foment.' The memorandum invited Davidson to consider 'whether the organisation had not better be wrapped in temporary obscurity and silence' and suggested that it should be left to the discretion of Maurice Hankey 'to raise the question of your successor, if any, with the Home Secretary of the new Government'.[11] Instead, Davidson decided to make a personal appeal to Josiah Wedgwood, the new occupant of the Duchy Office. 'I told him', Davidson has recorded, 'that, whoever was in power, it was his duty to protect the Constitution against a Bolshevik-inspired general strike... I begged him not to destroy all I had done and not to inform the Cabinet of it. This did not concern party but was a national matter. Josh said that he could not continue to build my organisation, but he promised not to interfere with the work we had done.' When Davidson resumed his duties after Labour's defeat, he was told by Wedgwood: 'I haven't destroyed any of your plans. In fact, I haven't done a bloody thing about them.'

Within a few weeks, Davidson was appointed Financial Secretary to the Admiralty, and replaced as Chief Civil Commissioner by Sir William Mitchell-Thompson, the Postmaster-General. Davidson, however, retained a close connection with his brainchild, whose work assumed critical importance with the onset of the mining crisis in the summer of 1925. Churchill wanted the Government to prove its determination to the unions by giving the Committee widespread publicity, but Davidson resisted, arguing that this would only provoke more trouble. This incident foreshadowed further disputes between the two men. There was also some disagreement between ministers on the eve of Red Friday about the Committee's ability to handle an immediate emergency, and according to Davidson : 'It was not until July 1925, when the threatened coal strike was averted only by the grant of a subsidy and the promise of a royal commission on the coal industry, that preparations were really put in hand.' These were placed under the general direction of a Cabinet committee chaired by Joynson-Hicks, the Home Secretary, and the details were left to John Anderson and the Supply and Transport Committee on which fourteen separate Government departments were represented, each with a clearly defined sphere of responsibility. The accumulation of reserve stocks of food and fuel was left, for instance, to the Board of Trade, and it was the function of the Ministry of Transport to make arrangements for long-distance distribution and to ensure electricity supplies.

The essence of the Government's strategy was regional self-sufficiency, and it was intended that in any large-scale disruption the civil commissioners should 'take drastic action of a comprehensive character'. This was provided for under the Emergency Powers Act, which Lloyd George had rushed through in 1920. Significantly, eight of the eleven junior ministers appointed as commissioners were officers of military rank and two were peers. Each had his own headquarters staff of specially selected civil servants to co-ordinate essential local services and liaise with a network of volunteer service committees set up under prominent and politically reliable local citizens nominated by the Government. Throughout the autumn of 1925, the senior officials of many municipalities were also sounded out, though in the vital London and Home Counties region those employed by Labour-controlled councils were not approached. On 20 November all local authorities received a confidential circular from the Ministry of Health which outlined the Government's arrangements and their role in them.

But however elaborate the schemes worked out by the Government and the local authorities, they could not be successful without sufficient volunteers to man the services vacated by strikers. Troops were to be used only in the last resort, and it was to be the job of the eighty-two volunteer service committees to provide the necessary manpower if and when the time came. However, an apparent rival announced itself through the Press at the end of September. Calling itself the Organisation for the Maintenance of Supplies, the new body declared: 'For many months past it has been evident that a movement is being organised to take advantage of a trade dispute,

exceptionally difficult to solve, in order to promote a general strike...
Numerous suggestions have since been made from various quarters
for organising those citizens who would be prepared to volunteer to
maintain supplies and vital services in the event of a general strike.
It seems, therefore, that the moment has come to announce publicly
that such an organisation has already been constituted and is at work
in many metropolitan boroughs, while steps are being taken to
create corresponding organisations in all the principal centres of the
Kingdom'.

The O.M.S., as the new body soon came to be known, disclaimed an
aggressive or provocative intent and emphasised its 'complete sympathy with any constitutional action to bring about a more equitable
adjustment of social and economic conditions'. But it warned that,
if 'an attempt is made to inflict severe privation on the great mass of
the people who have no direct part in the actual dispute, this
Organisation of Citizens, serving the interests of the general community, will place its entire resources at the disposal of the constitutional authorities'. Volunteers, the announcement added, were
needed for 'protecting the public services' and, if necessary, enrolling
as special constables; for manning the railways, tubes, trams, and
buses, and for general driving duties; for handling foodstuffs; and
for acting as clerks and messengers.

The *Daily Herald,* with piquant but unconscious irony, regarded
the O.M.S. announcement as an 'insulting intimation' that the Prime
Minister was 'unfit for his job'. It is unlikely that Mr Baldwin shared
this view. Far from rivalling the Government's efforts, the O.M.S.
was a valuable adjunct to them and was certainly launched with
strong ministerial support if not direct inspiration. Its president was
Lord Hardinge of Penshurst, a former Under-Secretary of State for
Foreign Affairs and ex-Viceroy of India, and its central council was
composed, not of obscure and choleric county worthies, but of
eminent and sober administrators who had spent distinguished careers
in the public service. The central council included Admiral of the
Fleet Lord Jellicoe, Major-General Lord Scarborough, director of
the General Territorial and Volunteer Forces from 1917 to 1921, and
Lieutenant-General Sir Francis Lloyd, food commissioner for London
and the Home Counties from 1919 to 1920. Joynson-Hicks favoured
*The Times* with his views on the O.M.S. on 1 October:

I have known of the inauguration of this body for many weeks
past; in fact, the promoters consulted me as to their desire to
form some such organisation... I told the promoters of the O.M.S.
that there was no objection on the part of the Government to

their desire to inaugurate the body to which you refer; that, if and when an emergency arose, the Government would discharge the responsibility which is theirs and theirs alone, but that it would be a very great assistance to us to receive from the O.M.S., or from any other body of well-disposed citizens, classified lists of men in different parts of the country who would be willing to place their services at the disposal of the Government. From this statement you will see that not only is there no reason why you should object to the O.M.S., but that you, and any other citizen who would desire the maintenance of peace, order, and good government in times of difficulty, would be performing a patriotic act by allying yourselves with this or any other similar body, formed for the sole purpose of helping the public authorities in the way I have suggested.

Less enamoured of the O.M.S. were the volunteer service committees, which felt that the newcomers would undermine their authority. The vice-chairman of the Wrexham Committee, for instance, protested to the Government after being informed by the local O.M.S. representative that it might be taken that the O.M.S. was 'supreme'.[12] It was vital that there should be no squabbling about 'supremacy' in a crisis and, although the Government was reluctant to be drawn into direct contact with the O.M.S., its principal officers were invited to meet Mitchell-Thompson, Davidson, and other members of the Supply and Transport Committee on 7 December. The Chief Civil Commissioner emphasised that in any emergency the Government must have absolute control of any organisation designed to maintain essential services. It was agreed that in such an emergency the O.M.S. would efface itself and hand over its personnel to the Government or its designated representatives—in effect the chairmen of the volunteer service committees.

Labour reaction to the O.M.S. ranged from smug contempt to fierce denunciation. Charlie Cramp, Thomas's chief lieutenant in the N.U.R., expressed the view of those in the Labour leadership anxious for a quiet life: 'Personally, I have not the slightest fear of these jokers. They are people who have never worked in their lives. If they started to do so in a strike they would make a very poor job of it.' For the Communist party, and for the Left in general, the O.M.S. represented 'the most complete scheme of organised blacklegging and strike breaking yet devised, and is the most advanced form of Fascism yet reached in this country'.[13] The menace of an imminent Fascist takeover was, of course, a recurrent theme in Communist and Left-wing propaganda. Hankey, a rather more dispassionate observer, had also expressed apprehension during the mining crisis of July, but overt Fascism was the least of the dangers facing Britain in 1925. Membership of the British Fascists, set up in 1923, and of the National Fascisti, a militant but minute splinter group of the parent body, numbered only a few thousands, and, unlike the Communist party, neither had any kind of base in the trade unions or popular support outside. The leaders of both groups consisted mainly of retired military and naval officers and extreme Right-wing Tory peers, far more concerned to preserve the *status quo* than to overthrow it. The activities of the two groups hardly invited comparison with their namesakes in Italy. The most spectacular coups of 1925 were the painless and temporary abduction of Harry Pollitt from a Liverpool-bound train by members of the British Fascists in March and the hijacking and crashing of a *Daily Herald* delivery van by members of the National Fascisti in October.

Far more significant than the incidents themselves was the judicial indulgence shown those who perpetrated them. Charged with unlawful conspiracy to assault and unlawful imprisonment, Pollitt's five kidnappers were all found not guilty by an exclusively middle-class jury. After consultations with the Attorney-General, Sir Douglas Hogg, the prosecution reduced the charge against the four *Daily Herald* hijackers from one of larceny to one of committing a breach of the peace. 'They all appreciated', said prosecuting counsel, 'that their conduct was not what it should have been, however meritorious it might have been from another point of view.' Binding over the defendants to keep the peace in the sum of £100 each, the magistrate remarked on the prosecution's leniency. A week later, the Bow Street magistrate ruled that a *prima facie* case had been made out against the twelve Communist leaders charged with sedition. Labour supporters drew the obvious conclusion. Oswald Mosley, Labour's bright new meteorite, denounced Government intervention on behalf of the National Fascisti as a public scandal and as one of the most shameful acts of injustice that the country had ever known. Bernard Shaw was constrained to observe 'that a mere withdrawal of the charge against these gentlemen was, after all, a very poor acknowledgment of their services to the Government; I think they might at least be given the O.B.E. at the first opportunity'. The Attorney-General and the jury of eminently respectable Liverpudlians were certainly not Fascists, yet their behaviour reflected an attitude which was not untypical of large sections of the middle-class in 1925: that a spot of mild political hooliganism was permissible, provided, of course, it was directed against the 'Reds'. To what extent this attitude might have been inflamed and harnessed by a determined Fascist organisation during the General Strike must remain a matter for speculation, for by May 1926, the British Fascists had virtually ceased to exist as a separate body. When the O.M.S. was launched, a majority of the party's leadership proclaimed that 'at the present moment effective assistance to the state can best be given in seconding the efforts of the O.M.S.'. They withdrew from the British Fascists to form the Loyalists, which as a 'non-political' group was then incorporated into the O.M.S. According to one of the leaders who refused to desert the British Fascists, they were offered money to change their name, abandon their military structure, and later their manifesto.[14] There is no independent evidence of this, but it is likely that Lord Hardinge, president of the O.M.S., had indirect contact with the British Fascists through his cousin, the Rt. Hon. Arthur Hardinge, who sat on the party's executive. Some members also offered to enrol as special constables, provided they could serve as a body under their own officers. Liverpool again distinguished itself by allegedly announcing its intention to accept the offer.

Despite evidence of O.M.S. and Government preparations, the trade union movement showed no inclination to make preparations of its own. The Industrial Alliance was formally constituted in November, but three of its most important components had still not balloted their members and by securing the last-minute withdrawal of the N.U.R., Jimmy Thomas managed to ensure that the Alliance was a still-born giant. It played no part in the events of 1926 and effectively lapsed after the general strike. The T.U.C. General Council was even less anxious to commit itself. It was not until 27 April, with three days to go before the mining subsidy ended, that the Council considered for the first time the problem of what was actually to be done. Meanwhile, it was left to the Industrial Committee, originally set up to liaise with the miners in July 1925, and reappointed at Scarborough, to handle the situation as it thought best.

This was presided over by Arthur Pugh, chairman of the General Council, who one contemporary observer thought 'might have made a fortune as a chartered accountant'.[15] An ex-steel smelter, Pugh typified many of the older and more conservative trade union leaders. Cautious and sceptical, he regarded the political wing of the Labour movement as a potential threat to the independence and integrity of the trade unions. Of the Industrial Committee's seven remaining members, only Alonzo Swales, of the engineers, George Hicks, of the bricklayers, and John Bromley, of the locomotive engineers and firemen, were avowed Left-wingers. Bromley, who was also an M.P., was an outspoken critic of MacDonald's premiership, and an

44

opponent of the ban which excluded Communists from the Labour party. He had provoked Jimmy Thomas's wrath in January 1924, by rejecting as inadequate a wages award which Thomas had persuaded the N.U.R. to accept. Thomas had expressed himself freely to the King when asked for his views on the leader of A.S.L.E.F. 'Speaking to you as subject to your Majesty, sir, or as man to man?' Thomas had inquired. 'As man to man, please, Mr Thomas.' 'Then you can take it from me, your Majesty, he's a bloody 'ound.'[16] After the general strike Thomas was able to declare : '...there was no better pal throughout the whole of this business than Bromley has been to me.'[17]

The other four members of the Industrial Committee—Jimmy Thomas, A. G. Walkden, of the Railway Clerks' Association, Arthur Hayday, M.P., of the General Workers, and Ben Tillett, of the Transport Workers—were all firmly opposed to militancy. As founder of the Dockers' Union and leader of the great dock strikes of 1889 and 1911, Tillett had himself been the focus of Labour ferment, but personal and political frustrations had soured his radical ideals and in October 1923, he had offered his services to the new Tory Premier, Stanley Baldwin. After the interview, John Davidson wrote to Admiral Sir Reginald 'Blinker' Hall, the ex-director of Naval Intelligence and principal Tory agent, that Tillett was 'absolutely broke; is going to fight Communism in the winter, and evidently wants financial help. The Prime Minister wondered whether you thought it might be worthwhile sending for Tillett. There is just a chance he might do business.' Hall, who was to play his own small though significant role in the events of 1926, was far from enthusiastic, but suggested to Davidson that the party chairman 'might be prepared to make a special grant of £1,000 if (the) P.M. decides it, but he feels as I do that we can't encourage all the derelicts—and if we began, there is no end'.[18] Whether Tillett managed to sell his services is not known, though he would have had difficulty earning his money at the end of 1925.

The Industrial Committee was no more anxious to plan for the probable crisis the following May than the General Council itself. After the Scarborough Congress it met only twice during the remainder of 1925. On 25 October it resolved merely to watch the course of events, and on 18 December it decided that the additional powers which Left-wing delegates at Scarborough had wanted the General Council to adopt were unnecessary. Mrs Webb's jubilant surmise at the end of December was that 'The General Council has been rescued by Thomas and Margaret Bondfield from out of the hands of the little knot of silly folk who led it into the Scarborough morass of pseudo-communism.' In fact, there was little need for Thomas to practise his rhetorical arts on either the General Council or the Industrial Committee. Despite the heated resolution-mongering at Scarborough, it was clear that most union executives were in no mood for a self-sacrificing struggle on behalf of the miners. Unemployment was high and trade union membership was falling. In the peak year of 1920 it had totalled over $8\frac{1}{4}$ million. In 1926 it totalled less than $5\frac{1}{4}$ million. It was clear, too, that the Government had made formidable preparations since Red Friday and that Baldwin could not afford to capitulate a second time.

Early in December Churchill admitted that in the summer 'the country as a whole was not sufficiently informed about the character and immense consequences of such a struggle as that with which it was confronted', but went on to warn that any further conflict 'between the community on the one hand, with the Government at its head, and many of the great trade unions on the other, could only end in one way, namely, by the community, at whatever cost, emerging victorious over an organised section of its citizens, however valuable, important, and even numerous that section was'.

The Industrial Committee took the Chancellor's warning to heart and for the next five months proceeded on the assumption that the best way of avoiding a clash with the Government was not to prepare for one. Only Walter Citrine, who acted as the Committee's secretary, questioned this assumption. Still only thirty-eight, Citrine had worked as an electrician in Liverpool before launching into a successful union career. After rising to prominence in the E.T.U., he had been appointed to the newly-created post of assistant secretary of the T.U.C. General Council in 1924, and had been made acting secretary when Fred Bramley died suddenly soon after the Scarborough Congress. Holding aloof from the sectional and ideological passions which surrounded him, Citrine was anxious to turn the General Council into a powerful and effective leadership for the whole trade union movement. Convinced that Red Friday marked the beginning, not the end of the struggle, he had attempted, unsuccessfully, to present a plan for streamlining strike procedure to the Scarborough Congress. At the end of 1925 he tried once more to force some unwelcome realities on the attention of his colleagues.*

* During the summer of 1927 Citrine spent a weekend with the Webbs. Mrs Webb described her guest as 'Under forty years of age, tall, broad-shouldered, with the manners and clothes and way of speaking of a superior bank clerk; black hair growing low on his forehead, large pointed ears, bright grey eyes set close together, big nose, long chin and tiny rather "pretty" mouth, it is difficult to say whether or not he is "good-looking". In profile he is; in full face he is not. When arguing his features twist themselves up and he becomes positively ugly. By temperament and habit of

46

In a carefully argued 'Memorandum on the Impending Crisis',[19] he raised precisely those issues which the Industrial Committee preferred to ignore. Recalling the Tory outcry which had greeted the coal subsidy in July, he observed that the Government would be under great pressure to refuse further financial assistance during any reorganisation period recommended by the Royal Commission. What, asked Citrine, did the Industrial Committee intend to do if the Government bowed to this pressure? 'I am conscious', he wrote, 'of the difficulties of making a decision on matters which must be to a large extent in the region of conjecture. Nevertheless, I consider there is a duty imposed upon the Special Industrial Committee to examine in the closest degree the situation and to determine upon some form of preparation.'

But what form of preparation? Was the Parliamentary Labour party to be excluded from discussions as it had been in July or was it to be invited 'to propagate throughout the country the necessary support to force the Government to a favourable decision?' The practical question to be considered was 'whether it is possible to keep the issue a purely industrial one while at the same time having the fullest consultation with the political wing of the movement'. Were any essential services and supplies to be maintained in the event of a national stoppage? If so, which were they to be and who was to maintain them? Should members of the Labour movement be urged to start storing essential commodities or could satisfactory arrangements be made with the Co-operative Societies? Finally, Citrine dealt with the crucial question of the relationship that was to exist between the General Council, working through the Industrial Committee, and the Miners' Federation. He urged that:

It is necessary to get an understanding as to which body is entrusted with the conduct of the dispute. There is at present no

life Citrine is an intellectual of the scientific type. He is sedentary, takes too little exercise for his health; he is assiduous, always improving himself by reading and writing and working at his job unremittingly – he has no "silly pleasures"; he is a non-smoker, non-drinker, small slow eater, takes a daily cold bath, sleeps with his windows open – altogether a hygienic puritan in his daily life . . . I think he is very ambitious – expects too much relatively to his faculties . . . He has the integrity and loyalty characteristic of the better type of British mechanic. I think he is too public-spirited and too intent on real power to go the way of Frank Hodges and become a hanger-on of the directors of capitalist industry. His pitfall will be personal vanity and the sort of conceit which arises from continuous association with uneducated and unselfcontrolled official superiors . . . Lying full-length on the window-seat in a free and easy way with his boots on my best Indian shawl he slightly annoyed me. But he has character, industry and intellect. He is the first "intellectual" to be at the centre of the T.U. Movement . . . what he will make out of the Movement, during the next ten years, raises my curiosity.'[20]

single authoritative body directing the policy which is to be pursued. Statements are being made with increasing frequency from the platform and the Press, none of which can be taken as expressing any real co-ordinated policy. It appears to me that if responsibility is to be taken by the General Council through its Special Committee for organising the trade union movement in defence of the miners' standards, then the General Council must determine the policy to be pursued. It would not only be inadvisable but even dangerous to allow individuals, whether they be miners' officials or politicians, to create a state of tension and lay down lines of policy to which the General Council might feel itself unable to subscribe. The mining situation has ceased to be exclusively a miners' question; it certainly is not purely a political question, and the imperative need is to get recognition generally that whatever policy is laid down by the General Council shall be the policy for all concerned.

Citrine's memorandum was never seen by the General Council as such, but a copy was submitted to the Miners' Federation and it was discussed when the Federation and the Industrial Committee eventually met on 12 February. The circumstances were not propitious. In December Arthur Cook had infuriated the Co-operative Union by assuring a meeting of South Wales miners that in the coming struggle, the Co-operative movement would be 'the victualling movement for the fighting forces of Labour'. Citrine had been holding talks with the Co-operative movement at the time and he received an irate letter from the secretary of the Co-operative Union. 'It is a great pity that Mr Cook cannot be "muzzled". See his statement again this week that an arrangement has been come to for the Co-operative movement to deal with the question in case of a crisis. This is causing a lot of discussion in the Co-operative movement, because no such arrangement has been come to, and I think he ought to be a little more guarded in his statements, as it is making our position more difficult every time statements like that appear in the Press.'

A public slanging match between Cook and Thomas had followed in January. Incensed by Cook's criticism of a new wages award for railwaymen which allowed for reductions in certain circumstances, Thomas wrote a bitter denunciation of the miners' leader in the *Daily Herald*:

'Like the majority of the members of our movement, I have long ceased to treat Mr Cook seriously, and my regret is that a great

48

organisation like the Miners' Federation should day after day have its case ruined by the childish outbursts of its secretary...one's sympathy for the miners is accentuated by the knowledge that they have to suffer under the double misfortune in having to tolerate as their leader Mr Cook, who has yet to learn the elemental principles of leadership...all those who happen to know most about events are praying that he will at least take a rest and so render a more lasting service to the cause of the workers.'

Cook's reply was equally venomous:

'It is true I do not possess a dress suit, and I do not attend dinners and banquets given by the enemies of the working class and make alleged witty after-dinner speeches there. Thomas may think that comes within the province of a trade union leader, but if it is one of the "elemental" principles of leadership, I am not going to adopt it. Thomas is giving vent to his personal spite because I have remained true to the cause of the workers. Along with other noble lords, dukes and gentlemen, he has long wished me in a very warm place.'

The two antagonists were in complete agreement, however, when they and their colleagues met to discuss Citrine's memorandum on 12 February. Although the miners were later to denounce the General Council for failing to prepare adequately for the May crisis, both Arthur Cook and Herbert Smith urged that no practical steps should be taken until the Royal Commission on the Mining Industry had issued its report. No doubt their suspicion of Thomas made them reluctant to hand over direction of policy to a body in which his influence was so considerable. Thomas was just as reluctant to see the Industrial Committee organising for a conflict which he was determined should be avoided. 'It was clear to me', says Citrine, 'that the meeting did not want to face the issues raised in my memorandum and would do anything to put off a decision.' This reluctance persisted at a second meeting a week later, although it was agreed to ask the Co-operative Union if they would be prepared to help. The Industrial Committee also gave a hostage to fortune. In a statement issued after the meeting, it declared: 'The attitude of the trade union movement was made perfectly clear last July, namely, that it would stand firmly and unitedly against any further attempt to degrade the standard of life in the coalfields. There was to be no reduction of wages, no increase in working hours, and no interference with the principle of National Agreements. This is the position of the trade union movement today.'

Other less comradely statements were also made after the meeting. Cook told Citrine that Thomas was completely distrusted, and Frank Varley, of the Nottingham miners, complained that there was too much jealousy among the miners. 'You may take it for granted', he lamented to Citrine, 'that everything I say Herbert Smith will contradict, merely because I say it.'

On 26 February the Industrial Committee and the miners met the Co-operative Union. Cook's misleading statement of December was not forgotten, but now the Co-operative Union raised an even more unpalatable issue. Recalling the heavy financial losses which some of the local retail societies had suffered during the miners' strike of 1921, the Co-operative Union refused to guarantee any further assistance unless the assets of the whole trade union movement were pledged in advance. Neither the Industrial Committee, nor indeed the General Council, had authority to give such a pledge and the one positive attempt to prepare for the May crisis ended in complete failure.

Gloomy and dispirited, the Industrial Committee and the miners trooped back to the T.U.C.'s headquarters in Eccleston Square, a house once occupied by Winston Churchill. Millions of workers might have to stare into empty larders, exclaimed Thomas. How were they going to be saved from starvation? Undaunted, Arthur Cook replied that working-class families, knowing that a strike was inevitable, should be laying in secret supplies of food. 'I mean it', he persisted in face of Thomas's scepticism. 'My own mother-in-law has been taking in an extra tin of salmon for weeks past.' After an astonished silence, Thomas was unable to restrain himself: 'By God! A British revolution on a tin of salmon!'[21] Still adamantly refusing to pursue any of the other initiatives urged by Citrine, the miners and the Industrial Committee settled down to wait and to hope. It was just possible that somehow the report of the Royal Commission on the Mining Industry, expected in March, would save them from a mutual embrace which neither wanted.

## Chapter Four

# *The Samuel Report*

'The desire to secure cheap coal by a lowering of wages in the coal mining industry is undoubtedly present and this, together with the urge for decreased taxation, must have considerable influence on the Government's policy. The outbreak of political opposition which succeeded the granting of the subsidy by the Government in July and allegations of pitiful surrender to the forces of anarchy make one reflect on the possibilities of the Government's declining further assistance. There seems a steadily growing tendency among the more vocal Conservative politicians to regard a struggle with the trade union movement as inevitable and imminent... There has been unmistakable evidence of preparation for possible public disorder next year, and the swearing-in of special constables is proceeding steadily. The Fascisti movement is drilling and organising its forces, and while as an economic factor this can be safely ignored, it is more in the realm of enforcement of law and order that the dangers lie... Preparations which have been made to meet previous Labour disputes, notably in 1919, have been perfected, and it is reasonable to suppose are very much more complete. Can we afford, in view of these obvious preparations, to delay in making our preparations?'

Memorandum on the Impending Crisis, presented by Walter Citrine to the T.U.C. Industrial Committee, 19 February 1926.

Unlike previous royal commissions on the mining industry, the present one contained no representatives of miners and owners. 'The P.M.'s idea', explained Clive Wigram, the King's Assistant Private Secretary, 'was to have a Government Commission composed of a few distinguished men of business who could take evidence of both sides and make recommendations. The P.M. wishes to avoid the repetition of a Sankey report, with three separate reports,* and he did not intend to pack the Commission with owners and miners. His one object was to have an independent tribunal.'[1] From the miners' point of view, however, the independence was a little one-sided. The Com-

---

* It will be recalled that the members of the Sankey Commission had, in fact, produced four reports concerning the mining industry's future ownership.

mission's chairman, Sir Herbert Samuel, a former Liberal Home Secretary and, until recently, High Commissioner in Palestine, was known to be opposed to nationalisation of the mines, and his three colleagues were unlikely to be any more sympathetically disposed to the miners' basic proposal.

Sir William Beveridge, the Liberal economist, had worked at one time as a leader writer for the *Morning Post*, whose proprietor was the pro-Fascist, coal-owning Duke of Northumberland. Beveridge had then gone into the Civil Service and, after a distinguished career, had resigned to become director of the London School of Economics. Both Samuel and Beveridge were, in Mrs Webb's somewhat enigmatic but clearly disparaging phrase, 'Typical Liberals'.

General Sir Herbert Lawrence, who had served as Haig's wartime Chief of Staff, was managing partner of Glyn, Mills and Co., the prominent banking house, and was also on the boards of several other leading companies, including the London, Midland and Scottish Railway. Kenneth—later, Sir Kenneth—Lee was chairman of the great Manchester cotton firm of Tootal, Broadhurst Lee and Co., and chairman of the District Bank.

Samuel was on holiday in the Italian Tyrol recovering from his exertions in Palestine and contemplating a philosophic work on the contemporary failure of belief when the Prime Minister's summons came. Unwilling to desert his own sunny and civilised pursuits for the gloomy and dispiriting world of coal, Samuel only accepted his new assignment at Baldwin's emphatic insistence. He was of Cabinet rank, the Prime Minister told him, and he was not identified with either capital or labour. Samuel argued that he had no special knowledge of the coal industry and that there must be people with better qualifications to chair the Commission. Far from any connection with the coal industry being desirable, replied the Prime Minister, it would be a disqualification, for it was essential that fresh minds should be brought to bear. 'No selection better or as good is possible.'[2]

The Commission opened its proceedings in public on 15 October 1925, in a large committee room adjoining Westminster Hall and once again miners and owners began the parade of well-known arguments. The miners made it clear that they were not prepared to accept any worsening of working conditions and urged that only a fundamental reorganisation of the industry under public ownership could solve its problems. The owners proposed the lengthening of working hours, a reduction in the wages of their own employees—and those of the railwaymen so as to cut transport costs—and a return to district settlements. 'The unrest in the mining industry', observed Evan Williams, chairman of the Mining Association, 'has not been the spontaneous expression of dissatisfaction on the part of the mass of the workers themselves, whose wages have been higher and employment more regular than those of workers in the other heavy industries; but it has been the result of a deliberately planned attempt on the part of the industry under private enterprise after de-control, in order to force upon the nation the political policy summed up in the phrase "The Mines for the Miners".'

It rapidly became clear to the commissioners that what they were witnessing was not simply a dispute about wages between one group of employers and their men, but the ritual battle-cries of two savage and implacable tribal foes. Generations of mutual hatred spilled out into the environs of Westminster Hall with the myriads of statistics, and journalists and public, drawn by the scent of blood, came crowding in to see what Beveridge called 'one of the free shows of London'.[3] Each side took full advantage of the right to question the other's witnesses, so that a devoted audience might see Herbert Smith and Evan Williams, or Arthur Cook and the Duke of Northumberland appearing together on the same bill.

There were some members of the audience, however, who felt that the star performances left much to be desired. The Socialist historian R. H. Tawney, who was also Beveridge's brother-in-law, had been a member of the Sankey Commission, and he was invited by the miners to prepare a scheme for nationalisation which they could then submit to the Samuel Commission. It did not take him long to become 'very sick with the way Cook is running the miners' cause'.[4] Unknown to Tawney, Cook had also asked the Communist-controlled Labour research department to draw up a nationalisation scheme. On the other side, David Davies, a Welsh Liberal M.P., former Parliamentary Private Secretary to Lloyd George, and a director of the Ocean Coal Company, wrote to Samuel privately regretting the attitude both of his fellow-directors and the officials of the Mining Association.

Davies sent a copy of this letter to his friend and compatriot Tom Jones, deputy secretary to the Cabinet. In a covering letter to Jones he was even franker. 'The evidence given by Evan Williams appears to be more stupid than one could possibly have anticipated. He has done his best to rile the miners. There is not a note of con-ciliation in the whole evidence. He has put the railwaymen on their guard, and cemented the alliance between them and the miners. He has boosted the royalty owners when there was not the slightest justification or reason for doing so, and he has not made a single constructive contribution towards the solution of the problem. One would feel inclined to dissociate oneself officially and in every other

53

way from the vapourings of these people. What they say is no doubt true, but it is the offensive way they say it; the evil spirit which appears to vitiate and befog all their utterances; and their total inability to realise that it is their business to attempt to help the Commission and not to make their task more difficult.'⁵ Jones thought this letter showed there were 'some decent and progressive coal owners ready to move forward'. Perhaps so, though none seemed able or willing to assert themselves against Evan Williams and the Mining Association.

Before a full month was out Samuel was already regretting his new assignment. 'I can do nothing so far as I can see, at present,' he wrote to his wife, 'nor can anyone else it seems.' Beveridge suggested that 'unrestricted conversation' with the miners' leaders might break the deadlock, and in December 1925, Arthur Cook and Herbert Smith were invited to dine with Beveridge, Lawrence, and Lee at Lee's flat. Samuel himself did not attend, believing that as chairman of the Commission his presence would be inappropriate. After an agreeable meal, the diners got down to what Beveridge called 'brass tacks'. Cook and Smith were informed that the commissioners would not feel it right to recommend any renewal of the coal subsidy after 30 April. It was wrong to ask the taxpayers to make up the difference when employers and employed could not come to terms, and if the principle were established for coal, then why not apply it equally to railways, shipping, cotton, or any other industry of national importance in which there were similar problems? Since any improvement in mining organisation could not bear fruit immediately, the miners must see that a temporary increase in hours or a cut in wages was inevitable: which was it to be? Beveridge has given his own sour account of how Smith and Cook reacted. 'We thought we must, by hook or by crook understand, if possible, what was in the minds of the miners' leaders, but we never got within sight or smell of an understanding. Herbert Smith's mind was granite. Cook's mind I described, after he had left that night, as having the motions of a drunken dragon-fly. "Not a minute on the day, not a penny off the pay" was the dreary rigmarole.'⁶

Dreary rigmarole it undoubtedly was, but Beveridge and his colleagues could hardly have expected the miners' leaders to pledge themselves to sacrifices without knowing more about both the Commission's positive recommendations and the Government's attitude to them. What form of reorganisation would be proposed? How long would it take? Would the Government accept the proposals, and, if so, would they force the coal-owners to carry them out? None of these vital questions could be answered until the Commission had issued its report, and Smith and Cook were not the players to reveal their hand before the others in the game had even opened the bidding. This was a perfectly reasonable negotiating position, but the miners' leaders chose to ignore those who were supposed to be their partners at the table, the T.U.C. Industrial Committee. Despite Citrine's warning that a serious crisis would almost certainly arise on 30 April if Baldwin refused to renew the coal subsidy, neither he nor the other members of the Industrial Committee were told by the miners that the Samuel Commission itself would be opposing any further subsidy. The deliberate suppression of this information arose presumably from a fear that it would bring about some intervention by the Industrial Committee—and hence by Thomas and his Right-wing supporters. Thus the miners and the Industrial Committee awaited the Samuel Commission's judgment, as distrustful of each other as of those they were supposed to be in alliance against.

The Commission's report was published on 10 March 1926, after what Samuel has described as 'the most strenuous six months' work I have ever done'. The Commission had held 33 public sittings— the last on 14 January, and heard almost 80 witnesses; it had visited some 25 collieries in person and over 40 by deputy. So great was interest in its 300-page findings, originally published at a shilling, that they had to be reissued at threepence. Over 100,000 copies were sold and it was not surpassed as an official best-seller until the publication of Beveridge's own *Report on Social Security* in 1943. The Samuel Report said little about the industry's basic problem that was not already well-known. Exports had fallen by a quarter compared with the period before 1914, yet the number of miners employed had actually increased by 10 per cent. The industry had enjoyed a temporary burst of prosperity in 1923 following the French occupation of the Ruhr, but this had ended just as quickly with the French withdrawal, and the industry was once again trying to sell to a world already glutted with coal. 'The industry as a whole', declared the report, 'has ceased to be remunerative.' Three-quarters of its output was being produced at a loss and the unprofitable mines were kept going only by means of the subsidy. This situation, declared the report, was due largely to the loss of the Russian market, to competition from oil and German lignite, and to modern inventions which reduced the overall demand for coal. But attention was also drawn to another important factor. 'We had not been well impressed by the existing organisation of the industry', Beveridge has written, 'or by the mine-owners as a body; I found myself saying harsh things about them to Steel-Maitland as Minister of Labour.' The report was more specific. Many mines, it observed, were old and badly designed, and efficient working was often hampered by divided ownership of the coal seams; too many collieries were small and ill-equipped; insufficient research was being devoted to the utilisation of coal and its by-products; distribution and selling arrangements were 'expensive and inefficient'; working conditions and terms of employment 'called for improvement'. The owners were admonished to 'discontinue charging the miners as a body with deliberate attempts to destroy the prosperity of the industry, in order to compel its nationalisation', and to stop accusing the miners of restricting output.

The remedy for this formidable list of ills was not, however, to be total nationalisation. 'We are not satisfied', stated the report, 'that the scheme proposed to us [by the Miners' Federation, Labour party and T.U.C.] is workable, or that it offers a clear social gain.' Beveridge's personal view was that it was 'too syndicalist'; the report was couched in less emotive language. 'We perceive in [the scheme] grave economic dangers, and we find no advantages that cannot be obtained as readily, or more readily, in other ways.' These were to include state acquisition of the mineral rights; amalgamation of many of the smaller mines into more efficient units; improved sales and transport arrangements; the right of local authorities to retail coal; state support for a vast increase in research; the closer co-ordination of the mining and allied industries under an advisory National Fuel and Power Committee; the setting up of a National Wages Board with representatives of the miners and the owners, plus neutral nominees. In addition, a series of welfare reforms was proposed, including family allowances, profit-sharing, baths at all pit-heads, and annual holidays with pay when prosperity returned to the industry.

But when and how would prosperity return to the industry? As the Commission pointed out, to put all of its proposals into effect would take years. Meanwhile, three-quarters of the pits in Britain were being kept open only by a subsidy which was due to end in less than seven weeks' time. The Commission's views on the subsidy had not changed since the meeting with Smith and Cook in December. 'We express no opinion whether the grant of a subsidy last July was unavoidable or not, but we think its continuance indefensible. The subsidy should stop at the end of its authorised term, and should never be repeated.' How, then, was the industry to survive the immediate crisis? The Commission's views on this had not changed since December, either. The owners' demand for an increase in working hours, as well as for district agreements and cuts in the wages of both miners and railwaymen, was firmly rejected. But some sacrifice by the miners was essential. Since longer working hours would only make the situation worse by increasing a supply that already exceeded demand, the Samuel Commission looked to wages to provide the answer.

Nothing about the mining industry was simple and straightforward, least of all its wages structure. To those outside the industry its complexities were often incomprehensible and added greatly to the difficulties and frustrations of the Government and the T.U.C. in the forthcoming negotiations. It was during the course of these that Baldwin declared, 'I do not believe that anybody understands it.' Throughout the thirteen wage districts the basic or standard wage rate varied. To this was added a fixed proportion of the sales proceeds from each district. But since this might be more or less, depending on sales performance, it was not to fall below a specified minimum percentage of the prevailing standard rate in any district. Under the wages agreement of 1924, signed when British coal exports were still booming as a result of the Ruhr occupation, the minimum percentage had been increased from 20 to 33⅓. 'If the present hours are to be retained,' the Samuel Report stated, 'we think a revision of the "minimum percentage addition to standard rates of wages", fixed in 1924 at a time of temporary prosperity, is indispensable. A disaster is impending over the industry, and the immediate reduction of working costs that can be effected in this way, and in this way alone, is essential to save it.'

What was contemplated, however, was not 'a permanent lowering of wage standards but a temporary sacrifice by the men in the industry, other than the worst paid, in order to avoid the possible unemployment of hundreds of thousands of them'. Even this, it was alleged, would still leave the coal-owners without adequate profits, and in many districts without any profits at all. 'If trade improves and prices rise, a profit will be earned. If prices do not rise, an adequate profit must be sought in the improved methods which should in any case be adopted.' The Commission recognised the need for continuing variations in district wage rates, but was emphatic that these should continue to be fixed by national agreement. 'Such agreements are entered into in all the other British industries of importance.' Finally, the coal-owners (and by implication the Government) were left in no doubt that their obligations were as great as those of the miners. 'Before any sacrifices are asked from those engaged in the industry, it shall be definitely agreed between them that all practicable means for improving its organisation and increasing its efficiency should be adopted, as speedily as circumstances in each case allow.' Convinced that the report was generally 'very favourable to the miners', Samuel departed speedily for Italy, taking with him two volumes of Pliny's Letters, a memento from his colleagues on the Commission. 'Returning to Lake Garda, I settled down, thinking I was now safe. But it proved not to be so.' For the time being, however, Samuel was free to enjoy the congenial pursuits of classical scholarship and Italian sunshine.

Following a request from the Prime Minister that there should be no official pronouncements on the Samuel Report until its contents had been fully examined by all the interested parties, the Miners' Federation and the Mining Association maintained a rare and discreet silence during the first weeks of March. The Coal Merchants' Federation felt themselves bound by no such understanding and immediately launched a strident campaign against the proposal that local authorities should be empowered to retail coal. Equally uninhibited were some of the unofficial reactions to other parts of the Samuel Report. Addressing a miners' meeting in South Wales on 14 March, Arthur Cook was unable to refrain from declaring that there were to be no wage cuts whatsoever. On the same day Sir Adam Nimmo, a powerful member of the Mining Association, told the annual meeting of his Fife Coal Company that a reduction in wages was the one practical proposal in the report. Preliminary sniping was not confined to the main antagonists. Ramsay MacDonald welcomed the report as 'a conspicuous landmark in the history of political thought' and as 'one of the strongest indictments of private enterprise that has ever been issued as an official paper. The stars in their courses are fighting for us.' Few of MacDonald's colleagues cared to express themselves quite so lyrically, though many of the Labour party and T.U.C. leaders shared his view that the report provided the best hope there had ever been of securing long-term agreement in the mining industry.

The Left-wing in general and the Communist party in particular immediately declared their opposition to the report. According to the Communist party, it was 'a declaration of war against the miners and the whole working-class movement', and faced the workers with two dangers. The first was the direct offensive of the mine-owners and the capitalists; the second was the hesitation and trepidation of reformist leaders in the Labour movement who called for reconciliation of classes and preached sweet reason to the workers. What the workers needed was united action of the type that had brought about the victory of Red Friday.[7] Criticism of the Samuel Report swelled the renewed upsurge of Left-wing turbulence in the winter of 1925–6. Following the arrests of the Communist leaders and the anthracite miners, a Free Speech and Maintenance Fund had been set up with John Bromley as chairman, George Lansbury as treasurer, and an executive including Alf Purcell, George Hicks, and, inevitably, Arthur Cook.

On 7 February—'Release the Prisoners Day'—massive demonstrations had been held in many parts of the country. In London, a crowd of 15,000 had marched from Clapham Common to Wandsworth prison, where Harry Pollitt and his comrades were serving their sentences. At the end of that month, Shapurji Saklatvala, the party's lone M.P., had presented Parliament with a petition for their release bearing 300,000 signatures. On 7 March, three days before the Samuel Report was published, a meeting at the Albert Hall— 'one of the biggest meetings ever held in London', according to Lansbury—had risen to its feet and repeated after Lansbury the slogans for which the Communists had been gaoled: 'We call upon all soldiers, sailors and airmen to refuse under any circumstances to shoot down the workers of Britain, and we call upon working-class men to refuse to join the capitalist army. We further call upon the police to refuse to use their batons on strikers or locked-out workers during industrial disputes.' A week later the slogans were repeated by another vast crowd outside Wandsworth prison.

The first big Left-wing attack on the Samuel Report came within a fortnight of its publication from the National Minority Movement. Launched during the summer of 1924, the Movement's rapid growth among the miners and engineers, and to a lesser extent among the railwaymen and transport workers, had caused serious concern to Baldwin and J. C. C. Davidson during 1925, and its secretary, Harry Pollitt, had been one of the arrested Communists to receive a maximum sentence. On 21 March 1926, the Movement convened a National Conference of Action in London, which claimed to speak on behalf of 957,000 workers. This was an exaggeration, since union memberships were counted several times over if separate delegations represented branches, district committees, and the national executives of the same union. The Conference was, nevertheless, an impressive tribute to Pollitt's hard work and skilful organisation.

With Pollitt in prison, Tom Mann, the Minority Movement's chairman, delivered the main indictment of the Samuel Report. 'The policy of splitting the workers is very cunningly continued. The Commission has recommended some changes, aimed at splitting the Labour movement, such as the family wage, municipal selling agencies and the nationalisation of minerals. They hope the reformist elements in the Labour movement will concur with their recommendations and lose sight of the attacks upon living standards contained in the report—which the trade unions must fight.' The 'reformist elements' had clearly been in the ascendant since Scarborough, but Mann went on to urge: 'The real body through which we must function is the General Council of the Trades Union Congress.' There could have been little doubt among Communist and Minority Movement leaders that most members of the Industrial Committee and probably also of the General Council, were determined to prevent not simply a revolutionary strike, but a large-scale strike of any kind. It was believed—or, more accurately, hoped—that the Left-wing trade union leaders would be able and willing to assert themselves when the time came. Their language, as R. P. Dutt, editor of *Workers' Weekly*, observed optimistically after Red Friday, 'is the closest indication of the advance of the British working-class to revolution'.[8]

To encourage this advance, the party had set up 'nuclei' in 300 pits and factories by the beginning of 1926 and these were producing 70 newspapers with a combined circulation of 70,000. Considerable attention had also been devoted to the trades councils, the local federations of trade union branches. These were not entitled to send delegates to Congress and they had no policy-making role in the trade union movement, but they did represent the rank-and-file in each area and they were free of the inter-union rivalry which so often manifested itself at an official level. The Scarborough Congress had ruled out of order a Communist-sponsored motion calling for direct affiliation of the trades councils to the T.U.C., but the party had no doubt of their potential in a widespread strike. They had already shown something of this during the Russo-Polish crisis in 1920, when some 300 of them had constituted themselves into councils of action and had urged the Labour party and T.U.C. to oppose British intervention not only in Russia but in Ireland, too.

More than fifty were represented at the March Conference of Action and they enthusiastically endorsed the blueprint laid down by Mann and the Minority Movement.[9] Councils of action were to be set up once again, and these were to establish food and supply organisations with their local Co-operatives. They were also to form workers' defence corps, which would protect working-class speakers from 'bourgeois terrorism', trade union headquarters from 'Fascist incendiarism', and strike pickets against 'police interference'. They were to build 'a powerful working-class force, capable of defending the political and industrial rights and liberties of the workers'. Finally, the General Council was urged to convene a National Congress of Action and to secure the support of the international trade union movement for the British workers in 'the struggles ahead'.

Meanwhile, the Cabinet was concerning itself with the more immediate realities of the Samuel Report. Anyone familiar with the submissions made by miners and owners to the Royal Commission could hardly have expected them to reach voluntary agreement on the vital but contentious issues of wage cuts and reorganisation. It was the miners' view that reorganisation without wage cuts would solve the industry's problems; it was the equally firm view of the owners that wage cuts without reorganisation were the answer. G. R. Lane-Fox, the Secretary for Mines, saw clearly that if any kind of agreement was to be reached it was necessary for the Government to declare that it fully accepted *both* parts of the report.[10] Tom Jones, who was appointed secretary of the reorganised Cabinet Coal Committee early in March, was also convinced that an initiative would have to come from the Government.

> It is no use the Government saying: You settle the immediate question (wages) and we will deal later with the larger question (reorganisation). The Report makes it clear...that discussion of wages reductions is dependent on previous undertakings to re-organise. If the Government take the opposite line, fat will be in the fire. The resistance will come from the owners and the Government must be prepared to quarrel with them, some of whom will say that 'the mines may as well be nationalised'. Miners unlikely to accept wage reductions in full proposed by Commission but bargain should be possible between masters and men to which miners will make a contribution. Government talks privately with the owners but not with the miners. Owners therefore have considerable political pull. Government must fight down owners' opposition to reorganisation. Once more miners will not discuss wage reductions until there is firm promise on this point. Federation does not want to keep open pits that ought to be closed and will be willing to override district opposition if Government gives them a chance.[11]

But Baldwin and his colleagues disliked the Commission's reorganisation proposals almost as much as the owners and on 17 March the Cabinet decided that it would accept the Samuel Report only if the miners and owners also accepted it. Sir Arthur Steel-Maitland, the Minister of Labour, and by chance himself a coal-owner, obligingly provided Baldwin with a memo for guidance in dealings with the Miners' Federation. '(1) You cannot ask for details of Bills, etc., from us first before you do anything. (2) We are going on the assumption that you and the (Mining) Association are going to come to an agreement on the lines of the Report. (3) If you *don't*, then a new situation will have arisen. (4) *But the ball is with you both now.*

(5) *Beyond 30 April the subsidy cannot go on* except for a taper of two or three weeks if an agreement has been reached.'[12] This virtual ultimatum was presented with rather more grace by the Prime Minister when he eventually met both sides a week later. The conclusions reached by the Commission, he told them, did not in all respects accord with the views held by the Government and there were some proposals to which, taken by themselves, the Government was known to be opposed. 'Nevertheless', he said, 'in face of the unanimous report of the Commission and for the sake of a general settlement the Government for their part will be prepared to undertake such measures as may be required of the State to give the recommendations effect, provided that those engaged in this industry —with whom the decision primarily rests—agree to accept the report and to carry on the industry on the basis of its recommendations. It is our hope that in that event, by the co-operation of all parties, it may be possible to find in the report a lasting solution to the problem.' Asked by Herbert Smith if this meant that both sides would be left to settle in any way they could, and that the Government would give no further subsidy, Baldwin emphasised that agreement must be reached by 30 April, but hinted that temporary assistance for a further three months might be forthcoming to ease the situation in those districts where 'the sacrifice required must be heavy'. Urged to reveal what plans the Government itself had, Baldwin replied that the Cabinet had not had time to consider them. 'If I speak and say anything my word goes, you see, and it will be done, and it is a very responsible position...it commits the Government and therefore to go into any question in detail at the moment would be difficult for me.' He did, however, promise to prepare a schedule of matters needing legislation. Finally, there was a characteristic appeal: 'If we all swallow this report, we are doing it for the sake of peace... my job is to get a great party to endorse what I am going to put before them.'[13]

That evening Arthur Cook told a meeting in London: 'We have made arrangements that not one ton of coal will be handled in this country unless the Government's decision is satisfactory to us miners. We have also made sure that no coal will enter this country from America or Germany. We are going to be slaves no longer and our men will starve before they accept any reduction of wages.' At a private meeting immediately after the Samuel Report was published Cook had appeared far less intractable. Wage concessions, he had admitted, might be conceivable, given immediate proof of the Government's determination to press the owners into actual and not merely tactical acceptance of the reorganisation proposals. But the miners were not again 'buying a pig in a poke'. During the remaining six weeks of the subsidy there were to be further signs of Cook's willingness to discuss concessions by the miners—provided the Government guaranteed that reorganisation would take place. Baldwin, however, continued to insist that voluntary agreement between the two sides must precede any legislative action by him. The entirely predictable result was total deadlock. At joint meetings on 25 March, 31 March and 1 April, the miners wished to discuss only reorganisation and the owners nothing beyond wage cuts, longer hours and a return to district settlements.

Announcing to friends that 'only a strike of miners, supported by the whole of organised labour, would force...concessions from a Conservative government and the Mining Association', Cook turned once again to the T.U.C. Industrial Committee. On 8 April, the day before a Special Delegate Conference of the miners was to meet in London to discuss the Samuel Report, the Industrial Committee was asked to reaffirm its support for the three principles: no wage cuts; no increase in hours; no return to district agreements. Although the Industrial Committee had publicly asserted the three principles throughout February, the miners were now told that matters had 'not yet reached a stage when any final declaration of the General Council's policy can be made'. Citrine set out the Industrial Committee's new attitude in a letter to Cook: 'It appears to them that negotiations are yet in a very early stage, and that efforts should be made to explore to the fullest extent the possibility of reducing the points of difference between your federation and the coal-owners, and for that purpose they advise the immediate continuance of negotiations.' Citrine did not explain *why* the Committee had changed its attitude; why, as late as 26 February, 'There was to be no reduction in wages, no increase in working hours, and no interference with the principle of National Agreements', but not on 8 April. The reason, though, was clear. On 10 March the Samuel Report had been published and Thomas and a majority of the Industrial Committee and the General Council seized upon it as providing the basis for 'an equitable settlement of outstanding difficulties'. But no bargain could be struck on the basis of the Report if the T.U.C. were forced, in Thomas's revealing phrase, 'to acquiesce in a mere slogan'.

A month of unproductive haggling with the owners and of washing of hands by the Government had already substantially eroded the chances of a peaceful settlement when the Miners' Conference met on 9 April. The mood of delegates was not improved by the account Cook gave them of his meeting with the Industrial Committee. 'I know from delegates who were at the conference,' Thomas later told a meeting of his own railwaymen, 'how bitterly disappointed the miners' executive were, and the miners' executive expressed their disappointment to the miners' delegates, because they had intended and assumed that we would adopt the slogan. Having refused to do it, they naturally and obviously were sore, and said so to their Conference.'[14] The Conference showed its angry defiance of owners, Government and T.U.C. by unanimously agreeing to recommend to the district federations the three principles which the Industrial Committee had just refused to endorse.

Considered by itself, the resolution ruled out any concessions by the miners, a point which the General Council did not neglect to make in their subsequent account of events. 'It will be clear that while the Miners' Federation were fully aware that the Industrial Committee declined to tie the hands of the General Council and the trade union movement in regard to negotiations on the [Samuel] Report, their confidence bound its officials to refuse any consideration of the possibility of revision of wages and working conditions.'[15] What the General Council omitted to mention was that the chances of a negotiated settlement would have been even slimmer had Cook and his executive not urged their resolution on the Conference. A week before, the Miners' Minority Movement, with strong support in many of the district associations, had resolved 'to work vigorously and perseveringly for the full and complete rejection of the Royal Commission's report', and had demanded nationalisation without compensation and full workers' control. The Lancashire delegates had come to the Conference prepared to put a similar resolution and this would certainly have been adopted if the executive had not moved a tough-sounding resolution of their own. By their action the executive had managed to keep the door, if not fully open, at least slightly ajar. Baldwin, however, firmly declined to push and on 13 April the owners announced that they would be approaching the district miners' associations for wage talks, knowing full well that the district associations would refer them back again to the national federation. Undeterred, the owners posted notices in most pits announcing that employment on existing terms would cease on 30 April, the day the subsidy was to end.

This was too much even for the Industrial Committee, which immediately condemned the owners for creating 'ill-feeling and suspicion at a critical time' and asked to see the Prime Minister. On 13 April Baldwin agreed to meet the Committee the following evening and then spent an agreeable half-hour or so with Tom Jones discussing 'literary work'. Baldwin was pleased with the preface he had just written to a book on Eton and Harrow cricket matches and Jones was full of praise for a forthcoming anthology of the Prime Minister's speeches, *On England and Other Addresses*. 'It is the Englishness of S.B. that emerges in these addresses', Jones noted in his diary, 'and I think (for a Welshman) I've played up to that very well!'[16] The early-morning exchanges on 14 April were perhaps less diverting, though certainly more relevant. The subject was coal. Jones told the Prime Minister that he took 'a quite cheerful view of the position so far reached', and that the miners' reply to the owners 'was quite as satisfactory as we had any right to expect'. But Jones warned that the owners' attempt to impose district settlements would have to be opposed and that what should be aimed at was a national minimum percentage for all districts with flexible additions above it in the wealthier districts.

In the afternoon Jones listened to the Mining Association putting the case for district settlements to Steel-Maitland and even his buoyant optimism sagged. The Minister of Labour, Jones discovered, was hardly the man to achieve a settlement.

> He has an aggravating manner. He starts off a sentence but loses confidence before he is half through it and either starts another or begins a string of qualifications which tie up the sentence in an awful tangle. He is most industrious and has laboured hard to get up the subject, but distracts himself, turns constantly to Horace Wilson [Permanent Secretary to the Ministry of Labour] at his elbow, apologises, protests that he is being frank and straight, which of course he is trying to be, but the total impression is one of weakness and cloudiness.

Jones found the chairman of the Mining Association no more inspiring.

> 'Evan Williams, who for the last seven years has been putting the owners' case, is an insignificant little man. He is by this time quite able to make a neat and measured statement in quiet and reasonable tones, and one hardly realises the full gravity of the issues at stake. What *he* lacks in emphasis, however, is promptly supplied by Sir Adam Nimmo who is never more than a few inches away from Evan Williams. Nimmo is chairman of the Fife Coal Company and is also, I believe, a local preacher. He is powerfully built and lays down the law in stern tones... He is one of the greatest stumbling blocks in the path of peace. Among the thirty or forty others there is hardly an outstanding personality... The

65

discussion centred on the determination of the owners to go into the thirteen wage districts where they could fix the wages they proposed to offer after 30 April and invite the local miners' executive to discuss the proposal. It is certain that their invitation will everywhere be rejected.'

Jones's optimism was somewhat restored later that afternoon when he hurried down to the House of Commons to report on the meeting to the Prime Minister. After talk of coal, cricket, and Kipling— 'I...said there was a certain hardness about his style which the P.M. escaped'—Baldwin left to vote in a division. As Jones wandered back towards the Lobby he saw Ramsay MacDonald's secretary approaching with a gangling, fair-haired man. It was Arthur Cook. As they passed, Cook turned to Jones and whispered, 'I'd like to see you tonight.' In equally conspiratorial tones, Jones gave Cook his Hampstead telephone number and was about to write it down when John Bromley appeared and took Cook off to a meeting with the Industrial Committee. The phone call never came, but Cook had provided a further hint of his anxiousness to open the way to a peaceful settlement.

An hour or so later, Baldwin received the Industrial Committee in his room at the House. The Committee warned that, unless the deadlock was broken, Cook and Smith would try to gain support at a weekend meeting of the Miners' International in Brussels, and that a flood of violent oratory would be loosed off on Sunday. Baldwin was unimpressed. Frank Hodges, secretary of the Miners' International, had already expressed his approval of the Samuel Report and his intense dislike of Cook was no secret. As for violent oratory, this was likely to gain as many supporters for the Government as for the miners. Baldwin did agree to see both sides in an attempt to get negotiations going again and arranged to receive the Miners' Executive at noon the following day. But he also left the Industrial Committee in no doubt as to his own position in the dispute. The Committee were mistaken, he told them, if they thought he had granted the coal subsidy out of funk. He had granted it because he was a pacifist, but if a pacifist was pushed too far he could be very combative and obstinate, and the Committee were not to think that the country's money was going to be poured out indefinitely.

Later that night Baldwin made an even plainer statement of his position. He met Jimmy Thomas privately and after hearing how Thomas 'had fought with beasts of Ephesus upstairs', warned that if there were a general strike pressure to restrict the powers of the trade unions would become irresistible. He would be driven to deal

66

with the political levy, the strike ballot and the Trade Disputes
Act, and the Labour party's chances of coming to power would be
thrown back for years.[17] Baldwin knew his man, and while Jones
'metaphorically took the Prime Minister by the hand' and marched
him off to bed, 'very glad, I am sure, to be led away', Thomas sought
out Ramsay MacDonald to tell him into what desperate straits the
miners' intransigence was leading them all.

## Chapter Five

# 'Not a Penny off the Pay, Not a Second on the Day'

'The Government, no doubt, would consider longer hours with pleasure, but that pleasure will never be theirs. We have got to prepare ourselves for the control of this industry. I will not accept joint responsibility for private ownership. There can be no co-operation with capitalism so far as I am personally concerned.'

A. J. Cook, speaking in Cardiff, 27 March 1926.

'Cook and Smith dare not take up any other attitude, because neither has any real personality, and they are simply trying to obtain a continuance of the subsidy and so discharge what they consider to be the duties of their position. They know there are many others ready and willing to take their places if they appear to falter. The situation is undoubtedly a very difficult one, and one which must be in some very important respects considered as a whole... If it is true that only a limited production is required, then all theories of increased output fall to the ground. I put this to you with all respect and humility because we collectively, owners and men, have failed to do what I earnestly hoped and prayed we could do, which was to join together and work out a solution of the problem. If our failure is due to deeper reasons than those which appear on the surface, it is for those outside the industry to diagnose the causes which are nullifying the best elements in the representatives of each side.'

Lord Londonderry, leading Irish coal-owner, writing to Stanley Baldwin, 13 April 1926.

Early next morning, 15 April, Sir Alfred Cope, one of the moderate coal-owners, who appears to have been in touch with the Labour leaders, phoned Jones to assure him that 'Ramsay MacDonald and Clynes were passing the word along that the miners were (to be) reasonable and conciliatory otherwise public opinion would be alienated and in the event of a strike the prospects of the Labour party severely damaged'. Cope added that the miners' executive 'were counting on the P.M.'s goodwill and the continuance of a substantial subsidy'. At 11.00 a.m. Jones, Steel-Maitland, and Horace Wilson discussed with Baldwin the line to be taken at the midday session with the miners. It was agreed 'to keep the pot boiling and moderate the extravagance of speeches on Sunday'. The weekend meeting of the Miners' International was mentioned and Jones dismissed the notion that a visit by Cook and Smith to Brussels would have any unfortunate consequences. 'No one would understand them there and as Frank Hodges is secretary of the International he would select his own interpreter of their speeches.'[1]

When the miners' executive arrived for their appointment with Baldwin they expressed concern about two immediate issues: the owners' insistence on district negotiations and their refusal to give details of the new wage rates they proposed to offer when the current agreement expired on 30 April. Smith then made a personal though somewhat cloudy appeal to the Prime Minister. 'We want to be absolutely straight with you. We do not tell you we accept the [Samuel] Report. We tell you now, if you ask us, we think we are too low, but when we have things put before us we have to give consideration to them and give a reason if we cannot accept them... We are dependent at the present time upon the Government making a move which will assist industry over this stage; it is no good saying we are not.'[2] What kind of move—whether legislation, renewal of the subsidy or both—Smith did not make clear, and Baldwin did not pursue the point. He declared that he, too, wanted figures from the owners—'and I want them quickly'—and brought the meeting to a diplomatic and soothing close by promising to urge national negotiations on the owners. As Jones noted, 'The P.M.'s attitude at these gatherings is always most friendly and sympathetic and teachable.'

After the meeting, Cook at last managed to see Jones alone for a few minutes. 'We are economically in the weakest position we have ever been in,' Cook admitted frankly, 'and while a lot of our chaps won't agree with me, we shall have to have a national minimum not only with pluses above it, but minuses below it.' He urged that Baldwin should meet the owners as soon as possible on the question of national negotiations and then preside at a joint conference of the two sides 'while they thrashed out the wages issue'. What Cook clearly envisaged was an initiative by Baldwin to secure reorganisation and a new national agreement, with possible wage cuts as the price to be paid. Whether Cook really would have recommended wage cuts to the miners and whether they would have agreed are matters for conjecture, but an attempt to reach a settlement on this basis could hardly have failed more disastrously than the initiative which Baldwin now began to contemplate.

Not only had the Samuel Report insisted that no sacrifice should be asked of the miners until 'all practicable means had been agreed for improving the industry's organisation and efficiency'; it had also emphatically rejected a longer working day as the sacrifice to be made, pointing out that this would only add to the surplus of unsold coal or lead to further unemployment, with a smaller working force producing the same output. It was to this 'solution' that Baldwin, nevertheless, now began to turn, though another six precious days were allowed to pass before the owners were given an opportunity of savouring such an unexpected enticement.

While the Prime Minister gave the matter of hours his leisurely consideration, Cook and Smith pleaded their cause in Brussels. The response from the Miners' International was far from enthusiastic. The British miners had shown little enough concern about the effects of the 1925 subsidy on the working conditions of the European miners and the European miners paid back their British comrades in much the same coin. The International agreed to discuss the possibility of a sympathetic strike but it was made clear to Cook and Smith that, if a stoppage did occur, direction of the *British* strike was to pass into the hands of the International Committee—which would mean into the hands of Frank Hodges. Such a prospect did nothing, however, to dim Arthur Cook's incandescent oratory when he returned to England on the Sunday. He travelled to London immediately to address an I.L.P. meeting at Clapham. There could be no help for the miners from the Government, he announced, who would certainly back the owners, and the coming struggle had to involve not merely the miners, but the whole of the working classes. 'We have got the whole trade union movement in the country pledged to defend the miners' hours, wages and national agreements. Abroad, we have made agreements that no coal shall come into this country. The Government and the owners know we have got the organisation that can fight and win. My last word to the Government is, count the cost. The cost of a strike of the miners would mean the end of capitalism.' No reference to the unpleasant realities of Brussels or to the fact that no pledge had been received to stop the export of coal to Britain, since the Miners' International had no control over transport, was allowed to mar the enthusiasm.

Cook vibrated even more fiercely at a meeting of South Wales miners on the Monday.

Let me warn the Government that there is a new mentality in the police, the army, the navy, and the air force. Ninety-seven per cent of the recruits for the past two years have come from the working classes and thousands of them miners, who will not shoot against their kith and kin when the order comes, and we shall not be afraid to advise them: this is a war to the death, and it is your death they are after.

Arthur Horner, then a leading member of the Miners' Minority Movement, has given a revealing account of Cook's platform manner at this time:

In the months before the 1926 strike, and during the strike, we spoke together at meetings all over the country. We had audiences, mostly of miners, running into thousands. Usually I was put on first. I would make a good, logical speech, and the audience would listen quietly, but without any wild enthusiasm. Then Cook would take the platform. Often he was tired, hoarse and sometimes almost inarticulate. But he would electrify the meeting. They would applaud and nod their heads in agreement when he said the most obvious things. For a long time I was puzzled, and then one night I realised why it was. I was speaking *to* the meeting. Cook was speaking *for* the meeting. He was expressing the thoughts of his audience, I was trying to persuade them. He was the burning expression of their anger at the iniquities which they were suffering.[3]

After attending one of Cook's meetings in April, 1926, Kingsley Martin noted in his diary that the miners' leader 'made a most interesting study—worn-out, strung on wires, carried in the rush of the tidal wave, afraid of the struggle, afraid, above all, though, of betraying his cause and showing signs of weakness. He'll break down for certain, but I fear not in time. He's not big enough, and in an awful muddle about everything. Poor devil and poor England. A man more unable to conduct a negotiation I never saw. Many trade union leaders are letting the men down; he won't, but he'll lose. And Socialism in England will be right back again'.[4]

While Arthur Cook raised weekend temperatures, Jimmy Thomas strove desperately to lower them. With Baldwin's warning of the previous Wednesday to prompt him, Thomas declared at a meeting in Monmouthshire on Sunday that 'To talk at this stage as if, in a few days, all the workers of the country are to be called out is not only letting loose passions that might be difficult to control, but it is not rendering the best service either to the miners or anyone else.' Instead of organising, mobilising and encouraging the feeling that war was inevitable, Thomas pleaded, they should all be concentrating on finding a solution honourable and satisfactory to all sides. The Mining Association's contribution to conciliation was a statement which it issued two days later: 'There is not the slightest foundation for the rumours that the coal owners have decided, or are prepared to agree to the principle of a national minimum wage.'

On Wednesday, 21 April, with nine days to go before the end of the subsidy, Baldwin was due to see the owners. In the morning Jones reported to him what Alfred Cope had just told him of the South Wales owners' plans to impose savage wage reductions. To Jones it seemed clear the owners were 'spoiling for a fight. The publication of terms like these would swing public opinion over to the men'. Baldwin said he was 'building his hopes on some concessions from the men in regard to hours', but when Jones asked him what procedure he had in mind for his afternoon meeting with the Mining Association, the Prime Minister was at a loss. 'He seemed to be quite blank about it, and asked what we did on previous occasions. I told him that while we had open and formal meetings with the full executives, a great many secret parleys were going on among the leaders between the meetings. I added that I did not think I could deal privately with Cook as I used to deal with Hodges and J. H. Thomas. They could be absolutely relied on, but Cook might proclaim to the world that I had been talking with him. I thought that the P.M. should aim at conducting the effective negotiations with four representatives of the owners, and four of the men, until we had made some progress.'

Later that morning Jones urged his chief to obtain 'more adequate ministerial support'. Steel-Maitland was 'very conciliatory but ineffective and uncertain'. Would it not be better, suggested Jones, to call in Sir Laming Worthington-Evans, the Secretary of State for War, or Lord Birkenhead, the Secretary of State for India. 'The former is a little bit rough and dogmatic', Jones noted, 'but quick at grasping a financial point. I would rather Birkenhead because he has all the ability required to grasp the situation, he only talks when he has something to say, and when he speaks does so with perfect lucidity.' Baldwin agreed to 'have a "good think" about the whole question after lunch'.

At 4.00 p.m. the Prime Minister received the Mining Association, armed with the 'Child's Guide to Knowledge on the Miners' Wages' which Jones had thoughtfully had prepared for him by the Ministry of Labour. The owners, too, came armed—with the detailed figures of wages they were prepared to pay in each district after 30 April. In Yorkshire, Nottinghamshire, Leicestershire, Cannock Chase, South Derby, Lancashire, and North Staffordshire they proposed to reduce the rate by between 1s. and 1s. 6d. per shift, and in Scotland by 2s. In Durham and South Wales the proposed rates were lower than those of 1914. The Durham miner was to lose 18s. 4d. a week and his comrade in South Wales was to have his weekly earnings reduced from 78s. to less than 46s. There was to be no *national* percentage minimum for the industry and it was made clear that the National Wages Board proposed by the Samuel Report was to be no more than a rubber stamp for settlements imposed in the districts.

Baldwin pointed out how difficult it would be to shift the miners from the national minimum and tried to tempt the Mining Association with the proposal which Cook had advanced in his private talk with Tom Jones; a national minimum with temporary provision for plus and minus adjustments. Evan Williams dismissed this as impractical and Baldwin then turned to what he believed 'may be the crux of the whole situation—hours'. How much difference would it make to the proposed rates, he asked, if the miners' working day, reduced from eight hours to seven in 1921, was extended once again to eight hours. 'I only want to take South Wales for the moment to get a comparison.' If the extra hour was added, he was told, it would then be possible to add 30 per cent on the standard wage instead of 5 per cent and it was probable that this could be applied over the whole country. The Prime Minister was extremely satisfied with this answer and the owners withdrew, equally well satisfied with the indications given by the Prime Minister, as, indeed, they had good reason to be.[5]

The Samuel Report had stated: 'We cannot agree with the view presented to us by the mine-owners that little can be done to improve the organisation of the industry and that the only practicable course is to lengthen hours and lower wages. In our view large changes are necessary in other directions and large progress is possible.' Yet, not only had Baldwin made no attempt to insist on reorganisation, he had also repudiated the Samuel Report's view by himself suggesting longer hours. The Report had stressed that sacrifices were not to be asked of the miners until agreement had been reached on means for improving the industry's organisation and increasing its efficiency, yet the talk was exclusively of the sacrifice to be made by the miners. The Report had declared in favour of national agreements, yet Baldwin had made only the vaguest attempt to secure the owners' support for continuance of a national minimum percentage.

Williams and his colleagues were able, therefore, to face the miners next day with considerable confidence. Copies of the proposed district wage rates had already been sent to the Miners' Federation 'for information' and Williams made it clear that the Mining Association had no authority to negotiate on the rates. Williams admitted that many of the district wage offers were undoubtedly low, and, taking his cue from the Prime Minister, added that if the workers would agree to longer hours 'all of the districts would be in a position to offer wages of which no reasonable complaint could be made'. With the miners' rejection of this offer and continued insistence on a minimum percentage, the familiar deadlock was rapidly reached. In the evening the Industrial Committee again saw the Prime Minister. While Arthur Pugh was urging him 'to take a firmer control of the issue; to meet both sides, and to bring about a resumption of negotiations under his direction', coal-owners from all parts of the country were settling themselves down for dinner half-a-mile away at the Savoy. Their host was Sir Alfred Mond, whose 'bias towards ruthless American methods' had enabled him to build up an immense industrial and financial empire.

He was a coal-owner himself, but was unable to reconcile his philosophy of industrial efficiency with the bloody-minded and futile negativism preached by Evan Williams and the Mining Association. Many of Mond's dinner guests agreed, but none of them was willing publicly to repudiate their official negotiators. The initiative had to come from another quarter. The next morning Mond wrote to the Prime Minister, outlining the difficulties, and the possibilities.

I had last night a dinner of representative coal-owners of practically the entire country to consider the question of co-operative selling... If the Government expresses itself strongly on the matter and *insists* on the Royal Commission report, I am confident that something can be achieved. I assure you the whole country is looking most anxiously to you to *force* a settlement. Among all the coal-owners present themselves last night, the opinion was that the attitude of their representatives in the negotiations was quite unreasonable, and they merely do not speak out as they do not want to hamper their side. The general industrial community is looking forward with interest to a solution being found, but I should think it will have to be *imposed*. If the responsibility was taken off the shoulders of the two contending parties they would be pleased.[6] (Author's italics.)

Baldwin remained unmoved, continuing to limit his effective role to that of unofficial advocate of longer hours. At 11.00 a.m. on Friday 23 April, he presided for the first time at a joint meeting of owners and miners. 'When he rose to speak', observed Jones, 'his nervousness showed itself in his rattling out his sentences in a sharp tone at three

74

or four times his usual speed. Evan Williams, who had hardly slept the night before, spoke for some twenty-five minutes in his careful deliberate manner but making no advance whatever on the offer of district negotiations, and what he himself described as miserable wages on the seven hours basis and a reasonable wage for an eight hours day. Herbert Smith followed for about twenty minutes in if anything a more uncompromising mood. In a speech without any sense of order, at one point he was willing to negotiate nationally, at another he was determined to keep wages precisely where they are.' The only light relief occurred when Smith became entangled in some statistics and Williams and Cook interrupted at the same time to correct him. Turning to Cook, Smith growled, 'I can deal with one Welshman, but I can't deal with two at once'.

Eventually, Baldwin suggested that he might find it easier to 'untie the knot' if he talked separately that afternoon with a small committee from each side. He met first with the miners and immediately produced a set of figures showing that if the subsidy was withdrawn and conditions remained as they were, virtually all the pits in Northumberland, Durham, South Wales, and Scotland would be forced to close, driving at least 200,000 miners out of work. Herbert Smith refused to be impressed: it needed little ingenuity to calculate that if working hours were extended the owners would be able to produce the same amount of coal with a much smaller work force. There was no possibility, Smith emphasised, of the Miners' Federation recommending a return to district agreements or an extension of hours. He then proceeded gently to reproach the Prime Minister. 'We met you last week. You did not commit yourself at all to us. You heard what we have to say. You told us, and rightly too, that you were going to consult the coal-owners and we were to be in readiness, and we rather think, using a Yorkshire phrase, that we have been sidetracked...because we met exactly the same coal-owners with the same statements that we met before we came to see you. Exactly the same position. They have not gone a single item away from it... While we are for peace, we are not out for peace at any price. The conditions of peace are that at the pit we will do our best, whether it is private enterprise or nationalisation, but the next thing is a respectable wage which we can live on.'[7]

The miners took no responsibility for the chaotic state of the industry, Smith declared, and if the Sankey Commission's report had been adopted it would have been possible to talk about reducing hours, not extending them. 'Sir, we are open to discuss wages nationally. We are not open to consider an extension of hours. I want that be clearly understood, so that we make no mistake here, because even with an extension of hours all districts apart from one would suffer a serious reduction in wages... If you look at Bristol, the Forest of Dean, and Somerset, they have got to work and live by excitement; it will be excitement.' Smith was too seasoned a campaigner to go beyond offering to *discuss* wages nationally, but the fact that he did not rule out wage cuts in the same breath as longer hours was one further sign that the miners' leaders, at least, were still holding ajar the door to a settlement. Before the meeting ended, further hints were dropped that if a definite agreement could be reached on reorganisation then it might be possible to come to terms.

After tea and a walk on the Terrace at Westminster, Baldwin received the owners' committee. 'It is impossible', Jones noted after the meeting, 'not to feel the contrast between the reception which ministers give to a body of owners and a body of miners. Ministers are at ease at once with the former, they are friends jointly exploring a situation. There was hardly an indication of opposition or censure. It was rather a joint discussion on whether it were better to precipitate a strike or the unemployment which would result from continuing the present terms. The majority clearly wanted a strike and during the strike Adam Nimmo asked that the Government should either repeal or suspend the Seven Hours Act. The P.M. said very little throughout beyond posing an occasional question.'

It was Evan Williams, as usual, who did most of the talking. In a speech from which was omitted the slightest reference to reorganisation, Williams once more insisted that wage rates were matters to be dealt with in the districts themselves and that only then should they be submitted to a national body. It was admitted, said Williams, that on the present hours of work it was absolutely impossible to offer a wage other than one which, in some districts, he did not shrink from describing as miserable. 'I say again that is the position: in those districts which have to suffer from foreign competition on the present hours of work there is no possibility...of providing a wage which is other than very low, but I indicated that if an extension of hours could be agreed upon, the wage-paying capacity in those districts would be so improved that they would be able to offer a wage against which no reproach could be levelled.'

It was quite clear, Williams asserted through the haze from Baldwin's pipe, that even if the miners accepted the proposed wage cuts as they stood, a large number of the colliery companies would still be working at a loss and that others—'to what extent it is impossible to say'—would not be able to carry on working at all. 'The only real salvation of the industry lies in a longer working day which would increase the amount of money which will go into the industry and will enable the wages to be paid by the industry to be correspondingly increased.' Precisely how this was to be achieved without mass sackings or glutting the market with even greater quantities of unsaleable coal Williams did not say and Baldwin did not ask. Nor was Williams pressed on the vital questions of national wage settlements and reorganisation.

Strolling with the Prime Minister through St James's Park to the Travellers' Club, where Baldwin was to dine that night with Evan Williams, Steel-Maitland and Lord Weir, a Glasgow industrialist and former Minister for Air whose hostile trade union views made him anathema to Labour, Tom Jones made no attempt to disguise his concern at the day's proceedings. 'I told [the P.M.] that I thought he was much too gentle in his handling of the miners and the owners, and especially the latter, and that there were a lot of things he ought to have said. I didn't like his allowing the interpretation of the Report on the powers of the central authority to go unchallenged.' Earlier that day, as secretary of the Cabinet Coal Committee, Jones had circulated a memorandum from Birkenhead interpreting the powers of the proposed National Wages Board. 'Birkenhead holds that the Commission meant the central body to have effective control over the district proposals and was not simply to be a rubber stamp, affixing its approval or disapproval.' Nor was Jones happy at the way Baldwin had allowed the owners to slide out of their other primary obligation. 'I pointed out that throughout the talk with the owners there was not the slightest sign that they appreciated the need for reforming their business.' Baldwin's reaction was to blame Lloyd George for sowing the seeds of the crisis. 'In this as in so many other things L.G. has left us a legacy of trouble.' Jones agreed that Lloyd George was 'an opportunist *in excelcis*', but added that a strike on 30 April without any attempt to put the coal industry in order would be on Baldwin's part a policy of opportunism.

Friday ended with formal announcements from both the Miners' Federation and the T.U.C. A delegate conference of miners would be held on Wednesday 28 April and a conference of executives of unions affiliated to the T.U.C. the following day, 'in order that the trade union movement...may be fully informed of the position'. It was this last announcement which provoked speculation among the informal gathering of ministers and officials at No. 10 Downing Street on Saturday morning. Steel-Maitland believed the trade union conference would go against the miners, but Horace Wilson and Tom Jones disagreed. The terms presented by the South Wales owners, argued Jones, would make it impossible for the trade unions to desert the miners. Wilson and Jones thought the Prime Minister should see the Industrial Committee that morning and were surprised when Baldwin suggested a meeting at 5.00 p.m. on Monday after the Budget Speech. This seemed so leisurely that Jones and Wilson took it upon themselves to bring the appointment forward to noon. Maurice Hankey, the Cabinet Secretary, was also concerned at Baldwin's dilatoriness. Jones found him 'shocked at the thought that the P.M. was rather neglecting to keep the Cabinet informed'.[8]

Baldwin showed little concern about either of the conferences which were to take place the following week. After attacking 'intellectuals' and 'theorists' such as J. M. Keynes, whose article on the coal crisis appeared in the current issue of the *Nation*, and pouring scorn on an article in the *New Statesman*, 'a paper which he greatly dislikes', the Prime Minister asked Jones to spend the weekend with him at Chequers. That evening Jones braved the returning Cup Final crowds at Baker Street Station and caught a train to Wendover, where Baldwin's chauffeur was waiting for him. During the three-mile drive to Chequers Jones was treated to an enthusiastic monologue on the Prime Minister's interest in cricket. A new pitch was being fenced in at Chequers and J. M. Barrie and a team of admirals were going to be brought down to play.

Jones found the Prime Minister in the Long Gallery, smoking and reading a novel. Baldwin began at once to talk about the walk they would have next morning and of the difficulty of growing bluebells in a place as cold and high as Chequers. They agreed to avoid the subject of coal for the evening, but Baldwin was soon fulminating against the miners' executive. 'He said his ideas were slowly clarifying and without saying so proceeded, I guessed, to reflect the ideas which had circulated round the table at the Travellers' Club last night... "It was all wrong that a small body like the miners' executive should be able to hold up the country. The question of the miners' ballot would have to be tackled." But he was all for trying to get the power of the executive broken without resorting to a strike.' Jones suggested inviting Tawney or even Cook to Chequers that weekend but Baldwin thought this would be unwise.

Coal soon gave way to cricket and during a dinner enlivened by two of the Prime Minister's young nieces, Mrs Baldwin announced that she belonged to no less than three cricketing clubs whose other notable members included Maud Lawrence, Dame Meriel Talbot, and Lady Willingdon. After dinner the Baldwins retired and left their guests to amuse themselves by listening to 'attempts of various parts of Europe to communicate with us through the loudspeaker'. Sufficiently amused by 10.00 p.m. Jones also retired, taking with him translations of Horace and the *Regional Survey of East Kent,* both of which he had found in the Prime Minister's study. After an early breakfast and more lively fun with the nieces, Baldwin and Jones set off for the promised tramp in the woods. There cricket gave way once more to coal. Anxious for some immediate action, Jones suggested another possible weekend visitor to Chequers: Arthur Pugh. 'I told him that there were signs in the Press of surprise at the leisurely way in which the negotiations were proceeding. We walked on and on with remarks about the weather, the beeches, and the bluebells, and after five or ten minutes he agreed that I should summon Pugh but should keep the visit secret.'

The chairman of the T.U.C. arrived with Horace Wilson at 4.30 p.m. and Jones got him to talk of the days he had worked at Cwmavon for Wright and Butler, 'a firm well-known to S.B. This set them at their ease'. Baldwin showed the visitors over the house and gave them tea in the Long Gallery—'the finest room in England'. The Prime Minister enhanced the amiable atmosphere by bringing out Cromwell's life mask and comparing the left eye to Kitchener's. Queen Elizabeth's ring and the letter which Nelson had written after the Battle of the Nile were also brought forth. After tea, Baldwin and Pugh finally 'got to business'. 'This coal industry', declared Baldwin, 'wants a new wage machinery and a new temper. For the last ten years my predecessors and myself have just been sticking plaster on a boil.' What did Mr Pugh think should be done?

Like most of his colleagues on the Industrial Committee, Pugh believed a settlement was possible, if all sides, including the Government, genuinely accepted the Samuel Report. He told Baldwin that, instead of concentrating on wages, the negotiations should begin with reorganisation 'and work slowly down to the former, and thus narrow the differences to be bridged. The P.M. should aim at a five years' policy, and should try to keep in mind the past history and psychology of the miners, and the intense distrust of the miners' leaders of each other. He rehearsed the sort of speech the P.M. might make to the Trade Union Committee tomorrow, and the importance of reducing the number of negotiators to one or two for each party. When the talk had been going for an hour, the P.M. rang for some whisky and soda and I beguiled Wilson to the lounge, leaving the P.M. alone with Pugh.

'After they had gone, the P.M. said the talk had been invaluable to him and he joined Mrs Baldwin in her room while I drafted the outlines of two speeches, one to the T.U.C., and one to the owners for tomorrow's meetings. At dinner there were just the three of us and when it was over we went to the Long Gallery where he at once began to play patience and Mrs B. read the proof of a character study of S.B. which is about to be published by the Central Office—what he called "a good piece of journalism"... At 9.30 p.m. the P.M. was still playing patience and he had plainly had enough of coal for the day, so I went to my room.'

The Prime Minister was clearly due for more than his ration of coal on Monday, too, and he and Jones breakfasted before 8.00 a.m. Over the toast and marmalade Baldwin returned to a favourite topic—the iniquities of the Lloyd George Coalition. 'You cannot imagine the impression the meetings of the Cabinet made on me. I had been in business for years. You must remember I was over fifty when I took up office. In business you discuss a thing and decide whether to do it or not, but as I watched L.G.'s Cabinet—watching each of its members under a microscope—I felt I was in a thieves' kitchen. Nobody seemed to have any principles. There was the most awful cynicism. Perhaps it was all due to reaction after the War.'

At Wendover Baldwin bought *The Times*, the *Daily Telegraph* and the *Morning Post*. Jones suggested that, with a coal crisis on, he should have bought the *Daily Herald*, but the Prime Minister settled down happily with the *Telegraph* crossword 'which he finished just as we steamed into Baker Street'. Baldwin met the Industrial Committee at noon and immediately assured them that the Government stood firmly by the Samuel Report.[9] The deadlock, he implied, was due entirely to Herbert Smith's obstinate refusal to negotiate over wages. For the benefit of the Committee, Baldwin proceeded to forecast what this would mean, not only for the miners themselves but for the workers of other industries as well. Closure of pits would wipe out Britain's export trade and this, in turn, would lead to a rise in the prices of foodstuffs. 'But Mr Smith remained quite firm on this point that, however many men went out, he thought it better economically that there should be no change in the existing rate of wages.' The Industrial Committee began now to show signs of impatience. Pugh spoke first, repeating the point he had made privately to Baldwin the previous day. 'You have to bear in mind that all that is before the parties is the mine-owners' proposition of wages. You cannot discuss on that. As a matter of fact, the question of wages was raised far too early... The only thing before them is the reduction in wages, and obviously the miners are not going to discuss wages with you on that basis. What you should get down to is the report.'

Jimmy Thomas warned Baldwin of what would happen if a formula was not soon found. 'We have called a special conference of all the executive committees for Thursday afternoon. The notices expire on Friday night. Nothing, in my judgment, would be more fatal on Thursday than if the question to be put to that Congress is merely on the one side a statement, "No increase in hours, no reduction in wages, national negotiations", and the coal-owners' proposals on the other. I can conceive of nothing that is so calculated to settle in two minutes on the basis of a very bad bust-up than any proposals of that kind, in other words, that being the issue. What we are trying to assert is that that is not the issue, because it will not be the issue on Friday even then. What we are anxious about... is that between now and when that conference takes place, there will be a much clearer issue, a much nearer approach... We know you are working, but you see the danger. Thursday will soon be here, and that is what I am worried about.'

Baldwin invited the Industrial Committee to nominate several of its own members to sit in on discussions when they resumed between the two sides—whenever that might be. Steel-Maitland was not anxious for a resumption that day. 'They would merely go at one another like terriers so to speak. Does not that really mean that each should be talked to separately in order to see whether they can advance along something that looks as if it would lead to a common meeting ground, a common point?' Would it not be possible for the T.U.C. to talk to the miners while the Government spoke to the owners? Thomas thought the suggestion worthwhile, but other members of the Industrial Committee were blunter about the elusive role which Baldwin appeared to be playing.

'I thought the object in meeting the Prime Minister', announced Swales, 'was to know where he stands, which would help us in our discussions. Does that mean we simply report to you? Will you not try in your efforts today to get them together?' Swales was not mollified by Baldwin's plea that 'both want a little preparation since last Friday'. 'They have had three days. Candidly, my opinion is that when you got them together you should have kept them together. Time is of importance, and there have been three days when nothing has been done. My own view is that you have not completed your work yet.' When Baldwin once again lamented that Smith was not prepared to negotiate on wages, Swales snapped back, 'He is backed by the whole movement. I am on that. The miner is as low as he ought to go and there ought to be another way of finding a solution. The miner has been denied having any voice or control in the industry.'

But it was mild Arthur Walkden, of the Railway Clerks, who exposed the true extent of Baldwin's failure since publication of the

Samuel Report. 'Apart from the wages question, it might help us if you would tell us whether the owners have definitely given you assurances that they are quite agreeable to the reforms recommended in the Report being carried out in full? Have you had that from them?' Baldwin was forced to admit that he had received no assurances from the owners about their willingness to carry out the reorganisation proposals. His knowledge, he confessed, was confined to their press statements. 'Obviously that is the line.' Walkden hammered home the obvious rejoinder. 'We think you should have got right off the wages question. We are of the opinion that there is a great deal to be inquired into the mining position, and the country is anxious that something should be done to reform the industry.' Baldwin declared that this was a point to be cleared up in the next three or four hours and again affirmed that 'we do stand firmly on the Report'.

The Industrial Committee would certainly have questioned the Prime Minister even more searchingly had they seen the private note dispatched by Conservative Central Office to newspaper editors earlier in the day.

You will no doubt be fully occupied with the Budget debate. Perhaps you will kindly pass on the enclosed to your Labour correspondent. The Government are particularly anxious to draw the attention of the public to the serious economic position of the coal industry as disclosed in the statistical table given in the House of Commons last week, showing the percentage of coal which is raised at a loss. *Reference may also usefully be made to the question of hours, upon which it is desirable to concentrate attention rather than upon the reduction of wages.*[10] (Author's italics.)

The most pressing problem which Baldwin now had to face was the one of blunting the Industrial Committee's obvious impatience and reassuring public opinion. If a general strike was to be avoided, the Committee had to be persuaded that the terms being offered to the miners were reasonable. If a strike could not be avoided, public opinion had to be convinced that the fault did not lie with the owners or the Government. There could be no repeat of the situation the previous summer when, as Hankey had informed the King, 'Public opinion is to a considerable extent on the miners' side.' Up till now, however, the owners had managed to win little sympathy for their attitude. As J. L. Garvin wrote in the previous day's *Observer*: 'The owners have been tactless and irritating to the last degree. No responsible body of men has ever seemed more lacking in the human touch... Now, as last July, if they wanted to "Get the men's backs up" and keep them up, the owners could not have gone better about it.'

At his meeting with Evan Williams and the Mining Association on Monday evening Baldwin took the opportunity to speak plainly of the dangers they and the Government would face unless the owners made at least the appearance of a concession.[11] Public opinion, he warned, lay heavily against the owners' case since publication of the new wage scales, and whereas a general strike with public opinion on their side would be short and sharp, a strike without its support would be long and difficult. People did not ask why the new wage rates were published, or on what basis they were calculated, they simply looked at the figures. In such a situation, the T.U.C. might stampede the public into seeing the strike as a struggle of the employer class to cut wages—'the worst ground *we* could possibly fight on'. (Author's italics.) To negotiate now on a national minimum would avoid that suspicion and out of the negotiations the owners would be able to draw the eight-hour day. According to Baldwin, there was strong support for this among the ordinary miners in preference to wage cuts, though the only specified source for this information was a survey conducted by the *Daily Mail*, a newspaper not noted for its impartiality to the trade unions. Evan Williams asserted that negotiations on a national minimum would only delay a fight and that it would be much better for the Government to restore the eight-hour day at once. Patiently, Baldwin explained that such a move would 'unite the whole of the Labour party against them', and promised that if negotiations went forward on the basis of a national minimum, the Government would pass an eight-hours Bill through 'in a day for you'. Eventually, Williams said that he had no authority to offer to negotiate on a national minimum. Baldwin asked him to try to obtain it, and the meeting adjourned.

At 9.20 p.m. Baldwin met the Industrial Committee to exchange progress reports.[12] 'I have had an hour-and-a-half with the owners trying to get common ground for a common meeting. They have got a meeting first thing in the morning and they are going to see me the moment they are through. If they follow the course I advised, so far as they are concerned a joint meeting will be possible and I hope might be productive of some good.' Thomas emphasised that the whole of the trade union movement was behind the miners' demand for national negotiations, 'because any attempt to depart from that means disintegration. You may take that as a fundamental position. You may take that as our view no matter what else happens.

That is the very last word. That has got to be done.' Time, he warned, was running out, and they had to get down to brass tacks the next day. Baldwin asked if the miners were prepared to come to brass tacks. The Industrial Committee had just met the miners and Thomas was able to assure the Prime Minister that they were prepared to discuss any proposal submitted to them from any side, provided only that it embodied the principle of national negotiations. But that did not mean, Thomas added, 'committing them to anything at all whatsoever'. Baldwin ended the meeting with his usual felicity. 'We both of us have a difficult task and we are none of us brought up as circus riders.'

Thomas and Pugh had evidently been working hard on the miners, for a statement by Cook published in Tuesday's *Daily Herald* summed up the Industrial Committee's own views precisely: 'I am convinced that a settlement can be reached by a straight return to the Commission's proposals, and from them to a discussion on the basis of a national agreement.' Whether the miners would have been prepared to accept wage cuts as part of such an agreement could only have been discovered by opening genuine discussions on all aspects of the Samuel Report. But this Baldwin still steadfastly refused to do. Why, he asked, did Jones 'always turn to that rag', when Jones drew the statement to his attention. It was not Arthur Cook's ideas on the crisis which Baldwin wished to discuss, but his own. He invited Jones 'to turn over this idea which I have not yet mentioned to a soul. Do you think on Friday night, when we are right up against it, the two sides would be willing to make me arbitrator in the dispute?' If so, Baldwin continued, he would ensure the present wage rates were retained for two years and introduce a Bill to suspend the Seven Hours Act; withhold any further subsidy, though provide some assistance for men displaced by pit closures; drop the municipal trading proposals, but 'propound' schemes for co-operative selling : finally, he would consider how best to deal with mineral royalties 'without damage to the country's finances and to the debt conversion which the Treasury have in prospect'. They were a set of proposals entirely consistent with the views he had already expressed privately to the owners; they also marked a total retreat from the spirit and letter of the Samuel Report, requiring as they did immense sacrifice on the part of the miners without a guarantee that even nationalisation of mineral royalties would be proceeded with. They were indeed a classic example of Arthur Cook's 'pig in a poke', as unlikely of acceptance by the Industrial Committee as by the miners themselves. Baldwin knew this as well as anyone, but as he told Jones, 'It is the normal person we must carry with us if there is a strike'.

When the Mining Association called on him at midday to give their grudging assent to renewed talks without preconditions, Evan Williams stressed once more the importance of the eight-hour day.[13] 'Don't think I haven't got it in my mind firmly', Baldwin told him, 'but I must decide the psychological moment and the time will come, I think, when that will have to be said.' Praise or gratitude came rarely from Williams and his colleagues and even Lloyd George had earned no thanks from them for sabotaging the Sankey Report in 1919 and standing up to the miners in 1921. But Baldwin was now told that there was 'no P.M. in our experience whom we would more readily trust', which was a revealing comment on the extent to which the owners believed the Prime Minister had pledged himself to their cause. Indeed, Baldwin felt obliged to remind them that the Government had not so far committed itself to the eight-hour day, although 'I see no solution apart from it', a view which Steel-Maitland readily endorsed.

The Industrial Committee found Baldwin very pleased with his own efforts when they called on him in the afternoon to hear the results of his mediation with the owners.[14] The owners, he told them, did not like the idea of the Committee being present during discussion, but he did have one piece of good news.

You will remember the difficulty of the question of the national minimum and district negotiations... What the owners told me this morning was that if I would ask them and the miners to meet: 'We are quite prepared to have the situation cleared up between us and the men, and we would not impose any limitation at all upon the discussions that might take place. We should be quite prepared to explore the whole question of the national minimum and any other question that they might wish to discuss. We should make no reservations at all.' So you see, I have got them to come into a perfectly open conference free of prejudice and free of anything that may have been said before.

He was intending to inform the miners personally of this, but would it be better, he asked the Committee, for him to see them that evening or after their delegate conference on 28 April. 'Before', Pugh and Thomas chimed in simultaneously. 'I am absolutely certain in my own mind', said Thomas, 'that it will be fatal not to meet them tonight.' There was just one other little point, the Prime Minister continued. 'You, Mr Pugh, are an expert—or ought to be—on human psychology. Is it better to ask them to come after a meal or before one?' 'It all depends', replied Pugh, 'on how long it is since they had

D

the previous meal.' Steel-Maitland and Horace Wilson were more concerned about the substance than the timing of the talks. Would the miners be free to consider every aspect which might arise? Thomas answered that he would make only one qualification: 'Do not start with phrases. Up to now their obvious answer has been that there has been nothing concrete put up to them except the coal-owners' terms. Start off on the general discussion rather than on the particular question. You see what I mean?'

Earlier that afternoon Thomas and his colleagues had attended a meeting of the General Council at which the question of what to do if negotiations broke down had been discussed for the first time. The mining problem had been left entirely in the hands of the Industrial Committee since its reappointment by the Scarborough Congress the previous September and it was not until 27 April, according to Bevin, that the full General Council 'were even asked to consider the position of a possible breakdown in negotiations'.[15] By now, however, it was impossible to avoid the issue any longer. The conference of executives was due to meet in only two days and the subsidy was to end in three. What practical support was the trade union movement to render the miners if agreement had still not been reached by 30 April?

Although Ernie Bevin had been a member of the General Council only since September, it was his voice which now became decisive. In previous coal disputes, sympathetic support had always been asked of, and given by, the transport unions, since a transport strike was the quickest and easiest way of bringing pressure to bear on the public and the Government. In 1925 the transport unions had been called on to impose a boycott on the movement of coal. But those members of the General Council who thought the same sanctions could be applied in 1926 quickly found they were mistaken. 'I took the line', Bevin later told officers of his own union, 'that what we did in the July previous [1925] we were not prepared to re- peat. They just meant that we should endeavour to hold up coal—to boycott it—and anyone who knew the Government's plans knew very well that would be absolutely ineffective and foolish. I found, too, that as usual there was a lot of talk on the General Council by people who thought they were not going to be involved.'[16] Bevin agreed that, if a satisfactory settlement was not reached, the miners would have to be supported, but by the trade union movement as a whole, not simply by the transport workers, who were particularly vulnerable to blacklegs and Government volunteers. 'I personally made up my mind that it had to be a much wider dispute than anything attempted before; that it would have to be practically every section represented on the General Council in it.' But if the trade union movement was to give its support, then control of the dispute, Bevin insisted, must pass into the hands of the General Council. Only it could have the right to call workers out and the right to decide the terms of a settlement, subject to consultation with the miners.

There was little common ground between Bevin and Thomas, but they were agreed on this and a six-man Ways and Means Committee, including Bevin, was appointed to draw up an appropriate plan of action. Purcell was chairman, but from the start it was Bevin's massive personality which dominated the committee's deliberations. It went into session immediately and by Wednesday was able to lay before the General Council a scheme of phased strike action by the biggest unions affiliated to Congress. However, like the Industrial Committee, the General Council believed it was still possible to avoid a dispute if only the talks could be shifted away from the single and divisive issue of wages and on to broader aspects of the Samuel Report. 'I must confess,' Bevin wrote at the end of May, 'that the Report had a distinct fascination for me; I felt that if minds were applied with the right determination to give effect to it, what with reconstruction, regrouping and the introduction of a new element in the management of the industry, there would in the end be produced a *higher* wage standard. It may have meant some adjustments in varying forms, but this is nothing new; everyone of us has had to face these problems in other industries across the table and meet and overcome conditions over and over again.'[17]

But how was reorganisation to be achieved? The Samuel Report had made no suggestion for implementing its own proposals and it was to this problem that the General Council turned on 28 April. Bevin had already drafted suggestions of his own earlier in the week and these formed the basis of the policy statement which was now adopted by the General Council. The statement urged the appointment of independent commissioners to determine the type and extent of reorganisation necessary in each colliery; the passage of an Act of Parliament giving the commissioners power to enforce their findings; Government assistance where new capital was required; alternative employment or continuous maintenance for miners displaced by unavoidable pit closures. The policy statement was rather less forthright about the obligation laid on the miners by the Samuel Report... In one paragraph it asserted that the wages and working conditions of miners were 'already so depressed as to render it imperative to seek for remedies other than a further degradation in their standards of life'. In the next, it quoted the Samuel Report's own stipulation that no sacrifices should be asked of the miners until agreement had been reached on reorganisation. In one paragraph wage cuts were decisively rejected; in the next, implicitly condoned. The apparent contradiction followed logically from the General Council's reaction to the Samuel Report. Like the Industrial Committee, it believed that the miners should be prepared to make a temporary sacrifice for reforms which would lead to higher wages in future. Bevin and other members of the General Council still hoped the Government might be persuaded to grant a last-minute subsidy to tide the industry over the reorganisation period. But if more Government money was not forthcoming, the policy statement left the Industrial Committee free to urge wage cuts on the miners.

Armed with this mandate, Jimmy Thomas and the Industrial Committee returned to Downing Street in the evening. They found the Prime Minister unusually pessimistic and irritable.[18] 'I would like to say that when we get through this trouble, however we get through it, it would be a mercy if we could get a simplification of their wages system. I do not believe anybody understands it... If anybody would come along with a broom and go right through that industry and say this man is getting so many shillings a day, then we know where we are, but really I have found that about the toughest thing I have ever been up against... I thought I would tell you of my troubles and see if I could get any sympathy.' They were, declared Pugh, all in the same boat.

Talks between miners and owners had started the previous evening and resumed that morning after an adjournment by the miners' delegate conference. After a session lasting all day, agreement was still no nearer. The owners insisted on rates below the national minimum in the hard-hit exporting districts; the miners refused to consider wage cuts without a prior guarantee of reorganisation. It was clear to the miners, Baldwin told the Industrial Committee, that there would be 'enormous unemployment' if wages were not reduced in the exporting areas, 'but they had no suggestion to make as to how that difficulty was to be overcome'. Thomas made it plain that the General Council would not oppose wage cuts if the owners submitted detailed figures to substantiate their case and provided legislation were passed to compel reorganisation where it was not undertaken voluntarily. This was a low price to ask for T.U.C. neutrality in the event of a miners' strike, but Baldwin was still not prepared to commit himself. Even a blunt reminder from Citrine that the conference of executives meeting next day would expect 'something' failed to draw a positive reply from the Prime Minister. 'We must talk it all over now and let you know as soon as we can.'

## Chapter Six

# 'A Case of Bare Fists'

'There has been a curious spirit about among many people who perhaps do not know as much about it as we do of that peculiar kind of optimism that all English people suffer from of thinking that the thing that they all rather dread and don't want to come about. I do not know what it arises from. It may be partly from a feeling that we shall not make fools of ourselves, and I think it may be partly from a feeling that there may be some kind of conjuring trick at the eleventh hour that is going to save the situation, a sort of rabbit that can be produced out of a hat.'

Stanley Baldwin, during a meeting with the T.U.C. Negotiating Committee, 29 April 1926.

'We have striven, we have pleaded, we have begged for peace, because we want peace. We still want peace. The nation wants peace. Those who want war must take the responsibility.'

J. H. Thomas, speaking at the Conference of Trade Union Executives, 30 April 1926.

'I am representing, Mr Prime Minister, men who have stuck it for 40 years against every force, against gaol and against police, and against armies and your navy... My soul is writhing when I think of the cold-blooded, callous attitude that has been adopted against ourselves... I do not want to trespass on the legal side. Lord Birkenhead has not had the trial of the college of the gutter and the street, and the roughing it and all the tension of public opinion, he has never been an Ishmael. We have been Ishmaels on our side, and may be again, but we ask you to think... Take Mr Herbert Smith's word, and we will back that up. If we prove our desire from first page to last of that Commission's Report, we will stand by that, and we will face any issue... We want peace in our time, Oh Lord. We do.'

Ben Tillett, during a meeting between the T.U.C. Negotiating Committee and the Prime Minister, 1 May 1926.

The Government was displaying no lack of vigour in other directions. On Tuesday 27 April the Supply and Transport Committee decided that J. C. C. Davidson, the Deputy Chief Civil Commissioner, should take charge of Government publicity from the afternoon of 30 April. Local authorities were also warned to stand by for a telegram from Whitehall bearing a single word—'Action'—upon receipt of which their emergency plans were then to be put into immediate effect. On 28 April the Cabinet drew up plans for the use of troops in the event of a general strike. To avoid provocation, no troop movements were to take place before a strike, but once it had begun troops were to be dispatched 'as unobtrusively as possible' to likely trouble spots. One battalion was to be sent to Scotland, one to South Wales, and two to Lancashire. A press statement was then to be issued 'making clear that the troops were intended for protection purposes only and not for taking sides in a strike'.[1]

On Thursday 29 April the General Council started its own mobilisation. More than 800 delegates, representing the executive committees of 141 trade unions affiliated to the T.U.C., gathered in the Memorial Hall, Farringdon Street, to hear how close they were to peace or war. Arthur Pugh spoke first, outlining developments since Red Friday.[2] The Samuel Commission, he reminded delegates, had stipulated that no sacrifices were to be asked of the miners until agreement had been reached on reorganisation. 'Now clearly all discussion of the problem should be governed by this condition. From that point negotiations should have started. When the report was produced many of us hoped that a concerted effort would be made to give effect to the Commission's findings and recommendations in the spirit of the declaration I have just quoted. Unfortunately, in the discussions that arose upon the Commission's report, the wage question was isolated and thrust into the foreground, and the more fundamental and far-reaching recommendations regarding reorganisation were obscured. Indeed, it is not untrue to say that the mineowners, at any rate, have sought to ignore them and to concentrate discussion upon the proposal to reduce wages.' Again, the inference was unmistakable: the General Council was prepared to countenance wage cuts provided the other recommendations of the Samuel Report were put into effect.

Finally, Pugh read out the policy statement adopted by the General Council the previous day. This, he informed delegates, represented 'the basic principles which have been agreed upon by our friends of the Miners' Federation and is submitted to you as a basis of policy, not for getting over the difficulty of 1 May, but of a policy which must be applied to the mining industry in due course'. A resolution was moved by Thomas calling for the adjournment of the conference and the continuation of negotiations 'provided that the impending lockout of the mineworkers is not enforced'. Just before he rose to address the conference Thomas turned to Citrine and whispered, 'Baldwin has told me privately that he is going to put up to the coal-owners that they should pay the minimum of 1921 and possibly a somewhat lower minimum in the poorer exporting districts. Do you think the miners will accept that?' Citrine did not believe the miners would accept. 'Neither do I,' said Thomas,[3] who went on to make a gloomy speech to the conference. 'I will defy anyone with inside knowledge, and certainly those who have been in close and daily contact with the situation, to challenge the statement I make that there never was such an attempt to mislead and blind the public to the real situation. If you were to judge by the Press reports of the last two days, you would imagine that, not only was the atmosphere clearing, but that there was every sign of an amicable settlement being arrived at. Well, I wish I could share that opinion, but I do not share it. I not only do not share it, but I do not believe there is a vestige of evidence on our experience to warrant any such assumption.' It was possible, Thomas added, that the negotiations would be prolonged over the following night. 'If they are, it will be useless; they will break down. They cannot be honourable if, whilst the negotiations are taking place, if they are prolonged over that day, the lockout notices are overhanging one side.'

It was Bevin, in seconding the resolution, who roused the Conference to enthusiasm:

You are moving to an extraordinary position. In twenty-four hours from now you may have to cease being separate unions. For this purpose you will have to become one union with no autonomy. (Cheers.) The miners will have to throw their lot and cause into the general movement, and the general movement will have to take the responsibility for seeing it through. But at the moment we feel that to begin wielding any sort of threat in connection with the negotiations, in the stage they are now in, would be to place a weapon in the hands of our opponents. We are asking you to stay in London. You are to be our Parliament, you are to be our assembly, our constituent assembly, an assembly where we will place the facts and the figures and the proposals and the problems that have to be submitted for calm judgment, and at the end take your instructions.

All this struck exactly the right keynote with delegates, but Bevin could not restrain his contempt for the Parliamentary Labour party, whose leader had been appointed to the Industrial Committee earlier in the week and who now shared the platform with the rest of the General Council. 'I am staggered,' he said, 'at the way this business is being carried on. Why does not the Labour party in the House of Commons itself make a pronouncement on the question of the inadequacy of the miners' wages? Let them declare themselves on that floor and their constituents will answer them, I believe, as to whether the country is prepared to see the wages of these men further driven down.'

Dissent among the delegates came not from spokesmen of the Minority Movement or the miners, but from W. J. Brown, of the Civil Service Clerical Association. 'We are asked to adjourn today on the night before what may be the last day of negotiations without any conclusive demonstration of where the movement stands on this particular issue. It recalls to my mind the situation at the outbreak of the European war, when our own Prime Minister, rather than say where this country stood, preferred to do exactly what the General Council is doing here today—to stand aloof and to leave the attitude of this country in doubt right up to the last moment.' Brown persisted against the shouts of an increasingly hostile audience. 'If we are going into this business, if it is in the mind of the General Council that the whole movement should back up the miners and if peace cannot be got, then, in my opinion, the time has come to say it... We are told what some of us have known for months past, that the industry cannot be reorganised in time for the present rates of wages to be continued after 1 May. That is a fact which has been obvious for months past, and it does seem to me that the General Council would be pursuing a wiser policy if they asked us to tell the Government where we stand, and above all, if they asked the Parliamentary Labour party to come into action on this matter in a way they have not done up to now. In my opinion, we have blundered. In my opinion, the time for us to declare our action is now and not after the trouble has begun.'

In a bitter reply, clearly meant as much for Bevin as for Brown, Thomas defended his Parliamentary colleagues. The Miners' Federation itself, he told delegates, had asked MacDonald not to raise the issue in Parliament. 'Therefore, do not let there be any sneers at the Parliamentary party, because that is the position. The other point is that this resolution means exactly what it said. It means that we must continue our efforts to get an honourable peace and report the situation to you tomorrow. No, this is not the time for bluff or a big stick. This is the time to face a serious situation in a serious way and do the right thing at the right time.'

Arthur Cook spoke for the miners, provoking more embarrassment than enthusiasm among delegates. According to Citrine:

> He worked himself up into a state bordering on hysterics, his face was flushed, and tears were standing in his eyes... Pugh, in an aside, whispered, 'This is not Arthur's usual audience.' 'No,' I replied, 'it is much more critical.' Even in the most intense moment in Cook's speech there was scarcely any applause. Watching the delegates, it was a bit difficult to judge what their impressions were. Looking round the platform, I noticed Ramsay MacDonald, leader of the Opposition, and Arthur Henderson, secretary of the Labour party, both of whom were keeping in touch with us. All this time Cook was going ahead with his perfervid oratory, but it appeared to me he was getting prolix. Pugh said, 'He is missing his audience, he is going on too long.' It was perfectly plain that the audience was getting restive... Cook, in conclusion said, 'Nobody can charge us with not having warned the country that this position must come about.' Thomas smiled sardonically and said to me, 'That is just the damned mistake which has been made.'[4]

The General Council's resolution was put to the vote and carried with only two dissentients and delegates dispersed gratefully into the warm spring evening while the miners and the Industrial Committee (now renamed the Negotiating Committee) made their way once more to the House of Commons. Representatives of the Mining Association, explained Baldwin, were travelling to London to discuss 'an offer that should form, in my mind, a fair basis for agreement'.[5] Hoping that the offer would be put to them that night, the trade unionists retired to a committee room to wait. While Tillett and Swales sang *John Brown's Body* and the miners shied balls of paper at each other or wrestled, Thomas spoke to Citrine of the forthcoming apocalypse. 'I am perfectly convinced, Walter, there is absolutely no hope. Stanley Baldwin talks to me just like a pal. There is going to be trouble and I can see no way out of it.' It was inevitable, he assured Citrine, that the Government should go to extremes. 'You must remember there is a lot of Russian money in this country. The Government are well informed. By God, you don't know! When I was in the Government the railway sectional strike was on—you know, Bromley's strike. Well, do you know that I had on my desk every morning full details, photographs of letters that had passed, speeches made at private meetings—oh my God! They have tested the feelings in different parts of the country, and they have made up their minds that there will be trouble. They are going to smash it. It won't last more than a few days. A few people will get shot, of course, (indicating the General Council members and the miners), more of them will get arrested. The Government will arrest the remainder and say it is a case of putting them away for their own safety. Of course, the shooting won't be done by them direct, it will be those damned Fascists and those fellows. You see, Walter, they have come to the conclusion they must fight. Who is this strike against? It is not against the coal-owners, it must be against the State. The money is not in the industry, so the strike is against the state. Well, Baldwin says that the State must be supreme, and he is right. Churchill is the man who will play the big part in this.'[6]

Just after midnight there was a further brief meeting with Baldwin, who promised to pass on the owners' offer later that morning. It was not, in fact, until one-fifteen in the afternoon, after a series of frantic phone calls from the Negotiating Committee, that the owners' terms were finally received. As Thomas had anticipated, they provided for a return to the 1921 national minimum, which meant a reduction of 13 per cent in standard wages. What Thomas had not anticipated, however, was the additional demand for an eight-hour day. Accompanying these arid terms was a blunt reminder from Baldwin that Government acceptance of the Samuel Report depended upon agreement between owners and miners, though by now a little over ten hours remained before the lock-out notices expired. Two-thirds of the miners were, in effect, already locked-out, having finished the afternoon shifts in the collieries.

Inevitably, the terms were rejected by the miners' delegate conference and in the evening the miners' executive and the Negotiating Committee, including Henderson and MacDonald, urged Baldwin to get the lock-out notices suspended so that talks could continue. The Prime Minister, who was joined by Neville Chamberlain and Lord Birkenhead, two of the leading Cabinet hardliners, insisted that further talks would be useless unless the miners gave first a prior undertaking to accept wage cuts.[7] The miners, declared Herbert Smith, after removing his dentures and wiping them with his handkerchief, were prepared to consider every item in the Samuel Report, including wage cuts, but he could not bind them to a reduction in advance. 'I want to see the horse and see if he is capable of carrying me first. When I see the picture put down and see that the Government and the owners intend doing that reorganisation, I am prepared to put a value on it and make some suggestions to my committee.'

94

Baldwin offered to set up yet another inquiry into amalgamations and selling agencies, but Smith required more tangible proof of the Government's intentions.

Four hours of talking made an impact only upon the nerves and tempers of both sides. Thomas produced a copy of an O.M.S. poster announcing the proclamation of a State of Emergency. 'Jimmy Thomas looked the Prime Minister straight in the eye', writes Citrine, 'and asked him had this poster been ordered by the Government and did it represent the mind of the Government? Baldwin flushed and then, after a few seconds hesitation, said that it was true that the Government had taken the necessary steps to prepare for the proclamation of a state of emergency, but the poster had not yet been published. The silence was ominous. Every one of us concluded that we had been badly tricked. We felt we could no longer trust Baldwin or anyone else and that they were simply playing for time to complete the arrangements which the Government had in hand.'

Thomas warned that the poster 'would remove any vestige of hope' if it was seen by either the miners' or the executives' conference. 'We have been battling against greater odds than you are aware of night and day with very little rest. We have been battling to surmount difficulties, but that is always the task of the peacemaker, and then we find ourselves faced with the risk of all our efforts being in vain. How long this will be kept secret I don't know.' Baldwin was in no mood for lectures. 'It is only on a par with the work you have been trying to do during the last week,' he flashed back at Thomas. Citrine joined in, referring to the confidential letter circulated by Tory Central Office to newspaper editors on 26 April. Baldwin disclaimed all knowledge of it, but the miners and the Negotiating Committee made little effort to disguise their disbelief. No doubt the atmosphere would have become even more uncongenial had they known that while they sat talking to Baldwin, the Privy Council, presided over by the King, was meeting at Buckingham Palace to draw up the proclamation of a state of emergency.

In an anguished but ungrammatical exhortation, Thomas shared his 'nightmare' with the Prime Minister. 'I shall leave this room tonight, if there is no hope, with the feeling that the gravest crisis, wrought with even more far-reaching consequences because of the peculiar time and circumstances, than of 1 August 1914.' Less than 1 per cent of the country would vote for revolution, Thomas declaimed, but in the situation they now faced, 'The man who votes anti-revolution, the man in his soul who thinks of his children and his wife in the sense of a revolution, forgets the consequences, forgets results. He does not think like you and me, does not realise his duty, and that some decent citizen then creates a revolutionary state of affairs. I have pictured this. I dream of it. My colleagues know I cannot be happy over this business. They know perfectly well it is a thing that is a nightmare to me.'

Chamberlain's diary note conveys the flavour of the meeting.

> F.E. [Lord Birkenhead, formerly F. E. Smith] and I trying to pin them down to some statement of how they proposed to fill the gap between cost and price... All that Herbert Smith would bind himself to was to discuss reduction of wages after we had put into operation the proposals for reorganisation... As this would take years it was clear that it provided no solution of the immediate difficulty. Again and again Thomas declared that Smith had answered in the affirmative... Each time he made this assertion there were angry and excited murmurs from Cook... Time went on, eight, nine, ten o'clock passed, and at eleven o'clock we broke off...having heard from Thomas one of his regular blood-curdlers, with his, 'My God, you don't know what this means; if we are alive this day week,' etc.[8]

At 11.25 p.m., with thirty-five minutes to go before expiry of the lock-out notices, the Negotiating Committee trudged wearily into the Memorial Hall, where delegates had been waiting since 11.00 that morning. They had relieved the tedium with solo recitations and community singing. Music hall ditties and Scots and Welsh ballads were popular, but the favourite was a hymn, *Lead, Kindly Light*. There was little that was bright or kindly in the Negotiating Committee's report. Pugh gave a factual account of the day's negotiations and the Press was then invited into the hall to hear Thomas. Hamilton Fyfe, editor of the *Daily Herald*, was duly impressed, 'It was a stirring, thrilling speech. It won back for Thomas almost all the affection and confidence that he has been losing during the last few years. It proved that, when the critical testing moment came, he stood without hesitation on the workers' side. I felt as I listened to it, "That man, if he lives, will occupy the highest office in the State".'[9]

It was not until 1.55 that afternoon, Thomas told his audience, that any definite offer had been made to the miners. 'Never in my life-long experience of negotiations', he declared, 'did I see such incapacity as this in a grave situation. Then a proposal was made which in its application, if accepted by the miners, would have meant such degrading terms that I refuse to believe there is any decent-minded man or woman who would tolerate it. (Cheers.) My friends, when the verbatim reports are written, I suppose my usual critics will say that Thomas was almost grovelling, and it is true. In all my long experience, and I have conducted many negotiations, I say to you—and my colleagues will bear testimony to it—I never begged and pleaded like I begged and pleaded all day today, and I pleaded not alone because I believed in the case of the miners, but because I believed in my bones that my duty to my country involved it.'

When the conference adjourned shortly after midnight, the general secretaries of the various unions were taken to an adjoining room, 'the doors of which were carefully guarded',[10] and each was handed a copy of the 'Proposals for Co-ordinated Action' drawn up by the Ways and Means Committee. At a time still to be specified by the General Council, work was to cease entirely in the transport, printing, iron and steel, metal and heavy chemicals industries. Unions connected with the supply of electricity and gas were to co-operate in cutting off power but not light. The builders were also to down tools, 'except such as are employed definitely on housing and hospital work'. Health and sanitary services were to be maintained and 'the trade unions concerned should do everything in their power to organise the distribution of milk and food to the whole of the population'. Once the General Council had decided on timing, the call-out was to be left to the unions concerned. The trades councils were to assist local union officials and were to organise strikers 'in the most effective manner for the preservation of peace and order'. A warning was given against 'spies', and 'any person found inciting the workers to attack property, or inciting the workers to riot, must be dealt with immediately', though how such a person was to be dealt with was not disclosed. Finally, if employers attempted to renege on agreements with their own employees once the mining dispute was settled, 'there will be no general resumption of work until those agreements are fully recognised'. Bevin and Purcell explained that, by accepting these proposals, unions would be binding themselves to carry out the General Council's instructions 'both regarding the conduct of the dispute and financial assistance'.

Early on Saturday 1 May, union executives met separately to consider the proposals before gathering once more in the Memorial Hall to vote on them. By now, every pit in the country was idle and almost a million miners were locked-out. The *London Gazette* printed the Emergency Proclamation signed by the King and the morning papers carried reports of the Government circular sent the previous evening to local authorities listing the civil commissioners and their principal assistants. For Thomas the situation was virtually the start of civil war and he spoke with familiar desperation at the meeting of his own executive, but not in the terms which had so impressed the editor of the *Daily Herald* only nine hours before. According to Thomas's own account, he 'urged and pleaded with the N.U.R. executive to keep out of it. Many asked me afterwards why I didn't resign my position as leader of the railwaymen when I realised that my advice would not be taken. I had to recognise that I was one of the Strike leaders, and if I had resigned it would have given the impression that I sided with the Government. That would have made matters worse for our men.'[11] A decision by the N.U.R. Executive 'to keep out of it' would have had an even more disastrous impact on trade union morale, though this is a point on which Thomas's memoirs remain discreetly silent.

At noon the conference of executives reassembled. Some unions had already sent in written replies and the first letter Citrine opened and read out was from the Asylum Workers' Union, which pledged its full support. 'No one laughed,' recalls Citrine. 'All were too deadly serious.' At the end of the roll-call only the seamen, numbering 50,000 members, rejected the General Council's proposals. The executives of several small unions had been unable to meet before the conference and deferred a decision. Membership of unions in favour of the proposals, however, totalled over $3\frac{1}{2}$ million. Amid the cheering Charlie Cramp, Thomas's principal lieutenant in the N.U.R., leaned over to his neighbour and murmured, 'Pure fatalism —we can't win'.[12] Bevin spoke first on behalf of the General Council.

> Sometimes, it is said that he who draws the sword perishes by the sword, and we all looked upon the action of the Government last night as equal in stupidity to the actions of the well-remembered Lord North and George III combined... We look upon your yes as meaning that you have placed your all upon the altar for this great movement, and having placed it there, even if every penny goes, if every asset goes, history will ultimately write up that it was a magnificent generation that was prepared to do it rather than see the miners driven down like slaves. (Cheers.)

Turning to practical aspects, Bevin informed the conference that no person employed in any of the trades listed in the General Council's instructions 'must go to work at starting time on Tuesday morning; that is to say, if a settlement has not been found. Those upon whom the call is made to take part in this struggle must refrain from working after the finish of the shift on Monday night... I rely, in the name of the General Council, on every man and woman in that grade to fight for the soul of Labour and the salvation of the miners.' (Cheers.)

The applause became frantic when Herbert Smith advanced to the front of the platform. At the same moment cheering and the sound of a band drifted in from the street outside as the May Day procession passed on its way to the traditional rally in Hyde Park. Smith repeated what he had told Baldwin the night before: he was willing to inquire into every aspect of the Samuel Report and accept the findings of such an inquiry. 'But I was asked to say that I was prepared to take my revolver and to let the other man shoot first at me, which meant a reduction of wages...I hope the Government will find it has made a mistake and send for the Committee to come back, and say to them, "We are prepared to go through this book from start to finish and accept its findings." ' The implication that the miners might accept wage cuts in return for reorganisation was sufficiently clear to provoke an embarrassing intervention from Arthur Cook. According to Thomas, 'To our horror, Cook suddenly sprang up and shouted that his president had "gone too far". He demanded that Smith should be given a chance to speak again and retract his words. Smith did speak again. He repeated word for word what he had already said. I was watching Cook's face: it was then that I felt he wasn't even anxious for a settlement but preferred a fight.'

This disquieting incident was immediately obscured by MacDonald's blinding rhetoric.

We have come to a time when the miner's wife had gone to meet her husband with tears in her eyes because she cannot fulfil her duties as a wife. The humblest miner's wife has to look at her child with an aching heart instead of a proud one. There are millions of men, flesh of my flesh, blood of my blood, who hold with me the same traditions of Britain—Scotsmen, Englishmen, Welshmen—who will say that this fight is a wicked fight, an unnecessary fight, a criminal fight... It is the whole life of the toiling masses that we have been working for, striving for, not to make enemies to society, but to make the very best of friends society has got—the miner, the engineer, the worker in the field, all toiling, toiling, toiling, all honest men, able men, skilled men, contributing to the commonwealth so that they themselves might live honourable and magnificent individual lives... On Monday we will raise a debate in the House of Commons, but I hope, I still hope, I believe, I must believe, that something will happen before then which will enable us to go about our work cheerily and heartily and hopefully during the next week. If not, we are there in the battle with you, taking our share uncomplainingly until the end has come and until right and justice have been done.

At this pitch of appropriate fervour, the conference rose to sing *The Red Flag*, in which the leader of the Labour party joined with gusto, though he personally regarded Labour's anthem as 'The funeral dirge of our movement'. While delegates poured euphorically into the sunny streets still swirling with May Day marchers, the General Council met to consider its historic mandate. As the Council interpreted it, the mandate authorised them to call out the men in the 'front-line' grade at midnight on Monday 3 May, if by then a settlement had not been found, and in the meantime to resume negotiations in the hope of finding a settlement. Telegrams ordering a stoppage after final shifts on Monday were accordingly sent to the unions concerned and at the same time the General Council dispatched two letters to the Prime Minister. The first offered, in the event of a strike, to co-operate in the distribution of essential food supplies; the second announced that the miners' case was now being conducted by the General Council and that the Council was ready to resume talks 'at any moment should the Government desire to discuss the matter further'. The charge subsequently made by the miners was that the General Council's mandate was limited to organising a sympathetic strike and that the reopening of negotiations in advance of the strike was an act of bad faith. But there was more passion than proof to this argument. Members of the General Council who addressed the conference on 1 May made no secret of their desire to achieve a peaceful settlement if this was at all possible and it was Herbert Smith himself who urged a resumption of talks on the Samuel Report.

Furthermore, the General Council's authority to deal direct with the government rested upon the specific consent of the Miners' Federation as well as the mandate given by the conference. Before the conference resumed on 1 May, the General Council called in the Federation's three leading officials, Smith, Cook, and Richardson, and asked them if they agreed to place the conduct of the dispute from then on in the Council's hands. They did agree, provided they were consulted during negotiations and particularly before any terms were accepted. The General Council's decision to communicate with Baldwin on 1 May was in no way a breach of this understanding. Texts of the letters were read over the phone to the Federation office and copies were immediately sent round by hand. No protest was received from the Federation and the General Council readily accepted the Prime Minister's invitation to meet him later that evening. As Bevin put it, 'We may have made all the mistakes in the world, but that does not affect the question of whether or not we had the power to do what we did.'[13]

What the Negotiating Committee did not realise, as it made its way to Downing Street at eight-thirty on Saturday evening, was that Arthur Cook had received neither the General Council's phone message nor the copies of its letters to Baldwin. Cook did not learn of the new initiative until he went for a walk on the Saturday evening and chanced to meet Mary Quaile, one of the T.G.W.U. representatives on the General Council. Immediately suspecting the worst, he phoned Eccleston Square but the T.U.C. headquarters was deserted except for a caretaker and Cook was forced to contain his impatience until the meeting at Downing Street ended. He had a long wait, for the issue dividing the Government and the T.U.C. remained precisely what it had been the previous night; the Negotiating Committee continued to insist that the lock-out notices should be withdrawn so that unfettered negotiations could proceed on the Samuel Report; the Government would not consider lifting the lock-out notices without a prior acceptance of wage cuts. After two hours of unfruitful skirmishing, Baldwin suggested that more progress might be made if each side appointed a small subcommittee to continue the talks. The Negotiating Committee agreed and talks resumed at 11.00 p.m. between Pugh, Thomas, and Swales on the one side and Baldwin, Birkenhead, and Steel-Maitland on the other. Citrine, Wilson, and the ubiquitous Jones were also present to take notes, but by agreement no official minutes were recorded. In this informal atmosphere both sides relaxed. Thomas and Birkenhead took to referring to each other as 'Fred' and 'Jimmy', and Birkenhead declared that he was not out of sympathy with the miners as his great grandfather had worked in the Wakefield pit and had been champion prize fighter of Yorkshire 'when it was a case of bare fists'. Thomas joined in the joviality by cracking a joke at Baldwin about the way he had been 'anticipating the succession' during Lloyd George's premiership.[14]

By one-thirty on the Sunday morning a formula of sorts had actually emerged. 'The Prime Minister has satisfied himself as a result of the conversations he has had with the representatives of the Trade Union Congress, that if negotiations are continued (it being understood that the notices cease to be operative) the representatives of the Trades Union Congress are confident that a settlement can be reached on the lines of the Report within a fortnight.' On the face of it, this was a considerable triumph for the

T.U.C.: it provided for a withdrawal of lock-out and strike notices and a renewal of the subsidy for two weeks while a serious attempt was made at last to get down to the Samuel Report. But what was to happen if, at the end of the fortnight, the miners still refused to accept wage cuts or longer hours? Baldwin and Birkenhead had no more intention than Arthur Cook and Herbert Smith of 'buying a pig in a poke' and they left the T.U.C. subcommittee in no doubt that the Cabinet would consider a renewed subsidy only on the understanding that the miners would accept wage cuts at the end of the fortnight. This time Thomas did not try to argue against the pre-condition. Instead, he assured the Government representatives that, if the miners accepted the formula, this would mean that they also accepted the Samuel Report, including a reduction of wages. He promised to put the formula to the General Council and the miners' executive and to let Baldwin have their reply by lunchtime that Sunday.

As the meeting broke up Steel-Maitland passed Birkenhead a note: 'A taper has been lit this day in England.' On which Birkenhead replied: 'If it's a taper without a wages agreement not even God's help will enable it to be put out.'[15] The assurance demanded by the Government was completely at variance with the call for free and unfettered negotiations which had been made by the conference of executives, but Thomas returned home to Dulwich convinced that there was now 'every chance in the world of averting a general strike. In fact, I never felt so certain of a settlement as at that moment in all my previous difficulties'.[16] His optimism was not shared by ministers. There was absolutely no reason to suppose that a temporary suspension of lock-out notices would make the miners any more inclined to give the pledge required by the Government, and Baldwin and Birkenhead were apprehensive about the Cabinet's reaction to a formula which contained no specific reference to reductions. Nor did Steel-Maitland or Wilson have 'any faith in the wisdom of what they had done'.[17]

There was a further problem to be faced. When Citrine returned home at 2.00 a.m. he found that Cook had been trying to reach him. Citrine rang back and, after explaining briefly the evening's developments, asked Cook to appear with his executive before the General Council that morning. Then came what Citrine describes as 'an absolute bombshell'. The whole of the miners' executive, explained Cook, had already left London and returned to their various districts under the assumption that there were to be no further negotiations with the Government. 'If the General Council had wanted us to stand by', Herbert Smith later declared, 'they could have said so.' The Council assembled at ten on the Sunday morning and telegrams were sent at once to the miners' executive instructing them to return to London for consultations that day. Then came the debate on the formula. Bevin, in particular, wanted to know if the General Council was expected to pledge a settlement in a fortnight and, if so, how it was to be brought about. He was certain that 'underneath it all...the settlement provided for a reduction of wages or an increase in hours' and rightly suspected that there had been a private understanding to this effect. 'I questioned Mr Thomas very closely on this last point, and while they kept saying it might or might not involve that, at the same time, to act in a perfectly straight manner, I came to the conclusion that was really what it meant...and that the Prime Minister would be satisfied in advance so far as the reduction was concerned, irrespective of what might happen afterwards.'[18] Cook was also convinced that the formula was a prelude to wage cuts and appeared before the General Council to denounce it. Most members of the Council shared these misgivings and it was decided that, although the formula could be accepted 'in substance', its interpretation should be discussed with the Government.

It was 7.00 p.m. when Citrine eventually phoned Downing Street to request a further meeting with the Prime Minister. The T.U.C. subcommittee had promised to submit a definitive reply by lunchtime, but no one had thought of informing Downing Street until 1.40 p.m. that the miners had left London and could not therefore be consulted. As a result, the Cabinet had been standing by since noon and when Citrine rang seven hours later he found that 'they were not very keen whether we came or not, but at all events, 9 o'clock was fixed as the time for meeting them'. The T.U.C.'s apparent tardiness added to the suspicion and resentment which had been mounting on the Government side all day. None of the Government representatives at Saturday's meeting had been happy with the formula and just before the Cabinet met at noon, Bolton Eyres-Monsell, Baldwin's Chief Whip, joined him in the garden of Number Ten and forecast serious trouble from the party if the formula was accepted. Maurice Hankey and Baldwin's private secretaries were 'aghast' and one of them, Sir Patrick Gower, took Horace Wilson and Tom Jones 'aside to a private room and in great confidence divulged some secret plot of which he had news, weeks ago, that Winston, Birkenhead, and (I think) J. H. Thomas, had all agreed to bring S.B. down in the crisis and seize the helm themselves'. Jones's reply was 'Bunkum', but Gower was not alone in suspecting the motives of some of the Prime Minister's principal colleagues. 'As the strike became more imminent,'

J. C. C. Davidson wrote in an undated memorandum, 'it became quite clear to me that it would give one more chance to the old gang (Churchill, Chamberlain, and Birkenhead) of getting rid of the "second-class" brains, for they really—as I used to point out continuously to S.B....had not forgotten their sense of superiority and indispensability.'[19]

The Cabinet held its meeting at noon and the violence of its reaction against the formula was so great that Hankey confessed he had never witnessed a scene like it. 'All who were not present when it was agreed reacted in the same way against it, and felt that it would be read by the whole country as a capitulation on the part of the Government to the threat of a general strike. There was nothing on the face of the formula to indicate acceptance of the report. Birkenhead admitted that it was not ideally drafted but pleaded 1.15 a.m. and the mental exhaustion of everybody.'[20] An announcement by Mitchell-Thompson, who combined his duties as Chief Civil Commissioner with those of Postmaster-General, did nothing to soften the mood. Telegrams calling for a strike, he revealed, had actually been sent out at six the previous evening. 'This order for a general strike, of course, made a deep impression on the Cabinet', noted Jones, 'and ministers more than ever felt that the P.M. was a helpless innocent moving amid dangers unrealised.' It was not innocence, however, which separated Baldwin from the majority of his Cabinet colleagues, but a desire that the General Council should be given enough room to manoeuvre itself out of a tight corner. The T.U.C. clearly wished to avoid a strike and the Prime Minister was anxious to do nothing which would impede their line of retreat. But it was becoming increasingly difficult for him to restrain his own 'activists', who seized on the T.U.C.'s failure to make contact at noon as evidence of prevarication.

At 6.45 p.m. the Cabinet met again and produced the final draft of a document which several ministers had been working on for most of the afternoon. This was to be handed to the T.U.C. negotiators 'if the P.M. thought it wise to do so'. The first part of the document disposed of any vagueness about the Government's price for a suspension of lock-out notices and renewal of the subsidy. 'His Majesty's Government believe that no solution of the difficulties in the coal industry which is both practical and honourable to all concerned can be reached except by sincere acceptance of the Report of the Commission. In the expression "acceptance of the Report" is included both the reorganisation of the industry which should be put in hand immediately and such interim adjustments of wages or hours of work as will make it economically possible to carry on the industry in the meantime. If the miners, or the Trade Union Committee on their behalf, are prepared to say plainly that they accept this proposal, the Government is ready to resume the negotiations and to continue the subsidy for a fortnight.' The second part effectively blocked the line of retreat which Baldwin had been trying to keep open for the General Council. 'But since the discussions which took place last night between ministers and members of the Trade Union Committee, it has come to the knowledge of the Government that specific instructions have been sent under the authority of the Trades Union Congress directing their members in several of the most vital industries and services of the country to carry out a general strike on Tuesday next. Such action would involve a challenge to the constitutional rights and freedom of the nation. The Government must therefore require from the Trade Union Committee an unconditional withdrawal of this threat before it can continue negotiations.' It was inconceivable that even those on the General Council most opposed to a strike could have agreed to such total and abject surrender but it was with this ultimatum in his pocket that Baldwin faced the T.U.C. subcommittee in what was clearly to be the decisive meeting.

Thomas arrived ahead of his colleagues and, after announcing to Jones that he was on the verge of a breakdown, confirmed Baldwin's deduction: that given an opportunity, the General Council would recommend wage cuts and leave the miners to like it or lump it. Jones told him that 'the situation seemed to me very black and that the only possible line was that the T.U.C. should itself sincerely accept the Report, try to make the miners do so, and if they failed then the T.U.C. should stand back from the miners and thus avoid a general strike. He agreed, and thought it possible to reach that objective in three or four hours' time'. Jones hastened to report this to the Prime Minister, but Baldwin had left Downing Street after the Cabinet meeting and when he returned he was surrounded by colleagues. 'I tried to tell him, but as others were talking around us, he said, "Tell me when we have adjourned this interview, it will be a short one", and at this moment in came Pugh, Thomas, Swales, and Citrine (9.10 p.m.).' While talks resumed between the T.U.C. subcommittee and Baldwin, Birkenhead, and Steel-Maitland, colleagues on both sides assembled like the well-drilled infantry of two opposing armies. The Negotiating Committee waited in one of the rooms at Number Ten; the General Council and the Cabinet gathered in different rooms at Number Eleven.

At first the atmosphere between the two negotiating committees was strained. The Government trio, recalls Citrine, 'looked rather resentful. Birkenhead sat back in his chair with an injured air, and said that a painful impression had been left on their minds by the fact that we had not met the miners. We explained the position. I said I realised I should have notified the Prime Minister's secretary earlier that morning that the miners' executive were not available. I pointed out that I had only received the information from Cook in the early hours of the morning, and in the stress of our meetings I had completely overlooked the possibility that the Cabinet would be meeting this morning. This statement seemed to reassure the Prime Minister and his colleagues, and they became intimate in explaining their own difficulties.' Birkenhead told the T.U.C. representatives that he and the Prime Minister 'had been going through it with the Cabinet' because the formula produced on Saturday was ambiguous. It was now essential for the miners to declare their unqualified acceptance of the Samuel Report, including wage cuts. The T.U.C. subcommittee balked at such brutal clarity and Thomas said the most they could do was to urge the miners to accept the Report as a basis for settlement on the understanding that it *may* involve wage cuts. Birkenhead drafted Thomas's comment into the form of a statement and it was this which became known thereafter as the Birkenhead Formula. 'We will urge the miners to authorise us to enter upon a discussion with the understanding that they and we accept the Report as a basis for settlement and we approach it with the knowledge that it may involve some reduction in wages.'

It is still far from clear whether or not the T.U.C. representatives agreed to submit this formula to the General Council and the miners. Thomas, according to his biographer, exclaimed: 'We accept it, never mind what the miners or anybody else say.'[21] Birkenhead, in his own account of the coal negotiations written several days later, claimed to have told the trade unionists: 'Well, if that is as far as you feel able to go, it would at least be useful that I should take down your exact words for the consideration of the Cabinet. I make it plain in my judgment there is no chance whatever that an assurance so vague and so limited will be accepted by them; but you are at least entitled that the words used by you should be placed before them for consideration.'[22] Horace Wilson's minute of the discussion also shows that the T.U.C. negotiators agreed to submit the formula to their colleagues. Pugh and Citrine, however, have always insisted that they declined to submit it. 'We never for a moment entertained the possibility of its acceptance,' Citrine wrote in his diary only five days later, 'and plainly said so.' Baldwin now raised the question of strike notices, though he still kept the Cabinet's ultimatum in his pocket. Pugh assured him that these would be automatically withdrawn as soon as the lock-out notices were lifted and here the matter was temporarily allowed to rest. At 11.00 p.m. it was announced that the miners' executive had joined the General Council in the Treasury Board room and both subcommittees went off to consult with their respective colleagues, Thomas muttering to Jones on the way out that Cook was 'A b——— swine'.

In all probability it was Thomas who left Government representatives with the impression that the Birkenhead Formula would be submitted to the General Council and the miners. But when Thomas and the other T.U.C. negotiators entered the Treasury Board room no reference was made to it. The only formula discussed was the one drawn up the previous night. This was immediately repudiated by the miners' executive and the General Council no longer felt able to support it. Bevin suggested that they should get away from 'these wretched formulas—taking a word out here and putting one in there', and began to draft a scheme for effecting the Samuel Report. His basic proposal was that a National Mining Board, including representatives of the Government, the miners, the owners and nominees of both, should decide the steps to be taken to reorganise the industry. This was similar to the proposal which the General Council had already put forward in its policy statement of 28 April. But whereas the policy statement had deliberately fogged over the issue of wage cuts during the reorganisation period, Bevin now suggested that the Board itself should determine 'what adjustments shall be made, if any, by all parties necessary to cover the interim period, subject to the maintenance of a national minimum and the Seven Hours Act'. *A* national minimum or *the* national minimum? The miners pounced on this small but significant difference in terminology. Before any decision could be reached one of Baldwin's secretaries arrived and asked the subcommittee to return. The miners and the General Council were anxious to press on with their discussion, but the secretary reappeared and announced that the negotiators were wanted immediately.

It was now 1.15 on the Monday morning and the T.U.C. representatives found the Prime Minister standing tense and alone in the Cabinet Room. 'The task of the peacemaker is hard,' he declared. 'Since we were here an hour ago, an incident has happened which the British Cabinet takes such a serious view upon that they have instructed me to break off negotiations and convey their decision in this letter which I now hand to you. But I felt, having regard to all you gentlemen have done, to try to effect an honourable peace, courtesy demanded that I should tell you personally.' It had been learned, Baldwin continued, that instructions had already been issued for a general strike and that the printers at the *Daily Mail* had refused to work on that morning's paper. 'It is a direct challenge, a direct challenge, Mr Pugh, and we cannot go on. I am grateful to you for all you have done, but these negotiations cannot continue. Goodbye. This is the end.' Pugh protested that the General Council knew nothing about the *Daily Mail* incident, but Baldwin insisted that 'the hotheads had succeeded in making it impossible for the more moderate people to proceed to try to reach an agreement', and after handshakes all round the bewildered representatives of the General Council found themselves being ushered to the door. 'Well, I have been happy to meet you,' Baldwin told Citrine, 'and I believe if we live we shall meet again to settle it.' Slight pause. 'If we live.'

The letter handed to the T.U.C. was a much tougher version of the Cabinet's original ultimatum. The necessity for immediate wage cuts or longer hours was repeated but the section dealing with strike notices carried a stern addendum.

...it has come to the knowledge of the Government not only that specific instructions have been sent (under the authority of the Executives of the Trade Unions represented at the Conference convened by the General Council of the Trades Union Congress) directing their members in several of the most vital industries and services of the country to carry out a general strike on Tuesday next, but that overt acts have already taken place, including gross interference with the freedom of the Press. Such action involves a challenge to the constitutional rights and freedom of the nation. His Majesty's Government, therefore, before it can continue negotiations must require from the Trades Union Committee both the repudiation of the actions referred to that have already taken place, and an immediate and unconditional withdrawal of the instructions for a general strike.

What had erupted at the *Daily Mail* was an entirely unofficial dispute. The printers objected to an attack on trade unions made in the leading article, 'For King and Country', and when Thomas Marlowe, the editor, refused to delete it workers in the machine room, foundry and packing departments downed tools. Although George Isaacs, the N.A.T.S.O.P.A. secretary, 'would have nothing to do with a strike', Marlowe, whose services in connection with the Zinoviev letter were by no means forgotten, phoned Downing Street and was put through to the Home Secretary. While the Cabinet ultimatum to the T.U.C. was amended to deal with the new situation, one of Baldwin's aides phoned the King's assistant private secretary at Windsor. 'The *Daily*

*Mail* has ceased to function. Don't be alarmed. Tell His Majesty so that he should not go off the deep end.' There was no need for concern, came the reply from Windsor. 'We don't take the *Daily Mail* or the *Daily Express*.'[23]

Did Marlowe's phone call provoke the Cabinet into sabotaging a chance of peace at the eleventh hour? Certainly, the Cabinet was still strongly divided over whether or not the time had come for Baldwin to hand over its original ultimatum to the T.U.C. when news of the *Mail* strike arrived. According to the Colonial Secretary, Leopold Amery, this 'tipped the scale'.[24] W. C. Bridgeman, First Lord of the Admiralty, wrote in his diary that the news arrived 'rather fortunately, as it brought the doubtful people right up against the situation that the General Strike had actually begun'.[25] * But even if the Cabinet had not felt itself bound at this stage to face up to the 'constitutional issue', it is apparent that talks would have broken down later on the mining question. Reluctant as they were to be drawn into a strike, the General Council were not, on Sunday night, prepared to underwrite any formula implying prior acceptance of wage cuts if this meant abandoning the miners. The notion that the T.U.C. had accepted such a formula arose out of the disingenuous account which Thomas gave in the Commons on 5 May. 'Mr Thomas is one of the most clever, glib and astute political strategists in the House,' Baldwin reported to the King on May 6. 'Yesterday he was almost machiavellian in his cleverness. He set out to convince the House that on the fateful Sunday night, the Parties concerned were actually on the point of arriving at a settlement on the basis of a formula agreed between the Trades Union Congress and the Prime Minister, which was to be submitted to the miners by the Trades Union Congress Committee for their doubtful approval, when negotiations were abruptly broken off by the Government, solely on account of the interference of the *Daily Mail*. The account Mr Thomas gave to the House of the events on Saturday and Sunday was incomplete and misleading.'[26]

In his own singularly inept account, Baldwin revealed the terms of the Birkenhead Formula and appeared to confirm Thomas's assertion that a settlement would have been reached on this basis had it not been for the strike at the *Daily Mail*.†

---

* Birkenhead's reaction on hearing the news was to exclaim, 'Hear, hear!' One of his colleagues pointed out severely that it was no time for 'flippancy'.[27]

† It was left to 'A Cabinet Minister' through the dubious medium of the Government's emergency paper, the *British Gazette*, to refute Thomas's contention that the disputing parties were on the verge of a settlement when the talks were broken off. The anonymous minister (who was probably Birkenhead) stressed that the Birkenhead Formula could never have formed the basis for an agreement because of its 'vague

When the T.U.C. subcommittee rejoined the miners and the General Council on Sunday night, Thomas read out the letter which Baldwin had handed over. Then looking round belligerently he declared, 'I have not been talking about this day coming. Some of those who have been talking have now got their will. They must control this from now. We should inform the Government that we regret any incidents that have happened and which have rendered the task of the peacemakers more difficult, but we cannot accept responsibility for them. You must control this thing, you who are on top or you will not be able to control it at all. You won't have the opportunity to issue instructions very long, I know. You won't have the power to issue instructions. I know, I know. War has been declared.'[28] Bevin raised his powerful voice above the indignant clamour. 'I propose we depute someone to draft a reply and that in the meantime we continue our discussions where we left off when the message came, for a basis of settlement has to be found sooner or later, and as we have made good progress on the job we had better go straight on and finish it.'[29] Bevin's suggestion was accepted and the discussions in the Treasury Board room continued for another hour. Pugh and Citrine returned to Number Ten with a resolution repudiating the *Mail* strike and protesting at the Government's peremptory refusal to go on with the talks. But Baldwin had gone to bed and they could find only the caretaker and the resident detective still on duty. There was no longer any point in remaining at Downing Street so the General Council made its way back to Eccleston Square where a full reply to the Prime Minister was drafted and dispatched at 3.30 a.m. on Monday 3 May.

A little over twenty hours now remained before the strike deadline and, after snatching some sleep, Bevin, Pugh, Citrine and the three miners' leaders continued the discussions on Bevin's plan for a settlement. The miners were perfectly willing to go along with the idea of a National Mining Board. But was it to secure *a* national minimum or safeguard *the* national minimum? Here in a new form was the question which the General Council and miners' leaders had been strenuously evading since publication of the Samuel Report. If

---

and limited' assurances on wage cuts. (It will be remembered that Birkenhead had objected in precisely these terms.) Had the Government accepted the formula, the minister declared, the General Strike would only have been postponed and the Government accused of submitting to trade union blackmail. For some reason an account by Hogg, the Attorney-General, which appeared in the 11 May issue, placed special emphasis not on the inadequacy of the formula but on the *Daily Mail* strike. On the same day Arthur Pugh wrote in the T.U.C. paper, the *British Worker*, that the Birkenhead Formula had never been dictated by, assented to or in the possession of the trade union negotiators.

genuine steps were taken to implement reorganisation, would the miners accept wage cuts in the interim? Bevin insisted that the time had now come for an answer. Smith, Cook, and Richardson finally agreed to the insertion of the words 'a minimum', but when they took Bevin's draft to their full executive, meeting in a room at the House of Commons, the phrasing was rejected by 12 votes to 6. Bevin, who attended the meeting, remarked: 'Well, if that is your decision the General Council must make its own decision. There are 3½ million men who must have their position considered.' The General Council accepted Bevin's draft unanimously, endorsing his argument that the miners had handed over their powers and must accept the General Council's ruling as final. No longer was there to be resistance to any settlement involving prior commitment to wage cuts. Instead, there was now recognition by the General Council 'that it could not demand the complete observance by the Government and the mine-owners of their obligations under the Report, and rule out the miners' obligations'.

Convinced that the way was now clear for a settlement, Bevin handed one copy of his proposals to MacDonald and another to Frederick Leggett, a contact at the Ministry of Labour, urging that the Prime Minister should put the scheme forward in the House that evening. If he did, Bevin assured Leggett, the Labour party would accept it. Citrine and Cook were in the public gallery when the debate began on the declaration of a state of emergency, but neither Baldwin nor MacDonald mentioned his scheme for it contained one fatal drawback: wage cuts were to be determined by a Board of miners, owners, employers, trade unionists, and Government representatives. How could they be expected to agree? MacDonald saw clearly that 'every constitution-monger will seize on the powers of the Board, and will destroy the whole thing at once on that. The Government will never accept it'.[30] Leggett consulted Horace Wilson, who confirmed MacDonald's opinion. Unless the T.U.C. were prepared, on behalf of the miners, to accept an immediate reduction in wages, said Wilson, the Government were just not interested.

The Commons debate centred on the constitutional issue raised by a general strike. (The term was not one which appealed to the T.U.C., who always steadfastly referred to 'the National Strike'.) Amid the loud approval of his supporters, Baldwin stated that the Government had 'found itself challenged with an alternative Government...I do not think all the leaders, when they assented to ordering a general strike, fully realised that they were threatening the basis of ordered Government, and going nearer to proclaiming civil war than we have been for centuries past...it is not wages that are imperilled;

it is the freedom of our very Constitution'. Although Baldwin was by now well aware that the *Mail* strike had occurred without the knowledge, much less the sanction, of the General Council, he emphasised that this had been decisive. 'We felt that this was more than a threat. It was direct action, and direct action, in my view, of the worst kind because it was suppressing, or trying to suppress, the possibility of the dissemination of news to the public. In these circumstances and with infinite regret, we had to take the stand that we could go no further.'

Outside the Chamber the Government was taking a rather less meticulous view of its responsibilities to the Press. Earlier that day, Sir Herbert Lawrence, one of the coal commissioners, had complained to the Attorney-General that he and his colleagues regarded as totally unreasonable the proposal to cut wages by 10 per cent *and* increase working hours. While the Prime Minister was asserting his eloquent defence of news dissemination, Jones wandered out into the lobby and learned from one of his Labour party acquaintances that William Beveridge intended to issue a denunciation of the owners' terms to the newspapers. Steel-Maitland was alerted. He immediately contacted Beveridge and prevailed on him to withhold his views from the Press.

Meanwhile, the Commons debate continued. Churchill, the main Government speaker apart from the Prime Minister, could detect 'no difference whatever between a general strike to force some Bill which the Country does not wish for, and a general strike to force Parliament to pay a subsidy...it is a conflict which, if it is fought out to a conclusion, can only end in the overthrow of Parliamentary Government or in its decisive victory'. The Labour leaders maintained that, since the strike had no political motivation, it could not be construed as a threat to the Constitution. 'I know the Government's position', said Thomas. 'I have never disguised that in a challenge to the Constitution, God help us unless the Government won...but this is not only not a revolution, it is not something that says, "We want to overthrow everything". It is merely, a plain, economic, industrial dispute...' MacDonald, who confided to Citrine that his hair had gone greyer since the morning, declared that 'with the discussion of general strikes and Bolshevism and all that kind of thing, I have nothing at all to do. I respect the Constitution as much as Sir Robert Horne [a former Tory Chancellor of the Exchequer].'

There was a more-in-sorrow-than-in-anger quality to these exchanges for it was apparent to the Tories that Labour's front bench were feeling acute discomfort as apologists for a strike they had always opposed and clearly dreaded more than the Government itself. In his report of Monday's proceedings to the King, Baldwin observed that 'The House of Commons rose to its greatest heights... So far from there being any disturbance, the atmosphere throughout the debate was grave, solemn, and impressive... The leaders of the Labour party were sincerely anxious of finding an honourable way out of the position into which they have been led by their own folly.'[31] No such gentlemanly reservations were shown to Lloyd George, who had derided the Government for being 'afraid to face cold steel' in July 1925, but who attacked the Government just as scornfully for its current position. In his report to the King, Baldwin referred to Lloyd George's 'vague and indeterminate vacillations, his niggling criticisms of the Government, and his insincere fraternisation with the Labour party'.

The debate ended at 11.00 p.m. and MacDonald and Henderson immediately sought out the Prime Minister, Churchill, and Steel-Maitland. 'Have you come to say that the strike notices are withdrawn?' demanded Churchill. 'If not, then there is no reason to continue this discussion. You tried it in Italy and failed, and you are not going to be successful in Great Britain.' 'It seems to me, Winston', Henderson retorted, 'that you are trying to give us a dose of Sidney Street.' Tempers began to rise and Steel-Maitland, who did not normally follow the Chancellor's hard line, declared that it was about time the Labour party and its friends were put in their place. Churchill ended the discussion. 'You will be better prepared', he told the Labour leaders, 'to talk to us in two or three weeks.'[32] Shortly after 11.00 p.m. Thomas emerged from the Commons with tears streaming down his face and pushed his way through the large crowd of sightseers, journalists and recruiting agents for the National Fascisti. 'I don't mind confessing that when I left the House that night, realising that all had been in vain and that a strike was inevitable, I gave way to tears. It was like seeing the fabric you loved smashed to fragments.'[33]

Chapter Seven

# *Battle Orders*

'The net impression left on my mind is that the General Strike will turn out not to be a revolution of any sort but a batch of compulsory Bank Holidays without any opportunity for recreation and a lot of dreary walking to and fro. When the million or so strikers have spent their money they will drift back to work and no one will be any better and many will be a great deal poorer and everybody will be cross.'

Beatrice Webb, writing in her diary, Monday, 3 May 1926.

'It is going to be interesting seeing if we can beat these fellows. I think we can, but it involves a big effort.'

Maurice Hankey, writing to his wife, Monday, 3 May 1926.

'As far as we can see we shall go on. I don't like general strikes. I haven't changed my opinion. I have said so in the House of Commons. I don't like it; honestly I don't like it; but honestly, what can be done?'

Ramsay MacDonald, quoted in the *Daily Herald* on Tuesday, 4 May 1926.

'The men are quite docile and taking very little interest in the situation. They have little idea of the merits of the dispute and say that everything is done in London. They will draw lying on pay on Friday and they are quite happy. They will keep all ready cash for their amusement and beer, and leave the feeding to be done, as far as possible, by others better off. After next Saturday they will be feeling the pinch a little and then I suppose we shall have to go through the same wearisome performance of feeding the children.'

Malcolm Dillon, Chief Agent to the Marquis of Londonderry and managing director of Londonderry Collieries Ltd., in a letter to His Lordship, Monday, 3 May 1926.

'Man, John, there's never been anything like it. If the blighters o' leaders here...dinna let us down we'll hae the Capitalists crawlin' on their bellies in a week. Oh, boy, it's the revolution at last!'

An I.L.P. enthusiast quoted in John Paton's *Left Turn*.

'Alvescot: All out here; God help us if we lose.'

Strike entry in *Oxford Railway Bulletin*.

Ever since Red Friday the Government had been working intensively to perfect plans for a crisis and ministers had good reason for feeling confident. As early as February the Home Secretary was reporting that 'little remained to be done before the actual occurrence of an emergency'.[1] The Government's two paramount objectives were the maintenance of essential supplies and the preservation of law and order. Both objectives were to be secured by the regional civil commissioners, aided by the local authorities and volunteer service committees in their respective areas and armed with the almost unlimited powers conferred by the Emergency Powers Act. Considerable quantities of food, coal and petrol had been stockpiled; the export of coal was banned and there was provision for fixing the retail price of all goods in the event of serious shortages. Distribution was in the hands of 150 local committees made up of the nation's principal haulage contractors and arrangements had been made to relieve them of their existing obligations by declaring legal priority in the transport of essential supplies. In extreme cases road officers appointed by the civil commissioners had the power to requisition, though the Government hoped this could be avoided by making businessmen themselves responsible for the operation of the haulage committees.

Local authorities were to assist the regional commissioners in controlling road transport and food and fuel supplies. The role they were to play had been outlined by the Ministry of Health in its confidential circular of November and transport and police arrangements were discussed at conferences between local authority and Government representatives in December, January, and March. Another ministry circular on 30 April listed the civil commissioners and their principal officers and local authorities were told that all emergency plans were to be put into effect on receipt of telegrams from Whitehall bearing the single word, 'Action'. The telegrams were duly despatched on the night of Sunday 2 May, by which time the commissioners and their staffs were ready at their headquarters.

Hyde Park was also taken over on Sunday to serve as a food depot for London and after thirty-six hours of frantic work was transformed, by Tuesday morning, into a miniature metropolis, with its own gas, light, heat, water mains and internal telephone system. From this depot the London Haulage Committee, whose members included Major Munro, of Covent Garden, James Paterson, of Carter Paterson, and Cecil Rickett, of Rickett Cockerell, was to distribute the capital's milk, meat, fruit, vegetables, groceries, wheat, flour and coal.

While discussions with the T.U.C. continued on Monday, the military precautions agreed by the Cabinet the previous week were being put into effect. All army and navy leave was cancelled and troop reinforcements were moved into London, Scotland, South Wales and Lancashire. The Cabinet had decided that troop movements were to occur 'as unobtrusively as possible', but in Liverpool two battalions of infantry landed from a troopship and marched through the city with steel helmets, rifles and full equipment while the battleships *Ramillies* and *Barham*, recalled from the Atlantic Fleet, anchored in the Mersey. Warships also anchored in the Tyne, Clyde, and Humber, and at Cardiff, Bristol, Swansea, Barrow, Middlesbrough, and Harwich. Servicemen were to be used, however, only as a last resort for the Government hoped that sufficient volunteers would be available to keep essential supplies moving and maintain law and order.

On Monday the O.M.S. officially handed over its organisation to the Government and its registered personnel, numbering some 100,000, were instructed to report to their volunteer service committees. Throughout the seven months of its existence the O.M.S. had always been careful to stress that it was motivated by patriotism not politics, but, to the disadvantage of the Government, it was the patriotism of the prosperous and the majority of volunteers lacked precisely those skills which were most needed. The great bulk lived in the south and east of England, the largest single number—over 7,000—being provided by the City of Westminster. The whole of Leeds, for instance, provided only 400 and there were none at all registered in Manchester or Liverpool. During the months preceding the strike the O.M.S. managed to provide discreet training for a limited number of volunteer drivers, telegraph operators and telephonists. But the total of skilled personnel handed over on 3 May was far from impressive. It included 1,322 lorry drivers and 250 Ford van drivers for the G.P.O. trained in O.M.S. 'schools'—usually the testing grounds of private factories—144 omnibus drivers, 1,345 car drivers, 640 railway operatives, 166 workers for inland waterways, 91 tramwaymen, and 351 mechanics. There were also 1,194 skilled, semi-skilled, and unskilled engineers for the electricity commission. The Government itself issued an appeal for volunteers on Sunday evening and recruiting stations were opened the following morning.

The sight of continual queues at the London enrolment centre, a temporary wooden hutment erected in the Foreign Office quadrangle in Whitehall, may have seemed impressive, but by 4 May only 6,000 volunteers had come forward and throughout the country the total was no more than 30,000.

On the other hand, it soon became clear that the response to the General Council's strike call had far exceeded even the Council's expectations. Tuesday dawned with uncharacteristic stillness in the streets and railway stations of the cities for there were no trains preparing to bring suburban cargoes to town and no buses getting ready to heave the city millions to their shops and offices. Clerks, typists, shop assistants, businessmen had to make their way as best they could and by 8.00 a.m. the stillness was gone from the streets. Pedestrians, cyclists, private motor cars, taxis, even ponies and traps, streamed into the centres of the towns creating a bedlam of noise and congestion. The main approaches to London were choked with cars stretching in unbroken convoys across the Thames bridges to the city centre, and from Marble Arch to Piccadilly traffic moved at the rate of only a few yards an hour. Strike action by members of the N.U.R. and A.S.L.E.F. was unanimous and even some isolated blacklegging by the white-collar members of the Railway Clerks' Association failed to make any difference to the number of trains that could be run. Passenger service on the L.M.S. was 3.8 per cent of normal on 5 May and freight service only 1 per cent of normal; on the L.N.E.R. the equivalent figures were 3.4 and 2.2 per cent, and on the Great Western 3.7 and 5 per cent.[2] At the twice-daily press conference given by J. C. C. Davidson at the Admiralty, the most he was able to say on Tuesday evening was that a limited railway service was being run and that 'from the north of England a train is being run daily, which stops at every station'.

On the London Underground 15 out of 315 trains ran on the first day of the strike and these covered short distances only. Of London's 4,400 buses, 300 were running with volunteer crews on Tuesday but the number was down to 40 by the end of the week.[3] The biggest operator, the London General Omnibus Company, moved its 3,300 vehicles into Regents Park, there to await any volunteer crews who might be brave or foolish enough to chance the unpredictable hazards of angry strikers and chaotic roads. Nine of the capital's 2,000 tramcars were operating. Outside London the situation varied and in a few provincial centres public road transport still functioned almost normally. In Oxford, Chatham, Cardiff, and Grimsby bus services were barely disrupted and in Southampton and Portsmouth the trams continued to run. In Bristol

E

and Maidstone both bus and tram services operated with virtually no cuts. But these were rare exceptions and in most of the towns and cities of Britain the paralysis of public transport was complete.

The response of other 'first line' unions to the General Council's call made less direct impact on the ordinary population but was just as overwhelming The dockers joined their fellow-transport workers and at the London Docks an immediate crisis arose with the threatened shutdown of electricity to the vast refrigerating plant, where three-quarters-of-a-million carcases were stored. It was not the kind of crisis which could be resolved by the jolly undergraduates and hearty middle-aged businessmen of the O.M.S. The Royal Navy had to sail to the rescue in submerged submarines which anchored in the King George V dock and linked their own electricity supplies to the refrigerating plant. Builders, printers, and workers in the iron, steel, metals and heavy chemicals industries were all out by the morning of 4 May. The London printers had already given an indication of their militancy earlier on Monday before cessation of the strike notices. When the London *Evening News* tried to quote part of the *Mail*'s 'King and Country' editorial, N.A.T.S.O.P.A. members halted production and both the *Star* and the *Evening Standard* failed to appear because the printing workers objected to the enthusiastic accounts which had been written of recruiting scenes in Whitehall. (Significantly, few members of the National Union of Journalists followed their executive's instruction not to work with blacklegs after 3 May. Only in Glasgow did the editorial as well as the printing staffs walk out.) Most of the morning newspapers could be bought on 4 May but the printing unions struck after final shifts on 3 May.

Severe complications arose, however, in the gas and electricity industries because of the General Council's directive that power but not lighting was to be cut off. It was an impracticable instruction which the unions concerned were left to interpret as best they could. Taking the line of least resistance, the A.E.U. directed its members to cease work only where others had already done so. The E.T.U. was less cautious and the General Council was horrified to learn just before midnight on 3 May that E.T.U. members had been ordered to strike, even if this resulted in a shutdown of lighting as well as power. Citrine immediately urged the E.T.U. to abandon its plan while the General Council reconsidered the matter. But he was unable to prevent the Labour-controlled Stepney Borough Council from going ahead with its own decision to close down the municipal power station between sunrise and sunset. This provided Davidson with some useful ammunition at his Tuesday evening press conference.

The Council's action, he alleged, had forced two hospitals in the borough to abandon operations and X-rays and to close their out-patient departments. Although the first two of these allegations were not denied, strikers blamed the out-patient closures on medical staff rushing off to enlist in the O.M.S. The General Council's revised policy on 6 May told strike committees to meet local authorities 'and offer to supply light and power for such services as house, street and shop lighting, social services, power for food, bakeries, laundries and domestic purposes'. Although a refusal by most authorities to negotiate led to an almost total withdrawal of union labour from the power stations, the Government was well able to cope. It had already received a pledge of support from the technically vital Electrical Power Engineers' Association and the non-technical jobs abandoned by strikers were filled with a ready supply of volunteers supplemented by naval ratings.

Confusion also followed on the General Council's directive that building workers were to come out with the exception of those 'employed definitely on housing and hospital work'. The most varied interpretations were placed on this phrase by the unions affiliated to the National Federation of Building Trades Operatives and solidarity gave way all too often to vicious squabbling between the national executives. The report of the Federation secretary at Wellingborough reflects the bewilderment and irritation of those who were expected to carry out the orders of the respective unions. 'I called a mass meeting, and if the instructions I had had from [Richard] Copock [Federation secretary] had been the only ones, I could have got a response. But each affiliated society secretary was on the platform with me, each with differently-worded instructions, each of which called on the members to cease work, and then went on to lay down rules and regulations which no one could interpret, but which made it impossible for the members to do so.'[4] Eventually, most areas resolved the problem by calling all Federation members out.

Further difficulties arose out of the General Council's decision not to interfere with the distribution of milk, food and medicines. The Government had ignored Citrine's offer of co-operation. 'What Government in the world', asked Churchill, 'could enter into partnership with a rival Government, against which it is endeavouring to defend itself and society, and allow that rival Government to sit in judgment on every train that runs and every lorry on the road?' The General Council had instructed the road and rail unions to grant permits and provide men for the movement of essential goods. The T.G.W.U. was agreeable, but the three rail unions refused to run a service for any commodity, arguing that up to 75 per cent of their membership would have to resume work and general morale would be broken. A National Transport Committee was set up to formulate a permit scheme for the movement of goods by road only, but this was effectively paralysed by open strife between the representatives of the transport workers and railwaymen, and the General Council was forced to leave the issue of permits almost entirely at the discretion of local transport committees. The chaotic results are described in a later chapter. It need only be said here that the problem of permits, like the problem of who was to remain at work in the power stations and on the building sites, flowed from a basic lack of preparation by the General Council. Its decision that each of the eighty-two unions affected by the strike should bring out its own members in its own way meant inevitable arguments over interpretation, arguments sharpened in many instances by ingrained craft prejudices and ancient sectional rivalries.

Most rank-and-file dissatisfaction, however, focused on the General Council's decision to divide strikers into a 'first line' and a 'reserve', which meant that the engineers and shipyard workers were held in check for another week. This plan came from Bevin, who argued that, if everyone was brought out at the same time, the strike would start to decline immediately from a maximum of strength, whereas keeping men in reserve was a guarantee that the strike could only become stronger. 'We must move as an army and bring our people in just at the right moment.' Citrine and Thomas opposed the strategy. Thomas, fearing the consequences of a long strike, believed the chance of a quick settlement would be improved if the unions demonstrated their full strength from the outset. 'Up to the evening of the strike the Government thought they knew our power, but the strike exceeded their greatest expectation. The position is that they are staggered. How does their mentality operate after the first shock? I can picture Winston—for he is dominating this—I can picture the Cabinet, I can hear him saying: "Wait until tomorrow, they will get tired. We will have our guns. We will have our volunteers. This cannot be a war of attrition. If it became that it would get out of hand in a week." '[5] Citrine also wanted a 'clean cut' instruction bringing everyone out, although I recognised fully the wisdom of the other strategy of bringing out the members in battalions. I cannot feel that our people are sufficiently disciplined and trained to understand that'.

Pressure from those who wished to join the strike immediately was certainly intense and the General Council was not exaggerating when it stated in its first strike communique on 4 May that 'The difficulty …has been to keep men in what we might call the second line of

defence rather than call them out'. Appeals were by no means confined to members of the big industrial unions. Operators at the
Central Telegraph Office, nerve-centre of the nation's telegraphic
system, were incensed that there were no plans at all for calling
them out and even the 310 members of the Goldbeaters' Trade
Society demanded to know what role they could play. The practical
effect of Bevin's strategy was to create a sense of isolation among
many of the 'first line' strikers, particularly in the big engineering
and shipbuilding centres like Coventry and the Clyde; to frustrate
the hundreds of thousands of trade unionists who, in spite of their
own inclinations, were forced to continue working; and to give the
Government another week's grace in which to improve its organisation and recruit more volunteers.

Bevin's attempt to weld the thirty-two individuals who sat on the
General Council into a co-ordinated and effective administrative
machine was more successful. A number of subcommittees had been
set up on 1 May to handle various aspects of the strike but these
broke down completely on 4 May under a mounting avalanche of
reports, inquiries, deputations and requests for rulings and instructions. The T.U.C.'s small staff were driven to the edge of hysteria
by the conflicting orders which rained in on them, while in what had
been the Churchill dining room the General Council sat debating
whether or not the reports from its subcommittees should arrive in
folders. By Tuesday evening Bevin had made up his mind that the
situation could not continue and, according to Citrine, 'rose in the
Council, with determination on his face, and offered to sacrifice
himself on the altar of duty. He was willing to undertake the whole
administration of the strike, and thus relieve the anxieties of his
colleagues. The lesser luminaries communed with themselves and
were wroth at the proposed usurpation, whereat Bevin was grieved'.
Elsewhere in his diary Citrine noted that 'there was a storm as a
consequence, and a good deal of straight speaking. Thomas and
some of the others were very sarcastic at Bevin's offer'. Nevertheless,
Bevin did persuade the Council to hand over the actual conduct of
the strike to a small Strike Organisation Committee and, although
Purcell was made chairman, it was under Bevin's assertive leadership
that the committee set about reshaping the T.U.C. for the most
important battle of its existence.

The National Transport Committee, representing Bevin's own
union and the railwaymen, moved out of the T.U.C.'s overcrowded
premises in Eccleston Square to Unity House, the N.U.R.'s headquarters in Euston. A Building Committee was formed to decide which
building operations should continue and transferred to the Clapham

offices of the Amalgamated Union of Building Trade Workers. A Political Committee, which included Thomas and Arthur Henderson, was set up to liaise with the Parliamentary Labour party. A Press and Publicity Committee was created to organise press conferences, issue statements on behalf of the General Council, and consider publication of a regular news bulletin, and a propaganda department arranged meetings and organised speakers to address them. An Intelligence Committee undertook the task of sifting and collating the scores of reports which arrived continually by post, telephone and dispatch rider from all parts of the country. An Interviewing Committee dealt with callers and deputations. A transport department established a daily courier service which, by the end of the week, covered most of the country.

Bevin was not solely concerned with efficiency, however, as Citrine's diary entry for Wednesday, 5 May makes clear : 'The [strike organisation] committee appointed practically every member of the General Council to a particular function; some of them of little use, I am afraid. Even the members of the Central Strike Committee, with the exception of Bevin and Purcell, were appointed to other duties, the net effect being to eliminate them from participating in most decisions, leaving only Purcell and Bevin to act. As Bevin remarked to me, "We must not have too many generals in this business".' Thomas naturally resented Bevin's emergence as the key figure at Eccleston Square and Citrine has provided a revealing contemporary account of the tensions which existed between them.

'Today, Sunday 9 May, I was thinking how, amid all our distress, the strike really has its lighter side. Take the personalities of our General Council for instance. There is Bevin, brawny of chest and broad of brow, swarthy of countenance, afflicted with the most becoming modesty. On the Saturday when the general strike was declared, he suggested that he should be added to the Industrial Committee. But Jimmy Thomas and his fellow conspirators had decreed that it should not be so... Then we have Jimmy Thomas— always discovering new situations, with mysterious side glances and knowing looks—endowed with facile entry into the innermost circles of Government. If we only knew what he knew! He had seen a Cabinet minister that day in the House of Commons, looking very worried. "By God, our stock is up, but we must remember the serious consequences of any hesitancy." Or perhaps a well-known capitalist, whose name he withheld for reasons which we would all understand, had winked at him, whereupon the said James required an urgent meeting of the Industrial Committee to debate the significance of the wink. Alternatively the transport and railway deities conduct a psychic and sometimes verbal warfare. One moment the gloom of depression settled on the one, and, strange to relate, the sunshine of optimism radiates its glow on the other. Bevin rises in the morning to make his reports, with lowering brow and serious mien. "Martial law has been declared in the East End. Serious clashes between the police and the populace. People getting short of food. We must have constructive proposals for a settlement." He had been talking to a prominent business man who exercised great influence in the City, and who had emphatically asserted that the Government had made a mess of the whole thing. "But we must not trust too much to that." Whereat Jimmy smiles sardonically and rises with pity in his look. Did anybody think he had entered in this business without recognising what it would mean? Why, he knew from the beginning the streets would be running in blood very soon. We were out of the stage of talking now. There was no compromise. The Government must fight until we are smashed. Of course, we all knew that we must be smashed. How could anybody think any different? Whereupon James sits down, leaving everybody in a state of gloom. Next day Bevin comes forward with a report that the whole movement is as solid as a rock; the dockers could not be persuaded back to work for weeks. Anyone who suggested in the East End that the strike should be stopped would be in danger of his life. The Government food organisation was *in extremis*. Their organisation had broken down at the docks and troops were trying to distribute food. The strikers, on instructions of the unions, were parading the streets in front of the troops in their war medals—and Bevin sits down, confident, determined to fight to the last transport worker and last worker. Then Jimmy slowly gains his equilibrium, looks round the Council, and with a drop in his voice says: "My God, my God, if only you knew! I was talking last night to Lord Reading.* He says Winston is out to smash the trade union movement. How can we win? We must find a bridge." This gives the necessary stimulus to Bevin, and he thunders in declamation that he always recognised that the strike could not be settled for at least three or four weeks. And so the show goes on.'

* Liberal Statesman and ex-Viceroy of India.

Chapter Eight

# *The Fourth Estate*

'The Soviet Press is jubilant over the non-appearance of some of the British newspapers and it is optimistically observed that one step further and the Soviet's *Izvestia* will be produced in the splendidly-equipped printing offices of *The Times*.'

A Reuter report from Riga, published in the *Manchester Evening Bulletin*, 8 May 1926.

'The field of battle is no longer transport but news.'

Winston Churchill, at the outset of the Strike, quoted in Basil Liddell Hart's *Memoirs*, Volume II.

'The most formidable and insidious attempt that has yet been made to cripple the freedom of the Press and to withhold essential news from the public has been frustrated. The *British Gazette* may have had a short life; but it has fulfilled the purpose of living. It becomes a memory; but it remains a monument.'

From the final issue of the *British Gazette,* 13 May 1926.

'One of the worst outrages which the country had to endure— and to pay for—in the course of the strike, was the publication of the *British Gazette*. This organ, throughout the seven days of its existence, was a disgrace alike to the British Government and to British journalism—in so far as British journalism can be said to have had anything to do with it.'

From the *New Stateman*, 15 May 1926.

While confusion reigned at Eccleston Square on Tuesday, serenity wreathed Downing Street. Calling at Number Ten in the morning Jones found the Prime Minister 'obviously rested, and happier in mind than he has been for some days'.[1] After discussing how badly MacDonald and the 'Goat'—Baldwin's epithet for Lloyd George —had done in Monday's debate, the Prime Minister hinted at legislative measures he intended taking against the T.U.C. 'We shall have to find some way to deal with all this trade union business, and revise its powers and machinery so far as the Government is concerned in the light of this tremendous centralising of their powers. We must get some way by which the voice of the rank-and-file can be made effective.' Before he could enlarge, a jubilant Churchill strode in and announced that he had commandeered the offices and machinery of the *Morning Post* in order to produce a Government newspaper.

The Chancellor was allowing himself some journalistic licence, for the *Morning Post* offices and machinery were commandeered not by him but by Davidson, who as Deputy Chief Civil Commissioner, supervised Government publicity arrangements. Nor did Churchill play more than a peripheral role in the events preceding the take-over. The idea that some kind of official news sheet should be published during the emergency was Davidson's. But how was it to be printed and distributed? Davidson believed that by pooling their resources, the owners of the national dailies could do the job and on 2 May he discussed the proposal with Lord Burnham, proprietor of the *Daily Telegraph* and president of the Newspaper Proprietors' Association. Burnham was sympathetic but had to report that, at a meeting that morning, the Association had decided that it could not undertake joint publication of a newspaper. Even the Bill Posters' Association, explained Burnham, had instructed its members not to post any Government bills and announcements on public buildings and hoardings, and 'the trade unions were introducing the Soviet system into all newspaper offices so that their agents could act as self-constituted censors and decide what to publish and what to suppress in the Labour interest'. He proposed, instead, that the Government should commandeer a suitable building and appoint an official editor of its own, promising that the Association would supply editorial experts.[2]

Davidson discussed the suggestion with Baldwin, who promptly recommended Churchill for the editorship. 'It will keep him busy, stop him doing worse things. I'm terrified of what Winston is going to be like.' 'So am I,' replied Davidson, 'but I've got my terms of reference, my instructions, and my position, and so long as I'm supported as being the executive head, I don't care a damn what Winston says; he's got no power except the power of personality which is very difficult to deal with; but he has no executive power, and I propose to censor. If Winston tries to turn the men into an army of Bolsheviks...I shall resist that.' Churchill, who considered that his front line reporting during the Boer War made him a veteran journalist, was enthralled with the prospect of running his

own paper and subsequently described the experience as 'a com-
bination of a first-class battleship and a first-class general election'.

The search for suitable premises was more protracted as it was
essential that they should provide an easy defence against militant
pickets. Churchill personally inspected the *Mail* offices but decided
that in the narrow streets which surrounded them the police would
be at a disadvantage in any confrontation with strikers. Lord
Beaverbrook offered the use of the *Daily Express* offices, but these,
too, were situated in a maze of narrow streets. Beaverbrook was
sure that the Odhams Press building in Long Acre would be ideal
and approached J. S. Elias, Odhams' managing director. But
although Elias opposed the strike, he had some sympathy for the
strikers and refused to allow his premises to be used. Even a hint from
Beaverbrook that his reward would almost certainly be a baronetcy
failed to change Elias's mind.³ Still hoping for some practical help
from the Newspaper Proprietors' Association, Davidson, joined now
by Churchill, met its representatives at noon on 3 May. Not only
did the Association again refuse to produce a paper of its own, but
it also cast doubt on the Government's ability to do so 'owing to
the lack of skilled mechanics and the absence of all the usual
channels for distributing papers when printed'. Davidson was particularly incensed by the attitude of Lord Riddell, proprietor of the
*News of the World* and chairman of the Association, who 'throughout
behaved, whether from design or merely because it is in his nature,
in a most obstructive manner'.

Thwarted by the Newspaper Proprietors' Association, Davidson
turned next to H. A. Gwynne, editor of the *Morning Post*. In a letter
dispatched immediately after the meeting with the N.P.A., Davidson
wrote: 'I do think that the men engaged in the production of
newspapers might volunteer to help the Government to produce
what they cannot produce themselves. If we could be free from the
responsibility of doing something we have never done before, i.e.
producing a newspaper, we will in turn, by the requisite financial
backing and providing protection, make your services to the public
and the State possible as newspaper proprietors. Do help. Do help...
It seems strange that from your office a four-page sheet cannot be
issued, i.e. printed and distributed.' The *Post* was the obvious target
for such an appeal. Owned by the Duke of Northumberland, it
outpaced even the *Mail* and the *Express* in its abuse of the strikers:
its Saturday headline read, 'Zinovieff Wins'; more importantly, it
occupied premises on an easily defended island site in the Strand
between the Lyceum and Gaiety Theatres. According to Davidson,
Gwynne was also angry at 'the defeatist attitude of Riddell and the

mugwumpishness of the leaders of the newspaper fraternity', and he replied the same day, offering his unconditional co-operation.

It was easy enough to requisition the offices of a sympathetic newspaper, but Davidson had no way of knowing whether enough skilled labour would be available to man the plant. That evening he and his advisers met in the Chancellor's room at the House of Commons to make a final decision. As an alternative to producing a full-scale newspaper it was suggested that a small bulletin 'about the size of a page out of a telephone directory' should be printed at the Stationery Office works in Harrow. But Davidson ruled this out because 'the obvious disadvantage of slow production and the distance between the editorial, printing and distributing staffs made the project one of doubtful success. In any case, Winston desired to produce a newspaper rather than a news-sheet'. Finally, Davidson made up his mind to take the risk and at 11.00 p.m., accompanied by Sir Malcolm Fraser, of Conservative Central Office and David Caird, the War Office press secretary, he arrived at the *Morning Post* to take possession on behalf of the Government.

Assistance from the *Post's* editorial employees was not in doubt and Gwynne was confident that the mechanical staff would also carry on working. Summoned by telegram and brought by car, their response seemed to justify Gwynne's optimism. Only the foundry overseer rejected his appeal to their loyalty and at 4.00 a.m. on Tuesday 4 May, work began on the first issue of the *British Gazette*. Davidson, however, thought it dangerous to rely on them and Fraser, whom he appointed to take charge of production and distribution, scoured the other newspaper offices for technical staff while the controller of the Stationery Office was instructed to arrange for duplicate type-setting by contract printers. Beaverbrook responded immediately, sending over Sidney Long, night superintendent of the *Express*. Long brought with him two other key members of the *Express* staff, the chief mechanical engineer and the head machine room overseer. 'By 6.00 a.m. on Tuesday morning', Davidson has written, 'we had collected a skeleton staff, and throughout the following morning and afternoon we picked volunteers for every department of the newspaper.' This effort was not wasted. At 3.00 p.m. on Tuesday afternoon representatives of the *Post's* own printing staff informed Davidson that the London Society of Compositors had strictly forbidden them to touch the work. This did not cause any immediate concern because of the arrangements which had been made to type-set in duplicate. But shortly after 3.00 p.m. news came that the outside compositors had struck and had also destroyed the type already set up. 'At this point', Davidson has recorded, 'Sidney

Long came to the rescue. It is not too much to say that without him the situation could not have been saved. Only five of the fourteen columns had been set, but he completed the rest with his own hands. By this point we had practically none of the mechanical staff left. Only six remained. However expert these men were, they could not be expected to run two rotary presses. Crews for each machine were required to handle the paper rolls, to oil and tend machinery, to clothe the cylinders with the stereo plates, and to remove the printed sheets. The editorial staff took over. They clothed themselves in dungarees and marched into the machine room, and even the art and music critics plunged into their unusual task with enthusiasm. The machines were late starting, and an accident in the foundry deprived us of the auto plates for two hours. It was nearly midnight before the last plate had been locked on to the cylinder, but, after a night full of anxiety, production difficulties and disappointments, about 232,000 copies had been rolled off the presses by six o'clock on the morning of 4 May.'

On Wednesday scores of additional volunteers were drafted in to help the willing but desperately hard-pressed *Morning Post* journalists. A few of the new volunteers were studying printing at London University but the vast majority had no knowledge of newspaper production and included undergraduates, clerks, artists, music professors, medical students, doctors, and coffee planters. To turn this assortment into reasonably proficient chargemen, brake and control men, flymen, reel-hands, boiler stokers, and office cleaners, Admiral 'Blinker' Hall, the legendary wartime Director of Naval Intelligence and former Tory principal agent, was brought in as organising manager and superintendent of personnel. Rapidly Hall assessed the skills and talents of his recruits, sorted them into shifts and gangs and arranged food and accommodation for them in the *Post* offices. He also imposed a system of strict security. On one occasion Birkenhead was not allowed through the strong police cordon mounted outside the building because he was unable to produce the appropriate purple pass.

The efforts of the new intake quickly became apparent. 'On the first night', Davidson has recounted, 'we had been forced to leave the two inside pages of our four-page sheet blank because of our difficulties. On Wednesday, we filled all four and doubled the number printed. From then on the quality increased rapidly. There were eight issues in all, and by the end of the strike the circulation was well over two million copies. It was a remarkable achievement, all the more so since in the early stages a few key men laboured under increasing strain to produce each issue. Many of them worked for seventy-two hours on end with only brief snatches of sleep. A number of them never left the building at all. We only had one linotype operator and so the work had to get under way at ten in the morning, only an hour or two after the previous day's printing had been finished. Nevertheless, with every day that passed the organisation was improved and the processes of production became more methodical.'

George Usher, one of Davidson's constituents, who owned International Combustion Ltd, loaned the firm's sizeable fleet of motor vehicles to distribute the *Gazette*. With the help of the Inland Revenue Authorities, a motor park was organised in the quadrangle of Somerset House and several rooms in the building were used to accommodate the *Gazette's* transport department. No serious attempt was made to obstruct production or distribution but, according to Davidson, intimidation of transport personnel 'was bad enough to make it necessary to put police guards over the wives and families of some of the key men at their private houses, and in one case transport a family to a safe place on the coast'.

As the *Gazette's* circulation increased, the organisational arrangements grew more elaborate. Somerset House and the Argus Press in Tudor Street, near the *Daily Herald*, were taken over as feeding and sleeping centres for the volunteers. W. H. Smith's dispatching warehouse in Carey Street was also commandeered and there the convoys from Somerset House would arrive throughout the night to be loaded with their wrapped and labelled cargoes. Packages made up to fit aeroplane fuselages were taken to Northolt and Biggin Hill to be flown to less accessible parts of the country. The *Gazette's* rapidly expanding circulation made heavy inroads on available stocks of newsprint. A shipload of 450 tons was therefore ordered by phone from Holland and the Bowater papermills at Northfleet were requisitioned and staffed with 200 volunteers who had to be given military and naval protection because the local population was so threatening. Within 36 hours of the takeover, the Northfleet mills were producing 50 tons of paper a day, sufficient for $1\frac{1}{2}$ million copies of the *Gazette*, and arrangements were made to produce paper at Aylesford, Grimsby, and Aberdeen. But before the ship from Holland arrived and the requisitioned mills could reach full production, the *Gazette* had already eaten its way through the available supplies.

It was Government policy to encourage other newspapers to publish in some form, but this did not deter the *Gazette* from seizing their stocks of newsprint for its own use. Even the loyal *Express* was not spared the *Gazette's* depredations and Beaverbrook's protest only provoked an insulting rebuke from Churchill. 'If any man living had used such outrageous language to me as he did on that occasion', Beaverbrook wrote, 'I should never have forgiven him. Churchill on top of the wave has in him the stuff of which tyrants are made.'[4] Geoffrey Dawson, of *The Times*, had a quarter of his newsprint seized and wrote indignantly to Baldwin that 'the broad effect of this action is to threaten the suppression of *The Times*, and presumably also of every other newspaper'. Dawson did not disguise his suspicion that the Government's real object was to deprive the T.U.C.'s *British Worker* of newsprint and added that this would seem to him to be an equally disastrous policy.[5] Graham Greene, then a young sub-editor on *The Times*, discerned a less sinister though scarcely more creditable motive. 'Our success aroused the jealousy of Winston Churchill, who seized a quarter of our paper stocks for his extravagent *British Gazette*. As the *Gazette* was badly edited, over-printed, and maldistributed, great bundles of his journal, manufactured with our paper, were dumped loose around the streets for anyone to pick up.'[6]

Many years after the general strike, Baldwin told G. M. Young, his biographer, 'Don't forget the cleverest thing I ever did. I put Winston in a corner and told him to edit the *British Gazette*.' Joynson-Hicks who, as chairman of the Cabinet Supply and Transport Committee, presided over the Government's emergency arrangements, shared fully Baldwin's desire to keep Churchill as far away as possible from the actual machinery of the strike, and giving the Chancellor a daily newspaper on which to expend his prodigious energies was meant to limit his scope in more sensitive areas. Davidson also recognised that Churchill was 'far too rich a mixture ...for the very carefully designed and delicately tuned engine which the Government were just starting on its full test', but soon found that his own difficulties were greatly increased. Davidson's intention was to supply the news 'censored when necessary, but undoctored'. Churchill, however, conceived it as not part of his duties to publish 'a lot of defeatist trash' and had no compunctions about distorting or suppressing any item which might be vaguely favourable to 'the enemy'. When a football match was played at Plymouth between a team of strikers and a team of policemen, Davidson was keen to publish the news. Churchill, who believed Davidson was 'a perfect ass' on the issue, appealed direct to the Cabinet. But there was little sympathy here for the Chancellor's well-known idiosyncrasies and readers of the *Gazette* were allowed to draw whatever subversive conclusions they wished from the fact that the strikers had beaten the police by two goals to one.

Churchill's efforts at falsification and distortion were more successful. Even the General Council was genuinely amazed at the unanimity of the strike, yet the first issue of the *Gazette* declared that it 'was by no means so complete as its promoters hoped'. The second issue asked, 'Why Walk to Work?' and assured bemused Londoners that the L.G.O.C. had 200 buses plying the streets, though the actual number was not more than 86. Weary commuters were further informed that a 'full service' was being maintained on the Central London Line and that other services were 'still improving'. Eight out of 29 trains were then running on the Central London Line and 43 out of a total of 315 Underground trains were operating. But these persistent falsifications were not Davidson's main concern. Far more serious was Churchill's attempts to slip in reckless and inflammatory comments. 'Birkenhead, who had been quite calm in the prior negotiations', Davidson wrote, 'was absolutely mad, and so was Winston, who had it firmly in his mind that anybody who was out of work was a Bolshevik; he was most extraordinary and never have I listened to such poppycock and rot.'

Foreseeing the kind of problem which would arise under Churchill's editorship, Davidson had appointed Caird as Government representative for editorial purposes and a direct telephone line had been installed between the editor's room at the *Morning Post* and Davidson's room at the Admiralty. 'After a great fight', Davidson has written, 'Winston agreed to be blue-pencilled, and from that moment my blue pencil was seldom idle. Caird, who exercised editorial supervision, submitted all copy to me where necessary, but despite all our efforts, a good deal of Winston's pugnacious spirit penetrated the *Gazette* and brought storms of questions in the House of Commons.' One such storm arose out of the *Gazette's* obvious attempt to suppress the manifesto issued by the Archbishop of Canterbury and other Christian leaders appealing for a negotiated settlement, which is discussed in the next chapter. Privately, Davidson had also insisted on keeping the statement out of the *Gazette*, but it was naturally Churchill who bore the brunt of the attack in the House of Commons. Type could only be set very slowly by amateurs, Churchill told his critics, and no doubt a number of pieces which should have gone in had been omitted. He had 'really not read this particular item' himself, but 'if importance be attached to it' he would see that it was published. The statement duly appeared two days later—the last day of the strike—as a small item on the *Gazette's* back page.

In the Parliamentary cut-and-thrust, Lloyd George delighted the Government's opponents by describing the *Gazette* as 'a first-class indiscretion, clothed in the tawdry garb of third-rate journalism'. Churchill gave equal delight to the Government benches with the comment that he could not 'undertake to be impartial as between the fire brigade and the fire'. The *Gazette*, however, was not devoted to the cause of the fire brigade and Davidson and the Government were embarrassed by its front-page pronouncement on Saturday, 8 May, that any action taken by the armed forces in aid of the Civil Power 'will receive, both now and afterwards, the full support of His Majesty's Government'. The King was so disturbed by this blatant incitement to violence that Lord Stamfordham informed the War Office that 'His Majesty cannot help thinking that this is an unfortunate announcement and already it has received a good deal of adverse criticism'.

Further difficulties were caused by Churchill's attempts to interfere in the production and distribution of the *Gazette*. 'The private secretaries at No 10', wrote Jones on Sunday 9 May, 'are all trying to get Winston to be put in charge of transport. Gwynne of the *Morning Post* has sent several messages begging that Winston should be kept away from that office where the *British Gazette* is printed. He butts in at the busiest hours and insists on changing commas and full stops until the staff is furious. Went to lunch with P. G. Grigg (Winston's private secretary) entirely out of sympathy with his chief's wild ways.' An undated memorandum from Davidson to Baldwin underlines the point.

The failure to some extent in the details of distribution of the *British Gazette* has been due entirely to the fact that the Chancellor occupied the attention of practically the whole of the staff who normally would have been thinking out the details. Of course he was anxious, but it was unfortunate that he tried so persistently to force a scratch staff beyond its capacity. So long as he does not come to the *Morning Post* offices again tonight the staff will be able to do what it is there to do, viz organising the printing, the production and distribution of the *Gazette*. I must depend on you, and the staff are relying on me, to find some means of preventing his coming. By all means let him put what pressure he can personally upon Sir Malcolm Fraser, who is in general control, and the Stationery Office, by interview or letter, but the technical staff should be left to do their job. He rattled them very badly last night. He thinks he is Napoleon, but curiously enough men who have been printing all their life [*sic*] in the various processes happen to know more about their job than he does. May I suggest that you enlist the services of Jix in urging that it is not safe for him to come.

Despite the problems which Churchill's editorship created, Davidson

Before the Strike: Ramsay MacDonald (right) with A. J. Cook, the secretary of the Miners' Federation, on his right. *Courtesy of Mrs Bennison*

Herbert Smith, President of the Miners' Federation, leaving the Federation headquarters in Russell Square during the General Strike. *Mrs Bennison*

Volunteers working the railways during the General Strike:
Mr Mowbray Bellairs, Major Barton and Major Bruce, the driver,
who had served in four wars and been wounded nine times.
*Radio Times Hulton Picture Library*

A lady volunteer transport driver during the Strike. *Radio Times Hulton
Picture Library*

Undergraduate volunteers in Fair Isle jerseys and plus-fours operating the signal box at Bletchley station. *Illustrated London News*

Volunteer porter at King's Cross station. *Illustrated London News*

The Civil Constabulary Reserve were recruited from Territorial Army units to assist the Metropolitan Police. *Communist Party of Great Britain*

The teams in the Police v. Strikers football match at Plymouth, 10 May 1926. The Strikers won 2-1, and the wife of the chief constable kicked off. *Radio Times Hulton Picture Library*

An armoured car in Oxford Street, 8 May. *Radio Times Hulton Picture Library*

A food convoy passing through Canning Town under military escort: 10 May, the seventh day of the strike. *Radio Times Hulton Picture Library*

Mounted police with batons clearing the road after an outbreak of
violence at the Elephant and Castle, London. *Illustrated London News*

A van overturned by strikers in Blackfriars Road. *Illustrated London News*

*Above* The attempt to wreck the 'Flying Scotsman' with 300 passengers aboard. 10 May 1926. *Illustrated London News*

*Below* The First Brigade of Guards returning through the City from Victoria Park to Aldershot after the General Strike. *Illustrated London News*

Stanley Baldwin in his hour of triumph at 10 Downing Street – 'Let us get the workers calm as soon as we can.' *Illustrated London News*

admired his energy and enthusiasm. 'Whether it was right or wrong he desired to produce a newspaper rather than a news-sheet. He, in fact, conceived that the *British Gazette* should be a better newspaper than any of the great journals whose operations had been temporarily suspended... He is the sort of man whom, if I wanted a mountain to be moved, I should send for at once. I think, however, that I should not consult him after he had moved the mountain if I wanted to know where to put it.'

At noon on Tuesday, 4 May, Hamilton Fyfe and his colleagues at the *Daily Herald* heard about the Government's plans to run a newspaper. The *Herald* itself was unable to publish because the compositors on other newspapers would agree to no exceptions to the ban on printing, but it was clear to Fyfe that the T.U.C. would have to run an opposition sheet. 'I have been urging this for some days. Now the need is urgent.'[7] That afternoon Fyfe met the General Council's Press and Publicity Committee and secured their agreement to the publication, at the *Herald* offices, of an eight-page evening paper to be called the *British Worker*. The General Council directed publication to begin the following evening and Fyfe believed 'we had plain sailing in front of us'. But when he returned to the *Herald* he found 'a tangle of difficulties, all resulting from the inability of some people to realise that there is "a war on".' The printing unions were not prepared to issue the necessary instructions to their members. 'These people want everything to be done as it is done in normal times', observed Fyfe in an agony of frustration. 'They would ask during an earthquake whether the letters were being taken to the four o'clock post; on the day when the Last Trump sounds they will complain that their shaving water hasn't been heated for them as usual.'

After an evening of fruitless discussion Fyfe returned to Eccleston Square and obtained an official authorisation from the General Council. This satisfied the printing unions and on Wednesday evening a large crowd gathered outside the *Herald* offices in Carmelite Street to await the first issue of the T.U.C.'s own newspaper. While Bob Williams, the *Herald's* general manager, was addressing them from a first-floor window more than 50 police suddenly emerged from the half-finished *Daily Mail* building opposite and mounted officers also rode up and began moving the crowd back. It was assumed the police had arrived to keep order but a number of plain clothes men headed by a detective inspector entered the *Herald* building and ordered that the machines should not be started. They also produced a warrant signed by the Home Secretary authorising them to search for and seize all copies of the *Daily Herald* for 4 May. The real purpose of the visit became clear, however, when the inspector asked for a dozen copies of the *British Worker* to be run off for submission to the City Police Commissioner. The copies were printed and the inspector departed with them, leaving some of his men in charge of the building.

Meanwhile, Williams had managed to put a phone call through to the General Council and while Pugh hurried over to the House of Commons to inform MacDonald of the situation, Citrine, Bevin, and Ben Turner of the textile workers dashed to Carmelite Street. Here they found the *Herald* staff and the crowd outside the building lustily singing the *Red Flag* while the detective inspector waited in Williams's office for a phone call from the Commissioner. 'I could not help reflecting on how easily a riot could be started', Citrine noted in his diary. 'Here were these people, normally friendly and peace-loving, suddenly converted into militant, menacing elements by the precipitate action of the police and the authorities. Men who probably had never heard the *Red Flag* sung before were joining in with gusto.' Just before midnight the inspector emerged smiling and told Fyfe, 'You can go ahead'. As the crowd in the street heard the rumble of machinery starting up they responded with cheers and another enthusiastic rendering of the *Red Flag*. A few minutes later Citrine and Bevin were presented with their first copies of the *British Worker*.

Under the Emergency Powers Act, the Government was able to close down papers which published seditious statements or false news. Since the Government and its agents alone had the right to decide what was seditious and what was false, the closure powers could be, and frequently were, broadly applied. But even the most zealous defender of Constitutional Government was hard-put to find anything objectionable, far less seditious, in the neatly printed columns of the *British Worker*. Apart from factual reports on the progress of the strike, it devoted most of its space to defending the General Council against the *British Gazette's* charges of revolutionary intent and to appeals for calm and order. Four of the seven issues printed before the strike was called off carried an identical declaration from the General Council that it did 'not challenge the Constitution. It is not seeking to substitute unconstitutional government. Nor is it desirous of undermining our Parliamentary institutions. The sole aim of the Council is to secure for the miners a decent standard of life. The Council is engaged in an industrial dispute. In any settlement, the only issue to be decided will be an industrial issue, not political, not constitutional. There is no constitutional crisis.' The three remaining issues carried an identical 'Message to All Workers'. 'The

General Council of the Trades Union Congress wishes to emphasize the fact that this is an industrial dispute. It expects every member taking part to be exemplary in his conduct and not to give any opportunity for police interference. The outbreak of any disturbance would be very damaging to the prospects of a successful termination to the dispute. The Council asks pickets especially to avoid obstruction and to confine themselves strictly to their legitimate duties.' For strikers with time on their hands the second issue listed seven suggestions. 'Do all you can to keep everybody smiling; the way to do this is to smile yourself. Do your best to discountenance any ideas of violent or disorderly conduct. Do the thing that's nearest: this will occupy you and will steady your nerves, if they get shaky. Do any odd jobs that want doing about the house. Do a little to interest and amuse the kiddies now you have the chance. Do what you can to improve your health: a good walk every day will keep you fit. Do something. Hanging about and swapping rumours is bad every way.'

To ensure that 'anything which might cause uncontrollable irritation and violence'[8] was kept out of the paper, the publicity committee appointed E. L. Poulton, of the Boot and Shoe Union, J. W. Bowen, of the Post Office Workers, and one of Arthur Henderson's sons to act as censors. Hamilton Fyfe was on excellent terms with them and fully accepted the need for 'moderation of language', but as an experienced newspaperman he wished to publish more than a mere catalogue of worthy strike reports and earnest General Council appeals. He believed the Council's decision to exclude general news was mistaken and in a letter to the publicity committee, a copy of which he sent to Bevin, he argued that even Labour supporters were turning to the *British Gazette* and that the circulation of the *Daily Herald* would suffer because potential readers would assume that it, too, excluded general news. 'I do not suggest much general news', Fyfe pleaded. 'A bit here and there will make readers think they are getting all there is. Cricket we certainly ought to give.' After consulting Bevin, the publicity committee replied with some haughtiness that it considered the *British Worker* to be 'a Strike Bulletin and not a newspaper. It also considered that the anxiety of the people generally to get hold of the *British Worker* needs no stimulus from the inclusion of cricket scores or any other matter of that kind... In the opinion of [the] committee, the only news that need be included in the *British Worker* is such as to show the spirit of our own people, the unity of our own action, and the enthusiasm and loyalty with which the General Council's instructions are being carried out.'[9]

Although Government requisition of newsprint forced a reduction from eight pages to four, publication of the *Worker* continued for eleven issues. Circulation also steadily increased—from 320,000 on 5 May to 500,000 on 17 May. But distribution was poor and, after more than a week, many parts of the country were still not effectively covered. It was reported from South Wales on 11 May that most areas were without copies and from Darlington on the same day that 'The great outcry of everyone is for the *British Worker* of which only odd copies have been received'. The official price was one penny, as it was for the *British Gazette*, but there were complaints of 'profiteering', for in some areas copies were being sold for as much as sixpence. The publicity committee tried to make up for faulty distribution by arranging for the publication of provincial editions, but none of these appeared until a day or two before the end of the strike. The delay was partly the fault of the General Council itself, which insisted that 'no additions, material alterations or omissions' were to be made to the copy sent down from London. Since this was invariably late, work was held up in the provinces. When the publicity committee discovered that the Glasgow edition had been set up with an unauthorised appeal for the extension of the strike, Poulton insisted that it be deleted. 'Will you see that all that stuff is kept out', he instructed the committee's local representative, 'and nothing provocative put in.' Wrangling continued throughout the weekend of 8–9 May and it was not until Poulton agreed to the inclusion of a page of Scottish news that work finally began on the Glasgow edition.

The attitude of the Typographical Association, which represented the compositors outside London, helped to impede the publicity committee's plans. The houses of the provincial dailies and weeklies were not as well organised as those in Fleet Street and even where the strike was solid, apprentices were not called out. As a result, the Association feared that even the publication of the T.U.C.'s own paper in towns where its members were particularly vulnerable would undermine morale and lead to a general resumption of work in the printing trade. It took much coaxing to secure the Association's co-operation and at Lowestoft and Norwich members refused to handle the *British Worker*. The Leicester branch also refused to help the T.U.C., though for a different reason. It contended that, since members of the Typographical Association had not voted for or against a general strike, the strike was unconstitutional. 'We do not see how smashing up the printing industry will help the miners, and call on members to honour their agreements with their masters.'[10]

The failure to exempt Co-operative enterprises from strike-action, which is discussed in detail in a later chapter, almost crippled production of the *British Worker* in the north and north-east. Fenner Brockway, who was in charge of arrangements in Manchester, found the local printing unions willing to help, but the Co-operative Printing Society refused to lend its premises because it was not permitted to fulfil its normal commercial contracts. The Co-operative Publishing Society, fifty miles away in Southport, proved more amenable, and the first Manchester edition of 50,000 copies appeared on Monday, 10 May and was distributed as far south as Derby, west to Holyhead, east to Hull and north to Carlisle. A fresh crisis arose, however, when the printers threatened to 'black' the *Co-operative News*. Fearing that the Co-operative Publishing Company would retaliate by refusing to handle the *British Worker*, Brockway persuaded the printers to carry on. By Wednesday 100,000 copies were being produced, but on Thursday the print was reduced to 60,000 because arrangements to distribute to outlying districts were cancelled. Brockway was not prepared to meet the 'excessive' mileage claims made by the volunteer drivers. Production of the Manchester edition continued up to Saturday, 15 May. 'Until the Strike was called off', Brockway later reported, 'the *British Worker* was immensely popular. The disappointment with the settlement reacted against the paper, as the organ of the T.U.C., but there was still a good demand. The attitude of the workers towards the *British Worker* in the later stages was reflected in the action of the printing chapel, when they were asked whether they would put through a Monday morning edition. They replied that they would not do it for the T.U.C. but would do it as a favour to the firm.'[11]

In Newcastle the difficulties proved almost insuperable. Arriving in the city at noon on Saturday, 8 May, after a twelve-hour car journey from London, A. W. Dawson, the publicity committee's representative, found the premises of the Co-operative Printing Society locked-up and the local Strike Committee away in Gateshead for a conference. By the time Dawson reached Gateshead, the Strike Committee was already on its way back to Newcastle. When he did make contact, Dawson found that the Committee had decided to produce its own bulletin. He persuaded them to support the *British Worker* instead, only to discover that Joe Tinker, the secretary of the local Typographical Association, was reluctant to help. Tinker feared that production of the *Worker* would cause a break in the ranks and that there would be 'a considerable amount of ratting'. Eventually, 'although it was against the grain', Tinker promised to do all he could to secure volunteers.

That evening Dawson travelled eight miles to Wylam to see the manager of the Co-operative Printing Society. But like his counterpart in Manchester, he too had received instructions not to handle the *British Worker*. 'This bombshell', Dawson reported to London, 'provided a disastrous ending to what had seemed a promising day.' On Sunday the prospects appeared brighter. Officials at Pelaws, the Co-operative Wholesale Society's printing works at Whitley Bay, were sympathetic, but then, according to Dawson, 'we met with another knock-down blow. The Newcastle Strike Committee had enforced the embargo on transport of food most rigorously, and included in that embargo Co-op Wholesale supplies to retailers. In view of this circumstance, the Co-operative directors in Newcastle retaliated by refusing to print the *British Worker*'. The only alternative was to use the printing shop owned by a Labour sympathiser in Sunderland. But suitable paper had first to be transported by car from Newcastle and the single flat-bed machine could print at the rate of only 1,000 copies an hour.

Despite all these difficulties, the first issue of 22,000 copies appeared on Tuesday, but the subsequent four issues averaged only 16–17,000 copies, since there was not sufficient transport to distribute a greater number. The cars, motor bikes and cycles had to drive twelve miles from Newcastle to Sunderland to pick up the issues and, instead of returning for fresh supplies when the first batch had been distributed, the drivers reported to their own strike committees and were usually sent elsewhere. Because of this, only 16,000 of the 22,000 copies printed on Tuesday were actually distributed. However, Dawson remained convinced that the venture was worthwhile. 'It will no doubt show a loss owing to the very heavy cost of transport, but the paper, though printed and distributed in such small quantities, was spread over a very wide area, and I believe its effect on the *Daily Herald* will be exceedingly good, if only our distribution methods in the North-East could be gingered up a bit.'[12]

The vacuum which the *British Worker* and the *British Gazette* were designed to fill was by no means as great as the General Council (and almost certainly Churchill) had hoped. Although only 40 out of 1,870 newspapers remained unaffected by the strike, many emergency editions were produced by skeleton staffs of managers, journalists, printing apprentices, and retired employees. In some offices technical overseers ignored the instructions of their unions and by the weekend of 8–9 May members of the Typographical Association were drifting back to work in substantial numbers. Davidson estimated that by 11 May, the day before the strike was officially called off, about 90 per cent of the provincial evening papers were publishing regular editions in some form or other. This may have been an exaggeration, but the T.U.C. Intelligence Committee's own assessment of the morning of 12 May was that 'there is a weakness so far as the printing trades are concerned. We have a number of reports indicating that newspapers either never stopped, or are reappearing, or are increasing the scope of their production'.

Although members of the London Society of Compositors held out until 16 May, many of the London dailies also contrived to appear in some form after the disruption to their editions of Wednesday 5 May. The Continental *Daily Mail* was flown over each day from Paris and at the weekend large numbers of the *Sunday Times*, printed by the *Newcastle Chronicle*, were brought by 'plane from Newcastle to Catterick. *The Times* published without interruption from the beginning of the strike. Multigraph machines were used to produce 48,000 copies of the single-sheet issue of 5 May and by Wednesday evening sufficient volunteers had been gathered to enable subsequent editions to be printed on the paper's own rotary presses. The number of copies produced on Thursday 6 May, was 78,000; on Saturday it was more than 166,000; on Monday the figure rose to 250,000 and on Wednesday 12 May, the last day of the strike, 342,000 copies were printed and distributed.

A number of weekly papers, such as the *Brixton Free Press, Streatham News* and *Hendon, Cricklewood and Golders Green Gazette*, also produced regular emergency issues, relying mainly upon the wireless, the *British Gazette* and the London dailies for their news. Davidson's organisation naturally did all it could to secure the widest publication of the Government's case and the local press was encouraged to make full use of official sources of information. The *Luton News*, for instance, was given a first-pull of the *British Gazette* each evening. This was then photographed on a reduced scale and the whole of it appeared as page 3 of the following day's *Luton News*. Many news-sheets, usually comprising a single page, were also published by individuals and enterprising commercial concerns. A news-sheet which circulated in the north London suburbs claimed that between 5 May and 8 May it had increased its print from 5,000 to 17,000. Most of these amateur publications simply contained items from the wireless news bulletins. Some, however, appeared to possess sources of news denied even to the *British Gazette*. A news-sheet circulated in the Strand assured its readers on 8 May that 'It is our endeavour to produce the news in this publication from reliable sources only' and went on to report that, during disturbances in Hammersmith, one policeman had been killed.

Several news-sheets rivalled the *British Gazette* for patriotic fervour. The *Emergency Strike Bulletin*, published by a Mr T. F. Moore, of Golders Green, discerned on 6 May that 'the same gallant spirit that was so prevalent in 1914 is again to be seen on every hand. Thousands of true sons of the Old Country and daughters also have given property and help to others. Yesterday we saw acts which showed only too clearly the grit that has built our wonderful Empire.' Determined, perhaps, not to show undue concern at the almost total absence of public transport, Mr Moore declared on 8 May that 'The very patriotic and courageous help given by women in every walk of life is one of the main features of this strike' and found further inspiration in the fact that every member of the Irish Rugby Football Team had enlisted in the special constabulary. The *Workers' Record*, which preferred to carry no imprint, displayed not only similar sentiments but a Union Jack and a portrait of the Prime Minister in the centre of its single page.

It was Fleet Street, however, which was supposed to have the glamour and many socially illustrious persons volunteered their services to the London nationals. Distinguished women sold copies of the *Sunday Express* in the streets as cheerfully as they sold Armistice Day poppies, and Lady Louis Mountbatten worked as a telephone operator at the *Daily Express*. Printing House Square was an even more fashionable resort than Fleet Street. Two Duchesses, a Viscountess, and the daughter of a Marchioness drove lorries for *The Times* together with directors of many of the leading banks and public companies. *The Times*, according to its own account of events, 'became the very centre of fashion. A strong contingent of the chairman's friends in the House of Commons came down at once, and continued to come night after night... Members of half the clubs in London offered their services. Undergraduates began to appear from the universities... A Governor-elect [of the Bank of England] put in some strenuous shifts as a packer in the intervals of packing his own boxes for the Antipodes.'

Nor was life in Printing House Square without its occasional dramas. During the afternoon of Wednesday 5 May, a stream of petrol was poured through a loading port into the machine-room and ignited. Graham Greene was relaxing with his colleagues after a tiring night of loading and packing that morning's issue when the fire alarm sounded. 'The bell rang once, twice, three times. Someone asked with mild curiosity, "A fire?" After a while the assistant chief sub-editor, Colonel Maude, rose and moved with his usual elegant and leisurely gait into the corridor...when he returned to the room and sat down, it took quite a time to realise that *The Times*—so he was telling us—had been set on fire... Maude obviously was not disturbed, there was no copy to deal with, and my fellow sub-editors chatted a little while on the subject of fires in general and the feasibility of burning down *The Times*. One of the sub-editors was an elderly man who ran a small farm in the country and therefore always dealt with the agricultural page. He told us a few anecdotes about rick-fires, which passed the time until the all-clear sounded.'

That night pickets tried to seize bundles of the second issue while it was being loaded into cars outside the building. The *New York Times* correspondent, who witnessed the incident from an upper window of the building, wrote: 'The assistant foreign editor, Mr Peterson, objected strenuously and got into a furious fist fight with three or four strikers sending smashing blows to his face and body. They finally knocked him into the mud, but not before he got home with some savage blows.' No further attempts were made at arson or serious violence. Security at *The Times* became almost as stringent as security at the *British Gazette* and loading operations were supervised thereafter by muscular members of the Sporting Department. To their colleagues these gentlemen became known as the 'storm troops'; to the pickets they became known as the 'Jazz Band' because of their Fair Isle sweaters. A dozen Tory M.P.s, including Duff Cooper (later Viscount Norwich), also descended on Printing House Square on Thursday night, seized with the urgent desire to act as well as talk. 'When the moment came', Duff Cooper wrote in his diary, 'and we sallied forth to fight we found there was practically no opposition at all. It was really a waste of time, but rather amusing.'[13]

Duff Cooper and his friends might have found possibly less amusing but more effective employment in the Northern Counties. The three morning papers published in Durham and Northumberland—the *Newcastle Journal* and *Chronicle* and the Darlington *Northern Echo*—continued to appear throughout the strike, but picketing of roads, particularly in mining areas, made distribution a hazardous operation. According to the *Northern Echo* 'vans were blockaded, supplies burnt and drivers injured, although none seriously. Sand bags, carts, wire ropes, railway sleepers, broken glass, sticks and stones were all used'. Early on Sunday 9 May, pickets attacked *Chronicle* vehicles carrying the *Sunday Times* and stole thousands of copies. But staff and police headed off the raiders outside Newcastle and forced them to reload the bundles. On another occasion a car driver bringing photographs to the *Chronicle* offices was attacked at Ferrybridgehill, in Durham, 'and came into Newcastle with his windscreen smashed, his bonnet and wings dented and broken, and his hands streaming with blood'.[14]

It was soon clear that, in attempting to silence the Press, the General Council had committed a grave tactical error. At the week-end Kingsley Martin reported to the Intelligence Committee that 'In Birmingham and at each place we visited we heard many expressions of the view that the calling out of printing unions was a mistake since it was extremely difficult for Labour opinion to grow and the pro-Government publications were much in evidence.' In addition to the *British Gazette*, all those national newspapers most hostile to Labour were continuing to appear. With the exception of *The Times*, which did not allow its opposition to the strike to taint the impartiality of its news columns, the London dailies published uncritically the Government's version of events and attacked the General Council with an immoderation which sometimes exceeded even that of the *British Gazette*. To counter this the General Council had only the inadequately distributed *British Worker* and the bulletins produced by local strike committees, which were unlikely, anyway, to influence anyone who was not already committed to the strikers' cause.

Ironically, the Liberal dailies, which had shown considerable sympathy for the General Council's position and could have had a powerful influence on middle-class attitudes during the dispute, were the ones most effectively suppressed. The *Manchester Guardian* published an emergency bulletin from 5 May but in London no newspaper favouring a negotiated settlement was available until the reappearance of a four-page *Daily Chronicle* on Monday 10 May. The other Liberal papers—the *Daily News, Westminster Gazette, Star* and *Sunday News*—were unable to publish in any form. On 3 May the General Council received a telegram from the *Guardian* urging that 'sane' newspapers be allowed to continue, but the Council was not prepared to discriminate.[15] Having taken the decision to call out the printers, this response was understandable; printers who remained at work would certainly have aroused the resentment of those on strike and it is unlikely that the printing unions would have agreed to such an arrangement. The General Council's error lay, not in its refusal to distinguish between the papers of C. P. Scott and those of Lord Rothermere, but in its original assumption that the Government would suffer if the Press could be paralysed. As the *New Statesman* tartly pointed out on 8 May: 'In a newsless world Governments must inevitably be almost omnipotent.'

# Chapter Nine

# *Stomping at Savoy Hill*

'The sensation of a general strike which stops the press, as witnessed from a cottage in the country, centres round the headphones of the wireless set.'

Beatrice Webb, writing in her diary, Tuesday, 4 May 1926.

'In London clubs on the first day of the strike crowds and members jostled each other around the boards where wireless bulletins were posted. They were desperately anxious for news of what was happening throughout the country... Those of us who have wireless sets, especially those of us who live in the country districts as I do, have been sitting up late at night to get any word over the wireless waves which might mean hope and peace.'

A report by Sir Philip Gibbs in the *Philadelphia Evening Bulletin*, Wednesday, 5 May 1926.

'The position was one of extreme delicacy and embarrassment throughout. It was impossible to give the lead which we should have liked, but it is a satisfaction to find an almost universal appreciation and recognition of the services rendered, and it may be only ourselves who feel that we might have done more with a freer hand.'

John Reith, in a confidential letter to senior B.B.C. staff immediately after the strike.

'The attitude of the B.B.C. during the crisis caused pain and indignation to many subscribers. I travelled by car over two thousand miles during the strike and addressed very many meetings. Everywhere the complaints were bitter that a national service subscribed to by every class should have given only one side during the dispute. Personally, I feel like asking the Postmaster-General for my licence fee back.'

Ellen Wilkinson, in a letter to the *Radio Times*, 28 May 1926.

'The universal feeling is one of gratitude to the B.B.C. for the admirable part their organisation has played during the recent happily-ended strife. Had it not been for this possibility of prompt and broadcast communication, the country might have become more uneasy, and been perturbed far more seriously than it has been. By the sending out of trustworthy news, and by the prompt denial of false rumours, the pulse of the country was kept calm and healthy... Both sides of the dispute ought to be grateful to the organisers of this new means of spreading intelligence.'

Sir Oliver Lodge, in a letter to the *Radio Times*, 28 May 1926.

As soon as it became evident that newspaper production would be affected by the strike, Davidson arranged to bring the British Broadcasting Company under his effective control. In theory, John Reith, the B.B.C.'s formidable managing director since the formation of the company in December 1922, was allowed to retain editorial discretion over all news except Government announcements; in practice, no news was broadcast during the crisis until it had first been personally vetted by Davidson. B.B.C. representatives moved into the Admiralty to receive and pass on news supplied by the press agencies and the headquarters of the civil commissioners, and Gladstone Murray, the deputy managing director, was installed in an office with Captain Gordon Munro, Davidson's liaison officer. Each of the five daily news bulletins plus a daily 'appreciation of the situation', which took the place of newspaper editorials, were drafted by Murray in conjunction with Munro and then submitted to Davidson for his approval before being transmitted from the B.B.C.'s London station at Savoy Hill.

The arrangement offended Reith's stern Calvinist integrity, but he was unable to resist for fear of provoking a direct Government takeover. A substantial minority in the Cabinet supported Churchill's view that the B.B.C. should be commandeered and used exclusively for the transmission of Government propaganda, and on 4 May the Chancellor told Reith that he wished to treat the B.B.C. as an offshoot of the *British Gazette*. On purely pragmatic grounds, Davidson was opposed to anything so drastic. He was no less aware than Churchill of the broadcasting medium's immense potential for influencing public opinion, but unlike Churchill he also recognised that the B.B.C. would retain its influence only so long as it was generally believed to be impartial. As he explained in a letter to Lord Irwin (later Lord Halifax) shortly after the strike, to have commandeered the B.B.C. would have been 'fatal...for the very simple reason that the people that you want to influence are those who would at once have ceased to listen had we announced that all news was dope, while on the other hand the die-hard element who criticised us for our partiality are on our side in any case.'[1]

From the outset the T.U.C. was convinced that wireless news would be tightly censored and the *Daily Herald* on 3 May carried a warning from the General Council urging trade unionists to ignore all broadcast statements. The paper also carried a suggestion that transmissions could be disrupted if enough listeners cause oscillations. (It was for such items that the police were looking when they raided Carmelite Street on 4 May.) Reith did his best to maintain some semblance of impartiality and since this fitted in with Davidson's plans, the B.B.C. was permitted to quote from the speeches of trade union leaders and from the *British Worker*. Against this, however, had to be reckoned the large number of totally inaccurate reports of returns to work which were broadcast. Although, in most instances, the unions concerned sent immediate corrections to Savoy Hill, these were never broadcast. Baldwin was perfectly happy with Davidson's covert control, but Churchill considered that the use of news from trade union sources was providing moral comfort to the enemy and he persisted in demanding outright Government control. At Baldwin's request, Reith attended a meeting of the Supply and Transport Committee on Thursday 6 May, at which the subject was discussed. Baldwin himself did not attend meetings of the committee, but Joynson-Hicks, who acted as chairman, stated that the Prime Minister preferred to trust Reith to do what was best. To Churchill's strenuous protest that it was 'monstrous' not to use such an instrument as the B.B.C. to the best possible advantage, Joynson-Hicks replied that, if anybody felt strongly on the matter, it had best be discussed at a full Cabinet.[2] Baldwin, however, skilfully deferred a Cabinet decision until 11 May, by which time there could no longer be any reasonable doubt of the B.B.C.'s docility and, despite the Chancellor's continuing opposition, it was agreed not to alter the existing position.

Had Reith been less compliant there is little doubt that Churchill would have got his way. The managing director faced his most crucial test on Friday, 7 May, the day after his appearance before the Cabinet committee. Randall Davidson, the Archbishop of Canterbury, phoned Reith to ask if he could broadcast a peace manifesto which had been drawn up that morning by a conference of Anglican and Free Church leaders. The Archbishop explained that, though Baldwin had told him he would not prevent the manifesto from being broadcast, he would prefer it not to be and he (Davidson) had been told to apply to Reith. 'A nice position for me to be in between Premier and Primate', Reith later recalled, 'bound mightily to vex one or other; at thirty-six years of age. I asked him to send it along.'[3] The manifesto, which MacDonald thought 'inspired',[4] contained three main points: cancellation of the strike; renewal of the Government coal subsidy for a limited period; and withdrawal by the owners of the new wage scales. Baldwin found none of these points exceptionable. What he objected to was the condition that they were to operate 'simultaneously and concurrently', for this ran counter to the Government's own condition that withdrawal of the strike must precede further negotiations.

On Friday afternoon, while Reith was still hesitating between Premier and Primate, he was visited by J. C. C. Davidson, who insisted that the manifesto could not possibly be broadcast as it would provide Churchill and his supporters with an ideal excuse for taking over the B.B.C. Reluctantly, Reith felt obliged to agree and he phoned the Archbishop to tell him that to broadcast the manifesto would 'run counter to his tacit arrangement with the Government about such things'. Had Reith had a hint from Downing Street, Davidson inquired. 'No', replied Reith unhappily. 'Downing Street knows nothing about it. I am speaking entirely on my own responsibility.'[5] The Archbishop was puzzled and offended by the ban and on Saturday morning wrote to Reith asking: 'Are we to understand that if the Churches desire to put something forth, their grave utterances must be subject to the approval of its wording by the Broadcasting Committee, and that without such approval we are confined, as we were yesterday, to utilising the scraps of publicity available by means of the few newspapers which have their limited circulation?'[6] Greatly distressed by the letter, Reith went immediately to Lambeth Palace to explain his dilemma. He agreed with the Archbishop that it was intolerable for the Churches to be muzzled at a time when they ought to be speaking to the nation, but pointed out that, if the manifesto were broadcast, it would weaken the stand which the Prime Minister was making against Churchill and Birkenhead. Appealing to Davidson to appreciate the difficulty of his own position, Reith added that it would be much easier for him to let the Government commandeer the B.B.C., but this would, he believed, be harmful to the public interest. Arrangements had been made to broadcast the Archbishop's address from St Martins-in-the-Fields the following evening and Davidson offered to show Reith his notes. Reith refused to look at them, refraining even from asking if Davidson intended to mention the manifesto.[7]

The Government was less concerned with spiritual susceptibilities. Colonel Lane-Fox, the Secretary for Mines, also visited Lambeth on Saturday. Coming directly to the point, he said that the Churches were asking 'impossibilities' in their manifesto and that it would be 'very unfortunate' if they were to insist upon negotiations before the strike was called off. Davidson assured the minister that he would not think of trying in a sermon to deal with the economic question. His object would be a spiritual one and an assurance that the Church was alive to what was happening and that its leaders were doing their best.[8] Davidson kept literally to his word. Without quoting from the manifesto, he described it as an attempt by Christian leaders to approach the problem in what seemed the true way, although it was open to anyone who so regarded it to describe it as mistaken. He condemned those who spoke of carrying on the struggle 'to the bitter end', defended the right of the workers not to endure worse conditions and pleaded for 'not only a reasonable but a generous settlement'. Fyfe was greatly impressed by the broadcast. 'For the first time in its history, I think, the Church of England has put itself on the side of the people against the privileged class. The old Archbishop has been splendid.'[9]

The Government did, however, pick up one crumb of clerical comfort. Although the Churches' manifesto did not carry the signature of Cardinal Bourne, the Roman Catholic Archbishop of Westminster, Bourne had sent a message to Davidson expressing his support for the document. But during High Mass in Westminster Cathedral on Sunday, Bourne declared, 'There is no moral justification for a general strike of this character. It is a direct challenge to lawfully constituted authority... It is therefore a sin against the obedience which we owe to God, who is the source of that authority... All are bound to uphold and assist the Government, which is the lawfully constituted authority of the country, and represents, therefore, in its own appointed sphere, the authority of God Himself.' J. C. C. Davidson naturally saw to it that both the *British Gazette* and the B.B.C. gave this pronouncement maximum coverage.

On Monday, 10 May, Lloyd George joined Labour M.P.s in attacking the Government for its suppression of the Anglican and Free Church appeal. The criticism was directed mainly at Churchill, though it was Davidson who had decided on his own responsibility that the manifesto should be given no publicity in the *British Gazette* or on the wireless. After the Commons debate and the publicity given to the manifesto by the *British Worker* and *The Times*, Davidson agreed to the inclusion of a brief reference in the B.B.C.'s afternoon news bulletins on 11 May. This stated simply that the leaders of the Christian Churches had issued a manifesto appealing for a resumption of negotiations and that a return to the *status quo* of Friday 30 April had been urged. The *British Gazette* published an equally cursory reference on 12 May. Many years later Davidson dictated a memorandum criticising the Archbishop for failing to realise that the Government was engaged in a constitutional struggle. 'I have no doubt in my own mind that by publishing the Archbishop's message on the back page [of the *British Gazette*] and having it read on the B.B.C. news a lesser number of times than that of Cardinal Bourne, I was only doing what the public would expect the Government to do (and to) carry out their general feelings and wishes: to call the Archbishop's message statesmanlike is a complete travesty of what the public thought at the time. The general criticism that I remember is that the Archbishop had better keep out of politics, and that his message was both weak and waffly.'[10]

Certainly, many Conservative M.P.s compared the Archbishop's attitude unfavourably with that of Cardinal Bourne and two of the most Right-wing did not hesitate to tell him that the Church would suffer discredit as a result of his activities. Nor were all of the telegrams and messages which poured into Lambeth Palace, once the text of the manifesto became known, favourable to the Archbishop. But there is no evidence for Davidson's assertion that public opinion was generally hostile to the initiative. During the weekend of 8–9 May public meetings were held in many parts of the country calling for a settlement on the basis of the Churches' manifesto. Preaching on Sunday at the City Temple, one of the most famous of London Free Churches, the Rev Dr F. W. Norwood reflected public sentiment more accurately than the Deputy Chief Civil Commissioner, when he declared: 'There is no attack on the constitution. It is impossible to witness the remarkable order on both sides and believe that we are in the grip of reckless revolutionaries. The conviction behind the strike may be mistaken, but it is honest and sincere.' As early as 5 May the Tory-controlled Newcastle City Council had passed a resolution in terms identical to those of the manifesto. Similar resolutions now came from other local authorities and from Rotary Clubs and trade union branches. In Birmingham the Lord Mayor and the Cadbury family tried to rally local businessmen behind the Churches' appeal, though with little success since the Chamber of Commerce and Engineering Employers' Association were against any compromise. A group of Cambridge dons sent a manifesto of their own to *The Times* pleading that the strikers should have 'fair play' and at Oxford a large number of Fellows, tutors and graduates met under the chairmanship of A. D. Lindsay, the Master of Balliol, to form an Archbishop's Committee. Oxford undergraduates produced on 11 May the first issue of the *British*

*Independent*, a duplicated paper designed to provide a daily platform for conciliatory views. 'The peacemakers,' wrote Professor Gilbert Murray in the second and final issue on 12 May, 'are far more numerous than the mischief makers; they only need to show themselves and to know one another.' Government supporters pointed to the victory of the Conservative candidate in the Buckrose (Yorkshire) Parliamentary by-election on 5 May, though in an exclusively agricultural and traditionally Tory constituency any other result would have been astonishing. A perhaps more significant indication of public opinion was the result of a Council by-election in the mainly middle-class London suburb of Chiswick, which was held on 10 May, after the Archbishop's intervention. A Tory majority of 272 was turned into a Labour majority of 664.

During the weekend the Archbishop became alarmed at the rift which seemed to be opening up between the Churches and the Government and at his own request he met Baldwin on Monday 11 May. 'I was afraid', Davidson has recorded, 'that he might be drifting into the same position as other people and regard me as hostile to him and his whole policy... I pressed on him that the responsibility must be his and that we had definitely said our say.' Baldwin's attitude was friendly and Davidson took the opportunity of referring to 'the truculent and fighting attitude' of some of the Prime Minister's colleagues. 'He did not in the least deny it and spoke of his difficulties as hourly very great. He took on the whole a rather more sanguine view of the situation from the Government point of view than I should be prepared to take at the present moment. We parted in the friendliest way.'[11]

While Reith was still trying to steer a delicate course between Lambeth Palace and Downing Street, further embarrassment arose from another quarter. Refusing to be bound by the T.U.C. boycott of the B.B.C., MacDonald requested on 7 May that a leading member of the Labour party should be allowed to broadcast. After consulting J. C. C. Davidson, Reith turned down the request. But MacDonald persisted and three days later he telephoned Reith to ask if he might make a personal broadcast. MacDonald said that he knew the managing director was not an entirely free agent and the draft he sent to Savoy Hill was accompanied by a friendly note offering to make any necessary alterations. Reith saw no reason why the speech could not go out as it stood, but again Davidson intervened, warning that it would set Churchill off. 'I do not think that they treat me altogether fairly', Reith confided to his diary. 'They will not say we are to a certain extent controlled and they make me take the onus of turning people down. They were quite against MacDonald broadcasting, but I am certain it would have done no harm to the Government.'[12] It was not until 14 May—two days after the strike was called off—that Thomas was allowed to broadcast on behalf of the Labour party.

MacDonald's desire to deliver a personal address was reinforced no doubt by Baldwin's own highly successful performance on Saturday evening. Baldwin had recognised the importance of the new medium from its inception and had made his first wireless speech during the 1924 election campaign. Now, with an expert blend of friendliness and firmness, he repeated that the strike had first to be called off before negotiations could resume, but repudiated the suggestion that the Government was fighting to lower the standard of living of the miners or of any other section of the workers. Once again, he professed his willingness to accept the Samuel Report if only the other parties would do the same. 'I am a man of peace', he concluded. 'I am longing and working for peace, but I will not surrender the safety and security of the British Constitution. You placed me in power eighteen months ago by the largest majority accorded to any party for many years. Have I done anything to forfeit that confidence? Cannot you trust me to ensure a square deal, to secure even justice between man and man?' The broadcast was delivered from Reith's house in Barton Street so that Baldwin could avoid crowds at Savoy Hill and Reith himself suggested the opening sentence of the peroration. As Reith was about to announce him, Baldwin struck a match in front of the microphone and lit his pipe. Whether this action was inspirational or instinctive, it is unlikely that even MacDonald could have equalled its wordless eloquence.

Shortly before Baldwin went on the air 'Fido' Childs, Head of the C.I.D., phoned through on his direct line to the Admiralty to tell Davidson that the Communist party was planning to interfere with the broadcast. Unfortunately, information about this is limited to two intriguing but scanty references in Davidson's papers. 'I sent for our communications expert John Somerville, who later became famous as the officer commanding Force H in the Second World War. We discussed counter-measures and it was agreed that the *Hood* (anchored in the Clyde) should jam any Russian attempts at interference. This was done most successfully, and we also made sure that the Communist party received no instructions from abroad.' In a later reference Davidson has written: 'We had only one complaint, from an old lady lying in bed with a crystal set and earphones, who was determined to listen to the Prime Minister; she claimed that she had had one of her eardrums burst when *Hood* got off the mark.'

On Sunday evening Lord Grey was to broadcast for the Liberals and Reith went to collect him from No. 11 Downing Street. The Chancellor invited Reith to join them for coffee and a polite but vigorous argument developed over the B.B.C.'s role in the crisis, with Mrs Churchill weighing in on the side of her husband and Grey supporting Reith. Churchill was particularly vexed that Saturday's news had contained an item about official collaboration with the T.U.C. in order that power could be restored to the London Hospital. (Reith had also turned down a request by Churchill that the sound of presses rolling at the *British Gazette* should be broadcast, though this was not raised.) As the Chancellor walked with his guests to the car, he asked Reith about his wartime wound. 'In the head wasn't it?' Reith replied that it was, but that his present attitude was not traceable to the wound.[13]

Chapter Ten

# *The Rank-and-File*

'Every day that the strike proceeded the control and the authority of that dispute was passing out of the hands of responsible executives into the hands of men who had no authority, no control, and was wrecking the movement from one end to the other.'

Charles Dukes, secretary of the General and Municipal Workers, January 1927.


'The men were not educated by any revolutionary feelings. They felt they were fighting the Government to get a fair deal for the miners... The instructions of the T.U.C. were accepted without question and the faith and confidence of the men in that body was a religion.'

The secretary of Dartford Divisional Trades Council.


Bevin was determined to impose discipline in the ranks as well as on the General Council. He shared with most of his leading colleagues a profound fear that Communist agitators might gain control of the strike in some areas and provoke violence, perhaps even revolution. 'What I dreaded about this Strike more than anything else was this', Thomas confessed in the House of Commons on 13 May. 'If by any chance it should have got out of the hands of those who would be able to exercise some control, every sane man knows what would have happened...That danger, that fear, was always in our minds, because we wanted at least, even in this struggle, to direct a disciplined army.' The 400 or so trades councils were regarded by Bevin particularly as potential sources of disaffection and in the *Proposals for Co-ordinated Action* their role was limited to that of working 'in conjunction with the local officers of the trade unions actually participating in the dispute' and to 'organising the trade unionists in dispute in the most effective manner for the preservation of peace and order'. In other words, they were to await their instructions from local union officials and not to take any initiative of their own.

Bevin's suspicions were undoubtedly aroused by the Communist party's campaign among the trades councils. More than fifty had been represented at the Minority Movement's Conference of Action in March and in a number of important industrial centres, including Glasgow, Edinburgh, Barrow, Doncaster, Sheffield, Liverpool, and Birmingham, councils of action had been functioning under Communist inspiration for almost a year.[1] In London there was at least one party representative on every trades council and five of the twelve members of the London Trades Council Executive were Communists.[2] Citrine had no more sympathy for the Communists than Bevin, but he recognised that the strike 'cannot be really effectively organised without the trades councils being made the nucleus of the strike organisation'.[3] He was unable to convince the General Council of this, though it made little difference : in most areas the trades councils did become the nucleus of the strike organisation. The intention was not to defy the General Council but simply to provide machinery for mutual consultation and support and it was the trades councils, composed as they were of delegates from the trade union branches in each area, which invariably took the lead.

By 4 May most of the trades councils had set up bodies which included their own executives, delegates from the strike committees of the various unions, and representatives of local working-class organisations such as Labour parties, I.L.P. branches and Co-operative guilds. Many of these improvised bodies assumed the title of joint or central strike committee, though in at least fifty-four towns they touched on raw nerves at Eccleston Square by calling themselves councils of action. Some of the local union officials shared the General Council's dislike of the title. At Dunfermline the council of action had to rename itself a strike committee and the editors of the *Cambridge Strike Bulletin* were forbidden to mention 'Government provocation and the words "Council of Action!"' In other areas the determination to avoid any kind of revolutionary connotation took more dramatic forms. The Widnes N.U.R. branch ended its meetings with *God Save the King* and the Dover Strike Committee requested strikers to sing *Rule Britannia* instead of the *Red Flag* when marching through the streets.[4]

In some districts, where one trade predominated or craft and industrial prejudices were strong, the unions concerned refused to co-operate with the trades councils. At Dorking, Llandudno, and Castle Cary, for instance, railwaymen were in an overwhelming majority and preferred to conduct their own affairs quite separately, and at Chesterfield, where the railwaymen were anxious for co-operation, they found that 'as usual with the rank-and-file miner, he remained apathetic'. At Southampton there was friction between the transport workers and the trades council and at Middlesbrough, Dunfermline, and Sheffield some individual strike committees were resentful of outside interference in what they regarded as their own affairs. At High Wycombe hostility between 'craft' and 'industrial' unions was intense, with the Furnishing Trades Association dominating the trades council and the N.U.R. running a completely autonomous strike committee. In Leeds no less than four rival strike committees were set up and spent much of the time quarrelling over the use of a single telephone.

Although the degree of co-operation achieved by the trades councils varied greatly, the examples cited above were rare and even in areas where co-operation was minimal, delegates from individual strike committees usually sat on the central strike committee or council of action. Joint activities helped to boost morale and made it easier to resolve difficulties when members of different unions in the same industry received imprecise or conflicting instructions from their head offices, which was frequently. At a Government factory in Lewisham workers came out and went back again three times in nine days.[5] In Dartford, members of the General and Municipal Worker's Union and the Public Works and Constructional Operatives' Union received no instructions at all. Such muddles were not unique. Although they had no official status, the central strike committees would often take it upon themselves to seek rulings from union executives or direct from the T.U.C. From many areas came bitter complaints about lack of direction from the centre. In Coventry the vehicle builders struck without waiting for an official ruling on whether they were included with the 'first-line' transport workers or the 'second-line' engineers. There was considerable pressure on the local strike committees to assume responsibility for calling out the engineers and building workers. As early as Monday 4 May, delegates to the Merthyr trades council decided that orders received through the various unions would lead to 'chaos and dissension' and the council executive was accepted as official interpreter. At the outset of the strike Macclesfield council of action held two sessions each day, 'principally to interpret instructions received by affiliated trade unions from their respective head offices'. Most strike committees, however, were unwilling to issue strike directives of their own and there is no evidence for Dukes's melodramatic assertion. Far from trying to usurp the powers of the General Council, the strike committees accepted it as an unpleasant but necessary part of their duties to restrain men who had not received official orders to cease work. Typical is the comment of Bethnal Green trades council, which was one of the most militant in London. 'Our nightmare was always pushing second line of defence back to work.'

Despite the limited mandate under which most of the strike committees chose to operate, they undertook an impressive range of activities, including the issue of permits, picketing, meetings, entertainment, relief of financial distress, communications, and publicity. Several defied the General Council's explicit instructions in one respect by forming workers' defence corps to protect meetings and pickets against interference from police and Fascists. At Methil, strike centre of the East Fife coalfields, a defence corps of 150 men was enrolled under the command of a former sergeant-major and this swelled rapidly to 700 after clashes between pickets and police. The corps was organised into companies under ex-N.C.O.s and these patrolled the area in columns of four armed with pick-shafts. The council of action noted that 'there was no further interference by the police with pickets'. The General Council feared that defence corps would behave provocatively and their apprehensions were no doubt increased by the fact that the Communist party and Minority Movement had been agitating for their formation since Red Friday. Some of the strike committees shared the General Council's concern that a workers' defence corps was only one step away from the Red Army. At Brighton, where members of the council of action were described by the council's secretary as 'mostly of "moderate" type', police charged a crowd outside the tram depot, 'hitting them with sticks, two feet long with knobs on the end'. The subsequent proposal to form a workers' defence corps was defeated, however. 'Reformists said it would make more trouble. I.L.P. and Co-op delegates said they would leave C. of A. if carried.' A similar situation in Edinburgh is recalled by J. P. M. Millar, who was secretary of the National Council of Labour Colleges and organised the office work of the Edinburgh and Lothian Central Strike Committee.[6]

Perhaps the most dramatic moment in the short history of the strike committee was when one day I heard an unusual noise in the stair leading to the strike committee boardroom. I went out and saw that four trade unionists, obviously very excited, were pushing their way past the stewards into the committee room. I followed them. I realised that three of them were Communists and the fourth, an older, more experienced non-Communist, was one of my old students. The excited deputation gave a short but graphic account of how mounted police, they said, had attacked peaceable strikers in the High Street, and demanded that the strike committee organise a workers' defence force. The effect of this report was electric. Only those who have experienced mob feeling can visualise how electric it was. I myself could hardly speak because of the flood of emotion. I realised, though, that in the highly emotional atmosphere the committee might be stampeded into some false step, especially as three of the deputation said quite bluntly that, if the strike committee didn't organise a defence force, the deputation and its friends would. I felt I had to jump in at once and, though I could, because of emotion, hardly speak, I said that while the committee were greatly concerned by the report, it was for the strike committee and the strike committee only to decide whether there should be a defence force, and it would certainly deal with any other group that tried to usurp its powers if it decided that a defence force was not advisable. Fortunately, at that point, the chairman of the committee, Tom Drummond, immediately stepped in and drove the point home and the Communists didn't get their defence force decision and the dangerous moment passed.

But where defence corps existed there appears to have been less trouble than in those areas where they did not. In Willesden, for instance, where a Maintenance of Order Corps with 200 men was formed, there was co-operation with the police and no arrests occurred, and at Selby the police and the defence corps 'worked in complete harmony'. On 10 May C. G. Ammon, who had served as a junior minister in the Labour Government, reported to the General Council that the Communists had 'captured' the movement in Camden Town and that 'there were nasty scenes...on Saturday when the police drew their batons'. However, he went on to record that 'Workers' Vigilant Corps, under control of the trades council, [are] doing wonderful work, and all is orderly now'.

The nature and effectiveness of local activities naturally tended to reflect the strength or weakness of the local Labour movement. Bridport had no strike committee and in the Lancashire market town of Ulverston, described by the secretary of the joint strike committee as 'a Tory-stricken place from one end to the other', it also proved impossible to organise any strike activities. 'Having representatives of the printing trades on the committee, I naturally thought these men would be a source of assistance in issuing bulletins of various descriptions; they were either afraid or incompetent, and proved useless for this purpose. From the very beginning I could clearly see the impotency of our committee as a corporate body to hold its end up on its own. I therefore got in touch, almost at the commencement, with the Barrow-in-Furness strike committee, and subsequently placed the Ulverston committee in their hands.' From the Suffolk coastal town of Lowestoft it was reported to the T.U.C. on Friday that 'the organisation is putrid, the spirit of the men is not good—a good deal of drinking, and fear that when the money is spent the greater number will return to work. Tramwaymen have now returned to work. Chairman of the strike committee has resigned and returned to work.' In Hampshire and the Isle of Wight no organised strike activities were even attempted.

The strike committees in traditional Labour strongholds usually displayed much more vigour and ingenuity. In Bolton, where the council of action was 'the sole authoritative body all through', nine separate committees were set up to handle office staff, organisation, transport, publicity, finance, public representatives, picketing, vital services and messengers. By the second day of the strike, 2,280 pickets had volunteered for duty. Each was provided with a white silk ribbon and worked in shifts of four hours a day. The transport committee mobilised 29 cyclists and 57 motor-cyclists who maintained daily contact with practically every town in Lancashire. Apart from pickets, the council of action kept strikers off the streets and no trade unionists were arrested in Bolton. At Merthyr the Central Strike Committee formed six committees and four district strike committees, each with four subcommittees of its own. The Methil council of action formed six committees and a courier service with three cars and 100 motor-cycles. The couriers worked under the Information Committee and covered the whole of Fife, bringing in reports, taking out information and carrying speakers as far north as Perth. A panel of 30 speakers was drawn up and meetings were always addressed by a miner, a railwayman, and a docker. Speakers' notes were issued by the propaganda committee. In the Labour-controlled borough of Stepney the town hall was placed at the disposal of the council of action and meetings and concerts were held every night of the strike.

Even in areas where solid support for the strike had not been expected, there was often a spontaneous and powerful upsurge of working-class solidarity. Johnstone and District strike committee, which operated a few miles outside Glasgow, found that 'Never before has such solidarity been shown in an industrial dispute in this locality; even our political opponents, Orangemen, being active pickets and taking part generally in the struggle.' At Wey mouth

Margaret Bondfield found Tories supporting the strike.[7] Reporting from Shrewsbury on 8 May, Ellen Wilkinson and J. F. Horrabin noted: 'Huge meeting. Everyone amazed at the way in which call has been answered. Prominent members of local Conservative party among the strikers... Everyone said, "Nothing like this could have been imagined in Shrewsbury."' Canterbury strike committee reported, 'The organisation here was perfect. No weakening whatever. Our difficulty was to keep the men not involved at work.' Oxford council of action considered that it had built up 'a model organisation'. The students and staff of Ruskin College and members of the University Labour Club helped with administration and propaganda and the council was able to extend its activities over a wide area, which included the towns of Chipping Norton, Witney, Abingdon, and Bicester. Hugh Gaitskell, then in his second year at Oxford, acted as chauffeur to Margaret Cole, who was in charge of the main courier service to London. 'Although my sympathies had always been on the Left', Gaitskell has recorded, 'I had not up to then taken any active part in politics. But there was never any doubt in my mind as to where I stood once the strike had begun. Most undergraduates responded to the call of the Government and left Oxford, with the permission of the authorities, to unload ships at the docks, or to drive buses and lorries. I remained behind and offered my services to the Oxford strike committee.'[8]

One of the most important tasks undertaken by the strike committees was the production of strike bulletins. Since the *British Worker* failed to reach many parts of the country, these became a vital means of encouraging morale and counteracting the flow of largely pro-Government sentiment on the wireless and in the newspapers. Wireless reports of alleged returns to work were particularly disturbing to strikers deprived of other news sources. Harwich and District trades council found that 'The B.B.C. had a most demoralising effect on our womenfolk, which reacted on their men.' But with only rare exceptions, the printing unions refused to handle the strike bulletins so that most had to be duplicated or cyclostyled with equipment borrowed from local Labour parties and trade union and I.L.P. branches. In Edinburgh, J. P. M. Millar took charge of producing a strike bulletin and installed a female typist and four duplicating machines in a basement passage of the Mid' East Lothian Miners' Association offices. He also managed to gather together several unwilling machinemen from the Scottish Typographical Association. On Tuesday 4 May the stencils for the first bulletin were cut and duplicating began. Millar was then called away for a short time.

When I returned I went down below to the 'printing shop' to see how production had progressed. At the end of the row of machines was the N.C.L.C. operator working her machine without difficulty and wearing the satisfied smile that a cat with a sense of humour might have had while consuming a large dish of somebody else's cream. The expressions on the skilled machinemen at the other machines was quite different. They looked decidedly upset and annoyed. The running of the duplicators had not turned out to be as simple as they had thought and the floor round about them was strewn with sheets that had not come up to standard. Their experience of the competition of skilled female labour in the form of the N.C.L.C. typist was such that they didn't turn up for any of the subsequent editions and I had to call on more female assistance. There is no doubt that it required very much more skill to run a printing machine, but running the duplicators also required a certain amount of skill, although of a different kind!

The editor of the *Wigan Strike Bulletin,* on being appointed, 'knelt by my chair, acknowledged our weakness and asked for Divine guidance'. In most other areas, however, the problems of news-gathering and production were approached in a rather more practical manner. The procedure adopted by the strikers who produced the duplicated *Sheffield Forward* is typical. 'A staff of volunteers working right through the night assisted the editor, who during the whole of the period of the dispute rarely got to his bed.' Individuals brought in news of events in their own areas and the editor and his assistants were in regular telephone contact with spokesmen in neighbouring towns. Barnsley, Rotherham, and Chesterfield provided news of the miners and Doncaster gave information about the railwaymen. The *Forward* also contained much comment on B.B.C. news reports and on items appearing in the *British Gazette* and the emergency editions of the *Sheffield Telegraph.* 'There were many rumours of collapses in various places', one of the *Forward* volunteers has recalled, 'and our main task was to check these and counter them by publishing denials "from our correspondent on the spot", so to speak. The paper was foolscap size, sometimes more than one sheet, and there was never any difficulty about selling it on the streets.'[9]

The small number of strike committees which induced members of the Typographical Association to work on printed bulletins received no thanks for their pains from Eccleston Square. A circular issued by the publicity committee on 5 May instructed local organisations 'to confine their statements on the situation to the material supplied by the committee and to add nothing in the way of comment and interpretation'. This was clearly intended to prevent the circulation of Communist propaganda and, although the publicity committee did not go so far as to ban duplicated bulletins, it actively discouraged those which were printed. Preston strike committee was ordered to cease publication of its printed *Strike News* and when the Bradford and District trades council sent a copy of its *Bradford Worker* to Eccleston Square it received, not the congratulations it expected, but a curt reprimand for violating instructions. Leeds council of action was given a similarly sharp rap over the knuckles, although the T.U.C. Intelligence Committee was forced to admit that it was 'a first-class strike bulletin'.

Fines were imposed on officials of the strike committees in Finsbury and St Pancras because of items published in their bulletins and in the militant mining areas of the north-east strike sheets became a regular target for the police. One of the most outspoken was the *Northern Light,* which circulated in the Durham coalfield. Its distributors were often arrested and the paper was produced from a different address each night. Most of the bulletins, however, whether duplicated or printed, consistently stressed the double theme running through each issue of the *British Worker:* that the dispute was purely industrial and that the strikers should conduct themselves in an orderly manner. 'It is not a strike run by Communists against the community', declared the first issue of the printed *Gloucester Strike Bulletin* on 6 May. 'It is a strike of the whole industrial Labour movement, organised by the Trades Union Congress, to defend the standard of life of one of its sections.' There was a decidedly familiar flavour to the *Cardiff Strike Bulletin*'s injunction to 'Keep smiling. Refuse to be provoked. Get into the garden. Look after the wife and kiddies. If you have not got a garden, get into the country, the parks and the playgrounds...There is no more healthful occupation than walking.' There was a religious rather than revolutionary fervour about some of the bulletins. The editor of the *Wigan Strike Bulletin* naturally had an appropriate message for his readers on Sunday 9 May: 'My Dear Public, Remember the Sabbath Day to keep it Holy. Thou shalt love the Lord thy God with, All thy heart, soul, mind and strength and, Thy neighbour as thyself. Daily bulletin. News from all points. Situation magnificent. Everywhere solid.' The Saturday issue of *Lansbury's Bulletin*, which circulated in Poplar, informed its readers that 'Tomorrow is Sunday.

You will come to our meetings at night, but I would like you to attend the Church services nearest your home... It is Christ's gospel of passive resistance which you are practising today.' *Preston Strike News* carried a special message from Canon Donaldson of Westminster. 'I earnestly beg that the workers will stand firm, they will win; but if they begin to doubt and quaver and to blackleg— all will be lost and lost for a generation.'

Where many of the strike bulletins differed significantly from the *British Worker* was in their frequent use of jokes, satire and even cartoons. Unlike the General Council, the strike committees realised, probably instinctively, that humour could be as effective as the earnest repetition of appeals and strike statistics. 'We understand', announced the *Westminster Worker* on 12 May, 'that luncheon cars are to be put on trains running between Westminster and Black-friars.' The *St Pancras Bulletin* reported on 12 May that notices posted on the walls of Highgate Cemetary called for volunteers and suggested that it should be 'picketed by Underground men'. *Kensington Strike Bulletin* announced on 7 May, 'The Strike is over. Only 400,000 N.U.R. men are now on strike, plus 1 million miners and 2 million others. But three trains are running in Manchester and there is a five minute service every two hours on the tubes. A bag of coal has been brought from Newcastle today.' The O.M.S. naturally came in for some heavy irony. 'Only 2 O.M.S. reported for pitwork', reported the *St Pancras Bulletin* on 11 May. 'Upon finding no baths at pithead and that they had left tooth-brushes at home they declined, and returned to London by the "Normal Rail-way Service".' Under the heading 'To Heaven by L.M.S.', the *Bristol Bulletin* published the following ditty : 'Early in the morning, per broadcast from London, see the little puff-puffs all in a row, D'Arcy on the engine, pulled a little lever, expansion of the boiler— UP WE GO !' The circular issued in Monmouthshire by the Eastern Valleys Joint Industrial Council favoured a more forthright approach. On 11 May it published an imaginary conversation between a striker and his young son. 'What is a BLACKLEG Daddy?' asks the innocent lad. 'A BLACKLEG is a TRAITOR my boy. He is a man who knows not Honour or Shame!' 'Were there many BLACK-LEGS in the valley, Daddy?' 'No, my boy! Only the Station Master at Abersychan, and two clerks at Crane Street Station.'

The *St Pancras Bulletin* was particularly ingenious at rhyming and in eight consecutive issues there appeared instalments of a complete 'Strikers' Alphabet' in verse. The first instalment of three verses was featured on 5 May. 'A is for ALL, ALL OUT and ALL WIN, And down with the blacklegs and scabs who stay in. B is for

Baldwin, the Bosses' Strong Man, But he's welcome to dig all the coal that he can. C is for Courage the workers have shown, Class Conscious and Confident that they'll hold their own.' The final three verses were published on 10 May. '*X* is for exit the whole boss class—*X*tra enjoyment for me and my lass. Y is for young workers to whom fighting is new; Yes, Young, but determined to fight with you. Z is for Zeal shown by the vigilance corps, Zealous that workers aren't trapped by the law.' A somewhat less lyrical item appeared on 11 May. 'The cab section, T. and G.W.U., going strong but regret that Brown's Garage, of Leverton St, Kentish Town, are still harbouring "blacks". All the Labour movement of St Pancras should centre on this "Home for Niggers" and see that they are made "white".'

The General Council's decision to leave the issue of food permits to the discretion of the railwaymen and transport workers in each area automatically gave the strike committees and councils of action a vital policy-making role to play. This was certainly not the General Council's intention, but since most of the Joint Transport Committees chose to operate as subsidiaries of a central strike committee the question of permits was invariably referred to the parent body. Finding themselves in a position to dictate terms to employers gave some of the strikers a rare and exhilarating sense of power. An Ashton sheet-metal worker wrote:

> Employers of labour were coming, cap-in-hand, begging for permission...to allow their workers to return to perform certain customary operations. 'Please can I move a quantity of coal from such and such a place' or 'Please can my transport workers move certain foodstuffs in this or that direction.' Most of them turned empty away after a most humiliating experience, for one and all were put through a stern questioning, just to make them realise that we and not they were the salt of the earth. I thought of the many occasions when I had been turned away from the door of some workshop in a weary struggle to get the means to purchase the essentials of life for self and dependants... The only tactic practised by some of them was bullying, and that was no use in a situation such as this; some tried persuasion, referring to us as *Mr Chairman* and *Gentlemen*, but only a rigid examination of the stern facts of the case moved our actions. The cap-in-hand position reversed.

Many of the employers who did obtain permits used them as a cover to move non-essential goods and the T.U.C. was deluged with reports of lorries labelled 'Essential Food' containing everything from bedding for blacklegs to toy rocking horses. 'People are often found masquerading as loaves of bread', observed the *Westminster Worker*. Other employers simply carried on their business without even bothering to apply for permits. The General Council and its National Transport Committee could hardly have failed to foresee this situation but no guidance was offered to strike committees faced with the question of what to do if lorries ran through their areas without permits. It was a question which had to be answered by each strike committee according to its own inclinations and resources. Where feeling was strong, mass pickets attempted to prevent the movement of unauthorised transport. This was particularly successful in parts of Scotland and the north of England and, during the first week, in London's East End. At Falkirk, for instance, blackleg drivers were formally placed 'under arrest' by pickets before being turned back and much of the traffic in and out of Edinburgh was controlled by the local strike committee. 'The effectiveness of our control over a very wide area,' writes J. P. M. Millar, 'was illustrated by the fact that a businessman called at the office for a permit. His son, who lived in a border town, had been taken ill and he was anxious to see him. I explained that he didn't need a permit as he was using a private car and he wasn't carrying any goods or passengers. He pleaded, however, for a permit as he feared that he wouldn't get to his destination without one. I set his mind at rest by giving him a special one!' Further proof of effective picketing was to be seen at Longcroft, outside Edinburgh, where the football park was filled with vehicles of all descriptions, 'impounded until a permit and a union driver are produced'.[10] Abe Moffatt, who later became Communist president of the miners, has described the situation at Cowdenbeath, in the Fife coalfield: 'All motor vehicles had to get permission from the trades council before travelling up the Great North Road. We had pickets on in various parts of the road to ensure that no one passed without the permission of the trades council. To ensure that no one would pass, miners had a rope across the road. If a motor vehicle had a pass it got through, if it had no pass it had to turn back.'[11]

Other parts of the country were less resolute. Throughout the eastern division of England, which included Cambridgeshire, Bedfordshire, Huntingdonshire, Norfolk, and Suffolk, road transport ran without serious interference and the docks and postal service functioned normally. Some strike committees also resented the lack of direction from the T.U.C. Coventry council of action found that 'Other difficulties were, to what extent assistance should be given to the local Food Controller, extent of permits for the movement of food supplies, the E.T.U. cinema operators wanted to know if they would be in order using "black" juice—many of the difficulties could have been easily dealt with if the council of action had been supplied with a statement which would have laid down general principles, and to which reference could have been made.' Paisley strike committee reported that its 'chief difficulty lay in getting accurate information from Headquarters, particularly in regard to the issuing of permits'.

Eventually, on 7 May, the National Transport Committee issued its first and only pronouncement of importance. This noted that the Government had ignored the T.U.C.'s offer to assist in the distribution of food supplies and drew attention to the 'gross abuse' of permits. Local transport committees were therefore requested 'to review all permits which have been issued'. 'Review' was generally taken to be a euphemism for 'revoke' and both the Government and the strike committees reacted accordingly. 'An organised attempt is being made to starve the people and to wreck the State', accused the *British Gazette*. This undoubtedly was not the intention but, characteristically, the T.U.C. did not think it necessary to state just what the intention was. Was trade union labour merely to abstain from working food lorries or were the lorries to be forcibly prevented from moving along the roads? Again, it was left to each strike committee to answer this vital question in its own way. Where the committee was militant, it usually attempted to enforce a total embargo on commercial road traffic through mass picketing. Where the committee was unwilling to go this far, it confined itself to securing the withdrawal of all transport labour.

A further question which had to be resolved was whether or not the Co-operative Societies were to be granted special exemptions. On the eve of the strike the Co-operative Wholesale Society had urged the retail societies to withhold credit from strikers and on 5 May Baldwin actually received a letter from the head of the London C.W.S. 'telling him to stand firm on the position he had taken up'.[12] Many of the local Co-ops were equally hostile to Labour. Bolton council of action observed that its local society was 'largely a Conservative body and non-sympathetic'. At Stratford-on-Avon the Co-op was 'not very sympathetic with Labour party' and Dunfermline council of action experienced 'great difficulties at times with certain members of the Board of Management, owing to their not even being trade unionists themselves'. There were a large number of areas, however, in which the Co-ops did advance credit to strikers and in several of them Co-op delegates even sat on the strike committees. But whether by design or default, no reference was made to the Co-ops in T.U.C. instructions until 10 May when, almost as an afterthought, the General Council announced that 'all men engaged in transport should now be on strike excepting men employed by Co-operative Societies solely for the purpose of delivering milk and bread direct to their members'.

Unlike other trading enterprises, the Co-ops were given no Government assistance in obtaining their supplies and, where the strike committee insisted on cancelling all permits, it was usually the Co-ops which suffered most. As a result, the C.W.S. was provoked into issuing another statement forbidding the granting of credit and in many areas there was intense bitterness between the Co-ops and the strike committee. In Northumberland and Durham 'Considerable difficulties arose over the withdrawal of all permits, as instructed by the T.U.C., which affected chiefly the Co-operative Societies. This problem continued unsolved throughout the strike, although partial and temporary arrangements were made to get over the most urgent difficulties'. In London nearly all the local Co-ops refused to advance credit. As Edmonton strike committee reported: 'It is impossible to make any arrangements with the London Co-operative Society, as they were more severely hit by the Transport and General Workers' Union than any other firm...and the action of the trade unions in further hampering the distribution of food supplies by these societies was much resented in this district.' Millar recalls that:

After a few days a number of Co-operative Societies across the water in Fife became desperate for supplies of food from the Scottish Co-operative wholesale warehouses in Leith. A deputation from the S.C.W.S. directors came to the office and asked to meet the Central Strike Committee, which controlled the issue of permits. They were not allowed to walk into the Miners' board room, where the strike committee sat permanently, but were stopped on the stairs by two stewards and referred to me in the office. Never had the board members received such a stiff reception... They put their case for food for industrial Fife and were told that they could have permits for one lot of vans. They must have thought, quite rightly, that this was the last lot of permits they would get, for I afterwards heard that they loaded up every vehicle they had and the cavalcade set off with a car in front with the permits so that the goods could get to their destination with the utmost speed just in case policy changed and the traffic was stopped.

In a few areas the strike committee and Co-ops did establish a fairly close relationship. At Sheffield the strike committee was generous in issuing permits for the transport of foodstuffs and even small private dealers were allowed to move firewood on condition they did not raise prices In Coventry the Co-operative Society placed a car at the disposal of the council of action, provided the council with duplicating facilities and verbatim copies of wireless reports, and gave an assurance that it would do everything possible to meet the council's demands. At a meeting of tradesmen, convened by the local food controller, the chairman of the Co-op announced that there would be no increase in his firm's food prices for at least fourteen days. The other tradesmen followed this lead, though according to the council of action, 'The local vultures were obviously disappointed.' In return, the Co-op secured permits for the release of food supplies and was given permission by the Warwick-shire Miners' Association to obtain coal from a local pit. The Co-op held the price of the coal well below that contemplated by other merchants, who again were forced to forgo some easy profits.

Where no arrangement was made between the Co-ops and the strike committees, Co-op stores found themselves starved of supplies while other traders were able to continue business as usual by courtesy of the Government-sponsored haulage committees. For despite the militancy of picketing in some areas, the Government's arrangements for transporting essential supplies by road were never seriously threatened. As the *Manchester Guardian Bulletin* observed on 12 May: 'The ordinary housekeeper would have no reason to imagine that a General Strike had been proclaimed, and to a large extent enforced, over a week ago. It is reflected neither in the price nor in the quantity of the food supplies of the shops.' This was the true measure of the Government's success. At midnight on 3 May food not coal was the ammunition which counted.

# Chapter Eleven

# *Reluctant Revolutionaries*

'By and large the Communist party [of Great Britain] passed the test of its political maturity. The attempt to present it as a "brake on the revolution" is beneath criticism.'

The Executive Committee of the Communist International, 8 June 1926.

'That lot run a revolution? They couldn't run a whelk stall.'

George Lansbury, quoted in Raymond Postgate's *Life of George Lansbury*.

The threat of renewed industrial upheaval and the timely arrest of twelve of its leading officials had provided the Communist party with an ideal political climate in the six months prior to the General Strike. Despite the I.L.P.'s stolid refusal to form an alliance with it, the party gained widespread Labour sympathy as a result of the arrests. By the end of the year, fifty local Labour parties were refusing to operate the ban on Communists adopted by the Liverpool Conference[1] and in January 1926, a Left-wing movement was launched to perform within the Labour party the kind of role that the National Minority Movement was already performing inside the trade unions.[2] It was with considerable optimism, therefore, that the Comintern Executive met on 4 March to debate 'The English Question'. The policy of the British party, declared Zinoviev, showed how united front tactics should be used and it was the British and Chinese comrades who had achieved the best results over the past year. A lengthy resolution prepared by Zinoviev noted that 'The methods used by the British capitalists to recapture their former position...are gradually making the British working-class more revolutionary'. Another factor 'pushing the British workers to the left' had been 'the fiasco of the MacDonald Government'. On the one hand, it had aroused to political consciousness broad masses of workers who had never before taken an active part in political life; on the other, it had 'brought no help to the working masses while openly supporting British imperialism'. Signs of this advance to 'a more revolutionary position' were to be seen in the support which had been mobilised on behalf of the miners on Red Friday; the resolutions passed by the Scarborough T.U.C.; the campaign for the release of the arrested Communists; the progress of the Minority Movement; the beginning of a similar organisation within the Labour party; and the pressure from rank-and-file members of the I.L.P. for a united front with the Communists.[3] Trotsky, who was already in conflict with the Stalinist faction in the Russian party, rejected the analysis. The Left at Scarborough, he pointed out with accuracy, remained Left 'only so long as it had to accept no practical obligations'. The Left faction on the General Council was ideologically shapeless and organisationally incapable of taking over from the dominant Right-wing and it was disposed 'either to direct betrayal or compromise, or else to a policy of wait and see with reference to compromises and complaints against traitors'.[4]

Ernest Brown, one of the British delegates, argued that his country still had 'immense resources and powers of resistance' and that the resolution proposed by Zinoviev painted the position in 'too gloomy colours'. Aitken Ferguson, another British delegate, was more confident. He claimed that, through the Minority Movement, the party was able, for the first time, 'actually to move the workers, not only to dig into the organisation itself, but to get them moving'. The Comintern Executive urged the party to continue giving its utmost support to the Minority Movement, to develop the Labour Left-wing and to make every effort to double its 5,000 members during 1926. But in attempting to win over the orthodox Left, the party was not to abandon its basic ideological commitment. 'Broad masses of the British working-class still cherish illusions about parliamentarianism and the traditions of liberalism. The party must wage an energetic struggle against the illusion that the British working-class can win its freedom through a bourgeois parliament.'

The British Communist party worked hard at its assigned tasks during the seven weeks which remained before the onset of the mining crisis. The Minority Movement held its National Conference of Action on 21 March and, despite the I.L.P.'s further rejection of an alliance 'so long as your party is committed to the...thesis...that an armed revolution is the only means of establishing socialism',[5] M.P.s belonging to the I.L.P. were at the forefront of the growing Left-wing movement. Although these developments were encouraging, the Communist party did not mistake them for signs of imminent revolution. Rather more than seven weeks would be required to demolish the cherished parliamentary illusions noted by Zinoviev and the party was justifiably resentful at Trotsky's assertion that it would 'let slip the revolutionary situation as the German party did in 1923'.[6] A realistic appraisal of the party's opportunities by J. T. Murphy, head of the industrial department, appeared in *Workers' Weekly* on 30 April.

> Our party does not hold the leading positions in the trade unions. It can only advise and place its press and its forces at the service of the workers—led by others. And let it be remembered that those who are leading have no revolutionary perspectives before them. Any revolutionary perspectives they may perceive will send the majority of them hot on the track of a retreat. Those who do not look for a path along which to retreat are good trade union leaders, who have sufficient character to stand firm on the demands of the miners, but they are totally incapable of moving forward to face all the implications of a united working-class challenge to the state. To entertain any exaggerated views as to the revolutionary possibilities of this crisis and visions of a new leadership 'arising spontaneously in the struggle', etc. is fantastic.

Realising that it was powerless to influence events nationally, the party executive dispersed itself throughout the districts on the eve of the strike, leaving only a small Working Bureau to keep the flag flying at headquarters in King Street. An attempt was made to keep in touch with the provinces through a makeshift courier service, 'but, during the short time that the General Strike lasted, the system had not the opportunity to advance very far beyond the rudimentary stage, and there is no doubt that some districts were almost entirely cut off after the first party lead'.[7]

The only practical option open to the Working Bureau was propaganda, and Tommy Jackson, acting editor of *Workers' Weekly*, was made responsible for producing a daily strike edition of the paper. The first issue of this emergency *Workers' Daily* on 3 May contained 'Four Slogans for Victory': 'Not a penny off the pay, not a second on the day; a council of action in every town; make friends with the soldiers; every man behind the miners.' By the crudest interpretation, none of these could be construed as a call to revolution. Nevertheless, on 5 May police raided the party press and effectively prevented further publication by removing vital parts of machinery. For the remainder of the strike the party had to rely on a duplicated *Workers' Bulletin* produced from frequently changed hideouts by Pollitt's wife, Marjorie, and Bob Stewart, the acting secretary. Despite grave transport difficulties and constant police harassment, the *Bulletin* was widely distributed and its circulation rose from 5,000 on 4 May to 20,000 on 13 May, the last day of issue. Its readership was probably nearer 100,000, since party branches and districts reproduced its contents in their own strike publications.

The *Workers' Bulletin* naturally marched boldly over ground shunned altogether by the *British Worker*. Arrests, troop movements, clashes between strikers and police, alleged disaffection in the army, were all prominently reported. The T.U.C.'s repeated assertions that the strike was a purely industrial dispute were also given short shrift in the pages of the *Bulletin*. The second issue on 5 May carried a party pronouncement on 'The Political Meaning of the General Strike'. The first watchwords remained 'Not a penny off the pay, not a second on the day'. But now that the struggle had begun, the workers had it in their power to put an end, once and for all, to the continued menace to their living standards and working conditions. Simply to beat off the employers' present offensive meant that they would return to the attack later on, just as they did after Red Friday. 'The only guarantee against the ravenous and soulless greed of the coal-owners is to break their economic power. Therefore, let the workers answer the bosses' challenge with a challenge of their own: "Nationalisation of the mines, without compensation for the coal-owners, under workers' control through pit committees!" ' The Government had dropped the pretence of being above all classes by allying itself with the coal-owners. 'Troops, aeroplanes and battleships are being used to overcome the workers, if possible, and to crush the General Strike. If the strike ends, though it be with the defeat of the coal-owners, but with the Government's power unshaken, the capitalists will still have hopes of renewing their attack. Therefore, the third essential slogan of the General Strike must be. "Resignation of the Forgery Government! Formation of a Labour Government!" ' It was still necessary for the workers to consolidate their defence through councils of action and defence corps and by arranging food supplies through the Co-ops. 'But the Communist party warns the workers against the attempts being made to limit the struggle to its previous character of self-defence against the capitalist offensive.' Battle had been joined and the only way to victory now was for every council of action to adopt the new slogans.

Although posing a direct political challenge to the Government, the new slogans fell far short of demands for a revolutionary takeover by the workers. The call for a Labour Government, explained Murphy, was made because the Labour movement 'was totally incapable of measuring up to the revolutionary implications of the situation'.[8] In its report to the Party Congress in October, the central committee developed the same theme. 'The party entered the General Strike with political and organisational slogans that were inevitably defensive in character... Once the masses were on the streets, the business of the central committee was to extend these slogans, at the same time making them more aggressive in character. The struggle was complicated by the fact that even before the strike began the party had to fight against the tendencies to surrender which were already making themselves felt amongst the leaders, i.e. to stress the need of maintaining even the defensive fight unbroken.'

Whatever impact the party was able to make, however, depended not upon a set of slogans coined in London but upon the hard work and initiative of individual Communists on the strike committees and councils of action. They were strongly entrenched in South Wales and industrial Scotland and well represented on councils of action on Merseyside and in and around Manchester and Middlesbrough. Party factions were also at work in all but ten of London's seventy councils of action and Communists dominated the councils in Poplar, Stepney, Bethnal Green, West Ham, Islington, St Pancras, Camden Town, and Battersea.[9] In all these areas activities such as picketing, publicity and workers' defence were undertaken with notable vigour. In most of them an attempt was also made to challenge the Government's emergency arrangements more effectively by co-ordinating strike activities on a regional basis.

On 4 May the London Trades Council Executive launched a Central London Strike Committee, but the lack of interest shown by district union officials and the formation by Bevin of a separate Permits Committee for London deprived it of any authority. As Duncan Carmichael, the Communist secretary of the London Trades Council, subsequently reported: 'It can be said that the organisation was of a most unsatisfactory character... No effective contact was maintained either with the local councils of action or strike Committees.' It was not until after the strike had ended that the first conference of councils of action was held.

Other attempts at regional co-ordination were more successful. Pressure from the five Communist members of Glasgow's Central Strike Committee ensured close liaison with fifteen local strike committees, in many of which Communists were also prominent. Airdrie and Coatbridge council of action, for instance, set up a workers' defence corps and organised mass pickets involving up to 4,000 men. Councils of action in the rest of Lanarkshire linked up under a Central Strike Committee of their own in which eight of the forty delegates were Communists, including the chairman.[10]

Methil council of action, which was under strong Communist influence, operated on a semi-federal basis throughout East Fife and regional federations with party backing were formed in the Manchester and Liverpool areas.[11] In Kent six strike committees grouped themselves under the Dartford council of action, though here the lead came from the Divisional Labour party.

In June 1926, the Comintern defended the British party against Trotsky's charges of passivity and indecision and went on to record that 'The councils of action organised by the trade unions actually developed into District Soviets. The departments organised by the General Council already resembled in their structure and functions the departments of the St Petersburg Soviet in the period of the so-called "dual power" (February–November 1917)'.[12] In a strictly limited sense this was true, for in attempting to control transport both the T.U.C. and the strike committees were clearly attempting to substitute their own authority for that of the Government. It is also probable that, if the strike had been prolonged, regional groupings of councils of action would have operated with an increasing indifference to the T.U.C. and they may well have evolved into embryo Soviets. But during the period the strike lasted there was no sign of a revolutionary initiative and the Communist party was too small to create one. Moscow seems to have been well aware of the actual situation and it is unlikely that the All-Russian Trade Union Council was surprised when the T.U.C. promptly returned its cheque for 2 million roubles (£200,000).* Robert Boothby, who was visiting the Russian capital at the time, was advised by Karl Radek to pack his bags for England immediately. 'It is more interesting now there than here. But make no mistake, this is not a revolutionary movement. It is simply a wage dispute.'[13]

Even in Durham and Northumberland, where the most effective exercise of power by strikers occurred, there was a determination to avoid any action which did not have T.U.C. approval. Events in the northern counties, recorded in unique detail on the trade union side,[14] deserve consideration for several reasons. They throw much light on Communist aims and tactics; they show the day-to-day

* The *British Worker* of 8 May stated: 'The report in the foreign press yesterday that an offer had been made by the Russian Trade Unions was confirmed this morning by a definite contribution being offered to the General Council. The Council has informed the Russian Trade Unions, in a courteous communication, that they are unable to accept the offer and the cheque has been returned.' Hamilton Fyfe wrote in his diary on 8 May: 'A very prudent proceeding! Had the money been accepted, the other side would have yelled that it was a "subsidy from Moscow". Of course, it would have been nothing of the kind. The Russian Trade Unions are often at loggerheads with Moscow. But the truth wouldn't have had a look in when once the lie started.'

difficulties which arose at a local level because of inadequate planning by the General Council; they indicate the potential of the regional strike organisations; above all, they are a graphic confirmation of Radek's point. On Saturday 1 May, Robin Page Arnot, director of the Labour Research Department and one of the twelve Communists imprisoned the previous year, arrived in the Durham mining village of Chopwell. After addressing a May Day rally, he spoke at a much smaller gathering in the Miners' Club at which it was agreed to summon a meeting of trade union officials, Co-op representatives and Labour councillors from Blaydon-on-Tyne for the following evening. Almost fifty delegates attended this meeting, which was held in Chopwell under the chairmanship of Will Lawther, a local check-weighman, who was an enthusiastic supporter of the Left-wing movement and a member of the Labour party's national executive. The 'Plan of Campaign', which Page Arnot had helped to draw up after weekend discussions with Communist organisers on Tyneside, was adopted unanimously. Its single object was 'To defeat the civil commissioner appointed for this region'. The commissioner, it was noted, 'is appointed by the Government and is armed with the Emergency Powers Act in order to break the strike. Our immediate aim is to prevent him doing that in this town. But in order to do that effectively we must offer a resistance throughout the whole region over which he has been given plenary powers. That is, we must defeat the civil commissioner and all his strike-breaking apparatus.'

Having outlined the formidable civil and military forces at the commissioner's disposal, the Plan declared: 'To meet all this we must improvise. The improvised machinery must be simple, easy to throw up, all inclusive. All activities in each locality should be centralised in a single body to be called council of action, strike committee, trades council or what you will; all such bodies should be linked up and centralised in the county capital town under a body responsible for the whole region.' The centralised body was to consist of district trade union officials—'men who, by experience and routine, are capable of thinking in terms of counties as a single whole'—and it was to assume an 'authority and scope on our side [which] would exactly answer to the civil commissioner'. Although the various municipal councils were to be incorporated in the commissioner's scheme, they were 'not necessarily to be handed over …in their entirety. A struggle may take place for the possession of the machinery of such authority as is possessed by Boards of Guardians or Urban District Councils. It may be possible to impede the operations of the civil commissioner and his officers under the

E.P.A.; perhaps even to transform part at any rate of the Urban District Council into strike machinery'.

Referring to the T.U.C. instructions that food supplies were to be maintained, the Plan observed that 'Whatever the intention of the General Council in laying down this instruction, it is clear that on this point depends the success of the general strike. Whoever handles and transports food, that same person controls food; whoever controls food will find the "neutral" part of the population rallying to their side. Who feeds the people wins the strike. The problem of the general strike can be focused down to one thing—the struggle for food control.' Finally, while all activities were designed 'for the purpose of defeating the civil commissioner's attempt to break the general strike', there was another object. 'That is the building up of our own morale both locally and nationally. Every officer who reports that picketing has stopped his transport, every military officer who reports that he cannot trust his men to act against the strikers because of effective fraternisation, is a means by which, when the report has filtered through to Whitehall, the morale of the Chief Civil Commissioner, and thence of the Cabinet, is impaired and weakened.'

Early on Monday Harry Bolton, chairman of Blaydon Urban District Council, carried out his role under the 'Plan of Campaign'. After interviewing all members of the council's staff, he ordered those suspected of being unsympathetic to the strike to take an immediate fortnight's holiday. Those who remained were placed, together with the council offices and duplicator, at the disposal of the strike committee. Meanwhile, dozens of young miners sped through Durham and Northumberland on pedal-cycles and motor-bikes spreading the appeal for local councils of action and in the evening Page Arnot met several prominent trade union officials to discuss plans for the regional co-ordinating body. Those attending were James White, area secretary of the T.G.W.U.; Ebby Edwards, financial secretary of the Northumberland Miners' Association; Ferguson Foster, an organiser of the National Union of Distributive and Allied Workers; and Charles Flynn, the union's northern divisional officer. Other officials who had been invited were busy with their own eve-of-strike arrangements.

A further meeting was therefore called at the N.U.D.A.W. offices in Newcastle on Tuesday and this time eleven unions were officially represented.* In addition, the Durham miners were represented

* These were: the Northumberland Miners' Association; the Northumberland Colliery Mechanics' Association; the National Union of Distributive and Allied Workers; the Transport and General Workers' Union; the National Union of

unofficially by Will Lawther and the National Union of Seamen by James Rogers, the local organiser. Delegates from Newcastle Trades Council and Gateshead Labour party also attended. After electing White chairman and Flynn secretary, the meeting appointed two representatives from each union to serve on a General Council for Northumberland and Durham and set up a joint strike committee composed of one representative from each union or group of unions involved in the dispute. Page Arnot was co-opted on to both bodies as director of the Labour Research Department. A series of sub-committees was then appointed to deal with routine matters such as propaganda, permits and defence.

The joint strike committee went into session as soon as the inaugurating meeting was over. Immediately it received a complaint that the miners' clubs were sending cars to collect beer while transport workers were on strike. Most of the evening, however, was devoted to interpreting and co-ordinating the sets of instructions which the various unions had received from their head offices. As a result of this discussion, it was decided to abandon subcommittees. 'Subcommittees must necessarily proceed from a body whose own movements have attained some degree of simple co-ordination, whose members know one another, and whose machinery has been tried and tested. The strike committee was not in this position.' The committee believed it could best overcome the problem by assuming direct responsibility for all activities and dealing with each issue as it arose. This 'meant of course an enormous accumulation of work. It meant that within a few days the committee began to sit in the morning and to continue from morning to after-noon, evening and midnight'. On the other hand, this con-centration of activities welded the committee into a cohesive body and enabled it 'to get the measure of what was important and what was relatively unimportant'. High on the list of the committee's priorities was the publication of a strike bulletin. Several unofficial sheets, such as the *Workers' Chronicle,* produced by Newcastle Trades

General and Municipal Workers; the Boilermakers' Union; the Federation of Engineering and Shipbuilding Trades; the Railway Clerks' Association; the National Union of Railwaymen; the Builders' Federation; and the Shop Assistants' Union. Shortly after this meeting, 11 other local organisations affiliated to the Northumberland and Durham General Council. These were: the Amalgamated Society of Locomotive Engineers and Firemen; the Electrical Trades Union; the Amalgamated Engineering Union (all of these were directly involved in the dispute and therefore also rep-resented on the Joint Strike Committee); the Plumbers' Union; the National Union of Clerks; the Lithographic Printers; the National Union of Bookbinding, etc., Workers; the Tyne Watermen's Association; the Gateshead Strike Committee; and the Newcastle Borough Labour Party and I.L.P.

Council, *Workers' Searchlight,* and Chopwell council of action's *Northern Light* rapidly appeared, but the committee wished to publish a bulletin of its own 'which would give accurate information, up-to-date information and local information to meet the extremely virulent poison that was being poured out from the blackleg sheets'. It continued to press for a permit from the Typographical Association until the weekend, when A. W. Dawson arrived in Newcastle to arrange for a local edition of the *British Worker*.

On Wednesday 5 May, the committee grappled with the difficult problem of permits. Having accepted from the outset that effective control of transport was vital to victory, the committee found that, by Wednesday afternoon, 'The abuse of permits was beginning to reach gigantic proportions... Unscrupulous contractors or employers were conveying any and every sort of goods under the aegis of "Food Only" or "Housing Materials Only".' It was decided to continue issuing food permits but all permits for the transport of building materials were immediately revoked. On the same day members of the General and Municipal Workers, unloading cargoes of food under permit at Newcastle docks, ceased work. Their objection was to a sudden influx of O.M.S. volunteers and to the mooring of a submarine and two destroyers beside a foodship. That evening the strike committee received a message that Sir Kingsley Wood, the civil commissioner, wished to see them, and shortly after he appeared in person at Burt Hall, the committee's Newcastle headquarters. The commissioner, who was received by White, Flynn, and James Tarbit, the Municipal Workers' organiser, claimed that the volunteers had appeared on the quayside without his knowledge or authority and gave an assurance that they would not be allowed 'to interfere with the habitual occupations of people who usually do this, so long as they will do it'. Tarbit warned that his men would object as strongly if the volunteers attempted to handle non-food cargoes and the deputation urged that ships with general cargoes should either berth in the river to await the end of the dispute or return to their port of origin. It was also emphasised that trade unionists could not return until the naval vessels had moved back to their usual anchorage at Jarrow, 'as it was impossible for us to agree that our men should be forced to work under the shadow of their guns'. Wood replied that the boats had taken up their present moorings solely for the purpose of dealing with possible riots or attacks upon power stations. He stated that he had no control over the Admiralty in the matter, 'but appeared to indicate that a suggestion from him to the commanders of the vessels might have the desired effect'. The commissioner added that he would like an opportunity of talking over the points which had been raised with his officers and it was agreed to adjourn the meeting to twelve-thirty the following afternoon.

When Wood returned on Thursday, accompanied now by General Sir Kerr Montgomery, the food officer, and R. S. Moon, the road commissioner, he repeated his guarantee that volunteers would not be allowed to handle food cargoes but refused to withdraw them completely. Instead, he proposed a system of dual control, with the volunteers working under official direction and not interfering in any jobs for which trade union labour was authorised by the strike committee. He also suggested that each side should appoint an officer to work in conjunction with his opposite number in supervising the work and dealing with any trouble which might arise. Montgomery stated that the utmost to which they could agree was that 'all men now doing their ordinary work should continue to do so' and Wood offered to clear the quayside entirely of volunteer lorry drivers. Flynn promised to put these suggestions fairly before the strike committee, adding that 'he would not be able personally to recommend the form of dual control proposed'. The committee endorsed Flynn's view and when Montgomery returned at 4.00 p.m. for an answer he was told that trade unionists could not be permitted to work under any form of dual control. Either all O.M.S. volunteers had to be withdrawn or the regular workers would stay out. Having reached stalemate in its negotiations with the commissioner, the strike committee decided that it had no alternative but to withdraw all permits. The feeling that it rather than the civil commissioner now controlled transport elated the strike committee and by Friday it was convinced that the success of the strike 'was completely assured. It was clear to everyone that the O.M.S. organisation was unable to cope with the task imposed upon it. The attitude of the population was favourable to the strikers and unfavourable to the Government. There were no disturbances, the trade unionists maintained an almost perfect discipline. There was no change from the ordinary except for the quietness in the streets and the absence of traffic'.

But, as usual, it was the Co-ops rather than the private traders who suffered in the general withdrawal of permits. The staffs of the retail societies ceased work to a man, while in Newcastle and Gateshead particularly, where picketing was least effective, private traders carried on much as before. 'There was no appreciable shortage of foodstuffs', reported the *Newcastle Journal* on Saturday, 'and prices seemed much as usual.' The strike committee recognised the difficulty the Co-ops were in and the retail societies in Newcastle and Gateshead were given permits for weekend deliveries of milk and bread. On Saturday the committee went further and authorised the release of all food supplies held by the retail societies. The Co-operative Wholesale Society urged that it, too, should be granted exemption: the committee promised to consider the request sympathetically but stressed that 'any general yielding on the question of removing the embargo on food supplies was at the moment completely out of the question'. The committee was reluctant to include the C.W.S. in the embargo and shared the opinion held by many of its counterparts that the T.U.C. was at fault in not reaching an understanding with the Co-operative movement before the strike began. The T.U.C.'s belated instructions on Monday that the Co-ops should be allowed to deliver only milk and bread to their members effectively ended the committee's discretionary powers to negotiate a more generous arrangement. The committee 'felt themselves bound to carry out the T.U.C. decisions to the letter no matter how many misgivings they might have' and the Northern Board of the C.W.S. was accordingly informed that the committee 'was impotent to afford them any further relief or to take any further steps towards the progressive realisation of that strategy which alone could guarantee nothing [anything?] more than a favourable draw for the strikers'.

From the N.U.D.A.W. offices in Newcastle Page Arnot co-ordinated Communist activities in the region, using members of the Young Communist League and other young Left-wing enthusiasts as couriers. 'By this means each day…it was possible', writes Page Arnot, 'to be at once in touch with the party in Newcastle and elsewhere, to receive reports and to have propaganda materials prepared, either (via the young volunteers) for the party or for the various daily meetings of the General Council at Burt Hall, which also had its own "courier" service: while by day and night the young miners and other motor-bicyclists of Blaydon sped over Durham county or up Northwards with whatever was necessary. The bike-less lads and lasses enrolled themselves in the mass pickets (200-strong at each of the two roads into Chopwell) which beset the Great North Road. Pickets used often to come and see me in Burt Hall with their problems (e.g. apparently unshatterable windscreens).' But the party's aim in the north-east went beyond picketing and propaganda. 'The intention was that the setting up of councils of action would enable the whole theatre of war from Tweed to Tees to be covered with a network of local councils. From these would arise a more revolutionary leadership, as things developed, than was possible from the ranks of local or district officials of trade unions.' It was hoped that such a leadership would emerge on Saturday 8 May, when delegates from eighty strike committees and councils of action in the north-east and from as far afield as Carlisle, Middlesbrough, and Workington convened at Gateshead Town Hall to hear a report from the joint strike committee. The committee made it clear, however, that it could accept instructions only from the T.U.C. or union executives and a federation linking the councils of action was not set up. The Communists had to nurse their disappointment while the conference devoted itself to more practical matters. Three issues dominated its deliberations: the failure of the Durham miners to send an official representative to the joint strike committee (they formed their own strike committee only two hours before the General Strike was called off); the absence of the *British Worker*; and the difficulties confronting the Co-ops.

Meanwhile, a garbled account of the strike committee's negotiations with the commissioner had been given to the House of Commons. On Thursday afternoon Martin Connolly, Labour M.P. for Newcastle East, outraged Tory members by declaring that the regional O.M.S. had 'entirely broken down, that the authorities have approached the trade unions and asked them to take over vital services, and that the trade unions have consented to do so on condition that all extra police, all troops, and all O.M.S. services shall be withdrawn. This has been done, and the city is going on all right'. Although most of these assertions were incorrect, the fact that the commissioner had made an approach to the strike committee caused the Government some embarrassment and not surprisingly it was denied by the Attorney-General. (It was denied again on Monday by Sir Harry Barnston, Comptroller of the Household, and Kingsley Wood stated much later that he had contacted officials of individual unions but not the Joint Strike Committee as such.) With further negotiations clearly out of the question, the strike committee feared that the authorities would resort to more drastic methods. In a phone call to Eccleston Square on Friday night, Flynn warned that force would be used against pickets or that serious incidents would be provoked in order to justify intervention by the armed forces. Events during the weekend seemed to bear out this warning. Trouble began on Saturday night when the police baton-charged a crowd of several thousand in Newcastle and made a large number of arrests. Dawson, who had arrived in the city at noon, informed the T.U.C. that 'The general situation is very good in this area, but there is a considerable danger of ugly incidents'.[15] There were further clashes on Sunday, and in a separate incident Will Lawther and Harry Bolton were arrested. By a suspiciously convenient chance, police escorting a food lorry happened to spot both men outside a pub. They were asked to help in distributing food and arrested, according to the police, when an argument began over permits. After a trial in which they were accused of establishing a 'reign of terror' in the district, they chose two months' imprisonment to the alternative of a £50 fine.

The T.U.C. Intelligence Committee noted on Sunday that the men were being 'restrained with difficulty' and the strike committee itself pointed out that its efforts to avoid provocation and maintain order had to be pursued without any sanction 'against disorder and overt violence on the part of the legally constituted authorities'. On Sunday night Dawson sent another personal report to London. 'The spirit of the strikers seems to be hardening and the only fear is that bitterness on their side and provocative action by the police may lead to some very unfortunate episodes.'[16] One such episode occurred on Monday afternoon when the engine and several coaches of the Edinburgh to Kings Cross Express were derailed passing over a section of sabotaged track at Cramlington, near Newcastle. Although no passengers were seriously hurt, several were taken to hospital and several more attempts were made to sabotage trains during the next few days. Violence did not end with the calling off of the strike. A large crowd which demonstrated outside Gateshead Police Court on 13 May during the trial of Lawther and Bolton was baton-charged by police and numerous arrests were made. Each side naturally blamed the other for starting the trouble. According to the account published on 15 May by the *Northern Light,* the demonstrators 'marched orderly into the town and settled themselves round about the police court to patiently await the result of the trial. This quiet gathering did not suit the police and one officer in particular did his best to cause trouble... Seeing what was brewing, and actually hearing some policemen say they wished to be given orders to charge the crowd, some of us did our best to keep order and succeeded after the decision of the court had been given in persuading the demonstrators to leave for home. They had proceeded some distance along Askew Road, on their way home, when a body of policemen, led by a well-known inspector and sergeant at their head, bearing the outward resemblance of gentlemen, went behind the peaceable and innocent procession with their brutally trained and uniformed bullies and belaboured people unmercifully'. The lie that it was the demonstrators who had attacked the police was 'exposed by the fact that not one policeman was injured, but a dozen or so of our men with wounds bore testimony to the brutality of the police'. The paper also carried specific allegations of violence against men held in custody and concluded that 'The lowest aim in life is to be a policeman. When a policeman dies he goes so low he has to climb up a ladder to get into hell, and even then he is not a welcome guest.'

By moving their duplicator to different premises each night, some-times hidden in the back of a maternity van, the staff of the *Northern Light* managed to keep up regular production. The paper's distributors, however, were frequently arrested and on 20 May Edward Wilson, a forty-year-old miner, appeared at Gateshead Police Court charged with contravening Section 21 of the Emergency Regulations by doing a certain act likely to cause disaffection among the civil population.[17] He had been arrested selling copies of the *Northern Light* for 15 May. According to counsel for the prosecution only one true statement was to be found in 'a deliberate chronicle of wicked falsehoods'—that every edition was eagerly awaited by the police. Ranging somewhat beyond his brief, counsel alleged that the crowd waiting outside the court during the trial of Lawther and Bolton the previous week was so hostile that 'the police had to send for reinforcements and to form their men up for a baton charge. There was this baton charge and it was a serious baton charge. Men were knocked out and so forth and others were locked up. These men used serious threats to the police, while his [counsel's] position, because he happened to be prosecuting in the case, was such that he had to close his office—which was a cowardly thing to force anyone to do—because he was simply carrying out his duties as a lawyer'. Those who behaved violently had to understand 'that no one would be allowed to over-ride the laws of this land; and if these men insisted in this course of action, so would the authorities persist in their course of action, and they intended to meet force with force'.

Selling copies of the *Northern Light* might not be violence, but clearly the council of action was 'resorting to this method of creating dissatisfaction amongst the civil population'. During the strike the police had been unable to find out where the paper was being printed so that they could 'raid the place and blot it out altogether in the same way as they hoped to be able to blot out this so-called council of action'. Counsel appealed to the court for the safety of the people of Chopwell, Blaydon, Ryton, and Spen, 'as there was no doubt about it that they were terrified to death' by the council of action. It was making their lives 'a perfect hell on earth' and should be 'stamped out'. At the outset, counsel for the prosecution stated that the defendant was a member of the 'Communist League', a contention promptly refuted by counsel for defence. Was the defendant a Bolshevist, inquired Sir Alfred Palmer, the presiding magistrate, or 'a Liberal, like myself?' His client, replied defence counsel, was a member of the Labour party and thought he was acting in a lawful manner. He had never been in a police court before and bore an unblemished character. After a short recess the Bench returned a unanimous verdict of guilty. Passing a sentence of three months with hard labour, Palmer commented that if he had had his own way he would have added a fine of £100. 'Why you and those who are associated with you don't go off to Russia I don't know... We don't want you...you are just a source of danger to the community and the sooner you make up your minds to either reform or get away, the better for all concerned.'

This trial and the police activity which preceded it suggest that the authorities decided on a much tougher line after Wood's failure to secure trade union co-operation. At the beginning of the week there had been only minor disturbances in Newcastle and on 4 May the Newcastle City Council had shown a token of its moderation by passing a resolution calling for a return to the status quo and resumption of the coal negotiations. It is reasonable to conclude, therefore, that the police received fresh instructions at the weekend. The motive is less easy to discern. If Connolly was correct in asserting that the Government organisation had lost control in Newcastle, this would certainly account for a new determination to smash the strike by force. But was he correct? One picture is drawn by the strike committee and the various strike journals; a totally different one is drawn by the region's three daily newspapers, which were all produced by blackleg labour and reflected strong Right-wing views. Neither can be relied on for an objective assessment of the situation. The increasingly energetic use of the police may have been a desperate attempt by the civil commissioner to break the stranglehold of the strike committee; it may have been calculated to avenge the committee's humiliating rejection of dual control; it may even have been part of a much wider official strategy, for more aggressive police behaviour was noted in many parts of the country during and after the weekend. Whatever the motive, the strike committee was in no mood to resist when it found that force was being used increasingly against its supporters. Resistance would have been uncomfortably close to revolution and revolution was for revolutionaries.

## Chapter Twelve

# A Struggle of Exhaustion

'Most people gloomy, but all uncompromising. General opinion that the fight would be short but violent. Bloodshed anticipated next week.'

Arnold Bennett, writing in his journal, after lunching at the Reform Club, on Wednesday, 5 May 1926.

'Before we are through, unless it is a quick finish, there is bound to be some outbreak of violence leading to stern and merciless suppression for the sake of law and order.'

Sir Philip Gibbs, writing in the *Philadelphia Evening Bulletin*, Wednesday, 5 May 1926.

'Already by the second day there have been ominous signs that this peaceful state of affairs is gradually giving way to a more dangerous temper. From various parts of the country incidents are reported which involve minor damage to property and in some cases in personal injury. Nothing that has happened so far is of serious consequence in itself, but is plain enough proof that every day the strike lasts the strain on the nerves will be greater, the number of incidents will grow and the danger to life and property become more serious ... Is this to be a struggle of exhaustion, like that of the Great War? If so, the symptoms of disorder which have already been noted can only lead in the end to rioting and bloodshed. A struggle of exhaustion on this scale can hardly end without scenes of violence on a scale of which for generations this country has had no experience.'

*Manchester Guardian Bulletin*, Thursday, 6 May 1926.

'The arm which is being served out to "Specials" and other volunteers is the handle of the "trench tool" which was so much used during the later part of the War.'

Hamilton Fyfe, writing in his diary on Sunday, 9 May 1926.

The incredulous comment of one French observer when he learned of the football match between strikers and police in Plymouth was,

'The British are not a nation, they are a circus'.[1] Dozens of similar diversions must have been as infuriatingly inexplicable to continental observers. The Mayor of Lewes put up the prize in a public billiard match between strikers and police. At Banbury joint concerts were arranged and both sides competed in a tug-of-war. At Norwich strikers and police organised a series of athletic matches under the auspices of the Chief Constable. In all of the eastern counties between London and the Humber, strike committees worked with police and civic leaders 'to keep the peace and organise recreations'. At Lincoln, where the Chief Constable was 'a consistent friend of Labour and absolutely refused the assistance of either military or mounted police', the strike committee provided all of the special constables recruited during the emergency. After marching along the Sussex coast from Newhaven to Seaford at the weekend, more than a thousand strikers 'passed a vote of confidence on the local police sergeant and his constables which was received with musical honours'. Bus strikers in Brighton presented their Chief Constable with a silver salver when the strike ended. Ilkeston Strike Committee found the local police 'very good and sooner assisted than interfered with us'. Leyton Strike Committee had a 'very pleasant relationship with the police' and Selby Strike Committee observed that 'Police assistance could not be improved upon; our strike police and local police worked in complete harmony'. At Yeovil, 'There was a good feeling exhibited by the town police throughout' and at Swindon the strike committee 'worked so well with the police that when our autocratic Mayor sent two tramcars on to the streets the police allowed our strike leaders to take charge of the situation. This was the only incident of excitement during the whole strike'. Bath Council of Action was 'complimented and thanked by Mayor and Chief Constable for maintaining perfect order; advised Mayor first day of strike to disband local specials as superfluosities'.

The explanation for this state of affairs was provided by John Anderson, who early on in the strike urged the Supply and Transport Committee to abandon any idea of using the police as blacklegs. 'How is public order being maintained today? Think of the mining villages of Yorkshire and Durham. In any such village there may be scores of miners and only one policeman. The miners are idle and many of them feel bitter. Street meetings are being held and angry speeches made. Yet there is no rioting, no violence against persons, no wrecking of property. Why not? I can tell you one cause. When at any such meeting tempers are rising and things are beginning to look ugly, the one policeman intervenes, and says: "Now then, Bill, that's about enough; time you went home to the missus."

And the meeting breaks up, because it is recognised that the police officer is not trying to help the "bosses", but is only doing his job of keeping the peace. Any impairment of the reputation of the police for impartiality is calculated to impair their power to maintain order.'[2] Much the same point was made retrospectively by William Paul, who organised propaganda for Lewisham Council of Action. 'The Left-wing members of our council were not averse to violence in theory, but they were Englishmen, too, with a constitutional aversion to it in practice, and certainly to the casual and unpredictable kind which results in broken heads and smashed windows, and alienates public opinion without furthering the cause. At heart, too, many of us were rather less revolutionary than we pretended to be and would have regarded arrest, no matter in what cause, as a disgrace which would cause the neighbours to talk.'[3] Tactful police behaviour and trade union restraint prevailed in most areas throughout the strike, but there is no basis for the myth that serious violence was lacking. In the working-class areas of London, Glasgow, and Edinburgh, and in many of the northern cities, vicious and often sustained rioting occurred.

Mass pickets gathered in the main roads of London's East End before seven o'clock on Tuesday morning and during the day scores of vehicles suspected of carrying goods or office workers to and from the City were stopped and quite frequently wrecked. Several vehicles were set alight, others thrown into the river. After a night of fierce street battles, thirty civilian casualties were taken to Poplar Hospital. One man allegedly died of his injuries early on Wednesday morning. According to the Associated Press report in Wednesday's *Philadelphia Ledger*, 'When the police intervened there was lively rioting. The constables rained blows on the rioters with their clubs and numerous disturbers of the peace were in bad shape when, with the aid of reinforcements, the police finally cleared the streets.' On Tuesday night there were also disturbances in Newcastle, and at Chester-le-Street, near Durham, mounted police broke up a crowd which had invaded the railway station. 'Despite rough play', noted the *British Gazette*, 'the crowd showed a sense of humour.' It is unlikely that any of the participants in Wednesday's events were amused. There were further baton charges in Poplar and Canning Town and violent clashes around the Blackwall Tunnel, where cars were smashed and set alight. In Hammersmith seven buses were wrecked, strikers and Fascists fought a pitched battle, and police made forty-three arrests. Attacks on trams and buses also led to sporadic clashes in Leeds, Nottingham, Manchester, Stoke, Liverpool, Glasgow and Edinburgh. In Sheffield four men were charged with unauthorised possession of a machine gun. On Thursday there were more clashes in the East End, and at the Elephant and Castle mounted police broke up an angry crowd after a bus, which was trying to dodge strike pickets, had crashed on to the pavement killing a man. In the same area another bus was set alight. The *Manchester Guardian Bulletin's* London correspondent reported that 'Things seem more serious today with the streets much emptier through the taxicab drivers joining the strike. There are more buses now, each with one or two policemen beside the driver. A new strikers' plan borrowed from the French Syndicalists has been tried this morning in Camberwell; some women laid their babies on the road in front of commercial vehicles and when the cars stopped, men jumped on the footboards and turned out the drivers and smashed the machinery of the cars.' There were renewed clashes in Nottingham when strikers tried to march on factories where work was still continuing and strikers and police fought pitched battles in Cardiff, Ipswich and Leeds. At Burnley strike pickets claimed that police brandished revolvers at them, 'which has not had a very good but rather an intimidating effect'; and at York police and strikers fought for possession of a level crossing. Further north rioting was more serious. A mob of 4,000 wrecked the goods and passenger stations at Middlesbrough and chained lorries to the railway line. While naval ratings struggled to clear the line, fighting also erupted at the bus terminus and outside a nearby police station. At Musselburgh, near Edinburgh, a number of passengers were hurt when their train was stoned and in Edinburgh itself twenty-four arrests were made after attacks on vehicles. In Aberdeen police baton-charged a crowd of more than 6,000 who were smashing the windows of passing buses and trams. Trouble started in the East End of Glasgow early on Thursday morning when 500 miners from Newton and Cambuslang tried to storm a tram depot housing student strike-breakers. Sporadic fighting and looting went on for most of the day. During Thursday night the rioting grew worse and a total of eighty-nine arrests was made.

On Friday there was fresh violence in Poplar, Ipswich, Cardiff and Middlesbrough and disturbances in Sheffield, Newark and Darlington. A mob of 1,500 demolished a brick wall in Wandsworth to obtain missiles and a member of the British Fascisti was almost lynched when he deliberately drove his van into a crowd of demonstrators on Wormwood Scrubbs, severely injuring a man. Further rioting erupted in Glasgow and Edinburgh. By midnight forty-eight arrests had been made in Glasgow and twenty-two in Edinburgh. In Hull nine people were hurt and a large number arrested after baton charges against a crowd interfering with volunteers offering their services at the City Hall. As rioting spread, trams were attacked and burned and the civil authorities appealed for help to the captain of the *Ceres*, the light cruiser responsible for protecting Hull Docks. While fifty of his men faced the crowd with rifles and fixed bayonets, the captain addressed them from the balcony of the City Hall. Explaining that it was his duty to safeguard the city's property, he warned that if another tram was attacked, he would man them all with naval ratings.[4] This appears to have been the only instance of direct military intervention against rioters.

Although most of the week's violence was sporadic and unorganised, it fed apprehensions in Pall Mall no less than in Eccleston Square. Lack of regular and reliable news also gave rise to a crop of melodramatic rumours. When Duff Cooper visited White's on Wednesday morning he found 'a lot of people discussing absurd rumours—one was that Winston had been assassinated'.[5] By Friday many were convinced that a Cabinet minister had at the least been seriously wounded; that certainly two and possibly four policemen had been killed; that troops had been forced to fire over the heads of rioters in Bermondsey; that armed blue-jackets were patrolling the corridors of the House of Commons; and that two divisions of the Red Army were on their way from Archangel to Wick. The General Council urged that 'no credence whatever should be given to the wild and malicious rumours, circulated probably with the idea of discrediting the workers in the public mind, of outbreaks of violence and similar disturbances'.[6] Even the *British Gazette* on Saturday felt bound to warn readers to 'Beware of Canards'. 'The spreading of rumours was found to be a useful weapon in the Great War, and many foolish people are trying to make use of this form of warfare today. Already the omnibus that has been thrown into the Thames is a familiar friend—sometimes it is Blackfriars Bridge, sometimes Waterloo, sometimes Hammersmith. Why not give this faithful friend a rest? Then there is the old yarn about the two policemen. They have already been killed in Bethnal Green, Battersea, Putney, Highgate and a few other districts. But they have not yet been absent from duty. Whatever alarming rumours you hear from either side, don't believe them. There are rumour-mongers of all sorts in various guises. Treat them with contempt.' There were few other rational appeals with which the editor of the *British Gazette* was associated. When he was not trying to slip material of a rather different kind past Davidson's blue pencil, Churchill was directing bellicose pleas at the Supply and Transport Committee. Samuel Hoare (later Lord Templewood), who sat on the Committee as Secretary of State for Air, has described the atmosphere of those meetings.[7] 'In the chair sat Joynson-Hicks, the very embodiment of a Victorian Home Secretary, frock-coated, eloquent, determined to rise to an historic occasion. On one side of him were Churchill and Birkenhead, no less conscious of the magnitude of the crisis, and bent upon bringing it to an end by bold and dramatic action. On the other side was John Anderson, an outstanding Civil Servant as yet unknown beyond Whitehall, but already showing the solid qualities of imperturbable resolution and sound judgement that were afterwards to distinguish his great career. From the first meeting of the Committee it was evident that he very well understood what should be done, and that, if left to himself, he intended to do it.' Churchill, of course, was determined that Anderson should not be left to himself, but quickly discovered that the Permanent Under-Secretary was not to be overawed. When pickets tried to prevent newsprint from reaching the *British Gazette's* offices, Churchill was outraged and demanded the immediate dispatch of Foot Guards armed with ball cartridges. 'I would beg the Chancellor of the Exchequer', retorted Anderson, 'to stop talking nonsense.' Apparently disconcerted, the Chancellor stopped.[8]

Prior to the strike there had been grave doubts in Whitehall and Westminster about Joynson-Hicks's capacity for rational conduct during a crisis. Known in official as well as unofficial circles as 'Mussolini Minor', Jix had a record for reckless utterances which rivalled even that of Churchill's.* According to Davidson, however, the Home Secretary 'Not only handled the Committee with supreme skill, but showed that he really understood his own countrymen. Jix was never rattled, was most business like and adopted a policy with regard to the police which it is not too strong to say was superb. Winston really acted as lead in Jix's boots'.[9] Jix entirely supported the view that it was the job of the police to deal with disturbances and that troops should be used only as a last resort. His main consideration was to ensure that sufficient numbers of auxiliaries should be available to back up the regular police when

* In 1908 Churchill, who was then a Liberal, had been beaten by Jix at a by-election in Manchester. Speaking at a dinner given in his honour by the Maccabeans, a venerable Jewish society, Jix declared: 'I could say you were a delightful people, that Jews were delightful opponents, that I am very pleased to receive the opposition of the Jewish community, and that I am, in spite of all, your humble and obedient servant. I could say that, but it wouldn't be true in the slightest degree. I have beaten you thoroughly and soundly and I am no longer your servant!' On a later occasion, Jix stated, 'We did not conquer India for the benefit of the Indians. I know it is said at missionary meetings that we conquered it to raise the level of the Indians. That is cant. We conquered India as the outlet for the goods of Great Britain. We conquered India by the sword and by the sword we should hold it.'

necessary. Although there were already 98,000 specials enrolled throughout the country and 11,000 in London alone when the strike began, the Home Secretary wanted still more. In a wireless broadcast on Wednesday night he appealed 'to all who are fit and strong to offer their services as special constables by going to the Police Station nearest to where they live. At the Police Station they will find a magistrate in attendance ready to swear them in. By becoming a special constable, they place their services at the call of the Government for the purpose of ensuring the maintenance of law and order, and the freedom and safety of the individual citizen'. The large London business institutions, he added, were answering with great vigour. 'From the Stock Exchange I am promised 1,400 or more special constables, and I am assured that I shall get a proportionate response from the Baltic, Corn Exchange, Lloyd's, Commercial Sale rooms and other big markets.'

The appeal was greeted with a mixture of derision and alarm by the *British Worker*. On Thursday, in a front-page 'Reply to Jix', it asserted that there was 'no need for the panic which the Home Secretary seems intent on provoking. The strikers are standing firm, and they mean to conduct themselves in a disciplined, quiet and orderly manner'. By Friday, however, the Cabinet was convinced that 'the first essential in the present situation' was more protection for those who were working and that 'the intimidation carried out and threatened' called for an expansion of security forces 'on a considerable scale'.[10] Troops were still to be used only in a serious emergency and neither Reservists nor Territorials were to be mobilised. Instead, more specials were to be called for and a new, full-time Civil Constabulary Reserve was to be set up, recruited exclusively from members of the Territorial Army, Officers' Training Corps and 'Ex-military men who can be vouched for at Territorial Army Unit Headquarters'. Members of the new force were to wear civilian clothes, but would be issued with armlets, truncheons and steel helmets, and the force would be 'so organised that members of the same Territorial Army unit who enrol for service will serve together and under their own officers'. It was arranged for recruiting to begin on Monday at T.A. drill halls throughout the City and County of London. On Friday night the Home Secretary broadcast another appeal for special constables. 'The matter', he stressed, 'is urgent; the sooner we can get a strong, indeed an enormous force, the sooner can I provide protection to individuals, particularly throughout London. May I say, therefore, I want 50,000 special constables by Monday morning. Over 20,000 have already enlisted. Surely there must be another 30,000 men in London willing and eager to serve their country for a few days or even weeks in this crisis. Even if things are quiet, I want men to roll up and be sworn in. Even if not used they would afford a steadying influence. It may be that men have a right to withhold their labour, but it is absolutely certain that in a free country men have a right to work if they wish to do so. I do not wish to be an alarmist, but naturally all the attacks on omnibuses, lorries, vans and so forth are reported to me. In the aggregate the number is small, but the law of England provides than no single man should be molested in the performance of his duties.'

The much tougher line taken at Friday's Cabinet meeting was aggressively reflected in the pages of Saturday's *British Gazette*. It was this issue which carried Churchill's provocative announcement to the armed forces that any action taken by them in aid of the Civil Power would receive full Government support. The situation, the paper declared, was becoming more intense 'and the climax is not yet reached. Orders have been sent by the leaders of the Railway and Transport Unions to do their utmost to paralyse and break down the supply of food and the necessaries of life. Intimidation both by disorderly crowds and picketing has occurred in many places, and may soon occur in many more. His Majesty's Government have directed all authorities to repress and overcome these criminal obstructions'. The General Council was accused of 'an organised attempt...to starve the people and to wreck the State', and the paper warned that 'the legal and constitutional aspects are entering upon a new phase'. This was certainly a veiled hint at the Cabinet's decision to enact punitive legislation against the unions.

A vital decision was also taken by the Supply and Transport Committee on Friday. For three days the London docks had been at a complete standstill, with traders unwilling to risk their trucks at the hands of the pickets who continually crowded the area. Strong protests were made by civil commissioners whose regions depended upon London for food supplies. Indeed, by Friday food shortages in the South Midlands were so acute that Lord Winterton, the local commissioner, threatened to resign unless his lorries were guaranteed adequate protection on their journeys to the docks. In London itself only forty-eight hours' supply of flour was left.[12] For practical reasons it was therefore essential that the docks should be reopened. Politically, it was equally important for the Government to demonstrate that it was capable of moving supplies from the area. It was clear, however, that police would be violently resisted and the committee resolved to break the strikers' blockade with troops. It rejected Churchill's demand that machine guns should be placed

along the whole of the route from the East End to the Hyde Park
depot and that tanks as well as armoured cars should accompany the
food lorries.[13] Saturday's display of military strength was nonethe-
less formidable. Each of the 105 lorries which set out from Hyde Park
at four-thirty that morning was loaded with Grenadier Guardsmen,
and twenty armoured cars, crewed by men of the Royal Tank Corps,
made up the escort. While the convoy lumbered through the deserted
streets, 500 volunteers, including a party led by Lord Burghley, the
Master of Magdalene College, Cambridge, were towed by lighter from
Westminster Pier to London docks. At 8.00 a.m. they began loading
lorries with flour under the protection of Lewis guns and two fully
armed Guards battalions. The convoy had been timed to begin its
return journey at 10.30 a.m., but an hour-and-a-half later the Supply
and Transport Committee was still waiting anxiously for news of its
departure. 'Gloomy forebodings had been laughed aside without
much conviction', Davidson has recalled, 'when a piece of paper was
put in front of Philip C-L [Cunliffe-Lister, later Lord Swinton,
President of the Board of Trade]. He read it: he smiled; he held it so
that I could read it as I was sitting next to him. He then threw it
across to Jix, who announced that he had just been informed that
the head of the convoy had left the docks about twenty minutes ago,
and that the convoy had been received with enthusiasm and cheering
as it proceeded on its journey.' Enthusiasm was less evident at the
outset. 'The sullen mass of strikers who congregated after dawn',
reported the *New York World* correspondent, 'were awed by the
military and permitted most of the moving on to be done by mounted
police, unarmed as always, but backed this time by enough artillery
to kill every living thing in every street in the neighbourhood.' But
as the head of the two-mile column, with its escort of mounted police,
armoured cars and cavalry emerged into the City, large crowds
gathered to cheer it on. The B.B.C. was put in mind of the Lord
Mayor's procession. To the *British Gazette* the convoy looked 'like
the commissariat of a victorious army'. A second convoy of 170
lorries loaded up and returned to Hyde Park just after midday and
on Sunday 267 lorries made the journey. Although an increasing
number of vehicles went to the docks without escort after the weekend, food was still not being moved in sufficient quantities.
Normally, foodstuffs were unloaded at the docks and floated by
lighters to the wharves, but the strikers would not allow the tugs to
operate. Colonel Moore-Brabazon (later Lord Brabazon), special
commissioner for London docks, appealed to Lord Beatty, First Lord
of the Admiralty: would he allow food tugs to fly the White
Ensign? Beatty consented and 17,000 tons of perishable foodstuffs

were delivered to the wharves within 48 hours. 'Such is the power of the Navy,' Brabazon later commented. 'John Jones's tug could be wrecked, but to touch anything flying the White Ensign—that could never be done.'[14]

The Government's calculated show of military force helped to reduce subsequent violence around London docks, but had little effect elsewhere. On Saturday there were baton charges in Wandsworth, Battersea, Lambeth, Deptford, Paddington and Camden Town. Outside London there were also ugly scenes. At Sidcup eleven strikers were injured during disturbances. Plymouth Corporation's attempt to run a skeleton tram service on Saturday morning led to clashes between strikers and mounted police and the service was withdrawn after a warning from the local strike committee that it 'would no longer be responsible for the good order of our people'. Clashes occurred at Southsea and Swansea, and at Nottingham water hoses were turned on strikers attempting to march on the Players' tobacco factory. Further north the violence was once again more serious and sustained. At Walton-le-Dale, near Preston, police baton-charged strikers interfering with buses and shots were fired at a train passing below a bridge at Crewe. In Preston itself a mob of 5,000 tried to storm a police station to rescue a striker arrested during earlier attacks on buses. After three baton charges local police had to call for reinforcements from the Lancashire Constabulary. Fighting lasted for a further two hours before the mob was finally dispersed. At York police baton-charged a crowd who were also trying to rescue an arrested comrade. Fresh disturbances, which began in Hull on Saturday afternoon, continued until the early hours of Sunday, and resulted in twenty-five arrests and forty-one hospital admissions. At Middlesbrough renewed fighting broke out around the railway station at 11.00 p.m. and went on for three hours. In Newcastle two baton charges and twenty-five arrests had been made by midnight. In Edinburgh magistrates ordered all pubs to close after 3.00 p.m. and the city had a fairly quiet night. Glasgow was less peaceful. 'The struggle', reported Monday's *Times*, 'was of the wildest description; pots and pans, iron bars, pickheads and hammers were used as missiles, but fortunately no police were injured. Over sixty arrests were made.' On Sunday rioting broke out in the city for the fourth consecutive night, bringing the total of arrests since Thursday to 269.

There was trouble in other parts of Scotland on Sunday. At Anstruther, East Fife, police made three baton charges to disperse strikers obstructing a railway line, and at Tranent, near Edinburgh, local police besieged in their own station had to be rescued by colleagues from other parts of East Lothian. There were fierce clashes in London on Sunday. At Camden Town forty strikers were taken to hospital after police broke up an attack on a bus. There were baton charges at Cricklewood and at Paddington, where sixty-two arrests were made. During fighting at Nine Elms railway depot a police sergeant was struck on the head with a hammer and a special constable stabbed in the back. Railway lines were also sabotaged in several areas during the weekend, though the only injuries occurred in Monday's derailment at Cramlington. On Friday an engine was derailed at Bridlington owing to interference with points and on Sunday bolts were removed from a section of track near a level crossing at Egham. According to the *British Gazette's* account, the missing bolts were noticed before the arrival of a train two days later, which says rather more for the effectiveness of the strikers than for that of the saboteurs. In fact, the hazards of riding on trains driven by unskilled volunteers were great enough in themselves. In six separate major crashes during the last week of the strike, four people were killed and more than thirty injured. On Monday the *Manchester Guardian Bulletin* placed the week's violence in some perspective by reporting that the casualties involved were far less than those arising out of Sunday's Joan of Arc celebration riots in Paris. That day's issue of the *British Gazette,* however, carried yet another appeal from the Home Secretary for special constables. 'Give the Government enough…to enable me to allot two to every vehicle that is, or thinks it is, in danger, thus releasing the regular police for perhaps sterner work. Give us men in such numbers that we may have mobile forces of young and vigorous special constables available in any London area where trouble is anticipated. Give us this and there will be little fear of serious trouble.'

Prompted by a class instinct as powerful as that which motivated the strikers, well-fed young men from the fashionable clubs, universities and business institutions responded to Jix's appeals in their thousands. At White's on Wednesday, Duff Cooper found half-a-dozen of the members in full police uniform, including the Honourable Lionel Tennyson, who had the rank of inspector. Sir John 'Buffles' Milbanke looked 'very smart as a sergeant'. The ninth Duke of Rutland, Duff Cooper's brother-in-law, was a special constable 'and works every night from six to nine'. On Monday Duff Cooper went to Buck's and found that 'They are all becoming special constables. Tom Trower was in the highest spirits, having become a whole-time constable and thus escaped from his office'. Others who responded to the call were Dr Arlington, the headmaster of Eton, and fifty of his assistants, and the 85-year-old Earl of Meath, founder of the Empire Day Movement, who announced, 'I box every morning and am still able to tackle a man'. The vicars of Seaview and St Helen's, Isle of Wight, added police truncheons to God's arsenal. In the South Midlands Lord Winterton was surrounded by young men imploring him to send them to Glasgow as specials so that they could 'have a crack at them dirty Bolshies on the Clyde'. Some of Jix's recruits were, like Graham Greene, impelled 'More from curiosity than from any wish to support the Establishment'.[15] Greene's task was to parade the length of Vauxhall Bridge every morning with a regular policeman.

> There was a wonderful absence of traffic, it was a beautiful, hushed London that we were not to know again until the blitz, and there was the excitement of living on a frontier, close to violence. Armoured cars paraded the streets, and just as during the blitz certain areas, Bloomsbury and Euston among them, were more unhealthy than others like Hampstead and St John's Wood, so Camberwell and Hammersmith were now considered more danger-ous than the City. Our two-man patrol always ceased at the south end of Vauxhall Bridge, for beyond lay the enemy streets where groups of strikers stood outside the public houses. A few years later my sympathies would have lain with them, but the great depression was still some years away: the middle-class had not yet been educated by the hunger-marchers. On the side of the Establish-ment it was a game, a break in the monotony of earning a secure living, at its most violent the atmosphere was that of a rugger match played against a team from a rather rough council school which didn't stick to the conventional rules. 'I'm almost sorry now that it's over', I wrote home, 'as we had as much free beer as we wanted at the office while it was on'.

By Tuesday 11 May, 200,000 specials were enrolled in the provinces and in London alone 40,000 were on duty, together with 18,000 steel-helmeted members of the new Civil Constabulary Reserve. The Cabinet's decision that specials instead of troops should back up the regular police was certainly wise, but the scale of recruitment, particularly in London, was out of all proportion to any violence which the authorities could reasonably have anticipated. For scores of thousands of specials there was little to do but ride as escort on the occasional bus or lorry or wander about the streets in police caps and plus fours. On Sunday Fyfe observed that 'The specials are becoming a joke, even among people who are on the side of the Cabinet. It is so obvious there is nothing for them to do. What did those who made such desperate efforts to enrol them think there would be for them to do?' The Home Office could probably have provided a three-fold answer: to reassure the general public; to disconcert the T.U.C. and the strikers, and to deal with any serious breakdown in public order. Where specials were used against strikers, however, they more often provoked trouble than deterred it. Their obvious class-consciousness, lack of tact and frequent indiscipline made them a dubious asset to the regular forces of law and order. In an assessment of police activities which it made after the strike, the T.U.C. Intelligence Committee observed that 'The worst feature was the wholesale enrolment, especially in London, of special constables, many of whom were irresponsible persons likely to create trouble. They were, unfortunately, provocative, and it says much for the discipline of the movement that collisions between the strikers and the police were relatively infrequent. Speaking generally, the areas which relied entirely upon the local police without any other assistance, passed through the crisis without any serious untoward incidents. In Liverpool, for example, where large numbers of dockers and others were on strike, and where disturbances of the peace might easily have occurred, neither special constabulary nor military were employed in the town and order was maintained. [The Fascists recruited as specials were apparently never used.] The employment of special constables created a situation similar to that which prevailed in Dublin in the early days of the Black and Tans.' This judgment was wholeheartedly endorsed by G. K. Chesterton. 'There are many things we should like to know about the free hand given to "specials" during the recent crisis. We should like to know, for example, how many of them had seen service in Ireland as Black and Tans, and if any person in authority knew that they proposed to serve the English strikers as they had once served Irishmen. We know that the ruling classes had determined on a Civil War, but we should like to know how far the police were prepared to go in helping them.'[16]

The comparison with the Black and Tans is perhaps an exaggeration, though the T.U.C. received much evidence of irresponsible and often brutal behaviour by specials. Sunday's fighting at Nine Elms railway depot, in which a special was stabbed, was almost certainly provoked by the police themselves. In a protest to the T.U.C., W. Wright, the local N.U.R. secretary, explained that congestion occurred each morning between 10.00 a.m. and 12.00 a.m. when union members went to their headquarters in Wandsworth Road to sign on for strike pay. 'On more than one occassion during this congestion baton charges have taken place, but what aggravates the men most is the sudden arrival of irresponsible youths called specials in motor cars, who jump out and commence clashing about with their batons without any discretion whatever. Several of our members have been batoned in this manner and a few have been arrested.' To his own union Wright submitted a detailed account of a clash which had occurred on Friday.

Whilst a small crowd of my members were waiting outside my committee rooms in Wandsworth Road they saw a railway lorry. This naturally upset the men who stopped it from passing. I heard of it in the committee rooms and went to where the lorry was. The police appealed to the men not to cause a disturbance and so did I and was thanked by the police afterwards. After the lorry drove away the men stood about in groups and I with them in a perfectly orderly manner. Half-an-hour afterwards a covered lorry drove up from which alighted two sergeants and about fifty constables. Without the slightest provocation they drew their batons and on the word to charge being given they unmercifully belaboured men, women and children, injuring many. It was a mercy that I moved my head in time or I should have been killed, and I was fortunate enough to receive only a severe blow on the shoulder from a constable's truncheon. Shortly afterwards, a motor ambulance arrived on the scene, but the injured had been removed to hospital. I hope I never witness again such a terribly brutal scene... I am very much afraid after what has happened the men will arm themselves and as there are about twenty thousand on strike in this neighbourhood, should the police again attempt such a thing it will be them taken to the mortuary and not the hospital.

On Saturday Tilbury strike committee reported: 'Trouble certainly has been experienced in the district, but we find it is entirely through provocative action on the part of special police who were convoys to oil tankers bound for the oil wharves. It appears that when passing these pickets these police flourished revolvers and sticks, accompanying these acts by unseemly gestures, and thus aroused resentment. Further, they were either driving very carelessly or they intentionally skirted our pickets with the result that three men were injured. The report of this "accident" spread and a huge crowd collected. On the return journey reprisals were taken against these police, *not by our pickets* but by the crowd and a wholesale disturbance were [*sic*] created with dire results to these police.' The neighbouring Strike Committee at Stanford-le-Hope reported that specials accompanying a convoy of tanks 'made grimaces and held up truncheons' as they passed pickets. 'This was followed by the leading car swerving to make men move who were standing in the road. Later two youths riding on their cycles were overtook [sic] by the convoy and a blue car number 2112 broke from the line of column, swerved across the cyclists and a special pushed one causing the...cyclists to fall into the hedge. On the return of the convoy, the crowd lost its temper and James Partridge was arrested.' On Monday there was an angry Commons row over the behaviour of specials, with Labour members denouncing them as 'blackguardly hooligans' and Tory members defending them against 'unfounded charges likely to prejudice the public'.

From the weekend the regular police also adopted a much tougher attitude. The T.U.C. Intelligence Committee assessment noted that

At the beginning of the strike the attitude of the regular police called for no comment. In many places, the relations between the police and the strikers were all that could be desired. In some towns the police and the strikers were on the friendliest terms, football matches being arranged and the police taking the initiative in promoting sports and entertainments. Towards the end of the first week, however, the reports which came to hand indicated some change in the attitude of the police. The police tended to become rather more rigorous and less conciliatory. No doubt, incidents had occurred, many of them resulting from the actions of hooligans quite unconnected with the strike, which led the police to adopt sterner measures, but it would not be surprising to learn that the Government was implicated in the more aggressive policy... During the first two or three days of the strike there did not appear to have been many arrests, but by the weekend arrests began to take place, and in the last day or two of the stoppage, took place in considerable numbers.

It is possible that the police were acting on fresh instructions issued after Friday's Cabinet meeting, though individual police authorities showed an emphatic reluctance to take orders from either Whitehall or the civil commissioners. Chief Constables resented the threat to their traditional autonomy, regarding even police who accompanied food convoys from other counties as encroachers.[17] It is probable, therefore, that the much tougher police tactics evident at the end of the first week were due as much to sore feet and short tempers as to Home Office directives.

On Friday Birmingham strike committee alleged that the police were taking an 'autocratic and unjustifiable attitude' and a deputation met the Lord Mayor to urge 'in the interest of peace, that definite instructions might be issued to restrain the activities of the police against people in the streets'. Reporting from the city after the weekend, W. A. Robson, Josiah Wedgwood, and Kingsley Martin stated that complaints of undue severity were being made against superintendents 'but not against constables, with whom there appeared to be good feeling... The Lord Mayor of Birmingham is well-known to be Labour in sympathy and has on one or two occasions protested effectively against undue police interference or excessive severity. He has incurred the enmity of the more bitter section of the employers... The Lord Mayor's views are shared by only a minority of the City Council'. A T.U.C. speaker reported that Friday's baton charges in Hull were 'without slightest provocation' and that in Saturday's disturbances 'men, women and children were scattered by foot and mounted police. Many people injured. At the busiest shopping time when the maximum number of people were in the centre of the city, two trams were brought out. The crowd simply looked on out of curiosity when suddenly a large force of police attacked them right and left with batons while mounted police rode into the crowd.' Paddington strike committee urged the T.U.C. to secure the removal of the divisional mounted police commander. 'On Saturday he was driving his horse on to the footways amongst the crowds of very orderly people and terrorising them to such an extent that a deputation of private people have waited on the local superintendent.' Before Sunday's outbreak of violence in Cricklewood the T.U.C. was informed that 'from the beginning of the dispute, trade union leaders [here] have offered the police authorities every possible assistance in maintaining order and have at all times urged the men affected by the dispute to do nothing that would be calculated to cause a breach of the peace. This advice has been accepted loyally by the men and until the police adopted a provocative attitude there was no cause for complaint. During the last day or two, however, the police authorities have adopted a different method. They have paraded large numbers of police without any apparent reason and men have been arrested for no apparent cause'. A resolution was forwarded to the T.U.C. on Monday from Plumstead strike committee protesting at the 'unwarrantable attacks upon our members in various parts of the surrounding districts by the police which have resulted in injuries and arrests'. It was alleged that police had forced their way into the homes of two strikers, batoning one and batoning the wife of the other. 'We feel it our duty', added the committee, 'to bring these happenings before the mass of people in this wonderful nation of ours.'

Only minor disturbances were reported on Monday, but on Tuesday there were violent clashes in Mansfield, Darlington, Wolverhampton, Newcastle, and Gateshead. A T.U.C. dispatch rider reported from Mansfield that the police were 'highly provocative and maltreating women'. The T.U.C. was also informed from Darlington that 'There had been no violence or rioting in any sense and no warning given' before police baton-charged. On Wednesday, the day on which the T.U.C. called off the strike, police made several baton charges against a thousand miners holding up traffic in the Doncaster area. More than eighty were arrested. During Wednesday evening the Poplar police apparently decided to seek recompense for their week's labours. Local Labour leaders were addressing a meeting of 500 dockers outside Poplar Town Hall at 9.00 p.m. when a police tender suddenly swerved into the road and raced through the crowd, injuring a number of people. When the tender stopped at the end of the road thirty police jumped out, doubled back and baton-charged the crowd. While the injured were still trying to drag themselves away a second baton charge was made. A total of twenty-five casualties was treated at hospitals in the borough, including a local clergyman who approached police with an upheld crucifix. Shortly after this incident, police with drawn truncheons stormed into the district headquarters of the N.U.R. in Poplar High Street, batoning anyone unfortunate enough to be within striking distance. The Mayor of Poplar, who was in the building playing billiards at the time, was admitted to hospital with serious head injuries. Drunken specials were also accused of numerous assaults in Poplar on Wednesday evening and of wrecking three public houses in the area.

Of the 3,149 prosecutions arising out of the strike, 1,760 related not to acts of violence at all but to acts of 'incitement' under the Emergency Powers Act. The courts invariably took a stern view of such offences. A Lambeth tram cleaner was fined £5 for shouting, 'We want the revolution'; a striker at Farnworth, near Bolton, received a month's imprisonment for tearing down a Government poster; another in north London was given six weeks with hard labour for telling a crowd that the Liverpool police were on strike; a Communist found chalking 'seditious' slogans on a pavement at Castleford was goaled for two months with hard labour and fined £200; at Penrith the local secretary of the National Union of General Workers went to prison for three months with hard labour for issuing a leaflet urging workers not to become special constables.*

---

* David Kirkwood, one of the Clydeside Brigade, infuriated Tory M.P.s by declaring that if the country had treated his wife as it had the miners' wives, he would blow up the whole House of Commons. Challenged by Joynson-Hicks to

Most charges brought under the Act concerned the production, distribution or even mere possession of literature which might contribute to sedition or disaffection among the armed forces or civilian population. One of the many rumours sweeping the country was that the Welsh Guards had mutinied and been confined to barracks; its reappearance in strike bulletins was a fairly common reason for suppression and imprisonment. Many of the most militant publications, however, including the Communist *Workers' Bulletin,* took the precaution of changing addresses each night and managed to carry on throughout the strike. Unable to discover where the *Workers' Bulletin* was being produced, the police had to content themselves with charging Marjorie Pollitt, the paper's publisher. Possibly because the final hearing of her case did not come up until after the strike, Mrs Pollitt was simply required to pay a £50 fine with costs. A much more typical sentence of two months imprisonment was imposed on a Manchester businessman found in possession of copies of the *Workers' Daily.* On 10 May police raided the offices of Birmingham strike committee, charging all twenty members of the committee with publishing a false statement. The statement, which had appeared that day in the local strike bulletin edited by John Strachey, was to the effect that the Government had been defeated in a debate on the Emergency Powers Act. Since the defendants were able to show that they themselves had been genuinely misled by a false message delivered to the Birmingham N.U.R., ten only were required to pay light fines, eight were bound over and two were discharged.

Incautious speeches incurred the risk of high penalties. At Saturday's May Day rally in Hyde Park Shapurji Saklatvala, the Communist M.P. for North Battersea, called on 'the army boys' to 'revolt now and refuse to fight, and then they will be the real saviours of their homes and the workers. I want navy boys to march behind every English housewife when she goes out to purchase food, and I want the army and navy really to protect the people instead of the rogues and thieves of the master classes'. Such 'curious language' earned Saklatvala two months in gaol. For a similar speech Pontefract magistrates sentenced Isobel Brown, a young Communist schoolteacher who offered 'Moscow, Soviet Russia' as her last permanent address, to three months imprisonment. A Liverpool

repeat this statement outside the House, Kirkwood did so at Cloan, near Sheffield, and was summonsed. He repeated the offensive words for the benefit of the court – in broad Scots dialect. 'But at Cloan it was English he spoke,' protested the police constable. Kirkwood was fined £25.[18]

Communist who told an open-air meeting that troops stationed at Chelsea Barracks and Aldershot had refused to entrain for mining areas and that all transport in the East End of London had been stopped by the workers in spite of repeated baton charges by mounted police, was also gaoled for three months. The police naturally paid close attention to Communist party activities. Raids on its London and provincial offices were frequent and some 1,200 of its members were brought before the courts,[19] a fact which certainly pleased the party quite as much as it did the Government.

Less obvious precautions were also taken by the authorities. Soldiers in civilian clothes were sent to some areas to mingle with the strikers and report on the situation[20] and special branch officers were undoubtedly involved in similar operations. Several strike committees suspected that they were the targets of *agents provocateurs*. Westminster Strike Committee, for instance, was convinced that the mysterious sympathiser who offered one of their bulletin vendors a box of ammunition was a police agent. At Lewisham the suspicions of the council of action were aroused by a man named Johnstone, who was local secretary of the Unemployed Workers' Committee Movement.[21] When Johnstone committed suicide a few months later, both his wife and his mistress signed sworn affidavits that he had, indeed, been a paid police informer and that he had killed himself when his weekly wage was cut off by the secret service.

On Sunday 9 May, two men in plain clothes claiming to be detectives entered and searched Arthur Cook's London hotel room while he was away for the day. No authority was shown for the search and Cook was not aware that it had taken place until he was told by the chambermaid. During the first few days of the strike the T.U.C. accumulated considerable evidence that letters addressed to Eccleston Square were being opened. On Saturday it was also informed that censorship of incoming and outgoing telegrams had been imposed. On the same day dispatch riders were instructed to wire all subsequent messages in code. Where strike arrangements were working well, the code word 'objective' was to be used; where arrangements were indifferent, the code word was to be 'subjective'; bad organisation was to be indicated by 'perspective'; good spirit by 'respected'; moderate spirit by 'constitution'; and bad spirit by 'challenge'. On Tuesday 11 May, dispatch riders received a further set of instructions from H. H. Elvin, chairman of the T.U.C. General Purposes Committee. 'I have found that a large number of telegrams ...have reached this office... From Wednesday 12 May please do not send telegrams, but when important events or changes in the situation have taken place, which were not known, as far as you are aware, at the T.U.C. at the time of your departure, you are immediately to telephone.' Elvin added a warning that T.U.C. telephones were undoubtedly being tapped and appended an elaborate list of fifty-two additional code words which could be used to describe any situation from blacklegging on the railways to troops firing at crowds. The code word for police was 'beauty'; for baton charges, 'beautify'; for troops firing on crowds, 'beautifully'. Strike committees were to be described as 'sweats'; strike committees under arrest as 'sweated'; police in charge of strike premises as 'sweat beauty'. How long it would have taken the authorities to break this ingenious code is a matter for speculation. In the event, they did not need to try: twenty-four hours after issuing the code, the General Council of the T.U.C. called off the strike.

# Chapter Thirteen

# *Liberals To The Left and Liberals To The Right*

'Somehow, in spite of general political agreement, I always feel slightly repelled by [John Simon]. An affection of cordiality which hasn't much behind it, great volubility in talking about what interests him and no attempt to talk about what interests you. An appearance of deference with no real desire to consult, except in so far as may be needful to find out what line you mean to take. Intellectually a Liberal without much of the stuff of it…he is second in command [to Asquith] and he is playing for the succession. He ought not to under-rate Lloyd George, whose star is at present under eclipse, but who may yet find himself.'

C. P. Scott, writing in his diary, 29 January 1923.

'John Simon is doing very well, and working very strenuously… He means to "get there" if he can!'

A. C. Murray to Lord Reading, 7 March 1923.

'The Labour people are pleased with [Lloyd George]. He has proved more of a friend to them than Ramsay MacDonald, who got cold feet, or even J. H. Thomas, who showed up very badly, and who [David] thinks is broken as a result of the strike. When D. spoke in the house the first week of the strike, the Labour people cheered him. Hartshorn overheard Ramsay MacDonald say to those next to him, "There they go, the b… fools, cheering him again'. D. is pursuing a definite policy, and the strike had helped him in forwarding it, though it has had the effect of making him temporarily unpopular in the country, whereas there is no doubt that Baldwin has temporarily made strides. D.'s idea is to go definitely towards the *Left*, and gradually to co-ordinate and consolidate all the progressive forces in the country, against the Conservative and reactionary forces. Thus he will eventually get all sane Labour as well as Liberalism behind him.'

Frances Stevenson, writing in her diary, 15 May 1926.

'We have read with much enjoyment the account of a new split in the Liberal party... Even Lloyd George's defection in 1915 could not have seriously weakened a party with a philosophy and a policy. It had neither, and his defection knocked the bottom out of it. The splits in the Liberal party since then have been nothing more than the attempts of certain individuals to cast loose from the sinking ark. But Mr George has been concerned about his next destination; he wanted to cling to the ark, if possible, until his dove came back with an olive branch. The Land Bill dove found no land, and did not return. The strike-speech dove may be more fortunate. It seems that Mr George has hopes; and has been clever enough to give the impression that he is being cast out of the party because he espoused the cause of the workers. Very neat indeed! But does Labour want him?'

*GK's Weekly*, 29 May 1926.

'The occasion of the split is admirably suited to Lloyd George's claim to be a democratic leader; Asquith and Grey pronounced in favour of the Government; he argued in favour of the men. Supposing Lloyd George were to go on the stump advocating the policy of a living wage obtained by state control of capitalist enterprise, and supposing he were incidentally to come over to the Labour party, what would happen then? Philip Snowden would certainly welcome him and he might get a following not only among Liberal and non-political electors, sick of the Government, but also within the Labour movement itself... Some time in 1919 Sidney wrote an article for the *New Republic* suggesting such a possible development of Lloyd George's career... It may still come true and it will not be the Left-wing trade unionists who will object—to them Lloyd George may seem preferable to Mac-Donald, Thomas, or even Henderson, as the exponent of a forward, perhaps of a demagogic policy. He has also a money chest; he might bring over brains.'

Beatrice Webb, writing in her diary, 31 May 1926.

While MacDonald and the leaders of the Parliamentary Labour party strove during the first week of May 1926 to disentangle themselves from a situation they privately deplored but dared not publicly denounce, the Liberals were embroiled in divisive passions of their own. Despite the formal reunion between the Asquithian and Lloyd George factions brought about by the Tariff Election of 1923, the two ex-premiers had never been genuinely reconciled. With his own political machine and treasury intact, Lloyd George paid scant regard to either the views or the sensibilities of the party's acknowledged leader, removed since his electoral defeat in 1924 to the Upper House as Lord Oxford and Asquith. There was ample justification for Oxford's view that Liberal reunion had:

> turned out to be a fiction, if not a farce. The control of the party has throughout been divided between two separate authorities: the Liberal Central Office and Mr Lloyd George's rival machine—the former very scantily, and the latter very richly, endowed ...I was driven myself last December to the humiliating task of making a personal appeal to the better-to-do among our followers to come to the rescue and provide us with a wholly independent fund of adequate amount... Meanwhile, the rival organisation, well supplied with material resources, is being enlarged in every direction, and has been recruited at its headquarters quite recently by an influx of skilled wire-pullers and propagandists. Under such conditions, to talk of Liberal unity as a thing which either has been, or has any fair prospect of being, achieved, seems to me to be an abuse of language.[1]

Oxford wrote this dismal account on the eve of his retirement in October 1926, by which time the General Strike had brought about —or had been used as an excuse for bringing about—a final and spectacular rupture between himself and Lloyd George.

The first signs were mild enough. Speaking in the Commons debate on 3 May Lloyd George condemned the strike as mistaken but scorned the Government's contention that it was a challenge to the Constitution. What incensed Government supporters was not that this coincided with the known views of Labour front benchers, but that Lloyd George had attacked the Government with equal ferocity only nine months previously for granting the coal subsidy. 'I never heard Lloyd George worse', Duff Cooper noted angrily in his diary. 'Every fact, every figure, every date was wrong.'[2] Next day the Liberal Shadow Cabinet—of which both Oxford and Lloyd George were members—discussed the strike. Although misgivings were expressed about the Government's handling of the crisis, it was unanimously resolved that 'society was bound with all the resources at its command to make certain of victory' over the T.U.C.[3] This was the theme of Oxford's pronouncements that day in the House of Lords and on Saturday in the *British Gazette*. The constitutional threat implicit in a general strike was similarly stressed by Lord Grey also in the *British Gazette* and in his wireless broadcast on Sunday. Far from retreating from his position of 3 May, however, Lloyd George went on to insist that the Government was 'equally, if not more, responsible' for the onset of the strike and that negotiations should begin immediately. He refused to attend a further meeting of the Liberal Shadow Cabinet called for Monday 10 May, underlining his differences with his colleagues in a letter to Sir Godfrey Collins, the party's Chief Whip. In his slyly pointed reply, Collins suggested that Lloyd George 'had probably overlooked, or had not had an opportunity of reading' Oxford's speech in the Lords and obligingly enclosed a relevant extract.[4] Oxford stated his own interpretation less subtly. Lloyd George, he wrote to a friend, 'was in the sulks, and had cast in his lot for the moment with the clericals—Archbishops and Deans and the whole company of the various Churches (a hopeless lot)—in the hope of getting a foot-hold for himself in the Labour camp'.[5] During the week immediately following the strike Oxford's resentment was inflamed by the promptings of his colleagues. By 18 May he was, according to one of them, *'far more* indignant at L.G.'s behaviour than I have ever seen him'.[6] Two days later Oxford wrote to Lloyd George rebuking him for not attending the Shadow Cabinet meeting on 10 May. Such conduct, Oxford declared, 'I find impossible to reconcile with my conception of the obligations of political comradeship'.[7] Without waiting for a reply, Asquith sent a copy of this letter to the Press, deliberately forfeiting whatever chance remained of healing the rift. 'I don't suppose', Laski observed, 'that since the Russell-Palmerston row over Louis Napoleon, one distinguished statesman has ever so written to another.'[8]

On 1 June, twelve of Oxford's closest supporters in the Shadow Cabinet, including Grey, Collins and Sir John Simon, signed their names to a savage condemnation of Lloyd George.[9]

Since [he] broke up the first Coalition and became Prime Minister he has played many parts, and when he rejoined [Lord Oxford] at the general election of 1924 it was obvious to everybody that nothing could make this reunion effective except a willingness to forget past differences and an identity both in machinery and in single-minded devotion to the party...but Mr Lloyd George has insisted upon retaining separate headquarters and a separate fund ...and his methods have often made us suspect that he has not abandoned the idea of a new Coalition. His action during the recent General Strike has to be regarded in the light of this record. It is obvious to us that his letter to Sir Godfrey Collins [of 10 May] was written with an eye to its possible future use if events had turned out as he anticipated with his communications to the foreign Press*... Practical suggestions for dealing with the coal dispute are welcomed by all of us, and have been made by none more clearly and usefully than [Lord Oxford]. But it seems to us to be pure opportunism to taunt the Government as Mr Lloyd George did nine months ago, with being 'afraid of facing cold steel', to refuse to meet his colleagues at the crisis of the strike on the ground that he was opposed to the demand for unconditional withdrawal, and when that withdrawal took place to tell his constituents that he was always in favour of the policy that he refused to discuss with [Lord Oxford]... We have done our best in the interests of Liberalism to work with Mr Lloyd George in the councils of the party, but we cannot feel surprised at [Lord Oxford's] feelings that confidential relations are impossible with one whose instability destroys confidence.

Although Oxford had widespread sympathy and respect from his party, it was not prepared to see Lloyd George excommunicated. By twenty votes to ten, Liberal M.P.s reindorsed him as their chairman and when the National Liberal Federation met in the middle of June it expressed its 'unabated confidence' in Oxford, but added significantly that it wished to 'retain the co-operation of all Liberals in pressing forward a vigorous and constructive policy of social and industrial reform'. Oxford did not attend the meeting, having suffered a stroke, and for the next three months he was in convalescence. When he next made a public appearance, in October, it was to reaffirm his view that the General Strike had been 'an offence of the gravest kind against both law and morals', and to announce his retirement from the leadership. He refused to contemplate a political future while Lloyd George remained; the party felt that it could have no political future if Lloyd George went. By the end of 1926 the Oxford dissidents had accommodated themselves as best they could to Lloyd George's inevitable supremacy.

The conviction that Lloyd George had deliberately chosen to open a rift with Oxford during the General Strike in order to place him-

---

* According to Colonel Tweed, one of Lloyd George's principal organisers, Lloyd George had written an article for an American magazine sympathising with the strikers. Tweed's explanation was that Lloyd George considered a revolutionary situation possible and was determined to be on the right side of the barricades.[10] Lloyd George's journalistic endeavours were also focused closer to home. 'With the object of pushing himself to the front,' wrote Fyfe on May 11, 'he tried to get a newspaper printed at Luton, combining the energies of the three Liberal journals in London (*Daily News*, *Daily Chronicle*, *Westminster Gazette*). The project came to grief. The Lloyd George organ ought to have appeared this morning, but the *Daily News* people broke away and so brought the scheme to naught. Lloyd George is furious.'

self at the head of Labour moderates was shared by observers as mutually antagonistic as Baldwin, Lansbury, and the Webbs. Lansbury believed as far back as June 1925, that MacDonald and Thomas 'were arranging some sort of concordat with Lloyd George by which a new party uniting the right of the Labour party with the Liberals would take office after the next general election'.[11] In the aftermath of Red Friday Mrs Webb was driven to much the same conclusion. 'That is what Lloyd George and Thomas are busy engineering. But they won't succeed—no one trusts them—"Taffy was a Welshman, Taffy was a thief".'[12] When the strike came a rumour that some such deal had been made was given wide currency by the chairman and secretary of the Liberal Candidates' Association, both avowed enemies of Lloyd George. They alleged that their *bête noire* had met three Labour leaders at Snowden's house in Surrey on 7 May and offered to pledge himself and his coffers to the Labour cause. Lloyd George rebutted the charge with a detailed alibi and a confirmatory letter from Snowden.* It is against this background of internal Liberal dissension that Sir John Simon's Commons pronouncement on 6 May that the General Strike was illegal should be judged. A coolly ambitious lawyer-turned-politician, whose role as

* Towards the end of May 1926, Joseph Westwood, Labour M.P. for Peebles and Southern Midlothian, stated that 'Labour members of the House of Commons were invited to give their views on the question of Mr Lloyd George definitely associating himself with their Party'. In February 1929—shortly before the General Election—H. A. Gwynne, the editor of the *Morning Post*, acting with encouragement from J. C. C. Davidson, who by then was the Tory party chairman, decided to follow up the story. Lloyd George himself flatly denied it. MacDonald refused to be interviewed but his Parliamentary Secretary told the *Morning Post's* reporter that, when asked about the story, MacDonald had 'laughed, held up his hands and said "What next? I neither affirm nor deny".' Henderson strongly denied the story, Thomas 'shook his head, but said nothing', and Lansbury was non-committal. Robert Williams, who had been chairman of the Labour party in 1926, and J. H. Hayes, an ex-Labour Whip, confirmed that unofficial sounding had been made, Williams alleging that the Snowdens had been involved, Hayes that Sir Henry Slesser had been the go-between. At first, Slesser refused to discuss the matter at all, but then relented to the extent of denying that he had taken 'soundings' in 1926. From the Rev. Herbert Dunnico, Left-wing Labour M.P., came positive affirmation 'that a private and informal meeting between certain members of the Labour party on the one side and Lloyd George on the other was held'. According to Dunnico, Lloyd George gave an assurance that he would be prepared to serve merely as Minister of Agriculture under MacDonald or any other Labour Prime Minister if Labour were the dominant party. Gwynne also had an anonymous Liberal informant who claimed to have had the story confirmed a year or two previously by the Labour leader himself. '[MacDonald] added that not only did Lloyd George make the proposition of amalgamation with the Labour party, but said that if they could come to an agreement he would put a large portion of his fund at the disposal of the Coalition. Ramsay described the conversation, but did not enter into details. He said that at the end he told L.G.: "You have put your cards very frankly on the table, but there is nothing doing".'[13]

Liberal heir apparent had been shattered by Lloyd George's return to the fold in 1923, Simon had cause for viewing the situation with less than legal detachment. Even Duff Cooper, who believed the speech to be 'most important and impressive', also observed that it could 'prove the way to [Simon] supplanting Lloyd George as [the Liberal] leader. The latter has missed another chance'. Simon contended that the strike was 'an utterly illegal proceeding' because it was directed, not against employers but against the State, and that consequently neither strikers nor their unions were immune, under the Trade Disputes Act of 1906, from claims for damages where contracts of employment had been broken. Every railwayman who was on strike in disregard of his employment contract was, according to Simon, personally liable to be sued in the county court for damages and every trade union leader who advised and promoted the strike was equally 'liable in damages to the uttermost farthing of his personal possessions'. Finally, trade unionists who ignored the strike call could not be deprived of their union benefits since the call was 'wrong and illegal'. Slesser, the former Labour Solicitor-General, himself a leading authority on trade union law, who was absent from the House during Simon's oration, wished to reply to it next day, but MacDonald forbade this.[14] During the next few days Simon's opinion naturally received wide publicity and on Monday, in spite of MacDonald's prohibition, Slesser rose amid Labour cheers to reply. It was doubtful, he claimed, if any employer could prove that the strike was directed against the State. If so, it must amount to seditious conspiracy and where was the evidence of that?

On Tuesday the High Court gave final hearing to an application from Havelock Wilson, president of the Seamen's Union, for an injunction restraining officials of the union's Town Hill branch from calling out members in support of the strike. His grounds were, first, that a two-thirds majority of all members was required for a strike call and, second, that the strike was contrary to the law. In granting the injunction Mr Justice Astbury delivered himself of the opinion that 'the so-called General Strike' was indeed contrary to law and that 'those persons inciting or taking part in it are not protected by the Trade Disputes Act of 1906. No trade dispute has been alleged or shown to exist in any of the unions affected, except in the miners' case, and no trade dispute does or can exist between the Trades Union Congress on the one hand and the Government and the nation on the other. The orders of the Trades Union Council... are therefore unlawful, and the defendants are at law acting illegally in obeying them and can be restrained by their own union from doing so'. In the Commons later that day Simon took issue with

Slesser. In his first speech Simon had suggested that the strike was illegal because it was aimed against the state. Relying strongly on Astbury's well-timed *obiter dictum* he now expounded this doctrine in more detail. 'You may do what you think proper in the exercise of your right to strike against your employer, but you are not only breaking the law, you are inflicting a most serious blow on the whole constitution of the country if you abuse that undoubted right with totally different effects, so that the result of what you do, whether you mean it or not, must be that you are putting pressure upon the community, the Government, the people as a whole.' As a corollary, Simon argued that, since a General Strike had not been envisaged by Parliament when it passed the Trade Disputes Act, the Act did not cover it.

These assertions may have been good politics: it is doubtful if they were sound law. They received support from Sir Frederick Pollock in the *Law Quarterly Review*, but were convincingly refuted by A. L. Goodhart, the journal's editor, who contended that sympathetic strikes inevitably brought pressure to bear upon third parties and that 'the coercion of the Government was merely incidental' to a strike which was genuinely in furtherance of a trade dispute.[15]* Simon's point that a General Strike had not been in the minds of M.P.s who voted in 1906 for the Trade Disputes Act may well have been true; it was also totally irrelevant. English courts are concerned, not with the intentions of the legislature but with the actual wording of the statutes they are called upon to interpret. Nor were Astbury's confident remarks legally decisive, for they were made without citation of a single authority, in a case where the defendants were unrepresented by counsel and related to a question not directly at issue—the constitutionality or otherwise of a General Strike. Furthermore, as Slesser subsequently pointed out, judicial authority had already established the legality of a withdrawal of labour for political ends.[16]

It would seem fair to deduce that MacDonald's reluctance to see Simon answered sprang from a hope that the recalcitrant trade unionists would be panicked into abandoning the strike. Sir Osbert Sitwell believed that, from the moment Simon first spoke, 'the strike leaders, in their blue serge suits, with their moustaches and bowler-hats, found that they had come perilously to resemble rebels, and must have felt from time to time on the verge of being proclaimed... Everywhere Sir John's declaration produced in the people of this

* The *Solicitors' Journal* on 15 May declared that, 'The learned K.C.[Simon] gives no reasoning or authority for this sweeping declaration and with due respect we suggest that none exists.'

country, tolerant and law-abiding by nature, an immediate response. "Good gracious!" they exclaimed primly, "what I'm doing isn't respectable!" and many of them longed in consequence to return quietly to work'.[17] Astbury frequently claimed thereafter that it was really he who had saved the nation. Slesser's view was that neither Simon nor Astbury had the least effect on the strikers. 'I have spoken to most of the leading characters in the affair and never found one who admitted it. Indeed, the matter of legality never had any part in their decision, though there was, and I believe still is, a strong belief in the middle classes to that effect.'[18] Almost certainly typical of the individual striker's reaction was that quoted by Ellen Wilkinson: 'If the British Constitution makes a man work underground for less than £2 a week, it's about time that constitution was challenged!'

The Government itself responded to Simon's speeches with considerable caution. Although they had been suggesting for months that a General Strike would be unconstitutional, ministers showed no inclination to confirm Simon's opinion. The Attorney-General was prepared neither to affirm nor dispute it, agreeing with Slesser that it was a matter for the courts to decide. The *British Gazette* on 8 May devoted a column of verbatim report to Simon's first speech, but its own comments, which did not appear until two days later, were uncharacteristically circumspect. 'It is understood that the law officers of the Crown do not dissent in general principle from [Simon's] conclusions. The constitutional and legal bearings of the situation are now being examined in the light of the unprecedented attack to which the community is at present exposed at the hands of a section of its citizens.' Some senior Conservatives had personal as well as legal reservations about Simon. Davidson's opinion was that 'One could never quite trust John Simon. He was really a *faux bonhomme*, and he spread around him an atmosphere of insincerity... His tactics always engendered distrust, and I always felt that he lacked moral courage. His famous speech in the General Strike, for example, was strictly a legal argument... His attitudes were always too clever, and they lacked either conviction or authority. He was a man who could never come to a decision.'

The *British Gazette*'s inference that legislative measures were about to be taken against the strike was no mere part of Churchill's psychological warfare campaign. On the first day of the strike Baldwin had spoken to Jones of his determination to revise trade union 'powers and machinery', and a small Cabinet committee consisting of Lord Cave, the Lord Chancellor, Birkenhead and Hogg, had been set up to draft the necessary legislation. Before the weekend they had produced an Illegal Strikes Bill which was to overrule all previous legislation on the subject. It had only four provisions: first, to make it unlawful to support strikes with any object other than the maintenance or improvement of conditions of labour in the industry or branch of industry in which strikers were engaged; second, the High Court was to be empowered, on the suit of the Attorney-General, to prevent trade unions or Co-op funds from being used in such a strike; third, neither trade union membership nor benefits could be withheld from those refusing to participate in a general or sympathetic strike; finally, the term 'strike' was defined.

By now, however, Baldwin had wisely concluded that the trade unions and Labour party would strenuously resist any attempt to destroy what they regarded as 'their most important charter'.[19] These misgivings were soon dispelled or overborne, for on Saturday the Cabinet unanimously resolved to pass the Bill through all its stages in the Commons on the following Tuesday, 11 May. Churchill had already been trying unsuccessfully to press Montagu Norman, Governor of the Bank of England, into freezing all union funds. On Sunday an additional Order in Council under the Emergency Proclamation gave the Government power to prevent the transfer of money 'for any purpose prejudicial to the public safety or the life of the community', pending the passage into law of the Illegal Strikes Bill. Chamberlain's view that 'the best and kindest thing now, is to strike quickly and hard' was not shared by Jones and others in the Cabinet secretariat. On Monday, while Baldwin perambulated the terrace at Number Ten, Jones pleaded with him to pause before rushing the Bill through Parliament.[20] Jones's alarm was increased by the discovery that the Prime Minister was not even clear about what it was designed to do. Jones told him that 'in my belief Eccleston Square was already beaten, and knew it was beaten; that it had taken some time to get the country to appreciate what the General Strike was, but this new Bill would come as a thunder-clap on the country which was utterly unprepared for it, and would greatly confuse its mind. It would be held to be an attack on trade unions, and would profoundly change the quite peaceful temper of the men now on strike. Could he not give two or three days more before introducing it?' Baldwin was non-commital, remarking only that Churchill had secured Simon's general support for the Bill. Jones conferred with other officials at Number Ten and it was agreed that some urgent lobbying was necessary. Waterhouse believed that the only way left of influencing Baldwin was through the King, and while he went off to see Lord Cromer, who had excellent Royal connections, Jones himself lunched with the Tory elder statesman and ex-Premier Arthur Balfour. Balfour disclosed that Lord Salisbury, leader of the Conservative peers, was also concerned at the Government's haste. Having assured himself that Jones was not against the Bill itself but only the timing, Balfour promised to raise an objection at that afternoon's Cabinet. Returning to Downing Street, Jones learned that Cromer intended to see the King at once and that a Royal message would be transmitted in time for it to have an effect on Baldwin and his colleagues. The King had already expressed alarm at Sunday's Order in Council, declaring that 'anything done to touch the pockets of those who are now only existing on strike pay might cause exasperation and serious reprisals on the part of the sufferers', and that, in his judgment, it would be 'a grave mistake to do anything which might be interpreted as confiscation, or to provoke the strikers, who until now had been remarkably quiet'.[21] The Strike Bill he regarded as the work of Baldwin's 'hot-headed colleagues' and feared that it could have 'disastrous effects, especially at the psychological moment when there is but little bitterness of feeling between the Government and the strikers and when the situation generally seems hopeful'. When Jones reached the Commons shortly after 4.00 p.m. he found Stamfordham already waiting with a message for the Prime Minister. Meanwhile, pressures in favour of postponement had been exerted from other quarters. Eyres-Monsell, the Chief Whip, had discovered that a majority of Tory M.P.s were against provocative legislation at such a moment and Walter Elliott, junior minister at the Scottish Office, made it known that any attempt to rush legislation through Parliament would give many Scots M.P.s the impression that the Government was panicking. Even Churchill was forced to conclude that it would be wiser to amend the timetable. After meeting for two-and-a-half hours the Cabinet agreed to defer the Bill. Party opinion and the King's appeal had obviously impressed the Cabinet. So, too, had the knowledge that, within a day or so, the immediate necessity for such legislation might well have disappeared.

H

Chapter Fourteen

# *Extrication*

'It is false economy to expect a man to go down a mine and do his best and come up at the end of the week with not enough—not enough in thousands of cases to feed himself, to say nothing of the wife and children who are depending on him, and the nation cannot slide out of this responsibility.'

Ernest Bevin, addressing the special Conference of Trade Union Executives, 29 April 1926.

'You are, I expect, quite in the thick of this fight. You know that I may not agree with you in politics, and I am incompetent to judge of the wisdom and the results of the General Strike. But as to the miners I am all with anyone who will fight for the mainten- ance of their wages. Our men are a decent lot, by no means wanting a fight for the sake of being nasty. They simply cannot live on less. They felt—and I fully agree with them—that much of the subsidy was grabbed. They see the wasteful luxury of some owners. Our men are not hotheads like some of the Celts may be but I am convinced they are going to keep their ends up desper- ately. However, you know more than I do, and as I feel you must be taking your share of the fight I wanted to let you know as their parson that I wish you Good Luck in the name of the Lord.'

The Rev H. Marshall, in a letter to E. F. Wise, of the I.L.P., Tuesday 4 May. [Wise passed the letter on to Tom Jones.]

'All's well! We are entering upon the second week of the general stoppage in support of the mine workers against the attack upon their standard of life by the coal-owners. Nothing could be more wonderful than the magnificent response of millions of workers to the call of their leaders. From every town and city in the country reports are pouring into the General Council headquarters stating that all ranks are solid, that the working men and women are resolute in their determination to resist the unjust attack upon the mining community... The General Council's message at the opening of the second week, is "Stand firm. Be loyal to instructions and Trust Your Leaders." '

The *British Worker*, Monday, 10 May.

On Thursday 6 May, a few hours before Simon rose to speak, another former Liberal Home Secretary landed at Dover. 'Watching the course of events remotely from North Italy', Samuel has recorded, 'I wondered from time to time whether, as chairman of the recent royal commission, I could possibly be of use. When the situation became serious, I telegraphed to a member of the Government—I have no record and forget who it was—asking whether it would help if I came back; the reply was appreciative but negative. Nevertheless, when the General Strike was actually declared, I decided to go, and reached England on Thursday, 6 May. As the railways had stopped I had telegraphed Mitchell-Thompson, the Postmaster-General, who was looking after Government transport, to ask if he could arrange to bring me from Dover to London. On arrival I found waiting for me Major Segrave, the most famous racing motorist of that day, with a powerful Sunbeam car. My sister was living in Folkestone, and I stopped a few minutes to see her; then we sped along one of the newly-built motor highways, all the roads empty of traffic because of the strike. At times we touched eighty-five miles an hour; and, although Segrave drove cautiously through the villages and suburbs, we reached the Reform Club in Pall Mall from Folkestone in one hour and ten minutes.'[1] Despite the Government's 'negative' response, Samuel speedily set about contacting other interested parties. He got in touch with his colleagues on the Royal Commission but they, too, were discouraging, feeling that even an informal initiative could do no good and might even do harm. A phone call to Thomas elicited a quite different response. Warmly welcoming Samuel's return, he promised to arrange a meeting with the T.U.C. Negotiating Committee, believing it possible that 'something might come of it'.

Samuel's intervention was exceedingly well-timed for by Friday Bevin as well as Thomas was urging the General Council 'to get negotiations going somewhere'.[2] Although the strike was still solid its disruptive consequences had been offset by the efforts of volunteers.* To be made effective the strike had to be extended

* According to Davidson, 'The workers' reaction to the strike call had been much more complete than we had expected. The railwaymen were out almost to a man and London Transport came to a complete standstill. The organisation of the maintenance of supplies which the Home Secretary had set up was quite unable to cope, but within a very short time volunteers had replaced the usual labour force ... The public response was overwhelming ... They came in their thousands and even some of the strikers volunteered for service away from their home districts. It was the hard work of these people, who felt that the Government must be supported, rather more than the organisation we had created that broke the General Strike.'[3] (*The British Gazette*, on 11 and 12 May, gave the total of enlistments as almost a quarter of a million.)

and on Friday a decision was actually taken to call out the engineers and shipyard workers the following Wednesday. But could the movement face let alone win a war of attrition? Would the strikers remain solid when strike pay began to run out? Would they remain peaceful if the Government resorted to more drastic measures? To Bevin the answer was clear. 'You could not sit in the strike organisation room, with deputations and committees coming in all the time from all over the country, without sensing pretty clearly how long we could carry it. I felt and said that we would reach the maximum of strength about the following Tuesday—then it would be a case of "holding out" and I thought approximately three weeks would be necessary after that to clean up.'[4] Bevin had already been encouraging his own business and religious contacts to form themselves into some kind of mediation committee but he willingly dropped these efforts in favour of Samuel's much more promising initiative.

On Friday afternoon the Negotiating Committee met Samuel in the opulent Bryanston Square home of Sir Abe Bailey, a South African mining millionaire friend of Thomas. Samuel left the committee under no illusions. After first emphasising that he was in no way authorised to speak on behalf of the Government, he gave his own view of the minimum requirements for a settlement. It was useless, he told the committee, to expect the Government to discuss conditions for a resumption of coal negotiations while the strike lasted; it was useless to resume the coal negotiations so long as the miners maintained an absolute veto upon wage reductions in any circumstances; it was useless to hope for any renewal of the subsidy beyond the strictly limited period already defined by the Government. Were the miners, asked Samuel, now prepared to face the prospect of wage cuts if talks were resumed? Yes, replied the Negotiating Committee, they were—provided they were convinced that the Commission's reorganisation proposals would be implemented. Having disposed of this crucial point, Samuel and the committee soon found themselves in agreement on more technical matters. It would be the task of a National Wages Board, comprising miners, owners, and neutral members, meeting under an independent chairman, to draw up the new wage scales. Any revision would be for one year only, during which time all reforms would be carried into effect. The board itself would ensure that there was no backsliding. After arranging to meet Samuel the following day, the committee returned to T.U.C. headquarters, entering the premises separately 'so as not to arouse suspicion, as so many press sleuths are hanging about, although no newspapers are appearing'.[5]

Wonderland would have been a more appropriate venue for

Friday's meeting than Bryanston Square. Not only had the miners not expressed their willingness to face wage cuts, they had not even been told of the Negotiating Committee's decision to see Samuel. By the weekend, however, they were convinced that some furtive plot was afoot. Their suspicions had been aroused on Wednesday by Thomas's unauthorised reference to the Birkenhead Formula and by Baldwin's disclosure that it had envisaged wage cuts. Press speculation fed the miners' suspicions. An agency report in Thursday's *Manchester Guardian Bulletin* stated, 'It is understood Mr Baldwin and Mr Thomas are again in formal conversation with a view to seeing whether some understanding can be reached without delay.' More newspaper speculation was inspired by MacDonald's indiscreet comment to reporters that he was 'keeping in continual touch with the Government side, and was hourly in conference regarding settlement of the strike'. The Labour leader had, in fact, been secretly to Downing Street on Friday morning with Sir Allan Smith, chairman of the Engineering and Allied Employers' Federation, to press for a settlement based on temporary wage cuts of 10 per cent pending final arbitration. Baldwin had turned down the scheme.[6]*
On Friday evening the *British Worker* carried a statement denying that any attempt had been made 'to re-open negotiations with a view to ending the General Stoppage. The General Council wish it to be understood that there is no truth in this assertion. No official overtures have been made to the Government by any individual or group of individuals with or without the sanction of the General Council'.

On Saturday the miners heard—though not from the T.U.C.— that contact had been made with Samuel.† At that morning's meeting of the General Council, Cook and Smith angrily demanded to be included in whatever discussions were taking place. Bromley responded with vigour. 'By God, we are all in this now and I want to say to the miners, in a brotherly, comradely spirit, but straight—

* Baldwin was more favourably disposed towards a scheme proposed by Lord Astor. This envisaged withdrawal of the strike notices, renewal of the subsidy for a fortnight while further negotiations took place, and arbitration on all points still unresolved after the two weeks. 'I proceeded,' says Jones, 'to argue for it with all my might . . . My policy was to split Eccleston Square in two with the aid of a gesture from the P.M. which would help the moderates.' Jones's policy was not welcomed by Churchill, who 'overwhelmed me with a cataract of boiling eloquence, impossible to reproduce. "We were at war. Matters had changed from Sunday morning. We were a long way from our position then. We must go through with it. You must have the nerve." I shouted back "I have plenty of moral nerve, but we want something besides nerve".'

† Cook told the Conference of Executives in January: 'We heard [the General Council] had been meeting somewhere; heard it by accident, and suspicion was created. We asked "Who?" On the Saturday we learned it was Sir Herbert Samuel.'

but *straight*—that this is not a miners' fight now. I am willing to fight right along with them and to suffer as a consequence, but I am not going to be strangled by my friends.' Smith's characteristic rejoinder was that if Bromley wanted to pull out, the miners would not try to stop him. Eventually, tempers subsided and Smith was persuaded to agree that there was no point in the miners participating until more tangible discussions began.[7] Thomas and his colleagues said nothing of the very definite proposals which had already emerged.

Meanwhile, Samuel was testing the somewhat cooler climes of Downing Street. In a two-hour meeting with Baldwin that morning he explained the essence of his proposals for a settlement of the mining dispute, but the Prime Minister refused to make any commitment of his own.[8] The Government's uncompromising attitude was set out in a letter drafted by Birkenhead and signed by Steel-Maitland which was dispatched to Samuel soon after his departure. 'We have repeatedly stated that we cannot negotiate until the General Strike has been withdrawn. For if we did so...the true situation sincerely faced would be that we had procured the end of the General Strike by a process of bargaining. It is therefore plain that [the Government] cannot enter upon any negotiations unless the Strike is so unreservedly concluded that there is not even an implication of such a bargain as would embarrass them in any legislation which they may conceive to be proper in the light of recent events. In these circumstances I am sure that the Government will take the view that while they are bound most carefully to consider the terms of any arrangement which a public man of your responsibility and experience may propose, it is imperative to make it plain that any discussion which you think proper to initiate is not clothed in even a vestige of official character.'

This was the reply which Samuel had expected and when he met the T.U.C. negotiators at Bryanston Square that afternoon he urged that the only remaining course was withdrawal of the strike and a public pronouncement of their agreed views on a settlement of the mining dispute. To give these views extra authority, Samuel promised to seek endorsement from his Coal Commission colleagues.* 'We had a long conversation amongst ourselves,' Citrine recorded in his diary, 'with regard to the position of the miners. Should we tell them all about what was happening? It was risky because they might say that they must consult their full executive. They might

---

* Samuel's ex-colleagues were not, in fact, prepared to give their endorsement, arguing that to do so would be constitutionally improper since the Royal Commission had completed its work.

even insist on calling their delegate conferences. Furthermore, if the word got out that Samuel was discussing matters with us, it would destroy his utility in later negotiation. He could hardly pose as an impartial person when, in fact, he had been consulting with us. We came to the conclusion that it was extremely unlikely that the Government could approach us and we decided to tell the miners so. Samuel undertook to let us have a draft of his letter this evening and we would send for it to the Reform Club. Then we would send him an intimation as to whether we could meet him again tomorrow.'

A notable absentee from the first part of Saturday's proceedings in Bryanston Square was Thomas. He was a guest at a luncheon party at Wimborne House, the gracious Arlington Street residence of Lord and Lady Wimborne.[9] Wimborne, a Liberal landowner and industrialist, and former Lord-Lieutenant of Ireland, had been prevailed on by his decorous and personable wife to bring together those whom she felt could perhaps produce a solution to the crisis. Thomas's fellow-guests were the coal-owners, Lords Londonderry and Gainford; the ex-Viceroy of India, Lord Reading; the editor of the *Westminster Gazette*, J. A. Spender; the poet and writer Osbert Sitwell; and Mrs Snowden,* who was deputising for her husband. Sitwell, whose friendship with Lady Wimborne dated from the publication in 1924 of *Triple Fugue,* his first book of short stories, clearly relished the atmosphere of high drama in which he was now immersed. 'We went into luncheon to the minute, passing through a vista of fine rooms on our way to the dining-room. Almost directly we sat down, the conversation took the turn we had so ardently wished it might... So important in its matter, so vehement in its manner, so frank was the talk, that the footmen, I recall, had to be told almost at once to leave the dining-room, and only return when summoned.' The excitement was caused by Thomas's glib assurance that the miners were ready to accept the Samuel Report, including the recommendations on wage cuts. There was no more substance to this assurance on Saturday than there had been on Friday, but Reading and Wimborne hurried at once to Westminster to apprise Churchill and Birkenhead of it. Both ministers remained un-

---

* She was, according to Beatrice Webb, 'a "climber" of the worst description, refusing to associate with the rank and file and plebeian elements in the Labour party. Hence every "class-conscious" Labour man or woman listens for the echoes of Ethel—climbing, climbing, climbing, night and day! out of the Labour world into that of plutocrats and aristocrats.... The only other climbers are Thomas and his wife and daughters; but Thomas drops his "h's" defiantly; and Mrs Thomas is a retiring and discreet climber and has never pretended to be specifically Labour, and the daughters are so far removed from Labour circles that one of them when asked ... whether she was a "Fabian" retorted indignantly "No: I am a 'Thomas' "!'[10]

impressed, maintaining, says Sitwell, 'that mere acceptance would not now be enough; we must engage in that blustering and platitudinous redundancy, "A fight to a finish".'

On Sunday morning a written draft of Samuel's proposals was placed at last before the miners' representatives. Smith dismissed them as 'a new suit of clothes for the same body', but agreed to summon his Executive for a meeting with the General Council that evening. Citrine wrote:

> It was evident to me that the General Council were coming to the conclusion that it was simply hopeless to continue the strike if the intention was that in no circumstances and in no conditions would the miners accept any reductions. We cannot see any possibility of winning on this negative issue, yet we are all apprehensive of what will follow after the miners have been told that they cannot, in the view of the General Council, hope to secure an undertaking that there will be no reduction... It will be a repetition of Black Friday, with the difference that we will have had the General Strike, and we will have realised either our strength or our impotence. Let me try to reason it out. Can we hope to force such a condition of things that the miners will be secure indefinitely against a reduction? I do not believe that any of us have thought in our innermost consciousness that we could secure such a definite guarantee. What we have thought is that we could make arrangements so that reorganisation would be pressed so insistently that the reduction would be minimised, if not escaped altogether. But for a period there must quite evidently be some reduction, pending fructification of reorganisation methods, unless we can, through the General Strike, force the Government to grant a subsidy during the reorganisation interval. I do not think we are likely to succeed in this.

A clear hint of this mood was given by Thomas that afternoon at a rally in Hammersmith. He declared that he had never been in favour of the principle of a General Strike and that, whatever the outcome, the nation was bound to be the worse for it. 'The responsibility', he concluded, 'is indeed a heavy one. But there will be a graver responsibility on whichever side fails to recognise the moment when an honourable settlement can be arrived at. That moment must be accepted and everyone must work to that end.' The significance of these remarks was not lost on the Government: they were quoted in the B.B.C.'s 9.00 p.m. news bulletin and given prominent coverage in two consecutive issues of the *British Gazette*.

Sunday evening's meeting of the General Council and the miners' executive confirmed the worst apprehensions of both. The General Council insisted that no settlement was possible unless the miners accepted wage cuts; the miners insisted just as firmly that no settlement was possible unless it excluded wage cuts. The issue, said Pugh, was no longer the miners' exclusive concern; the whole trade union movement was involved and the miners had a responsibility to that. Smith was unmoved. 'Our men in the coalfields have given us our instructions and we cannot depart from them.' Later that night Thomas renewed his exchanges with Wimborne. Before 9.00 a.m. on Monday he was back in Arlington Street for a prolonged session with both Wimborne and Reading. The result was yet another formula, based upon his persistently wilful misrepresentation of the miners' position. This stated that if an assurance could be given by 'some person of influence, not a member of the Government' that the Samuel Report would be effected without delay, it was 'possible that the T.U.C. might call off the General Strike and indicate that the miners accept[ed] the Report unconditionally with all its implications'.[11] The formula was immediately read over the phone to Tom Jones and conveyed by him to Baldwin. Baldwin tossed it impatiently aside, saying that he had already provided the necessary public assurances, and that it simply remained for the T.U.C. to call off the strike. It is unlikely, however, that Baldwin failed to detect the T.U.C.'s increasingly desperate desire for a settlement and it would be surprising if this was not one of the factors which weighed in the Cabinet's decision later that morning to postpone the Illegal Strikes Bill.

From Arlington Street, Thomas hurried to Bryanston Square, where Samuel and the Negotiating Committee were joined this time by Cook, Smith, and Richardson. As Samuel began to recite his proposals, Smith interrupted, 'You are not reading that through; we are not agreeing with that'. Until now Samuel had been under the impression that the miners would be prepared to accept wage cuts if they received adequate guarantees of reorganisation, and it came as a shock to find that he had been misled. 'I hate this business,' he exclaimed. 'I was content in Italy writing on philosophy, and I have come here not at anyone's invitation, but merely to try to do my best as a good citizen, and as chairman of the Coal Commission, to see whether I can put things straight. No one else is doing anything at all. The Government has closed the door and you have done the same. I am not at all happy. I was brought into this business of the commission against my own inclinations and I had to record the facts. It is not that I want the miners' wages reduced. I think they are too horribly low altogether.'[12] On this last point Smith agreed, but on no other. In a letter which he wrote to the Prime Minister on Tuesday but never sent, Samuel observed that 'So far as the Miners' Federation is concerned it is Herbert Smith and not Cook who is the dominating influence and his position is up to the present quite immovable. The T.U.C. were deceiving themselves when they informed me that there was no longer an absolute veto upon any kind of reduction in any circumstances. My own clear view is that the veto remains exactly the same now as it was throughout the negotiations. This is due not only to the suspicion, which is undoubtedly a real one, that reconstruction will not eventuate to any full extent or in the near future, but also to the conviction that the miners' wages are not susceptible of any further reduction at all.'[13]

The argument was resumed that evening between the General Council and the miners' executive. Pugh announced that the Council regarded Samuel's proposals as 'a satisfactory basis' for the reopening of negotiations on the Coal Commission's report. In the heated exchanges which followed, Bromley spoke of a mass drift back to work on the railways.* 'Unless the strike is called off now there will be thousands of trains running. The result will be that there will be a debacle. It is no good; we cannot go on any longer. We are busted.' He warned the miners that if the strike was not called off immediately, he would order his A.S.L.E.F. members to resume work on Tuesday. 'Take them back', replied Smith contemptuously. 'Are you people simply going to cry like this?'[14] After a private discussion among themselves, the miners returned after three hours with the uncompromising declaration that 'there should be no revision of the previous wage rates or conditions, because if the measures for re-

---

* This was a theme continually stressed by Bromley and Thomas, but it had no basis in fact. Official figures showed that out of a total of 39,421 locomotive engineers employed by the four main companies, 742 reported for duty on Tuesday 11 May. The proportion of firemen and signalmen returning to work was similarly low and, although there were substantial defections by members of the Railway Clerks' Association, more than 99 per cent of all railway staff remained loyal to the strike.[15] Such precise information was not, of course, available to the T.U.C., but the Intelligence Committee observed on 12 May that Government claims of a massive return to work by the railwaymen were not confirmed by reports 'coming into this office. In many places ... the original response of the R.C.A., though good, was not absolutely solid. Moreover, it should be remembered that, though we are receiving reports from a large number of well organised industrial centres, the information to hand from the rural districts is so slight as to be of no real value at all .... Some of the reports with regard to railwaymen returning to work are clearly untrue .... It may be that the Government are making big claims on the basis of a staff consisting in the main of supervisory grades, clerks, and more or less isolated railwaymen in the rural areas. It may also be that they are including voluntary workers in their total.'

organisation are actually put into effect such revisions would be unnecessary'.

After his meeting with the miners Samuel was certain that his initiative had failed and on Tuesday morning he wrote to the Prime Minister explaining the reason. 'The T.U.C. would be glad to settle on the terms suggested. They are, however, convinced that their constituents would violently resent any desertion of the miners. Whatever might be their own views as to the probable outcome of the strike and as to the hardships and dangers which it brings they are not in a position to end the strike without the miners' concurrence.' But Samuel had underestimated the General Council's determination to end the strike: before the typed copy of his letter was ready for signature he was informed that the T.U.C. were 'on the point of separating themselves from the miners' and that the Negotiating Committee wished to meet him again that afternoon to obtain a final draft of his proposals.[16] News also reached the Cabinet that morning, via Tom Jones, that 'the moderates were in the ascendant and that they would probably win in the course of the day'.

Jones's optimism stemmed from a report he was given of early-morning exchanges at Wimborne House. Wimborne and Reading had made a 'sustained and passionate' appeal to Thomas to call off the strike immediately. Thomas had replied that they were 'preaching to the converted' and that the General Council would make its final decision that night. The two ex-Viceroys had an urgent reason for their appeal, though they did not disclose it to Thomas: they had just been told that the Government planned to arrest trade union leaders on Wednesday if the strike continued. Although the information was inaccurate, rumours of impending arrests had been circulating for several days. Swales believed the warrants had been issued for himself and Bevin as early as Sunday. Bevin and the rest of the General Council, however, had a higher regard for Baldwin's political acumen and it was not fear of arrest which prompted their decision on Tuesday.*

In the evening the Negotiating Committee returned to Eccleston

---

* On Monday 10 May, Fyfe wrote in his diary: 'There are stories about today that Churchill and N. Chamberlain have prevailed on Baldwin to order the Banks to refuse to pay out trade union funds, to arrest the members of the General Council, and take various other "strong measures" to bring the strike to an end. There is no truth in any of this, so far as I can learn. Baldwin is very anxious that the Samuel intervention shall succeed. He is nervous about what may happen if the strike goes on. But he is not so rattled as to be misled into doing these foolish and dangerous things.' In a note on 22 May, Fyfe added: 'It is stated that the General Council was "largely influenced in its final decision" by these rumours. This is untrue.'

Square with a final draft of the Samuel Memorandum. This proposed:

1. that a National Wages Board, including representatives of the miners, the owners, and neutral members, should be set up under an independent chairman to settle disputes in the industry;
2. that there should be no revision of previous wage rates unless there were sufficient assurances that reorganisation would be effectively adopted, and that any revision should only occur after consideration of every practicable means of meeting immediate financial difficulties;
3. that a committee, including representatives of the miners, should be established to co-operate with the Government in the preparation of all necessary legislative and administrative measures and that this committee or the Wages Board should ensure that the reforms were not being neglected or unduly postponed within the industry;
4. that if a new wages agreement was found to be necessary it should be on simplified lines, with no reduction for the lower-paid men and an irreducible minimum for all colliery workers;
5. that new workers over 18 should not be recruited if unemployed miners were available;
6. that workers displaced by pit closures should be given alternative employment and housing or special grants in addition to unemployment pay;
7. that the subsidy should be renewed for the duration of negotiations;

When the miners' executive arrived at 8.30 p.m. Pugh told them that the General Council had decided unanimously to adopt the Samuel Memorandum and that the strike was to be ended that night.[17] Why, asked Smith, had the miners been excluded from the afternoon talks with Samuel? And why was the strike to be called off in such haste? Pugh pointed out that all the amendments to Samuel's proposals were in the miners' interest and that the General Council had an obligation to the whole movement to secure a settlement as quickly as possible. The miners, he urged, had an equal obligation to preserve trade union solidarity by accepting the Memorandum themselves. To Smith's inquiry as to whether the Memorandum could be amended, Pugh snapped, 'No. You must take it or leave it'. Smith persisted. 'Do you people realise the serious position you are putting yourselves in? Are you going back without any consideration for the men who are going to be victimised in

224

this movement? Are you not going to consider them at all?' The matter, he was told, had been considered and need not concern the miners. Cook wanted to know what guarantee there was that the Government would accept Samuel's proposals. 'You may not trust my word', Thomas replied with pained dignity, 'but will you not accept the word of a British gentleman who has been Governor of Palestine?'

After an hour of futile wrangling Smith waved his colleagues out of the room for separate discussions. 'Immediately they had left', says Citrine, 'indignant conversation broke out among the members of the General Council.' Bevin's comment reflected their mood. 'I am not concerned what the miners may think about it. They can say what they like about me. My union came into this business on very definite terms, and I have told my men so. The dockers will stick out for weeks, and so will the miners, but I don't think it is right to go on asking the men to make sacrifices if we can get justice any other way.'[18] But could justice be got any other way? Irritation gave way to apprehension. 'With others I categorically questioned the Negotiating Committee', Bevin later recounted.[19] 'We asked, "Does it mean, if we call the strike off, that the Samuel document is to be made public, that the Government is to accept it, and that lock-out notices are to be withdrawn simultaneously with our ordering resumption of work?" Categorically, these questions were asked three times and in each instance the answer was "Yes". Well, you have negotiated and I have negotiated, and you know you have to take the word of negotiators. We took their word. I have since heard things that made me uneasy.'*

Just before midnight the miners' executive returned. The proposals, they said, implied wage cuts for a large number of mineworkers and were, therefore, unacceptable. 'Moreover, if such proposals are submitted as a means to call off the General Strike such a step must be taken on the sole responsibility of the General Council.' After the miners had withdrawn, there were more angry outbursts. Hayday and Thomas castigated the miners for their parochial self-interest and indifference to the rest of the trade union movement. 'Those men', declared Jack Beard, of the General Workers' Union, 'have

---

* Ben Turner's diary provides confirmation of Bevin's account. 'It was definitely put: "If Strike called off would lock-out notices be withdrawn and men resume work at old wages and hours?" The Negotiating Committee said yes, that was their opinion and belief.'[20] Fyfe's diary also records: 'The General Council members who are not among the negotiating seven have been anxious to be assured that the terms provide for "simultaneous" calling-off of the strike and withdrawal of the lock-out notices. Three times, I hear, this was raised; each time the required assurance was forthcoming.'

never readily put themselves into the hands of the General Council. I am not prepared to put everything our unions have into the pawn shop and feel that it is not appreciated by these people. As far as I am concerned, I will not accept any longer the contribution of the poorest section of the work-people without the consent of [my] Executive. I have trusted the Negotiating Committee, I believe they have worked like Trojans in this. But I pay my tribute especially to the work that Thomas has done. There is nobody who has been more maligned than he and nobody has done more for the miners.'[20] Bevin urged that one more attempt should be made to secure the miners' agreement. 'We were tired and had given no thought to demobilising. I felt, in view of the heated nature of the miners that night, we should see them next morning and really try to get a united body.'[22]

At this point Citrine was called to the phone. At the other end was Sir Patrick Gower, Baldwin's private secretary. 'The Prime Minister wants to know whether you have any news for him. He has been sitting up for you. Do you want to see him this evening?' Citrine explained that the General Council were still in session, but that if Gower would not mind waiting, he would go and ask them. A few minutes later Citrine returned with a positive assurance that the Council would be ready to see the Prime Minister at noon on Wednesday. 'All right,' replied Gower, 'we may take that as fixed.'[23] The phone call reassured Bevin. 'I concluded that what we had been told of the Prime Minister being in possession of the information was correct and that he was actually waiting in Downing Street to know whether we accepted the document or not. No suspicion entered my mind at all, but I did suggest that we ought not to see the Prime Minister that night ...I have heard since that the Prime Minister was told from our side that we might be wanting him early in the evening, but still, when the Prime Minister's secretary rang up Citrine as to whether we would be wanting to see him that night, having listened to the report of the Negotiating Committee, I came to the conclusion that everything was as reported and I voted for the calling off like any other man would have done under similar circumstances.'[24]

Turner was puzzled. 'How did P.M. know we wanted to see him? Strange and unexplained mystery. Who had told him?'[25] The informant appears to have been Wimborne's hard-working secretary, Selwyn Davies. During the talks at Wimborne House it had been arranged that Davies should mingle with the crowds in Eccleston Square that night, there to await news from Thomas of the General Council's final decision. Between 10.00 p.m. and 11.00 p.m. Thomas asked Davies to announce to the Prime Minister and Wimborne that 'though he was encountering the most formidable obstacles, he would, he thought, by 2.00 a.m., be in a position to say that his colleagues had given him authority to call off the General Strike'.[26] Soon after midnight Davies returned to find the miners' executive boarding their charabanc and bearing on their faces 'unmistakable symptoms of the most profound dejection'. A few minutes later Thomas emerged from the T.U.C. building and walked for a short distance, discreetly trailed by Davies. At a quiet spot Thomas stopped and asked Davies to tell the Prime Minister, Reading and Wimborne that the General Strike would end at noon on Wednesday, by which hour he and his colleagues would be at Downing Street.

T.U.C. leaders subsequently denied that a decision to end the strike had been taken before Tuesday's meeting with the miners. There was, Thomas indignantly told the Special Strike Conference in January 1927, 'no suddenness about it. After a four hours' debate [the miners] returned to us and gave the decision Mr Smith has mentioned, not hastily, but after four hours' discussion. [The miners had, in fact, debated among themselves for just over two hours.] We did not even then accept it as final. We said : "We will send a deputation to the miners", and we did and you have the result.' Citrine was even more assertive. 'We called off the strike, definitely and finally made up our minds at the General Council at about ten minutes before we met Mr Baldwin on Wednesday 12 May... What was the object of sending a deputation to meet the Miners' Federation next day but in order to get, if possible, an eleventh hour agreement, and it was not until then that the General Council finally said: "We must close this matter down". So much for the facts as I understand them in that connection.' Rather different facts emerge, however, from Citrine's diary entry for 11 May. After speaking to Gower, Citrine wrote: 'Our fate was decided in those few seconds. Our decision to see the Prime Minister meant plainly to them the calling-off of the General Strike. It was an eventful decision, and one cannot see how it will turn out. I hope we have decided rightly. It was agreed later that the chairman of the council and the members of the strike committee should go along to the Miners' Federation offices tomorrow and meet the executive to try to induce them to accept the council's decision.'

Chapter Fifteen

# *The Surrender*

'Fellow Workers, the Government have given the game away completely. Judging by the wireless and their press one would suppose that they are able to nullify the effects of the General Strike. But now they are compelled to admit that the supply of special constables is not sufficient. They are also attempting to bribe us to return to work by exhibiting posters offering us protection against our unions after the Strike, if we will only "scab". If there were anyone sufficiently foolish to help to break our defence against the employers' greed, he could not rely upon their assurances. Cast your mind back only to 1914 onwards, and remember the pie-crust promises such as "A Land Fit for Heroes", etc., *ad nauseam*. This is a trap set to catch any weak-kneed people there may be about. By the response there are so few as to be negligible. So much for their trick. It is conclusive proof of their inability to carry on. But we can carry on. Our organisations are our strength.'

*Tottenham Strike Bulletin*, Wednesday, 12 May 1926.

'Eighth day! Steady boys! Sticking does it! Do you remember those horrible days in France, Flanders and Gallipoli where on occasion you were bombarded from land and air? Often you could not move, all you could do was to "stick it". You did so, and won the admiration of the world! Today, you suffer from a bombard-ment of lies and lots of provocation, and your trade union leaders' call to you is—Stick it, boys; hold on, altogether—women, men and children. We are winning by "Doing Nothing". Don't be bothered by the broadcasting news or the statements in the official papers... We are not attacking the Constitution. We are struggling to prevent British Labour being driven down to a Coolie level. We know that if the miners lose, we shall lose. We know that all Rise or Fall Together! So, once more, *Altogether! Altogether! Altogether!* Stand Firm and Fast by one another. No disorder. Troops, horse, foot, artillery, machine guns, armoured cars, aero-planes, these are only on parade. You can now see where our taxes go. The men who man the cars, or ride the horses, police or soldiers, navy or airmen, are our flesh and blood. Don't get into trouble with them. Let the world see you as true sons of Britain—great descendants of those who held the field at Waterloo, in the Crimea, and throughout the Great War, from one end of Europe to the other. Today you fight with your brains and just stand still. No one can harm you while you remain passive, and as you stick and stand by one another, you may be quite sure *Victory Will Be Yours*. You cannot be defeated by the Government, only treachery, disloyalty, or disorder could beat us.'

*Lansbury's Bulletin,* Wednesday, 12 May 1926.

'We have had our General Strike. Imperfect as it has been, mechanically and in the evolution of policy, it has been the most magnificent effort of rank-and-file solidarity that the British movement has ever displayed. Never again will the Congress undertake the custodianship of any movement without the clear, specific, and unalterable understanding that the General Council, and the General Council alone, shall have the free untrammelled right to determine policy. How can we, with the millions of interests and considerations to review, allow our policy to be dominated entirely by considerations of one union only? Were we to continue the disruption and dismemberment of the railway and transport unions? To bleed white the organisations who had thrown their all into the melting pot? To sacrifice the individual members who, faced by heavy penalties for breach of contract, had responded with an unparallelled loyalty to the call of the movement? The outstanding lesson of the General Strike of 1926 is that authority must be invested exclusively and entirely in the directing body.'

*Thoughts on the Termination of the General Strike,* written by Walter Citrine at midnight on Wednesday, 12 May 1926.

'What was the situation with which we were confronted? Before myself and my colleagues an abyss had opened. It was the culmination of days and days of faintheartedness ...When the truculence of the Tory Cabinet thrust them willy nilly into the General Strike [the Negotiating Committee] had not ceased in their endeavour to "smooth it over". Only a few days of magnificent working-class effort had passed before they were once more trying to get peace at any price. Then, gradually, an incredible thing happened. They began to win over one after another of their colleagues on the General Council. Bit by bit the process of "persuading" the others went on until the situation of complete surrender had been reached, the situation with which we were now faced. It was more than a surrender on their part. It was an ultimatum to us miners, bidding us surrender, too.'

From *The Nine Days,* A. J. Cook's own account of the General Strike.

On Wednesday morning Labour party and T.U.C. leaders made one final effort to secure the miners' agreement. Ramsay MacDonald urged Cook to avoid making a 'tragic blunder' and asked if he could address the miners' executive himself. 'No', Cook replied. 'You have already taken your stand in appealing to us to consider reductions and the full acceptance of the Samuel report, which meant reductions. That has been your attitude throughout, and we do not want you to come to our meeting.'[1] Shortly after, the six-man T.U.C. deputation headed by Bevin and Purcell arrived at the Miners' Federation offices in Russell Square.[2] (Neither Pugh nor Thomas joined the deputation.) The miners, said Bevin, might not agree with the Samuel Memorandum, but they should accept it in their own interests and that of the Labour movement. If they stuck to rejection they would split the movement and almost certainly be offered worse terms in the future. A similar appeal was made by Purcell and by Ben Turner, who claimed that Intelligence Committee reports showed the strike was already on the 'slippery slope', especially in the railway centres.*

Smith, whose humour was not improved by a severe bout of gastritis, replied, with truth, that there was more enthusiasm for the strike amongst the rank-and-file than the General Council, and attacked the Council for having been 'continually on the doormat of the Prime Minister since and before the strike began' without the miners' knowledge. He agreed to put the latest appeal before his executive, but warned that they would be unlikely 'to "swallow something" after all the intrigues behind the Speaker's Chair in the House of Commons'. Within half-an-hour Cook returned with a resolution expressing 'profound admiration of the wonderful demonstration of loyalty as displayed by all workers who promptly withdrew their labour in support of the miners' standards'—and reaffirming the miners' repudiation of wage cuts, longer hours and

* The Intelligence Committee's Wednesday morning assessment of the rail strike has already been quoted. The committee described the situation generally as one 'in which we are holding our own. But the Government's organisation is improving, and its policy is gradually becoming more aggressive. Every day the intensity of the struggle will increase'.

district agreements. It was now 11.45 a.m. and Bevin had just time to dash by cab to Downing Street to join the Negotiating Committee for their noon meeting with Baldwin. When he arrived, the committee —and Baldwin—already knew of the miners' decision, for Cook had issued an immediate press statement emphasising that the miners were 'no party in any shape or form' to the strike's cessation. 'I ask you', Thomas besieged the Conference of Executives in January, 'with such a situation, was that playing cricket with us?'

Although Baldwin could have little doubt of his visitors' mission, they had to submit to an interrogation by Horace Wilson before he would agree to receive them. Earlier that morning Baldwin had been warned by Joynson-Hicks and other hard-liners on the Supply and Transport Committee not to risk 'even appearing to enter into any negotiations with the T.U.C. until there has been an unconditional withdrawal of the General Strike'.[3] * Wilson met the T.U.C. at the door of the Cabinet room. 'You want to see the Prime Minister?' Told that they did, Wilson asked why. 'To discuss the position', said Thomas. 'You know the Prime Minister will not see you', came the reply, 'before the strike is called off.' From the back of the group Bevin growled, 'For Christ's sake let's call it on again if this is the position'.[4] But the necessary assurance was given by Thomas and the party was finally ushered into the Cabinet room, where Baldwin was waiting with Birkenhead, Chamberlain, Steel-Maitland, Bridgeman, Lane-Fox, and Worthington-Evans.[5] The Prime Minister was tense and without any preliminaries asked Pugh to make his statement. The strike, said Pugh, was to be terminated forthwith. 'That is the announcement which my General Council is empowered to make.' Relief showed plainly on the faces of Cabinet members. 'I thank God', replied Baldwin, 'for your decision.'[6]

Before going to Russell Square, Bevin had agreed with the Negotiating Committee on the points to be settled at Downing Street. 'First, the Strike to be called off. Secondly, we had to discuss the resumption of work in an organised manner, and thirdly arrangements for negotiations on the basis of the Samuel Memorandum.'[8] To Bevin's intense alarm, no reference was made to either of the

* 'So overwhelmed were the Conservative members by the news', Baldwin reported to the King on 13 May, 'that they found it difficult to believe that the surrender of the T.U.C. was unconditional . . . . Some Conservatives were afraid that the Government had accepted conditions until Cook repudiated the Samuel proposals. Their nervous apprehension and suspicions, however, were merely indications of the tremendous importance attached to the constitutional issue by every member of the Conservative party and the feeling which might have been aroused by any word or action which might have been interpreted as a sign of weakness on the part of the Government.'[8]

last two points. Thomas contented himself with an appeal for generosity, informing Baldwin that the T.U.C. had 'done a big thing' and that they felt sure it would be responded to 'in a big way'. 'We trust your word as Prime Minister. We ask you to assist us in the way you only can assist us—by asking employers and all others to make the position as easy and smooth as possible, because the one thing we must not have is guerrilla warfare. That must be avoided, and in that both sides have to contribute immediately. Nothing could be worse than that this great decision which we have taken should be interpreted otherwise than as a general desire to do the right thing in a difficult moment for the industry of the nation.'

Bevin tried to obtain a more precise commitment. He told Baldwin:

We have taken a great risk in calling the strike off. I want to urge it must not be regarded as an act of weakness, but rather one of strength...it took a little courage to take the line we have done. I want to stress Mr Thomas's point, and ask you if you could tell us whether you are prepared to make a general request, as head of the Government, that facilities, etc., ready facilities for reinstatement and that kind of thing, shall be given forthwith ...It would be very helpful to us before we left the building if we could have some indication in that direction because we shall have to send telegrams to unions whose headquarters are not in London, with whom we cannot converse, and coupling with it a declaration from yourself would, in a way, give the lead as to how the thing is to be approached. You said, sir, also you were going to call the parties together in order to effect a just settlement. Now, we have called our show off, and work will be resuming pretty quickly. I do not know whether I am overstepping the bounds, but I would like you to give me an idea of whether that means that there is to be no resumption of the mining negotiations with us, or whether all the negotiations have to be carried out while the miners still remain out ...I really felt in the event of our taking the lead in assuring you we were going to play the game and put our people back, that it was going to be free and unfettered negotiations with the parties very speedily, because thousands of our people cannot go back if the colliers are still out, and if the colliers are still out it is going to make it extremely difficult to get a smooth running of the machine. Those are the two points I wish to put to you.

Baldwin's reply demolished any lingering notion held by the T.U.C. that this was to be a negotiating session. 'I cannot say more here at this meeting now ...You know my record. You know the object of my policy, and I think you may trust me to consider what has been said with a view to seeing how best we can get the country quickly back into the condition in which we all want to see it... I shall do my part and I have no doubt you will do yours. In regard to the second point, there again, I cannot say at this moment what will happen, because I shall have to see the parties... I cannot say until I have seen them exactly what the lines will be upon which my object can best be attained, but you may rely on me and rely on the Cabinet that they will see no stone is left unturned... Now, Mr Pugh, as I said before, we both of us have got a great deal to do and a great deal of anxious and difficult work, and I think that the sooner you get to your work and the sooner I get to mine the better.' Pugh willingly assented and rose to leave, but Bevin again interjected.* 'I am a little persistent. I do not want to take up your time, but shall we be meeting on these points soon?' Baldwin answered with brisk finality. 'I cannot say that, Mr Bevin. I think it may be that whatever decision I come to, the House of Commons may be the best place in which to say it.' Even Birkenhead felt something akin to compassion for the T.U.C. leaders as they trooped dejectedly out of the Cabinet room. Their surrender, he wrote later to Halifax, was 'so humiliating that some instinctive breeding made one unwilling even to look at them'.[9]

The ritual was not quite finished. Citrine had first to agree a press statement with Tom Jones, which was then taken into the Cabinet for approval. The Cabinet wanted the word 'forthwith' added to the declaration calling off the strike. 'I refused point blank to do this,' Citrine wrote in his diary, 'and said that our members were being given instructions to return by arrangement with their unions, and we were not going to have a stampede back to work. Finally, we agreed to put in the word "today" ...While I was completing the wording, Eyres-Monsell...came in, and I heard him say to Jones, "Just give me the message will you, for my broadcast?" I appreciated the significance of this at once. They were going to broadcast a message, stating that the general strike had been terminated, and our people would be left wondering what had happened. So I pressed him to allow a strike message to be broadcast, saying men must not resume work except on the instructions of their unions. I

* Baldwin and Jones had already agreed that 'Bevin was the most powerful member of the T.U.C. The P.M. said that Steel–Maitland and Wilson had seen a lot of him and were well-disposed to him, but the P.M. himself was doubtful. "Ramsay is a Kerenski and Kerenskis have lost control. Bevin may well picture himself as the Napoleon of the trade union movement. We must wait for the strike to wear itself out." '[10]

was very suspicious of them, and despite their assurances I waited while Davidson...dictated my message over the telephone to the Broadcasting Corporation. [It was, of course, the Broadcasting Company.] Then I arranged for priority to be given for our telegrams to the head offices of the unions.'

This anaemic victory, however, could hardly be set against the Negotiating Committee's abject surrender over the questions of the mining lock-out and guarantees against victimisation. As Citrine recognised, 'the net result of our efforts from a public point of view is the calling-off of the strike without any definite knowledge that the lock-out would be withdrawn'. Turner, who had remained totally silent throughout the meeting with Baldwin, wrote in his diary: 'G.C. flabbergasted at nothing being settled about miners' lock-out notices. Retired and felt dismayed...left at 1.10 p.m. disappointed and disgusted. Papers out soon about T.U.C. surrender.'[11] * Bevin's conclusion was 'that either the Government had let Samuel give assurances he ought not to have given, or Samuel had overestimated what he could do, or we had placed too great an importance on the Samuel position. Certainly the proceedings were not in conformity with the arrangements of a quarter-to-one the night before.'[12] He chose to believe the Government had reneged on a private agreement with Samuel and a letter which he and two other members of the General Council sent to the press a few days later charged Baldwin with bad faith and called on Samuel 'to speak out and to speak without any reservations. Will he deny that consultations took place between Mr Baldwin and himself on the terms of the memorandum?'[13] Bevin and his two colleagues might have been better-informed had they read the letter which Samuel attached to his Memorandum: 'I have made it clear to your committee from the outset that I have been acting entirely on my own initiative, have received no authority from the Government, and can give no assurances on their behalf.'

By the time the Negotiating Committee returned to Eccleston Square on Wednesday afternoon the Government had issued the

---

* The T.U.C.'s abject surrender even caused some surprise in the Ministry of Labour. There was, stated a confidential memorandum by C. W. K. MacMillan[15], 'something unsatisfactory about it. Why, for instance, is it necessary to animadvert on the miners' attitude after the strike began as one of the reasons for their action? It was equally the miners' attitude before the strike began. If their policy was so clear cut, why was it not stated more definitely exactly why the strike was being called? Why – as Mr Lansbury afterwards complained in his journal – was there no definite statement as to "the length to which the strike would be pushed or upon the precise terms on which it would be called off?" Finally why did the Council, before they called the strike off, not make more certain that the Samuel terms would be agreed to by the Government? And why when they met the Prime Minister was their attempt to impose any conditions with regard to return to work so very half-hearted?'

ominous statement that they had 'no power to compel employers to take back every man who has been on strike, nor have they entered into any obligation of any kind on this matter'. Bevin warned that the Movement was facing the worst disaster in its history. 'Talk about Black Friday, it isn't in it. Something has happened and the best way to describe today, if we are not quick, is that we have committed suicide. Thousands of members will be victimised as the result of this day's work.'[14] Bevin instructed his own union members to stay out until further notice and waited apprehensively for Baldwin to address the House of Commons later that afternoon. The speech added nothing to what the Negotiating Committee had already been told, and in the evening Bevin and other members of the General Council returned to Downing Street. According to Bevin's own account: 'Worthington-Evans said: "You called the strike off at twelve o'clock, but now you have called it on again." I replied, "We have called off the strike against the constitution as you put it, but now we have called a constitutional strike to defend our wages and agreements." We discussed the position with the Prime Minister and he indicated that he was broadcasting a message that night. I asked him whether I might read it. He permitted me to do so and I told him it was very sentimental but not very effective. I asked him to put in the phrase that trade unions and employers should meet forthwith to arrange a resumption.'[16] To his credit, Baldwin did include such a phrase in his broadcast, but it was over shadowed by his statement that the strike had ended 'without conditions entered into by the Government. No government confronted by such a menace could enter into a conditional negotiation, the very undertaking of which would involve treachery to the accepted basis of our democratic constitution'.

To the strikers this was the first official indication that they had not won a magnificent victory, for what had been plain to the General Council since noon was certainly not reflected in the pronouncements which flowed from Eccleston Square during the rest of the day. The *British Worker* ran three editions, each redolent of triumph. The first edition, announcing termination of the strike, carried the headline, 'General Council Satisfied that Miners Will Now Get a Fair Deal' and printed the text of the Samuel Memorandum without comment. Under the heading, 'Miners' Thanks to Their Allies', the second edition quoted that part of the miners' executive resolution which expressed 'profound admiration' for the support which had been forthcoming from individual unions. A three-line reference to the fact that the miners had been instructed to stay out pending the decision of a Delegate Conference on Friday was the only indication of disagreement between the General Council and the miners' executive. The final issue featured a manifesto by the General Council asserting that 'assurances' they had been given had enabled them 'to terminate the general stoppage in order that negotiations could be resumed to secure a settlement in the coal-mining industry, free and unfettered from either strike or lock-out'. The manifesto, which was also sent to all affiliated unions, trades councils and strike committees and reprinted in Thursday's *British Worker*, concluded: 'The unions that have maintained so resolutely and unitedly their generous and ungrudging support of the miners can be satisfied that an honourable understanding has been reached.' Thomas assured the Parliamentary Labour party that the Government was bound by the Samuel Memorandum, while George Hicks was equally emphatic that 'the strike had been called off on this binding understanding'.[17] A letter sent on Wednesday to all branches of the Railway Clerks' Association, signed 'Yours in Victory' by A. G. Walkden, the Association's general secretary, stated that the T.U.C. had received 'an undertaking for the withdrawal of the lock-out notices and the continuance of the subsidy for such reasonable period as may be required for completing the negotiations'. It was, added Walkden, 'part of the understanding on which the General Strike was concluded that there should be no victimisation on either side'.[18] The telegram sent by Cramp to members of the N.U.R. claimed not only that the lock-out notices had been withdrawn but that 'There are to be no wage cuts whatever for the miners'.[19]

Some strike committees took these bogus declarations at face value. Birmingham, for instance, printed a special 'Victory Bulletin' and even the militant committees in Islington and St Pancras thought there was cause to celebrate. Others were puzzled but felt certain that, in the words of the Wealdstone committee, 'whatever the conditions, it means that justice has triumphed'. Aldershot was also convinced that the ending of the strike 'was for the best, although we cannot understand it yet, as we all thought we had won'. To most strike committees, however, the realities were clear long before Baldwin's evening broadcast. In London, some of the T.U.C.'s volunteer drivers had bundles of the *British Worker* thrown back into their faces, while others were cornered by irate strikers and ordered to give information they did not possess. In the Vale of Leven the news from the T.U.C. was greeted with 'furious boos and hissings'. At Oxford there was 'bitter disappointment at "cave in".' At Ripley, in Derbyshire: 'Everybody furious when settlement was known'. At Wolverhampton: 'The whole of the workers stood solid and were prepared to fight to the bitter end, so that when the news came through…that the strike was over it came as a shock'. At Wakefield: 'The spirit was magnificent, and consternation and dismay prevailed when the news came that the strike was called off had been confirmed'. Hull reported: 'Alarm—fear—despair—a victorious army disarmed and handed over to its enemies.' At Long Eaton the T.U.C.'s wire was thought at first to be a forgery because it came via the local police station. Manchester shared the disbelief. When Fenner Brockway placed the General Council's telegram before the strike committee, they asked him if he was sure it was not a hoax. 'One delegate,' he says, 'even suggested that I had been "got at" by the other side! Finally, they adjourned for a midday meal whilst their secretary telephoned London, sending out messages that meanwhile the men were to stay out. Everyone was confident, if the news proved true, that the Government must have climbed down. The next news to come through to me was a summary of "terms". They were wired as though they had been accepted by the Government; there was no indication that they were an unofficial memorandum prepared by Sir Herbert Samuel and not binding on anyone. The "terms" represented a considerable advance, though a clause providing for a temporary reduction in miners' wage was not pleasant. There was no suggestion that the lock-out of the miners was to go on. Then fuller reports came over the wire. When they revealed the truth we could not believe our ears. My first reaction was that the T.U.C. General Council had become either demoralised or corrupted. With a heavy heart I sent the "special" of the *British Worker* on to the streets.'[20]

Leslie Paul recalls that Lewisham council of action 'collapsed into wretchedness' when they received the General Council's wire. 'It was too early to shout that we were betrayed but privately that was the only thing of which we were certain. That for which the strike had been called had not been achieved... We kept saying to each other, in an agitated way, "We must keep calm" and we handed out this wonderful phrase to enquirers, and repeated it at all the public meetings. But what were we going to do on the morrow? Go back to the boring daily round after this intoxicating taste of power?'[21]

For the strikers of Lewisham, as indeed for those elsewhere, the boring daily round did not begin on the morrow. The Government's announcement that it could not compel the reinstatement of every man who had been on strike was seen by employers as an invitation to smash the power of trade unionism and put an end to collective bargaining. Many of the men reporting for work on Wednesday night and Thursday morning—including engineers, who had only entered the strike at midnight on Tuesday—were refused employment. Others were offered terms which might include wage cuts, loss of seniority and pension rights, and a ban on union membership. The railway companies were especially determined to exploit the situation and employees offered reinstatement were required to sign an acknowledgment that they were not relieved of the consequences of breaking their service. American observers saw clearly what was happening. The New York *Herald-Tribune* headlined its dispatch, 'British Employers' War on Unions'. The *New York Times* correspondent cabled that the strike was over 'but the lock-out has begun...it is now the turn of the employers to strike'.

In the instructions approved by the Conference of Executives on 1 May the General Council had directed that 'in the event of any action being taken and trade union agreements being placed in jeopardy...there will be no general resumption of work until those agreements are fully recognised'. The trade union movement was now informed 'that it would be better for each executive council itself to make arrangements for the resumption of work of its own members'. In effect, the movement was asked to surrender its ultimate bargaining power at precisely the time it was most needed. At the Conference of Executives in January 1927, there was bitter criticism of the General Council both for its failure to secure guarantees against victimisation and for its decision to call out the second line unions on the eve of its visit to Downing Street. Bevin's reply to the latter point was that orders had gone out to the engineers and shipbuilders on Friday and that it had not been possible to cancel them. 'We had cut our lines of communication, as you must do in a general strike... It was not quite so simple as sending telegrams. The trade that is referred to is the engineering trade, and in the engineering trade I think there are forty-one unions, and of those forty-one unions not all the executives are in London. A large number of organisers and others had to be got in touch with all over the country, and it was not quite so ready as the rest of us.' Pugh dealt with the question of victimisation. 'The General Council could not, obviously, obtain guarantees from the Government as to what would apply in respect of agreements between organisations of employers and workers in the country. The General Council could not undertake to discuss those agreements. It was clearly recognised that in respect of those agreements the matter must be one between the parties responsible for them. That course was followed right throughout the country. There are no circumstances under which the General Council could take the place of the union executives in arranging what should follow the national strike so far as the unions are concerned.' Asked by a delegate why, in that case, the principle had been adopted by the Conference of Executives on 1 May, Pugh replied by throwing the whole blame on to the miners. 'To illustrate what I mean, I will take my own industry, seeing that eighty-five per cent of my people could not start work owing to the mining dispute being continued. I would ask my friend if it was possible for the General Council to secure that the whole of those men should be reinstated?' In so far as it went, this was a fair comment, but it did not explain the General Council's failure to guard against the wholesale assault on wages and working conditions. It is probable that Pugh and his colleagues simply did not envisage a vindictive reaction from employers. As Beatrice Webb observed, 'they drifted into the general strike, and suddenly closed it down, in both cases swayed by the impulse of the moment without any consideration for the necessities and interests of those with whom they were co-operating. And yet they mean so well! They are so genuinely kindly in their outlook; they would gladly shake hands with anyone at any time, whether it be a Tory Prime Minister, a Russian emissary or their own employers. They play at revolution and they run away from the consequences with equal alacrity'.[22]

Had the men returning for work succumbed to the pressure of their employers, the unions would have been able to do little about it. As one group of strikers wrote later: 'The bosses in all trades felt, in fact, that now they had the trade union movement at their feet, and all they had to do was to stamp on it.'[23] It was anger, however, not panic that motivated rank-and-file trade unionists. Without waiting for a lead from either the T.U.C. or their own executives, they refused to accept the humiliating terms which employers were trying to dictate. As a result, 100,000 more men were out on Thursday than on any previous day. Anger was reinforced by the now certain knowledge that the General Strike had been called off without the miners' assent or a withdrawal of the mining lock-out. The *British Gazette*'s headlines proclaimed, 'Unconditional Withdrawal of Notices by T.U.C. Men to Return Forthwith. Surrender Received by Premier in Downing Street.'*

Reaction in Lewisham and Manchester was again typical. Paul recounts that Thursday in Lewisham was 'all confusion. Strikers were trying to get from branch secretaries, who were trying to get from district secretaries, who were trying to get from executives the terms on which they should go back. More men than ever were out of work. Some transport workers took the broadcasts that the strike was off as a personal instruction and reported back to work, so that in our borough we heard of strike-breakers and strikers jointly running vehicles. This so infuriated the local busmen that they formed a procession to march on the local bus garage and demand the terms upon which work was to be resumed. They had not got halfway before police barred their way and when a tram came along

* This was the last issue of the *British Gazette*. On Wednesday 12 May, Churchill convened a meeting of newspaper owners at the Treasury to canvass their views on the *Gazette*'s future. It 'was sentenced to immediate death'.[24]

and broke the police ranks a wild melee and chase developed through the streets. We began to think things might go our way after all, and a soldiers' battle develop now that the generals had left the field to parley, and so we thought of strengthening rather than weakening our council of action'. Brockway writes of Thursday in Manchester as 'chaos. The *Gazette*, the Government sheet, chortled over the great surrender but the temper of the workers was more militant than ever and in Manchester there was no thought of going back. Telephone inquiries came to me from all over Lancashire as to whether it was true that the General Strike had been declared "on" again. For the first time feeling was bitter—bitter against employers who were everywhere victimising the local strike stalwarts, and bitter against the T.U.C. General Council. It looked as though the end of the strike might be the beginning of the revolution'.

To the General Council, inundated with indignant telegrams and phone calls from strike committees, it seemed also that the dreaded day of revolution was about to dawn. All over the country strike committees were reacting to the letter if not the spirit of the Communist party's call for a continuation of the struggle independently of national union leaderships. In some areas a rent strike was developing; in others, which had hitherto been peaceful, there were outbreaks of violence. There was, for instance, a major riot at Swindon on Thursday when a crowd of thousands, including women with aprons full of stones, prevented the first trams from returning to the streets.[25] The Intelligence Committee reported on Thursday: 'Feeling is running frightfully high all over the North.' Desperate to regain the initiative, the executives of the three rail unions ordered their members not to resume work until previous agreements were recognised and the General Council issued a belated 'Stand Together' appeal of its own. After further assurances that the ending of the strike had made possible a resumption of negotiations in the coal industry and a renewed subsidy, this latest statement went on to warn workers against signing individual agreements with employers. 'Consult your union officials, and stand by their instructions. Your union will protect you, and will insist that all agreements previously in force shall be maintained intact.' A much tougher statement, issued several hours later, reflects the General Council's increasing alarm. 'Those employers who imagine that the calling off of the General Strike means the failure of the trade union movement are making the mistake of their lives …It is not beaten. It is not broken. Its strength is unimpaired, and reinforced by the solidarity which the response to the General Strike revealed. If one class of employers, misinterpreting the calling off of the strike, thinks it can seize the opportunity to disrupt and degrade the Trade Union movement the situation is grave indeed; for to that the movement cannot and will not submit.'

Baldwin was due to speak in the House of Commons on Thursday evening and both Laski and Snowden privately urged him to take a stand against victimisation. Other pressures were exerted by several members of the Cabinet who 'were very nervous of the P.M. showing undue magnanimity' and Birkenhead drafted an unyielding speech for the Prime Minister.* Baldwin, however, saw as clearly as the General Council the dangers of an unofficial strike led by local militants and he rejected Birkenhead's draft as 'not being in [my] style'.[26] In the Commons Baldwin reaffirmed the Government's pledges to stand by the volunteers, but also denounced any attempt to destroy trade unionism or undermine working conditions.

> I will not countenance any attack on the part of any employers to use this present occasion for trying in any way to get reductions in wages below those in force before the strike or any increase in hours ...There can be no greater disaster than that there should be anarchy in the trade union world. It would be impossible in our highly developed system of industry to carry on unless you had organisations which could speak for and bind the parties on both sides ...We know that in all these great organisations there are some who are of little help. At a time like this there are some who like fishing in troubled waters. Let us get the workers calm as soon as we can, lest their work spoils the work of half a century.

Government hardliners including Hoare, Amery and Joynson-Hicks, 'professed themselves satisfied with the P.M.'s speech'. Duff Cooper, who was perhaps closer to Tory backbench opinion, was less grudging. 'Ever since the strike began until yesterday morning', he wrote in his diary after Thursday's debate, 'I have had a sensation of sick anxiety. This afternoon it returned, but the Prime Minister's speech dispelled it for good... I came home and dressed for dinner for the first time since the trouble began.'

Baldwin's appeal and the grim determination of the strikers to stand fast had their effect and by the weekend agreements were reached in all disaffected industries. Terms were better than those originally offered, but still involved considerable hardship for many workers. The London newspaper proprietors settled for a ban on chapel meetings during working hours and a guarantee against further interference with the contents of newspapers. In Glasgow the powerful Outram Press, which controlled four dailies and one weekly, was more obdurate. All its employees were required to re-

* Churchill was not part of this particular Cabinet faction. According to Jones's diary for Thursday 12 May: 'Winston, strange to say, is now for being generous and has drafted a passage on wages for the P.M.'

nounce their union membership and journalists were even forbidden to join union colleagues at a dinner. The Stationery Office declared an 'open' shop and the *Manchester Guardian* seized its chance to impose a 'company' union on employees. The settlement concluded by Bevin on behalf of the dockers contained an admission that they had broken their original agreement and an assurance that the union would refrain in future from attempting to persuade supervisory grades to join in strike action. Bevin's efforts on behalf of the bus and tram workers were far less successful. Many were dismissed or suspended, while others lost their superannuation claims or were forced out of the union. (In Brighton alone the transport workers lost at least a thousand members.) In spite of this, Bevin was able to report at the end of May that out of 353,000 members who had gone on strike, the union had failed to secure reinstatement for less than 1,500.

The railwaymen were not so fortunate. Cramp's telegram to N.U.R. branches on Friday afternoon claimed: 'Complete reinstatement secured without penalties.' But under the agreement signed that day, men were to be taken back by the railway companies 'as soon as traffic offers and work can be found for them'. The agreement also provided for the removal to other jobs of strikers who had held supervisory posts, contained an admission by the unions that they had committed 'a wrongful act against the companies', and denied reinstatement to 'persons who have been guilty of violence or intimidation'. In return, the companies dropped their demand for £100,000 as security against any further 'wrongful acts'. (They had originally demanded a fine of a week's wages per striker.) The leaders of all three rail unions appeared to regard this harsh settlement as an achievement. Bromley described it as 'very satisfactory' and Walkden praised 'the magnanimous spirit' of the railway managers.[27] In his broadcast that night—the first by a Labour leader since the commencement of the strike—Thomas also paid tribute to their magnanimity. 'If any words of mine can help, may I say to every employer: Follow the example of the railway companies. Do the big thing.' Five months later Thomas told the Labour party conference that 200,000 railwaymen were working three days a week and 45,000 were still waiting for jobs. To some extent these figures reflected the general decline in railway freight trade due to the continuing coal lock-out. To an even greater extent they were the result of a prolonged and vindictive campaign of retaliation on the part of the railway companies.*

* On Monday 10 May, Sir Guy Granet, of the L.M.S.R., and Sir Felix Pole, of the G.W.R., told the Permanent Secretary to the Ministry of Transport that 'they did not want to destroy the unions, but only wanted power to select the men who should return after the Strike so as to eliminate undesirables.' Both represented themselves as being for 'moderation'.[28]

On the day after the agreement Fyfe wrote in his diary: 'I am afraid that Thomas has lost again the popularity he won back by his speeches just before the strike began. The feeling against the General Council is bitter, and, because of the general belief that he was more desirous than the rest of the G.C. of ending the strike, against him in particular...many are inclined to think that most of the blame for what has happened should be laid at the door of the miners' representatives who wouldn't agree to anything, so members of the G.C. are saying. But this has no bearing on the pitiful plight of the many strikers who are losing their jobs, or the harsh terms employers are imposing on those who return to work... In fact, the counter-attack by employers has failed, but has nevertheless, caused casualties. There is a lot of victimisation going on, I am afraid.' There was also resistance to victimisation. More than 30,000 railwaymen, printers, engineers and dockers remained on strike in Hull until 16 May to force the reinstatement of 150 tramway employees. In Eastbourne, members of all trades who stayed out until 17 May were also protesting against victimisation of tramwaymen. Workers at Erith stayed out until 24 May 'owing to the employers' attitude in not taking all the men back together'. But a week after the T.U.C.'s visit to Downing Street, anger had given way in most places to bitter acceptance of the inevitable. Brockway writes that in Manchester, where on 14 May 30,000 railwaymen had marched through the streets demanding unconditional reinstatement: 'A spirit of fatalism came over the workers. The T.U.C. had ordered them back; there was no hope of concerted resistance—so back they went ...Of course a General Strike must be revolutionary; it is of necessity a conflict between the workers and the capitalist state. The strike of 1926 was led by a General Council who did not realise this when they reluctantly authorised the struggle. And they drew back from it as soon as they understood its full implications.' Paul records that the Lewisham council of action 'melted away'. 'Who was willing to work for it any more? The temporary unity of the local movement, a source of happiness and pride...collapsed. The Right-wing, for the most part silent during the struggle...were relieved to see the strike out of the way so that they might continue once again the parliamentary work in which they believed, and history was to bear them out, the true future of the Labour movement to lie'.

Chapter Sixteen

# *Spoils of War*

'Mr Baldwin's proposals for a Mines settlement have been presented to the two parties for consideration. They include some but not all the points of the Samuel Memorandum; they suggest reductions of wages.'

From the *British Worker*, Saturday 15 May 1926.

'The Government has gained immense prestige in the world and the British Labour Movement has made itself ridiculous. A strike which opens with a football match between the police and the strikers and ends in unconditional surrender after nine days with densely-packed reconciliation services at all chapels and churches of Great Britain attended by the strikers and their families, will make the continental Socialists blaspheme ...Let me add that the failure of the General Strike shows what a *sane* people the British are. If only our revolutionaries would realise the hopelessness of their attempt to turn the British workman into a Russian Red and the British business man and country gentleman into an Italian Fascist! The British are hopelessly good-natured and common-sensical—to which the British workman adds pigheadedness, jealousy and stupidity... We are all of us just good-natured and stupid folk. The worst of it is that the governing class are as good-natured and stupid as the Labour Movement!'

Beatrice Webb writing in her diary on 18 May 1926.

'It is said on the Continent that the English and especially the working-men, are cowardly, that they cannot carry out a revolution because, unlike the French, they do not riot at intervals, because they apparently accept the bourgeois *regime* so quietly. This is a complete mistake. The English working-men are second to none in courage; they are quite as restless as the French, but they fight differently. That courage is required for a turnout, often indeed much loftier courage, much bolder, firmer determination than for an insurrection is self-evident. It is in truth, no trifle for a working man who knows want from experience, to face it with wife and children, to endure hunger and wretchedness for months together, and stand firm and unshaken through it all... And precisely in this quiet perseverance, in this lasting determination which undergoes a hundred tests every day, the English working-man develops that side of his character which commands most respect.'

From *The Condition of the Working Class in England*, by Friedrich Engels, first published in 1845.

'Since May 12th we have been left to continue our struggle alone, but not alone, as the rank and file are still with us. They did not let us down. Our bus-men, car-men, rail-men, and dock-men, men from the desks—pens laid aside—printers and pressmen, engineers and electricity men from the rank and file. All joined together with one motto: "Solidarity for Ever—and Capitalism defied!" As miners we thank them. For us they refused to bend; for us they struck our rights to defend. With such support our cause will not fail, for we all believe right will in the end prevail... We hope still that those leaders of the T.U.C. who feel that a mistake has been made will rally to our cause and help us to victory.'

A. J. Cook in *The Nine Days*, May 1926.

'One cold, brutal, inexorable fact stands out clear and distinct. Over one million mine workers together with their womenfolk and children are starving—yes, comrades, starving in the midst of plenty, starving in a land at the centre of which, here in this great Metropolis, wealth produced by the toilers of Britain is being poured out like water in an unparalleled orgy of wanton extravagance and luxurious pleasure.'

*Lansbury's Labour Weekly*, 29 May 1926.

'In this fight we have everything against us. The fight is absolutely unequal. It is not of our seeking. There will be no hunger in the homes of any colliery owners, their children will be fed and clothed, housed and educated just as usual, no matter how long the stoppage continues. On our side, there is privation, there is hunger and there is untimely death caused by this dispute. Therefore, we are not on equal terms. I want, even in face of the speech delivered by the Chancellor of the Exchequer, to say that there is another force against us besides the employers. The Government of the country is on the side of the mine-owners and against the miners in this dispute.'

Robert Smillie, miners' leader, speaking in the House of Commons, 31 August 1926.

245

I

Immediately after his Commons speech on Thursday, Baldwin met the miners' leaders at Downing Street. He emphasised that the Government was bound in no way by the Samuel Memorandum and that he would be tabling proposals of his own next day. 'There was never at any time,' Cook complained to the Conference of Executives in January, 'any shred of a hope of the miners having an opportunity of accepting the Samuel Memorandum as a basis for negotiations. That is a challenge I make.' But the miners themselves had not the slightest interest in the Memorandum. 'I understand they had rejected it, when discussing it with the Trades Union Council,' Baldwin told the Commons on 1 June, 'and they made no attempt after that to press its adoption on the Government. I say that in order to clear away certain criticisms which have been made against the Government for not having adopted that Memorandum as it stood. The Miners' Executive had publicly rejected that Memorandum and they adhered to that view when they saw me. I, therefore, informed Mr Herbert Smith and Mr Evan Williams, and the colleagues of each of them, that in the circumstances—I think I informed the House in the same sense—I had no alternative at that moment but to put forward to both sides proposals which appeared to me, or which should appear to me, to offer a reasonable basis of negotiations for settlement.' The miners' attitude allowed Baldwin to extricate himself from a potentially embarrassing situation, for as the General Council later argued, a decision by the miners in favour of Samuel 'would have thrown upon the Government and the mine-owners the responsibility for any continuance of the deadlock, a policy on their part which would have been opposed by public opinion'. Since the Memorandum, as it stood, was wholly unacceptable to most of the Cabinet, Laski was probably right in believing that Baldwin would have chosen to resign in such circumstances.

On Friday 14 May, the Government published Steel-Maitland's letter of disclaimer to Samuel and presented its own scheme for a settlement. This envisaged immediate wage cuts to be eased for a short time by a £3 million Government subsidy, while a National Wages Board, whose chairman was to have a casting vote, laid down the principles for a permanent fixing of the wage rates in each district. The Government rejected nationalisation of mining royalties and municipal trading but promised to give legislative effect to the Samuel Commission's other reorganisation proposals. The Government also stated its willingness to amend the Seven Hours Act, 'If the parties agree that it is advisable that some temporary modification should be made in the statutory hours of work.' Finally, the whole scheme was made conditional on its acceptance by both miners and owners, which naturally invited a repetition of the deadlock existing prior to the strike.

On 19 May the adjourned delegate conference of the miners expressed its agreement with the Government's reorganisation proposals, but rejected those dealing with wages and hours. The owners were even more uncompromising. In an interview with Steel-Maitland on 21 May they urged that wage cuts, longer hours and 'freedom from political interference' were all essential to the survival of the industry. Privately, Evan Williams warned the Minister of Labour that the Government's attempts to end the dispute were merely prolonging it and that, in any case, the owners could not be compelled to co-operate with a National Wages Board.[1] Confident that no Tory Government would interfere with their independence, the owners did not even try to disguise their contempt for those urging reform of the industry. Their political adviser, Austin Hopkinson, described the Royal Commission's proposals as 'sloppy eyewash' and informed readers of the *English Review* that the owners had, from the start, pursued a clearly defined policy designed 'to make the position of interfering politicians so unpleasant that they will for the future think twice before they meddle with the basic industries of the country'. Even Birkenhead was irritated. 'It would be possible to say without exaggeration of the miners' leaders that they were the stupidest men in England if we had not had frequent occasion to meet the owners.' Official Government reaction was vigorous but unconstructive. It 'deplored' the owners' attitude, warned the miners that it no longer held itself 'bound by the terms of an offer which had been rejected'—and, for the time being, left it at that. Its only other initiatives at this stage were confined to arranging for massive imports of foreign coal, issuing regulations restricting domestic coal consumption to 100 cwt a month, and renewing the State of Emergency.

Attention was also given to the future of the O.M.S. The Organisation, which wanted to secure a permanent status for itself, suggested to the Home Secretary that it should be allowed to maintain an up-to-date file of volunteers for use in future emergencies and that a public appeal should be launched for funds. A memorandum initialled by John Anderson firmly quashed both suggestions. This argued that a public appeal for funds would be politically divisive at a time when the Prime Minister himself was appealing for unity and tolerance and that O.M.S. assistance had, anyway, been of 'comparatively small importance'. The Supply and Transport Committee agreed with these conclusions and the Home Secretary wrote to Lord Hardinge pointing out that what was required were lists of key men such as train drivers, electricity workers and motor drivers. Since there were always sufficient railway volunteers and the electricity commissioners had their own lists, this left motor drivers 'on which the O.M.S. would hardly think it worth their time concentrating their efforts.'

Meanwhile, bitter controversy was still raging in Labour circles over the General Council's decision to call off the strike. The rail unions' refusal to impose a coal-handling embargo and the T.U.C.'s decision not to raise funds for the miners through a compulsory levy added to the miners' sense of grievance and betrayal. 'We have been fighting,' Cook told a mass rally of South Wales miners on 23 May, 'not only against the Government and the owners, but against a number of Labour leaders, specially the political leaders, whose position has been compromised... I have had experience of being bullied in colliery offices; I have had experience in 1920 and 1921 of meeting various Prime Ministers, but never have we been bullied by the employers or the Government to the extent that we were bullied by certain trade union leaders to accept a reduction in wages. The Government knew that and the coalowners knew it. One man on the other side said to me, "The T.U.C. will help us", and the Prime Minister on more than one occasion publicly thanked the T.U.C.'

Of the trade union leaders, Bevin alone was willing to try and help the miners out of their predicament. A week later he brought Smith and Cook with him to meet Baldwin. The Prime Minister told the miners bluntly that if they went on with the strike they would be beaten and that they should agree to longer hours. But as he confessed later that day to several of his colleagues, 'I did not move them.'[2] Churchill, who felt considerable sympathy towards the miners now that the strike had been defeated, argued that the Government could not afford simply to stand aside from what looked like a policy of starvation and that it should bring in an Eight Hours Bill at once for all pits above a certain wage level. Birkenhead agreed, but Baldwin disliked the idea of legislating without the prior agreement of both sides in the dispute and recalled Lloyd George's refusal to intervene in the coal crisis of 1921: 'He was successful.' Churchill's rejoinder that this had been after twelve weeks 'at a frightful cost' failed to convince Baldwin. 'We've got to guard against a settlement which is not a settlement. No time wasted so far. Our proposals turned down ten days ago. There are mutterings in various parts of the country. That process will quicken. I am not clear in my own mind on what we should butt on. I see nothing but a stone wall.'[3]

During the early part of June, Churchill's view gained ground rapidly in the Cabinet and was privately encouraged by Frank Hodges, secretary of the Miners' International. Those who advocated an eight-hour day did so because they were convinced that this would entail less sacrifice for the miners—and particularly for their families—than a cut in wages. 'If you substitute a longer working day for wage reductions,' Neville Chamberlain noted in his diary on 13 June, 'the women and children come out of the picture altogether. The whole burden then falls on the man, and he is not going to get a lot of sympathy if he is obliged to work as long as a railwayman.' This had a persuasive ring but entirely ignored the Samuel Commission's findings: 'The gain through the lengthening of working hours is not a net gain, either to the country as a whole, or to the mining industry, if that be taken to include the miners themselves. There is a heavy loss, in unemployment and distress and expenditure to relieve distress, which must be set against the apparent gain.' Baldwin, who had long been an adherent of the eight-hour day, was by now also convinced that the Government should take the initiative and a Bill to suspend the Seven Hours Act for five years was formally presented to the Commons on 21 June—with the owners' support. A second Bill introduced at the same time made only the merest concessions to the Samuel Report. It provided for a welfare levy on royalties and facilitated but did not compel amalgamations.

The Miners' Federation and the General Council had been preparing to submit their respective pleas to a conference of trade union executives called for 25 June. Both agreed, however, that the time was not right for an unpleasant inquest and the conference was deferred 'so that a united policy may be adopted to resist to the fullest extent the Government's action'. All sections of the trade union movement were also called upon 'to avoid statements, either in speech or writing, which create friction, misunderstanding and divert attention from the purpose in view'. But the miners' repeated appeal for a trade union levy and a coal-handling embargo were both rejected and the Labour party was unable to prevent the passage of a Bill which would, MacDonald declared, equip the owners with 'knuckle dusters'. On 30 June, the day before the Eight Hours Bill passed its Third Reading, Beatrice Webb observed that the Cabinet had now become 'parliamentary agents to the coal owners... The House of Commons today is in fact a tied house; but tied not as a body but in two mutually hostile groups, each pledged to fight out, in the government of the country, the struggle which is being carried on, openly or covertly, throughout industry at a fearful cost to the country... Ought the *capitalist* or the *organised workman* govern the country? Alas! for the plain citizen and the long-suffering consumer! Or it might lead to bloodshed. Out of this turmoil might emerge Lloyd George as arbiter; or Winston as Mussolini. It is clear that in their own imaginations, each of these two active politicians sees himself as *The Man of Destiny*! Of the two I back the Welsh Wizard—a stronger and bigger fighter.' The Eight Hours Bill received the Royal Assent on 8 July and four days later the owners posted up fresh wage rates, which meant cuts in most districts.*

Another bitter controversy involving the miners also reached its climax at the end of June. At the beginning of the month a British note had been sent to Moscow protesting at the large sums of money which Soviet unions were donating to the Miners' Relief Fund.† 'The King', wrote Lord Stamfordham to the Home Secretary, 'is a little anxious with regard to our remonstrances... His Majesty is sure you and the Government will differentiate between money sent in aid of the General Strike (to which we could unquestionably take exception) and that contributed on behalf of those suffering from the Coal Strike. It would be disastrous if the Government's action could in any way justify a cry from the Socialist party that the former were attempting to stop financial aid from Russia or from any other country to save the miners' women and children from starvation.'⁴ The Government would have been happy to let the matter drop, but its Right-wing supporters, ever eager for an excuse to denounce trade and diplomatic relations with the Soviet Union, forced a Commons debate on 'Russian Gold'. Although, by a curious omission on the part of Mr Speaker, no miners' M.P.s were called, Lansbury voiced their sentiments with abrasive eloquence: 'I do believe in the class war. I believe the class war is responsible for the starvation of my kith and kin, people who are bone of my bone and flesh of my flesh, down in the coalfields of Britain. The only thing that is being asked today by the Government and the capitalists is that the workers should sacrifice. I hope to God that the workers will be able to stand out and with their women defeat the most nefarious campaign that has ever been waged against them.'⁵

Few Tories were prepared to accept that the miners were starving. 'They are not within sight of starvation, hardly of under-nutrition, so well are they looked after by the guardians,' Chamberlain noted in

---

* Owners in the wealthy West Yorkshire area not only posted up lower wage rates but also attempted to alter the former wages/profits ratio to their advantage. Lane Fox was dispatched to warn them that the Government would not countenance a departure from the 87:13 ratio and would legislate, if necessary, to prevent it.

† Of the £1.8 million contributed to the Miners' Relief Fund for the 14 months up to 30 June 1927, more than half came from Soviet trade unions. Individual British trade unions raised £191,000, the T.U.C. General Council £164,000, and the Women's Committee for the Relief of Miners' Wives and Children £112,000.

his diary on 20 June. 'They are not living too uncomfortably at the expense of the ratepayer, while the nation is gradually overcome by creeping paralysis.'* A similar assertion was made publicly by Baldwin when fund-raising groups from the Miners' Federation arrived in Europe, Russia and America. A survey conducted by the N.S.P.C.C. also claimed that there was no urgent need among miners' children. Beatrice Webb was of the same opinion. She wrote in her diary on 18 June that letters from the women of Seaham Harbour—her husband's Durham mining constituency—'reveal no distress and some light-hearted enjoyment of the strike; the children, one mother tells me, regard the school feeding "as a picnic that happens every day", the food being better than they got at home— the relief provided by the guardians is nicknamed "Kind Joe", and some women, at any rate, are better off than they were before the lock-out. Miss Purves, the Federation secretary, an able and experienced woman—the daughter of a local tradesman—is puzzled to know what to do if the Central Women's Committee send down any funds—"the families are amply provided for".' After a visit to Seaham as late as 24 October Mrs Webb was able to note that 'The surface facts show no exceptional distress : indeed the pit villages look clean and prosperous and the inhabitants healthy (death rate unusually low). Various people told us that the men and boys had benefited from the rest, sun, and open air and abstinence from alcohol and tobacco... And the women freed from coal dust and enjoying regular hours : whilst the school-children, through the ample supply of first-class food (eleven meals each week at a cost of 3s 6d. per child at wholesale prices) were certainly improved in health and happiness... There was certainly no sign of strain. As I looked at the gathering of 400 miners' wives and daughters, in their best dresses, and the prettily decorated tea tables, with piles of cakes and bread-and-butter, it might have been a gathering of prosperous lower middle-class women—in appearance these women looked as comfortably off as Mrs Anderson Fenn [wife of the Labour party organiser for the north-east] and myself—their clothes certainly were quite as respectable and attractive. Neither were they gloomy—they were in a jolly talkative state of mind; they were enjoying their lives.'

Starvation may not have been a threat in Seaham, but the neatness and gaiety of its women were a reflection of pride rather than prosperity. Nor were all mining communities as fortunate. Where the

* The guardians did not pay relief to miners on strike, but only to their wives and children. The amount of poor relief paid out in the six months ending 30 September 1926, was £13 million—almost double the amount paid out in the same period of the previous year. On 1 May 1926, just over one million people were on poor relief. By July the total had risen to 2½ million.[6]

local authorities were less sympathetic, relief rates were cut, and services such as free milk for babies and free meals for necessitious school-children, suspended. 'The work of every Relief Committee is made a hundred times more difficult,' an official of the Women's Relief Committee told the Labour party conference in October, 'by the fact that we have to turn our backs on three-quarters of the distress for lack of means. Every week the need for funds becomes a hundred times more urgent. Every week some new Board of Guardians stops giving relief altogether. Every week some new Education Authority stops feeding the school-children ...A few days ago I saw a little grey-faced baby die in a home denuded of every comfort, with its mother half starved, sobbing her heart out because she had not the means to give it the necessary nourishment to save its life ...It would be a lasting disgrace to the Labour movement if the miners were beaten to their knees and defeated by the hideous and intolerable suffering which is being inflicted on their helpless wives and children.' It was undoubtedly increasing hardship among the mining communities and the General Council's adamant refusal to impose an embargo on coal-handling which finally induced the miners' executive to yield in their attitude to wage cuts. On 15 July it decided to recommend to a delegate conference a scheme proposed by a number of eminent Churchmen led by the Bishop of Lichfield. This provided for an immediate resumption of work and a renewal of the Government subsidy for four months while a new national agreement was negotiated. If the negotiations failed, an independent arbitrator would fix the award. Meanwhile, the Samuel commissioners would draft Bills giving effect to their reorganisation proposals.

The arbitration clause was a notable concession on the part of the miners' executive, but it failed to impress the Government. When the Bishop and his colleagues met Baldwin on 19 July they were told that a further subsidy was completely out of the question. The coal industry had been taught to expect public money whenever it howled, said Baldwin, and he was determined to end that. 'Plainly the Government wished that we would keep out of it,' wrote Dr Temple, then Bishop of Manchester, 'and are disposed to say that if we encourage the miners we prolong the strike. They expect a break fairly soon.'[7] Baldwin told Jones that he wished the bishops would go back to look after their flocks. 'What [they] do not seem to realise is that what they will do is to keep in power the latent atheist bolshevists, like Cook, and of whose leadership no good can come to the miners.' On 30 July a delegate conference of miners endorsed what by now had become known as the Bishops'

Memorandum, thereby giving the Government a splendid opportunity of securing a settlement on the basis of the Samuel Report, including wage cuts. But Baldwin would not shift from his refusal to hand out another subsidy and the opportunity was lost. The Miners' Minority Movement and the Communist party were naturally opposed to the provision for compulsory arbitration on wages and the miners' executive were forced to submit the whole scheme to a district vote. This resulted in rejection by the narrow majority of 34,000. The Government immediately pointed to this as a vindication of its own refusal to consider the Bishop's Memorandum, but had they responded imaginatively in the first place it is highly probable that the result of the vote would have been different.

Another indication of the miners' willingness to reach a compromise came on 17 August when a delegate conference empowered the executive to reopen negotiations with the owners and the Government without prior conditions. The owners, however, interpreted this merely as a sign of weakness and made it brutally clear in their meeting with the miners' executive on 19 August that they would accept nothing short of total surrender. 'I do not know whether, with your recent ecclesiastical associations, you have developed the habit of starting the proceedings with prayer and a hymn,' gibed Evan Williams, 'and I hope you will not find it strange if we do away with that this afternoon and get straight to business.' It was essential, Williams continued, for there to be changes in both hours and wages, and furthermore, these had to be carried out in each district since national agreements were 'deleterious and detrimental'. Smith replied that the miners had made a sincere offer. 'Would to God I had not made it now, as far as I am concerned, because it is wrong... We said we did not intend to increase our working day; we made that clear to you. We said we were prepared to inquire into the particular point, utilise it to the best advantage, and do all we possibly can to save our faces if we have to have reductions, and ask the Government to play their part. It is no good saying you are anxious to get a settlement; if you ask me to say the truth, I do not think you are. I intend putting a bit more fight into this than I have done; I have to do it whether I want to or not. I get no younger, but I will fight on while there is a bit left of me. If there is a feeling that you are the only persons on earth and we have to do this and that, I want to say I have not been bred that road. A fair deal I will put up with, but I will not have it crammed down me — that I will resist. Good afternoon.'[8]

On 24 August the miners' executive turned to the Government. Churchill, who was in charge of the Cabinet Coal Committee during

Baldwin's holiday excursion at Aix, immediately informed them that 'the question of giving any financial help to the industry has long passed out of the sphere of practical politics', but that, if the miners had any new suggestions to make, the Government would gladly help to resume negotiations with the owners.* Although the possibility of wage reductions had clearly been in Smith's mind the previous week, he now refused to go beyond his original promise to examine the Samuel Report 'page by page and accept its findings'.[9] Cook, who had protested fiercely when Smith first made the promise in May, now himself wanted to go far beyond it. Jones noted that the miners' secretary was especially anxious to get out new proposals 'but Herbert Smith had his feet on Cook's neck. When the meeting was over Cook in unmistakable language told Gowers and me what he thought of Smith and he tried to make our joint communiqué to the Press say that the men were prepared to face a reduction in wages. This I had to turn down as it went beyond what took place and would have justified Smith in denouncing it'. The miners' leaders decided to thrash the issue out at yet another delegate conference, which was fixed for 2 September. On the day before, Ramsay MacDonald travelled to Chartwell for a private discussion with Churchill. The Labour leader explained that the miners did not know—and would not know—of his visit. 'But he had been with [them] that day and was confident that he had much influence with them, especially with Mr Herbert Smith. If, however, he was to undertake the task of trying to persuade the Delegate Conference to "make proposals", he thought that it was only right that he should have some private assurance as to what the Government would regard as proposals of such a nature as to fulfil their promise to call a conference.'

Churchill summed up the Government's requirements in the following formula: 'We are prepared to negotiate on wages and hours to meet the immediate needs of the industry. We stand for a national settlement, in accordance with the established custom of the Federation, but we recognise the need for district variations.' He warned, however, that even if such a formula were accepted by the men, the Government could do nothing to ensure acceptance by the owners. 'If they put themselves in the wrong in this way, the Government would make no secret of their opinion that they were in the wrong, but the powers of actual coercion that the Government

* Before the meeting with the miners, Birkenhead dispatched a note to the Coal Committee urging that Cook 'should be sharply reminded that his own perverse obstinacy has greatly altered the position to the prejudice of the Miners so that the terms obtainable in May are no longer open. He might also usefully be reminded of his insulting references to the Prime Minister'.[10]

possessed were very limited. Mr MacDonald said that he quite understood that all the Government were committing themselves to was an
invitation to a conference, and was quite content with that.'[11]

The miners' delegate conference on 2 September had to face up to
several grim facts. They were in the 125th day of the lock-out with
funds in hand amounting to 1s 8d per head. In Derbyshire and the
Midlands there was a serious drift back to work and in Nottinghamshire a 'non-political' union was threatening to break away from the
federation. Above all, with imports of coal freely entering the country
they were left with no effective weapon to wield against the Government. Lancashire and South Wales alone voted against a resolution
empowering the executive to submit proposals for a new agreement,
provided only that it was national. After a further flurry of confidential meetings at Bailey's house in Bryanston Square involving
Churchill, MacDonald and the miners' officials, Cook embodied the
following formula in a letter to the Chancellor on 3 September:
'We are prepared to enter into negotiations for a new national agreement with a view to a reduction in labour costs to meet the immediate
necessities of the industry.' As Churchill had feared, Evan Williams
refused to discuss this or, indeed, any formula with the miners, and
he and other officials of the Mining Association were summoned
before the Cabinet Coal Committee on 6 September. Williams
repeated his refusal and went on to suggest that members of the
Cabinet, including the Prime Minister, had given both public and
private assurances that no further national negotiations would take
place. Churchill's angry refutation provoked a 'Ding-dong debate...
the verbatim report of which ran into fifty-six foolscap pages'.[12]
The Association was, Churchill declared, 'narrowing...the possibilities
of peace'; had the Government known that the introduction of the
Bill to extend hours 'would synchronise with a decision on your part
the moment you got it to close the national door, never should we
have allowed ourselves to be placed in that position'.

Williams made it clear that no co-operation could be expected
from the owners since a complete victory for them was already in
sight. 'There are districts where the owners' offer has been accepted
without reference in any way at all to national agreements. That
movement is spreading rapidly.'[13] Churchill's attitude was a revelation to the owners. According to Boothby, who was shortly to become
his Parliamentary Private Secretary, the Chancellor said of the
miners privately, 'I am all on their side now.' As Jones noted, 'The
way to make ministers moderate is to put them in the Chair.' But
Churchill's evident antagonism towards the owners and sympathy
with the miners aroused misgivings among several of his colleagues.

That day Steel-Maitland wrote to Davidson, who was holidaying with Baldwin at Aix, complaining that the Chancellor had allowed the miners to put 'us...into an anti-owner position'. He pointed out that Churchill had also been persuaded to modify the formula which had been drawn up for MacDonald's benefit on 1 September. 'It may do no harm, but it opens a serious loophole. He's jolly difficult when he's in a napoleonesque attitude, dictating instructions in military metaphors, and the spotlight full on him. He threw himself all over J.R.M., who is an untrustworthy beggar. But with these vagaries, he generally, after a lot of talking to, swings round to safety after all.'[14]

Two days later Steel-Maitland followed this up with another letter, pointing out that Churchill's 'impulsiveness and combativeness are an awful danger in negotiations. He has been more than a little trying as you would find if you could get Wilson or Gower or Lane-Fox to talk... Our trouble is that we jumped too soon... The miners were nearly down and out and ready to agree to anything... A few days more and perhaps the Notts and Derby agreement would have clinched it. As it was Winston jumped in too readily and was impossible to stop. With his impulsiveness he was all over the miners. Cook is able to quote him as ready, with them, to make peace and of course the miners have in turn stiffened a lot. On the other hand, the interview with the owners was lamentable. The strong hand may need to be shown, but not in a way that put all their backs up. If they were in a weak position (as during the passing of the Eight Hours Act) it would be different. But they are not, and coercive measures by the Government are not *at all* easy and they probably know it... What has also put their backs up is that they think W.C. is actuated by political and not industrial reasons and of course it is true. He thinks out industrial policy in terms of making a political speech ...He is a most brilliant fellow, but his gifts aren't those of judgment, nor of appreciating industry, nor of a negotiator.'[15] Davidson received a much more reassuring intelligence report from Patrick Duff, Baldwin's private secretary. 'Winston, considering the very disingenuous and provocative attitude of the owners, was comparatively restrained, although he always put his points aggressively and every now and then jumped on Evan Williams... I don't think Winston's activities are at present beyond what the circumstances of the situation call for, or are actuated by any desire for self-advertisement.'[16]

During the same week the Trades Union Congress opened at Bournemouth with scenes of spectacular drama revolving around John Bromley. He had infuriated the miners by publishing in his

A.S.L.E.F. journal extracts of the report which the General Council was to have presented to the Conference of Executives in June. The report was highly critical of the miners and its publication was seen as a deliberate breach of the agreement to defer criticism while the lock-out continued. It was Bromley, however, who was chosen by the General Council to second the miners' appeal for funds. As soon as he rose to speak the miners' delegation kicked over their chairs and squared up in expectation of a free fight. Some of them even tried to storm the platform. Pugh suspended the sitting for an hour and the miners marched out singing the *Red Flag*. But an attempt by Minority Movement supporters to force a debate on the General Council's decision to call off the strike was headed off by Cook, who urged that there should be no washing of dirty linen in public while the miners were still out. On the Monday after the conference the Webbs were chatting in their hotel with Lansbury and Ammon when they were joined by Cook. 'Sidney had represented him to me,' wrote Mrs Webb, 'as rude and unpleasing in manner. But with us that afternoon he was friendly—even confidential—and poured out an incoherent stream of words—vivid descriptions of Winston Churchill, J.R.M. and recent negotiations—at least his narrative would have been vivid if it had been coherent... Today he is in a funk : he sees that the miners are beaten and that all his promises of speedy and complete victory will rise up against him. "I shall tell them that we must have our Mons; a well-led army must retreat before a stronger army; *we shall win* like the British army did—perhaps four years hence." If it were not for the mule-like obstinacy of Herbert Smith, A. J. Cook would settle on *any* terms. He has led his army of a million miners into a situation where they must surrender—at discretion on any terms Winston can impose on the mine-owners.'

Churchill's attempts in this direction were proving to be notably unsuccessful. On 7 September Evan Williams had reluctantly agreed to refer the question of national negotiations to the owners' district organisations. A week later he informed the Chancellor that 23 of the 24 districts had 'clearly and emphatically' declined to give the Mining Association authority to negotiate with the miners. 'I desire to add that the decisions of the districts, which reaffirm the declarations made to you last Monday, arise from a deep and earnest conviction that settlements on a national basis, by linking the industry with politics, inevitably take the consideration of purely industrial questions out of their proper economic sphere, have been destructive of peace and prosperity to those engaged in the industry, and, as experience of the immediate past has shown, are a menace to the community as a whole.'[17] Williams's reply came as no surprise to those involved in the problem. In a summary of the situation, which he had sent to Baldwin on 10 September, Jones had spoken frankly of the dilemma which was bound to arise. 'The newspapers ask: Is it conceivable that a Conservative Government will coerce the owners, however foolish, and the assumption is, No ...What compulsion can the Government put on the owners, assuming the Cabinet agrees to go ahead? There's the rub... You will not like travelling into this region, but the Government cannot recede now without throwing over the Chancellor and his approving colleagues ...One purpose I have had in mind in recounting the above is to bring out the fact that though the language of the Chancellor has been more vigorous than some of his colleagues would use, the course he has followed has had their approval and cannot now be disowned.'[18]

On 15 September, Baldwin returned from Aix and took personal charge of the situation. Two days later he wrote to the miners suggesting an immediate resumption of work on the basis of district settlements. The one dubious concession was to be a National Appeal Tribunal with power to fix wages where more than seven hours was worked. The proposal was naturally rejected by the miners, who pointed out that it involved 'the entire surrender of the principle of national negotiations and agreements, a principle which the Commission stated to be essential, and which was endorsed in the letter of the Chancellor of the Exchequer'. That evening the miners' officials met Baldwin at Downing Street and stated the considerable lengths to which they were now prepared to go: an immediate resumption of work at rates prevailing under the 1921 agreement while an independent tribunal drew up the terms of a fresh agreement and decided ways of effecting the Samuel Report. Baldwin favoured the idea of a tribunal, with the powers of a full judicial inquiry, to settle hours nationally and a minimum percentage wage by districts. The necessary Bill was rapidly drafted, but the National Confederation of Employers' Organisations had got wind of it and they urged Baldwin not to proceed.[19]

Alarm at any form of compulsion applied to the coal-owners also spread rapidly in Government and Tory party circles. Jones summed up the sentiments expressed by Baldwin and members of the Coal Committee on 24 September: 'Suppose Tribunal formulated wages rates and owners refused to open pits, the result would be a demand for nationalisation and it would give men right to demand unemployment benefit. Is every industrial dispute to come to the P.M. and lead ultimately to arbitration? Better for Government to disinterest itself and refuse to see Evan Williams or Cook again. These and many more difficulties emerged in the course of the discussion and the opposition to positive action grew as the obstacles to making the Bill work were envisaged. Birkenhead felt it was the most difficult decision since the evacuation of the Dardanelles. On the whole he came down against action and that became the finding...' The Cabinet endorsed the finding and later that day the miners were informed that 'the Government are not prepared to go beyond the maturely considered proposals conveyed to you in the Prime Minister's letter of the 17th instant. These proposals cannot of course remain open indefinitely, but your Federation are still free to avail themselves of them by taking the practical step of ordering district negotiations to be set on foot subject to the subsequent review of an independent tribunal, where any departure from the old hours is involved'. As Jones noted, 'In their hearts the Cabinet hate this offer, and are dreadfully afraid it may be accepted.' But the Cabinet had no need to worry. The offer was contemptuously rejected and a miner's delegate conference on 7 October decided to call out safety men from the pits.

'The miners' decision to continue the dispute is heroic,' Robert Williams, the Labour party chairman, proclaimed at the party's annual conference in Margate on 11 October. 'They may be likened to the sightless Samson feeling for a grip of the pillar of the Temple, the crashing of which may engulf this thing we call British civilisation.' But hunger, cold and despair were gnawing at the miners' defiance. By the middle of October, 218,000 had returned to the pits and early in November the breakaway faction in Nottingham began negotiations for a district settlement. The T.U.C. initiated fresh talks between the miners and the Government, but the Government's original offer to set up a national arbitration authority was now modified by the proviso that it would operate for six months only. Although a coalfield ballot rejected a return to work on these terms by a majority of almost 150,000, the delegate conference despairingly recommended all districts to open negotiations. By the last day of November work was resumed in all the important coalfields. After a lock-out lasting seven months, the men had to face longer hours, lower wages, and loss of their national agreement. Birkenhead was elated. 'The discredit of the Miners' Federation,' he wrote to Halifax, 'is now complete. Torn by internal dissension they have been unable to prevent what are practically unfettered separate negotiations in each district.' After all, he concluded, there had been no point in 'losing about £30,000,000 in this insensate struggle without coming away with some trophy'.[20]

Birkenhead's sum did not include the indirect cost to the nation.

Lost coal production alone amounted to £97 million and a further £42 million had to be spent on imports of coal. The *Economist* in November put the total trade loss at between £300–£400 million. Strike pay cost the T.G.W.U. and the N.U.R. £1 million apiece and the accumulated reserves of all unions dropped from £12½ million to £8½ million in a year. In the coalfields, conditions continued to worsen. As the miners (and the Samuel Commission) had predicted, longer hours led simply to increased unemployment. In January, 1927, 200,000 were out of work. By July, 1928, the figure had risen to more than 300,000. The wages of those still fortunate enough to have jobs also slumped. Average weekly earnings in 1927 totalled 47s. Two years later they were down to 45s. When Hugh Dalton arrived in Bishop Auckland in the autumn of 1928 to seek Parliamentary nomination by the local Labour party, he found that 'human values had depreciated almost to nothing. White-faced women who starved themselves to feed their children; children certified by doctors as "suffering from malnutrition"—that meant having been half-starved long enough for it to become obvious—being fed at school; men sitting silent in Workmen's Clubs, too poor to buy either a drink or a smoke; every second shop in Newgate Street, the main street in Bishop Auckland, shuttered up and the shopkeeper ruined, because the people had no money to spend; old clothes and old boots being collected and distributed by charitable persons; others organising the departure of boys and girls, as soon as they left school, to be bell-hops in London hotels or kitchen maids in rich private houses'.[21]

The anger and frustration of individual trade unionists in the immediate aftermath of the strike enabled the Communist party to boost its membership from 6,000 to 10,000, but mass backing for the National Minority Movement was no longer forthcoming and a vigorous Left-wing campaign led by Cook and Maxton failed to rouse Labour from its caution and apathy. Trade union membership slumped below 5 million for the first time since 1916 and many unions disaffiliated from Congress. As Mrs Webb noted, the General Strike was 'a proletarian distemper which had to run its course and like other distempers it is well to have it over and done with at the cost of a lengthy convalescence'.[22] The long-delayed Conference of Trade Union Executives, which was finally held in January 1927, endorsed the General Council's report on its handling of the strike by 2.8 million votes to a little over 1 million. Since the miners themselves disposed 800,000 votes, the result was a substantial victory for the General Council. There was much partisan bitterness between Thomas and the miners' leaders, but it was Citrine's cleverly pitched appeal which stirred the Conference as a whole. 'I hope the time will come when, instead of looking at whether the miners were right, we shall sit down and look at the thing objectively and see what are the defects. Until we do that, neither getting rid of your leaders nor delivering the head of Jimmy Thomas on a charger, will be of any avail... Neither the Miners' Federation nor the General Council can be held entirely blameless for what happened. I ask you to try to dismiss personalities as far as you can, and to look at this thing objectively and to say to yourselves, what was wrong? Could, in the circumstances, any other set of men have acted differently?' Few, apart from the miners, were prepared to answer affirmatively.

During 1927 Birkenhead and the other Tory hardliners gained two more conspicuous trophies to place beside the ruination of the miners. Diplomatic relations were broken off with Russia because of unsubstantiated charges of misconduct against the Soviet Trade Delegation in London and a Trade Union Bill designed to outlaw the sympathetic strike was presented to Parliament. The Bill also contained a clause providing that trade unionists who wished to pay the political levy of their union would have to 'contract-in' instead of 'contract-out' and was clearly meant to deprive the Labour party of funds. Both the party and the trade unions resented the Bill as a threat to their traditional rights and it was only forced through the Commons by means of the closure, imposed for the first time since 1921. 'Call all your meetings,' taunted Birkenhead, 'blow all your trumpets, make all your speeches, unfurl all your red flags—and when you have done it all, the Bill is going through Parliament.'[23] *
Its immediate effect was to reduce Labour party income by a quarter. Its second and more important effect, however, was to bind the industrial and political wings of the Labour movement much more closely together than at any time since the war. The failure of the General Strike put paid to the notion that the unions could 'go it alone'; the Government's vindictive Bill convinced them that the alliance with the Parliamentary Labour party had to be made to work and to endure.

The swing away from industrial action was also reflected in the series of informal talks between trade union leaders and influential employers, culminating in the establishment of a National Industrial Council through which both sides of industry could discuss their common problems. The Council achieved little of practical significance, but the fact that trade union leaders felt able to support it was, in itself, a measure of the isolation imposed on Left-wing militants

---

* In the midst of this controversy Peggy Thomas married. With a sublime lack of tact which no other Labour leader could have equalled, her devoted father invited many Tory notables to the wedding, including Baldwin, who signed the register.

in the wake of the General Strike. 'J.R.M. and Henderson and the Evolutionists,' noted Mrs Webb in October, 1928, 'have swept Communism and left-wingism out of the way, Maxton and Cook agitation has fizzled out and Liberalism shows little sign of being a powerful rival for progressive support. All's well for election purposes. Whether all is equally well for the business of government, if or when the L.P. gets into power, is another question.' All was not well for the business of government when Labour formed its second administration following the election of 1929. It had to rely once more upon the Liberals for support and was plunged almost immediately into the maelstrom created by the Wall Street Crash.

After two years of rising unemployment and financial chaos, MacDonald managed to manoeuvre himself into the leadership of a National Government with Tory and Liberal backing. Repudiating their former Labour colleagues, MacDonald, Thomas and Snowden joined Baldwin, Samuel, Reading and Simon on the flag-draped election hustings of 1931. The results were an unimagined triumph for the new saviour of Britain, whose allies now included not only Baldwin, but the Archbishop of Canterbury and the King himself.[24] National candidates had 556 seats in the new House, providing the Government with a majority of 497. The Labour party returned 46 members, of whom only Lansbury was a former Minister. 'In effect,' wrote Davidson on November 5, 'the British nation has done through the ballot box what Continental countries can only do by revolution. We have a Dictatorship ...The causes of the defeat of the Socialists were in the main the profound contempt, especially of the women electors, for the men who ran away from the crisis and would not face up to it; secondly a keen disgust of the trade unions, who had again tried to dictate, as they did in '26, to the Government of the day; and thirdly a well-grounded fear on the part of the working-class elector that his savings were not safe under the control of the Socialists.'[25]

On the day Davidson wrote this account to his Uncle William in South America, a distinguished group of trade union and Government representatives gathered at Golders Green Crematorium for the funeral of A. J. Cook, whose death had finally occurred, following a long illness, six days after MacDonald's electoral triumph. As the mourners emerged into the fog to the strains of the *Dead March,* the large crowd waiting outside sang the *Red Flag.*[26]

# Appendix I

After the meeting between the T.U.C. negotiators and the Prime Minister at Downing Street on 12 May 1926, the following documents were issued by the General Council:

*Sir Herbert Samuel's letter to the general council, dated 12 May*

As the outcome of the conversations which I have had with your committee, I attach a memorandum embodying the conclusions that have been reached. I have made it clear from the outset that I have been acting entirely on my own initiative, have received no authority from the Government, and can give no assurances on their behalf. I am of opinion that the proposals embodied in the memorandum are suitable for adoption and are likely to promote a settlement of the differences in the Coal Industry. I shall strongly recommend their acceptance by the Government when the negotiations are renewed.

*The reply sent by Arthur Pugh and Walter Citrine to Samuel, dated 12 May*

The General Council having carefully considered your letter of today and the memorandum attached to it, concurred in your opinion that it offers a basis on which the negotiations upon the conditions in the Coal Industry can be renewed. They are taking the necessary measures to terminate the General Strike relying upon the public assurances of the Prime Minister as to the steps that would follow. They assume that during the resumed negotiations the subsidy will be renewed and that the lock-out notices to the miners will be immediately withdrawn.

*The Samuel Memorandum*

1. The negotiations upon the conditions of the Coal Industry should be resumed, the subsidy being renewed for such reasonable period as may be required for that purpose.
2. Any negotiations are unlikely to be successful unless they provide for means of settling disputes in the industry other than conferences between the mine-owners and the miners alone. A National Wages

263

Board should, therefore, be established, which would include representatives of those two parties, with a neutral element and an independent chairman. The proposals in this direction tentatively made in the Report of the Royal Commission should be pressed and the powers of the proposed Board enlarged.

3. The parties to the Board should be entitled to raise before it any points they consider relevant to the issue under discussion, and the Board should be required to take such points into consideration.

4. There should be no revision of the previous wage rates unless there are sufficient assurances that the measures of re-organisation proposed by the Commission will be effectively adopted. A committee should be established as proposed by the Prime Minister, on which representatives of the men should be included, whose duty it should be to co-operate with the Government in the preparation of the legislative and administrative measures that are required. The same committee, or, alternatively, the National Wages Board, should assure itself that the necessary steps, so far as they relate to matters within the industry, are not being neglected, or unduly postponed.

5. After these points have been agreed and the Mines National Wages Board has considered every practicable means of meeting such immediate financial difficulties as exist, it may, if that course is found to be absolutely necessary, proceed to the preparation of a wage agreement.

6. Any such agreement should :
   (i)   If practicable, be on simpler lines than those hitherto followed.
   (ii)  Not adversely affect in any way the wages of the lowest-paid men.
   (iii) Fix reasonable figures below which the wage of no class of labour, for a normal customary week's work, should be reduced in any circumstances.
   (iv)  In the event of any new adjustments being made, should provide for the revision of such adjustments by the Wages Board from time to time if the facts warrant that course.

7. Measures should be adopted to prevent the recruitment of new workers, over the age of eighteen years, into the industry if unemployed miners are available.

8. Workers who are displaced as a consequence of the closing of uneconomic collieries should be provided for by:
   (i)  The transfer of such men as may be mobile, with the Government assistance that may be required, as recommended in the Report of the Royal Commission.
   (ii) The maintenance, for such period as may be fixed, of those who cannot be so transferred, and for whom alternative employment

264

cannot be found; this maintenance to comprise an addition to the existing rate of unemployment pay under the Unemployment Insurance Act, of such amount as may be agreed. A contribution should be made by the Treasury to cover the additional sums so disbursed. (iii) The rapid construction of new houses to accommodate transferred workers. The Trades Union Congress will facilitate this by consultation and co-operation with all those who are concerned.

# Appendix II

The Manifesto sent by the General Council on 12 May to the secretaries of all affiliated trade unions, trade councils and strike committees and reproduced in the *British Worker* on 12–13 May.

The General Council, through the magnificent support and solidarity of the trade union movement has obtained assurances that a settlement of the mining problem can be secured which justifies them in bringing the general stoppage to an end.

Conversations have been proceeding between the General Council representatives and Sir Herbert Samuel, chairman of the Coal Commission, who returned from Italy for the express purpose of offering his services to try to effect a settlement of the differences in the coal mining industry.

The Government has declared that under no circumstances could negotiations take place until the General Strike had been terminated, but the General Council feel as a result of the conversation with Sir Herbert Samuel and the proposals which are embodied in the correspondence and documents which are enclosed that sufficient assurances had been obtained as to the lines upon which a settlement could be reached to justify them in terminating the General Strike.

The General Council accordingly decided at their meeting today to terminate the general stoppage, in order that negotiations could be resumed to secure a settlement in the coal mining industry, free and unfettered from either strike or lock-out.

The General Council considered the practicability of securing a resumption of work by the members in dispute at a uniform time and date, but it was felt, having regard to the varied circumstances and practices in each industry, that it would be better for each executive council itself to make arrangements for the resumption of work of its own members. The following telegram was despatched to you today:

> General Council TUC have today declared General
> Strike terminated. Please instruct your members as
> to resuming work as soon as arrangements can be
> made. Letter follows.
>
> Pugh. Citrine.

Throughout the negotiations and during the whole of the stoppage, the General Council have declared that they have been fighting to protect the miners against an intolerable degradation of their standard of life and working conditions. It was with this object, and with this object alone, that the General Council assumed the grave responsibility of calling upon its affiliated organisations to unite in strike action to enforce the cancellation of the lock-out notices and the withdrawal of the new wages scale posted in the mining districts. No attack was at any time contemplated upon the established political institutions of the country, and it is a testimony to the loyalty and discipline of the movement that disorders have been practically unknown.

The unions that have maintained so resolutely and unitedly their generous and ungrudging support of the miners can be satisfied that an honourable understanding has been reached.

The General Council accept the consequences of their decision with a full sense of their responsibility not only to their own membership but to the nation at large. They have endeavoured throughout the crisis to conduct their case as industrial disputes have always been conducted by the British trades unions, without violence or aggression. The General Council feel in taking the last steps to bring the crisis to an end and that the trade union movement has given a demonstration to the world of discipline, unity and loyalty without parallel in the history of industrial disputes.

# *Appendix III*

On the morning of 12 May the T.U.C. Intelligence Committee submitted the following apprisals to the General Council:

GENERAL SURVEY

1. The Reports received from all quarters including those of the Labour M.P.s who have been on speaking tours, show a remarkable spirit in the country. At the same time there is evidence to show that there is a discernible leakage back to work, and it is not improbable that this will grow.
2. The numbers who are standing continue to grow. Every day adds to the number of idle factories and workshops.
3. Yesterday saw the arrest, or the appearance before the magistrates, of a considerable number of people engaged in the dispute. In Chesterfield, Birmingham, and London, for example, local strike leaders or pickets were arrested or brought to court. Even the chairman and vice-chairman of the Shoreditch Borough Council Lighting Committeee were threatened with arrest. It is clear from yesterday's events that the Government is becoming more aggressive and determined.
4. Little has been heard of any military movements yesterday, but the Government appears to be handling food supplies in increasing quantities.
5. The Government has endeavoured to impress the country with the improvement in railway facilities. The actual improvement, though real, is very small. The amount of goods, including food, being conveyed is very small. The Government is still relying on road transport and the supplies in the docks.
6. Though it is uncertain whether there is a real food shortage in any areas, there is an undoubted fear in many areas that food supplies are short. In some towns—for example, certain Midland towns—there is estimated to be two to three weeks' supply of staple foodstuffs.
7. In general, the situation is one in which we are holding our own. But the Government's organisation is improving, and its policy is gradually becoming more aggressive. Every day the intensity of the struggle will increase.
8. The flow of resolutions regarding the basis of a settlement continued

yesterday, and included a telegram from the Bishop of Salisbury conveying a resolution. Sir John Simon and other Liberal members tabled a motion in the House of Commons on the lines of the Archbishop's appeal. The growing desire for peace amongst the general public is shown by the large number of communications received from people who offer their services as mediators or suggest solutions of the miners' crisis.

SURVEY OF THE STRIKE POSITION as regards solidarity and the effect of the strike on workers not immediately engaged.

1. The reports to hand from local strike committees and independent observers indicate no real breach in the solidarity of the strike. The Government admitted this in its official communique on Monday evening, when it stated 'while there are many individual cases of strikers in various trades and services returning to work, the General Strike continues unabated throughout the whole country. The success of the authorities in maintaining the feeding and vital services of the people must not obscure the grave fact or its increasing wasteful consequences for all classes'. In other words, although the Government claims that the nation is able to maintain its life, with the assistance of improvised services, it does not claim that the nation is able to get on with its work. In yesterday morning's 10.00 a.m. wireless bulletin the B.B.C. stated that 'although there have been important defections from the ranks of the strikers, particularly among railwaymen, the main body still holds aloof'.

2. The Government and its supporters put forward a constantly recurring claim that a considerable number of railway workers are going back to work. For instance, *The Times* yesterday morning speaks of 'the steady return to duty of railway workers'. The 1.00 p.m. bulletin of the B.B.C. yesterday gave out the following : 'The L.N.E.R. states that their men are returning to work in good numbers and eight hundred resumed work Monday.'

The 10.00 a.m. bulletin yesterday stated : 'That throughout the West Riding a certain number of railwaymen were drifting back to work including some signalmen.'

Monday night's 7.00 p.m. bulletin claimed : 'That one fifth of the regular staff of the Railway Companies is at work.'

The reports coming in to this office do not confirm or explain the Government's claims. In many places, of course, the original response of the R.C.A. though good was not absolutely solid. Moreover, it should be remembered that though we are receiving reports from a large number of well organised industrial centres, the information to hand from rural districts is so slight as to be of no real value at all.

The R.C.A. originally reported that 50,000 of their 67,000 members were out.

Some of the reports with regard to railwaymen returning to work are clearly quite untrue. For instance, we have a message from Sittingbourne, dated 9 May, saying that 'rumours stating that railwaymen have returned to work here are entirely false. A few clerks have gone back and that is all'. The *Slough Observer* issued Monday evening stated that the local station master reported 'A steady flow of our men back to work', and this was broadcast over the wireless, according to a report from Slough (1 May). This steady flow consists only of one signalman and one porter (father and son) and one platform inspector.

It may be that the Government are making big claims on the basis of a staff consisting in the main of supervisory grades, clerks, and more or less isolated railwaymen in the rural areas. It may also be that they are including voluntary workers in their total.

3. As was stated in an earlier report there is a weakness so far as the printing trades are concerned. We have a number of reports indicating that newspapers either never stopped, or are re-appearing or are increasing the scope of their production.

4. A few reports have come in showing that in one or two places men have resumed work. Portsmouth, for instance, reports (10 May) that of 200 employees of the Tramway Committee who ceased work, over 100 reported back on Wednesday. A report from Southampton (10 May) states that 'odds and ends of men are dribbling back to work'. Kingston reports that two railway workers have gone back at Surbiton and Malden. Bristol states that a few have gone back but that they have been more than counter-balanced by the men brought out. At Bridgewater 1,000 brick and tile workers resumed work Monday, but they struck owing to the dismissal of nine men for refusing to load transport. The nine men have been re-instated and the 1,000 have therefore gone back. They will, no doubt, however, appear in any official figures that may be issued of men who have abandoned the General Strike. Birmingham reports that Cadbury's workers are wavering and that numbers are expected to go back on Tuesday. Wolverhampton reports that typographical men have gone back by persuasion of the editor.

The few reports of this kind that we have to hand are completely swamped by a large mass of messages indicating a solid position.

There is, however, evidence that a slight leakage is beginning to take place, which may, or may not, tend to spread. Rugby reports (11 May) a little weakness due to a return to work of a printer who was secretary of a Rugby Labour party. Reading reports wavering on the part of tramwaymen and other transport workers unsettled. There is no real evidence of wavering on the part of the trade unionist core of the strike, but the position on the fringes is probably not quite as firm as it was. This is due, no doubt, to various causes. The strike has now lasted eight days and propaganda against it has been insistent. The uncertainty of the printers and the reappearance of the newspapers may have had an effect. There are, moreover, a number of non-unionists on strike, who are not entitled to benefit. There have been difficulties, also, in some places owing to lack of co-ordination between local strike committees and the local bodies in control of the unions concerned. Many districts, moreover, have complained of the lack of reliable news and in isolated places the workers must have been without any source of information except the wireless. As a whole, the strike is perfectly solid but these elements of uncertainty cannot be altogether disregarded.

5. While there are no indications of any important tendency on the part of men on strike to resume work, many reports show that the strike is extending and the factories and workshops not directly involved are slowing down or shutting down. There have been a number of strikes on the part of men not originally called out, but who have in one way or another become involved in the dispute. Prescot, for instance, reported on the sixth instant, that Workers' Union and Brass and Metal Mechanics' Union have refused to work on blackleg power. Leeds reported on 10 May the complete stoppage of engineering firms. Other messages of the same kind could be quoted.

In the meantime many factories are stopping owing to shortage of fuel, shortage of raw material, lack of power, or inability to get their output transported. The Amalgamated Union of Upholsterers report 400 men shut out owing to factory closing down, these numbers increasing daily. Coventry reports most of the foundry workers out through closing of factories. Nelson reports that yarn for cotton mills is brought by road but the supplies are diminishing and mills are closing down. *The Times* yesterday morning states that in the Textile and Boot and Shoe industries work is gradually stopping because of the withdrawal of fuel and materials. Mr Pethick Lawrence reports from Leicester a gradual shutting down of factories as there is no work for them to do. It is so obvious, however, that this must be happening that the point scarcely needs elaborating.

It is worth noting that Mr Churchill in the House of Commons, Monday, referred to a possible shortage of paper. He said that it had become necessary to requisition provisionally all news print available which was adapted to presses employed by the Government newspaper. The increasing circulation of the Government newspaper was making very large demand on the limited supplies now available. On this point we have a report from Brighton saying that local stocks of paper cannot go very far and that the proprietors are admitting that they will have to close down soon. According to Mr Churchill arrangements are being made both for the manufacture and importation of further supplies.

# *Appendix IV*

The following report was made by the T.U.C. Intelligence Committee to the General Council shortly after the strike:

The Intelligence Committee appointed by the General Council consisted of: Mr A. B. Swales (Chairman), Mr R. B. Walker, and Mr Arthur Greenwood. The functions of the committee were two-fold.

1. It was its duty to make enquiries regarding the large number of rumours which were afloat during the stoppage.
2. To examine reports and information dealing with the General Strike situation, and to investigate special problems.

As regards the first point, the committee was able to disprove the truth of many of the rumours which were circulating, and to ascertain the real facts regarding others. The greater part of the committee's work, however, fell under the second head. The reports which began to flow in to the General Council did not contain information regarding many essential points. The committee, therefore, asked that reports should deal with certain specified points of fundamental importance which were set out. It also asked the Members of Parliament who were sent into the country during the week-end 7–10 May, to collect information regarding the matters on which light was needed.

The main points to which attention was specially directed were the following :

1. The numbers affected directly by the strike.
2. The numbers who during the progress of the strike became unemployed through the operation of the strike owing to lack of materials, coal shortage, transport difficulties etc.
3. Cases of a return to work on the part of workers who had been called out.
4. The real position with regard to transport and especially the transport of goods.
5. The situation regarding food.
6. The attitude of the police.
7. The movement of troops.
8. Particulars of arrest.

The material which passed through the hands of the committee included the following :

1. Reports of trade unions to their branches.
2. The reports of local strike committees and councils of action.
3. The reports of the general council's despatch riders.
4. The reports of Members of Parliament and other speakers.
5. Information received from members of the Labour movement.
6. Special investigations.
7. Miscellaneous letters, telegrams, etc.
8. Resolutions passed by local authorities, religious bodies, etc. in favour of the Archbishop's appeal.
9. Proposals for the settlement of the dispute.

Unfortunately, a good deal of the information which came to hand was too general or too undiscriminating to be of very much service. The actual situation from day to day would have been much clearer had all reports been submitted in a standardised form under clearly defined headings. Moreover, the reports which were received from certain areas were very few, and in consequence, it was impossible at any given time to be able to present a complete statement of the whole position.

Again, many of the reports had to be discounted to some extent. There was a disposition on the part of at least some of those who made the reports to paint the situation in a too favourable light.

The broad facts as to the development of events did, however, emerge from the large mass of material which passed through the hands of the committee. It is, of course, agreed that the response to the call was magnificent. Cases were reported from some districts that non-unionists had come out on strike with the unionists and that new members of unions had actually been enrolled. On the other hand, there were cases of men not having struck although they were called out by their unions. One of the remarkable features was the response made by the non-manual workers, more especially those on the railways and at the docks.

In addition to the groups called out at the beginning of the strike, unofficial action was taken by other workers in some areas, and men were called out in advance of any instructions from the general council.

The result of the cessation of work began to make itself felt upon the available volume of employment in a very few days. Before the end of the week in which the strike was called, reports were being received of the closing down of factories and workshops in consequence of a short-age of raw material or transport difficulties. In other places half time began to be worked in order to conserve coal supplies. The indirect stoppage due to the pressure of the first grades called out would undoubtedly have been greater had the organisation of the workers engaged in commercial road transport been stronger. In the cotton area, e.g. where both yarn and cloth is now normally transported by road, the strike made little difference during the early stages of the dispute. So far as can be gathered, the strangulation of industries and trade due to the strike increased steadily during the whole period of the stoppage, and reached its effective maximum on the last day of the stoppage. The calling out of further groups of workers could not have had as substantial an effect as would seem to have been the case, as numbers of those in the second group were already standing because of shortage of materials etc., and because in some places the men had already come out.

The workers directly involved in the dispute may be divided into three main groups :

1. Those who had experienced long stoppages, as for example, the miners and the dockers.
2. Those who had experience of strikes of a shorter duration, e.g. the railway workers.
3. Those who had not previously taken part in a strike, e.g. railway clerks, and other supervisory workers.

It became clear that solidarity could not be maintained for an indefinite period. As regards the dockers and miners there was no sign whatsoever of any drift back to work. As regards the second group, however, there were unmistakable signs of a drift back before the stoppage was brought to an end. This movement was also clearly visible in the case of the third group. By the time the strike was called off, it is beyond question that a movement back to work had begun. The numbers were not large relative to the total numbers on strike, and though each day the additional number of people who came to a standstill was much greater than the numbers who sought to return to work, it is clear that the drift back was sufficient to create serious perturbation before the strike was withdrawn.

The reasons for the cracks which began to appear may be summarised as follows :

1. As already indicated above, many workers engaged in the struggle had experienced only strikes of a limited duration or had never been on strike before.
2. The sight of an increasing amount of transport had a depressing effect.
3. The Government pledge of protection to workers who remained at or returned to work also had an effect.
4. Sir John Simon's speech also influenced a number of people.

5.  In some parts of the country the absence of intimation as to progress of affairs cannot be ignored.

It is, of course, impossible to assess the value of these various factors. One thing is certain, however, the display of force had no influence whatever in weakening the resistance of the workers.

The information which was obtained with regard to the transport of goods showed that during the first stages of the dispute the amount of goods traffic on the railways was negligible. As will be pointed out below, such traffic as developed before the end of the strike was devoted primarily to milk and vegetables. Consequently, those districts which did not normally rely upon motor transport for their raw materials and for the carriage of finished products found themselves, where stocks were low, in increasing difficulties. They were, moreover, unable to move finished products. It must be pointed out here, however, that one of the weak links in the chain was the inadequate organisation amongst commercial transport workers. The difficulties of organising commercial transport where only two or three men are employed by a business firm are obvious, and even where commercial transport workers were members of trade unions there were cases where they did not respond to the call. As regards passenger traffic, this was an unimportant factor in the struggle. Its gradual improvement did, no doubt, exert a psychological influence, but the mere transfer of people from place to place did nothing to assist the maintenance of production in the essential industries. In some towns the tramway and motor services were entirely suspended. In others, an attempt was made to carry on a skeleton or partial service. In a few areas, e.g. Maidstone, a full service was continued by regular employees. In London the direct intervention of the Government brought out on the roads a number of the older type of L.G.C. buses, and also a number of pirate buses. But even in London this traffic was concentrated in certain districts. A suburban passenger train service was established, but even at the end of the strike the number of suburban trains running was but a fraction of the normal and the number of steam trains very few.

The chief commercial traffic was that which carried foodstuffs, and though a portion of the milk supply was carried by rail, the greater part was conveyed by road. A certain amount of foodstuffs, almost entirely fresh vegetables, were carried on the railways. As regards London, the majority of the food entered by road under strong military escort accompanied by armoured cars and tanks. A certain amount also was brought from the docks, but the total amount of food actually made available each day was below the normal, and there are strong reasons for believing that the food supply in London occasioned the Government considerable anxiety. It is understood that the amount which could be made available was not sufficient for more than a very short time. In other parts of the country, however, such information as was available showed that the food supplies were adequate. This, however, does not apply to Newcastle, where food permits had been withdrawn, and where the only food entering the town was from the docks.

At the beginning of the struggle, the attitude of the regular police called for no comment. In many places, the relations between the police and the strikers were all that could be desired. In some towns the police and the strikers were on the friendliest of terms, football matches being arranged, and the police taking the initiative in promoting sports and entertainments. Towards the end of the first week, however, the reports which came to hand indicate some change in the attitude of the police. The police tended to become rather more rigorous and less conciliatory. No doubt, incidents had occurred, many of them resulting from the actions of hooligans quite unconnected with the strike, which led the police to adopt sterner measures, but it would not be surprising to learn that the Government was implicated in the more aggressive policy. The worst feature was the wholesale enrolment, especially in London, of special constables, many of whom were irresponsible persons likely to create trouble. They were, unfortunately, provocative, and it says much for the discipline of the movement that collisions between the strikers and the police were relatively infrequent. Speaking generally, the areas which relied entirely upon the local police without any other assistance, passed through the crisis without any serious untoward incidents. In Liverpool, for example, where large numbers of dockers and others were on strike, and where disturbances of the peace might easily have occurred, neither special constabulary nor military were employed in the town and order was maintained. The employment of special constables created a situation similar to that which prevailed in Dublin in the early days of the 'Black and Tans'. Though there are, of course, exceptions in most cases, so far as can be ascertained, where disturbances occurred they were the work of people who were not connected with the unions on strike.

The use of troops and naval ratings does not seem to have been as large as might have been expected. During the early days of the strike, there were fairly considerable movements of troops by road, troops from the southern area being transferred to the north and west, whilst it is believed that some bodies of soldiers from the north were transferred to the south. The troops were primarily used at the docks and for the transport of food. The naval ratings seem to have been chiefly employed for the maintenance of services, for example, electricity.

During the first two or three days of the strike, there did not appear to have been many arrests, but by the week-end arrests began to take

277

place, and in the last day or two of the stoppage, took place in considerable numbers. The four chief grounds of arrest were :

1. Irregular picketing.
2. Breaches of the peace.
3. Sedition.
4. Publication of false news.

As regards the first, the chief cases seem to have arisen from mass picketing, which developed into the stoppage of vehicles etc. Breaches of the peace were created by the attempts of people who were not pickets to hold up vehicles by the collection of large numbers of people and by precipitate action on the part of the police. The cases of sedition were mainly concerned with statements likely to create disaffection amongst the troops. The publication of false news was the cause of one or two cases of arrests of persons concerned with the publication of strike bulletins, as, for example, at Birmingham.

The general attitude of the independent section of the public towards the dispute may be gauged by the resolutions of religious organisations and local authorities, in general, support of the Archbishop's appeal. A good many local authorities and a very large number of churches and public meetings passed resolutions calling for :

1. The withdrawal of the General Strike.
2. The cancellation of the lock-out notices, the continuance of the subsidy and the maintenance of existing rates of wages pending negotiations on the lines of the Commission's Report.

A very large number of telegrams was received containing these resolutions, and similar telegrams would no doubt have been forwarded to the Prime Minister. As this body of opinion was representative of an intelligent public, it is curious that the Government should not have acted more in the spirit of the resolutions.

The general sympathy of the public with the miners, and the widespread desire to bring the dispute to an early and honourable end was illustrated by the large number of people who sent schemes for solving the difficulty and offered their services as mediators.

The general impressions left upon the committee by the material which passed through its hands may be briefly summarised :

1. In general the response was magnificent and the discipline of the rank-and-file remarkable.
2. But there were amongst the strikers considerable numbers who had either no experience or little experience of strikes, or who were unlikely to stand the strain of a long strike.
3. Though the publication of the *British Gazette* had little influence

on public opinion, the wireless and the newspapers which improved day by day as the strike proceeded, did exert some influence.

4. The Government was unnecessarily aggressive. As is shown by the movement of troops, the use of naval ratings, the enrolment of special constables, and the character of the *British Gazette*.

5. It is clear that a general strike requires a more elaborate organisation than can be improvised at the last moment. This is especially necessary in order to ensure the fullest contact with the strikers. This contact was undoubtedly defective largely because of inadequate local organisation.

As regards the post-strike situation, three factors are creating perturbation amongst the rank-and-file in the country:

1. The sudden calling off of the strike.
2. The slow return to work of many strikers and the fear of victimisation.
3. The present position of the miners.

So far as the first point is concerned, the impression in the country was that on the Tuesday evening before the end of the strike everything was 'going strong'. By midday on Wednesday the workers received the news that the strike was called off. This created bewilderment, and led in many places to the cry of 'sold again'. If the workers could be told in explicit terms that the decision to call off the strike was the culmination of some days of discussion, it would clear away the feeling that the withdrawal was a sudden decision to capitulate. Moreover, if there is a speedy settlement of the mining dispute on reasonable conditions, it can be argued that the miners have obtained better terms than they could have done had they fought alone, the general stoppage will be justified in the eyes of the strikers.

The fact that numbers of men have not yet been recalled to work and the petty attempts at victimisation which are occurring outside of the large industries which have concluded agreements are creating a spirit of unrest and dissatisfaction which must adversely affect the trade union movement.

The continuance of the mining stoppage after the withdrawal of the General Strike, coupled with the suddenness with which it appears to the rank-and-file the strike was called off, is certainly giving rise to the view that the miners have been 'let down'.

On these points it is necessary to clear up the attitude and position of the General Council.

In conclusion, it should be noted that a definite campaign is now in progress with the object of securing an alteration in the law relating to trade unions, and one case has been reported of a firm taking steps to sue a trade union for damages in respect of breach of contract on the part of members of the union employed by the firm.

The whole question of the present position of the trade union movement and the reaction upon it of the General Strike call for the fullest consideration by the General Council.

# References

*Chapter 1*

1. HAROLD NICOLSON : *King George the Fifth*, p. 403.
2. NICOLSON, p. 386.
3. ibid.
4. NICOLSON, p. 380.
5. NICOLSON, p. 403.
6. KEITH MIDDLEMAS and JOHN BARNES : *Baldwin, A Biography*, p. 97.
7. MIDDLEMAS and BARNES, p. 98.
8. KEITH FEILING : *Life of Neville Chamberlain*, p. 109.
9. For a full account of the Tory leadership crisis see Robert Rhodes James : *Memoirs of a Conservative: J. C. C. Davidson's Memoirs and Papers, 1910–37*, pp. 150–166.
10. MARGARET COLE : *Beatrice Webb's Diaries, 1924–32*, p. 15

*Chapter 2*

1. W. GALLACHER : *The Rolling of the Thunder*, pp. 39–40.
2. LORD CITRINE : *Men and Work*, p. 210.
3. WEBB, p. 116.
4. CITRINE, p. 77.
5. THOMAS JONES : *Whitehall Diary, Volume II, 1926–30*, p. 19.
6. G. M. YOUNG : *Stanley Baldwin*, pp. 94–96.
7. MIDDLEMAS and BARNES, p. 280.
8. MIDDLEMAS and BARNES, p. 281.
9. ROBERT RHODES JAMES : *Churchill: A Study in Failure, 1900–1939*, p. 184.
10. *Churchill: A Study in Failure, 1900–1939*, p. 153.
11. ibid.
12. ROBERT BOOTHBY : *I Fight to Live*, p. 40.
13. *Churchill: A Study in Failure*, pp. 162–163.
14. KINGSLEY MARTIN : *Father Figures*, p. 162.
15. CITRINE, p. 139.
16. MIDDLEMAS and BARNES, p. 387.
17. FEILING, p. 156.

18. NICOLSON, p. 415.
19. CITRINE, p. 142.


*Chapter 3*

1. Speaking at a Miners' Delegate Conference, 19 August 1925. Quoted by R. Page Arnot : *The Miners: Years of Struggle*, pp. 383–384.
2. *Manchester Guardian*, 4 August 1925.
3. WEBB, p. 61.
4. ALAN BULLOCK : *The Life and Times of Ernest Bevin, Volume I*, p. 260.
5. NICOLSON, pp. 415–416.
6. WEBB, p. 74.
7. *Lansbury's Labour Weekly*, 10 October 1925.
8. *Lansbury's Labour Weekly*, 24 October 1925.
9. *Sunday Worker*, 6 December 1925.
10. *Memoirs of a Conservative*, pp. 227–228.
11. *Memoirs of a Conservative*, pp. 179–180.
12. PRO : HO 45/12336.
13. *Workers' Weekly*, 2 October 1925.
14. ROBERT BENEWICK : *Political Violence and Public Order*, p. 35.
15. HAMILTON FYFE : *Behind the Scenes of the Great Strike*, p. 31.
16. GREGORY BLAXLAND : *J. H. Thomas: A Life for Unity*, p. 168.
17. J. H. THOMAS : *My Story*, p. 136.
18. *Memoirs of a Conservative*, p. 188.
19. CITRINE, pp. 146–153.
20. WEBB, pp. 147–149.
21. THOMAS, pp. 105–106.


*Chapter 4*

1. MIDDLEMAS and BARNES, p. 389.
2. VISCOUNT SAMUEL : *Memoirs*, pp. 183–184.
3. LORD BEVERIDGE : *Power and Influence*, p. 217.
4. JONES, pp. 2–3.
5. JONES, p. 3.
6. BEVERIDGE, p. 220.
7. Communist Party Statement on the Samuel Report, 19 March 1926.
8. L. J. MACFARLANE : *The British Communist Party: Its Origin and Development until 1929*, p. 155.
9. JAMES KLUGMANN : *History of the Communist Party of Great Britain, Volume II*, pp. 101–104.
10. MIDDLEMAS and BARNES, pp. 395–396.

11. Note from Tom Jones to Stanley Baldwin, 24 March 1926. Quoted in JONES, pp. 9–10.
12. JONES, p. 9.
13. MIDDLEMAS and BARNES, p. 397.
14. THOMAS, p. 114.
15. Report of General Council to Special Conference of Trade Union Executives, 20 January 1927, p. 6.
16. JONES, p. 11.
17. JONES, p. 13.


*Chapter 5*

1. JONES, p. 15.
2. MIDDLEMAS and BARNES, p. 399.
3. ARTHUR HORNER : *Incorrigible Rebel*, p. 72.
4. MARTIN, p. 162.
5. MIDDLEMAS and BARNES, p. 400.
6. JONES, pp. 17–18.
7. Report of Meeting Between the Prime Minister and the Miners' Federation, 23 April 1926.
8. JONES, pp. 19–20.
9. Report of Meeting Between the Prime Minister and the Miners' Federation, 26 April 1926.
10. R. PAGE ARNOT : *The General Strike*, p. 121.
11. MIDDLEMAS and BARNES, pp. 402–043.
12. Report of Meeting Between the Prime Minister and the T.U.C. Industrial Committee, 26 April 1926.
13. MIDDLEMAS and BARNES, p. 403.
14. Report of Meeting Between the Prime Minister and the T.U.C. Industrial Committee, 27 April 1926.
15. BULLOCK, p. 299.
16. ibid.
17. BULLOCK, pp. 295–296.
18. Report of Meeting Between the Prime Minister and the T.U.C. Industrial Committee, 28 April 1926.


*Chapter 6*

1. PRO : Cab 23/52, 19/26, 20/26.
2. Report of Special Conference of Trade Union Executives, 29 April–1 May 1926.
3. CITRINE, p. 155.
4. CITRINE, pp. 155–156.

5. Report of Meeting Between the Prime Minister and the T.U.C. Negotiating Committee, 29 April 1926.

6. CITRINE, p. 157.

7. Report of Meeting Between the Prime Minister and the T.U.C. Negotiating Committee, 30 April 1926.

8. FEILING, p. 157.

9. FYFE, p. 15.

10. CITRINE, p. 162.

11. THOMAS, p. 104.

12. WEBB, p. 99.

13. Report of Special Conference of Trade Union Executives, January 1927, p. 45. Hereafter referred to as *Report*, 1927.

14. CITRINE, p. 165.

15. JONES, p. 27.

16. THOMAS, p. 102.

17. JONES, p. 28.

18. BULLOCK, p. 309.

19. *Memoirs of a Conservative*, p. 231.

20. JONES, pp. 28–29.

21. BLAXLAND, p. 192.

22. Birkenhead's Memorandum on the Coal Negotiations. Quoted in JONES, pp. 34–36.

23. JONES, p. 33.

24. L. S. AMERY : *My Political Life, Volume II*, p. 483.

25. MIDDLEMAS and BARNES, p. 408.

26. MIDDLEMAS and BARNES, p. 409.

27. JONES, p. 33.

28. CITRINE, p. 172.

29. BULLOCK, p. 313.

30. CITRINE, p. 173.

31. NICOLSON, p. 417.

32. CITRINE, pp. 175–176; W. H. CROOK : *The General Strike*, p. 425.

33. THOMAS, p. 104.

## Chapter 7

1. PRO : CP 81 (26).

2. CROOK, pp. 393–399.

3. CROOK, p. 390.

4. R. W. POSTGATE, ELLEN WILKINSON and J. F. HORRABIN : *A Workers' History of the Great Strike*, p. 25.

5. CITRINE, p. 180.

## Chapter 8

1. JONES, p. 36.
2. *Memoirs of a Conservative*, p. 234.
3. R. J. MINNEY : *Viscount Southwood*, pp. 194–196.
4. LORD BEAVERBROOK : *Politicians and the War*, p. 284.
5. JULIAN SYMONS : *The General Strike*, p. 166.
6. GRAHAM GREENE : *A Sort of Life*, p. 172.
7. FYFE, p. 25.
8. FYFE, p. 33.
9. T.U.C. Files.
10. ibid.
11. T.U.C. Files; See also FENNER BROCKWAY : *Inside the Left*, pp. 189–190.
12. T.U.C. Files.
13. DUFF COOPER (VISCOUNT NORWICH) : *Old Men Forget*, p. 151.
14. Quoted by A. MASON : 'The Local Press and the General Strike : An Example from the North-East'. *Durham University Journal*, June 1969.
15. CITRINE, p. 177.

## Chapter 9

1. *Memoirs of a Conservative*, pp. 247–248.
2. J. C. W. REITH : *Into the Wind*, p. 108; See also Reith's article in *The Listener*, 7 December 1967.
3. REITH, p. 109.
4. G. K. A. BELL : *Randall Davidson, Archbishop of Canterbury*, p. 1307.
5. BELL, p. 1308.
6. BELL, p. 1309.
7. BELL, p. 1310; REITH, p. 110.
8. BELL, pp. 1311–1312.
9. FYFE, p. 59.
10. *Memoirs of a Conservative*, p. 249.
11. BELL, pp. 1313–1314.
12. ASA BRIGGS : *The History of Broadcasting in the United Kingdom, Volume I*, p. 376.
13. REITH, pp. 111–112.

## Chapter 10

Unless otherwise indicated references to local Strike Committees are based on information in POSTGATE *et al*; EMILE BURNS : *The General Strike, May 1926: Trades Councils in Action*; T.U.C. Files.

1. MACFARLANE, p. 155.
2. MACFARLANE, p. 158.
3. CITRINE, pp. 177–178.
4. *Manchester Evening Bulletin*, 8 May 1926.
5. LESLIE PAUL : *Angry Young Man*, p. 87.
6. J. P. M. MILLAR : 'The 1926 General Strike and the N.C.L.C.'. *Bulletin* of the Society for the Study of Labour History, Spring 1970.
7. MARGARET BONDFIELD : *A Life's Work*, p. 267.
8. Quoted in SYMONS, p. 69
9. Quoted in SYMONS, p. 174.
10. CROOK, p. 411.
11. ABE MOFFATT : *My Life With the Miners*, p. 45.
12. JONES, p. 38.

*Chapter 11*

1. *Workers' Weekly*, 11 December 1925.
2. *The Left Wing: Its Programme and Activities*. Issued by Greater London Left Wing.
3. JANE DEGRAS : *The Communist International, 1919–1943: Documents, Volume II*, pp. 262–265.
4. MACFARLANE, pp. 156–157.
5. KLUGMANN, p. 264.
6. MACFARLANE, p. 162.
7. Report of 8th Congress of CPGB, October 1926, pp. 6–11.
8. MACFARLANE, p. 164.
9. T.U.C. Files; KLUGMANN, p. 154; MACFARLANE, p. 165; RODERICK MARTIN : *Communism and the British Trade Unions, 1924–33*, p. 72.
10. KLUGMANN, p. 154; MACFARLANE, p. 165.
11. KLUGMANN, pp. 155–157.
12. MACFARLANE, pp. 305–307; See also DEGRAS, pp. 301–306; KLUGMANN, p. 197.
13. BOOTHBY, p. 81.
14. *An Acount of the Proceedings of the Northumberland and Durham General Council Joint Strike Committee*. A general summary of the Committee's work appears in BURNS, pp. 152–154 and a more detailed account in *The Miners: Years of Struggle*, pp. 436–443. For Page Arnot's activities in the region on behalf of the Communist party see *The General Strike in the North-East* (History Group of the Communist Party, 1961); KLUGMANN, pp. 162–163. Unless

otherwise indicated, references to the strike in the North-East are based upon these sources.

15. T.U.C. Files.
16. ibid.
17. A full report of the trial appeared in the *Newcastle Chronicle* on 23 May 1926 and the *Blaydon Courier* on 22 May 1926. Extensive extracts are quoted in *The General Strike in the North-East*, pp. 17–18; See also KLUGMANN, p. 169; ALLEN HUTT : *The Post-War History of the British Working Class*, pp. 162–163.

## Chapter 12

Unless otherwise indicated the account in this chapter is based on contemporary newspaper reports, T.U.C. Files and information given by BURNS and POSTGATE *et al.*

1. JONES, p. 55.
2. JOHN W. WHEELER-BENNETT : *John Anderson Viscount Waverley*, p. 106.
3. PAUL, pp.95–96.
4. *Memoirs of a Conservative*, pp. 251–252.
5. DUFF COOPER, p. 150.
6. *General Council Bulletin No. 4*, 7 May 1926.
7. LORD TEMPLEWOOD : *Nine Troubled Years*, p. 31.
8. WHEELER-BENNETT, p. 106.
9. Davidson to Irwin, 14 June 1926. Quoted in *Memoirs of a Conservative*, p. 243.
10. PRO : Cab 23/52, 25/26. Cab 27/260 ST (24) 15.
11. EARL WINTERTON : *Orders of the Day*, pp. 139–140.
12. LORD BRABAZON OF TARA : *The Brabazon Story*, p. 158.
13. *Memoirs of a Conservative*, p. 243.
14. BRABAZON, p. 159; See also *Memoirs of a Conservative*, p. 253.
15. GREENE, pp. 174–175.
16. *GK's Weekly*, 29 May 1926.
17. WINTERTON, p. 139.
18. R. K. MIDDLEMAS : *The Clydesiders: A Left Wing Struggle for Parliamentary Power*, p. 197.
19. *Workers' Weekly*, 22 October 1926.
20. SYMONS, pp. 112–113.
21. PAUL, pp. 91–102.

## Chapter 13

1. THE EARL OF OXFORD and ASQUITH : *Memories and Reflections, Volume II*, pp. 240–241.

2. DUFF COOPER, p. 148.

3. ROY DOUGLAS : *History of the Liberal Party, 1895–1970*, p. 193.

4. DOUGLAS, p. 194.

5. TREVOR WILSON : *The Downfall of the Liberal Party, 1914–1935*, pp. 355–356.

6. WILSON, p. 356.

7. ibid.

8. ibid.

9. OXFORD and ASQUITH, pp. 236–237.

10. Private information quoted in DOUGLAS, p. 197.

11. WEBB, p. 63.

12. WEBB, p. 69.

13. *Memoirs of a Conservative*, pp. 260–261.

14. SIR HENRY SLESSER : *Judgment Reserved*, p. 156.

15. *Yale Law Journal*, February 1927.

16. SLESSER cites the case of the Queen v. Cooper, 1842. See pp. 161–166.

17. OSBERT SITWELL : *Laughter in the Next Room*, p. 206.

18. SLESSER, p. 155.

19. MIDDLEMAS and BARNES, p. 413.

20. JONES, p. 47.

21. NICOLSON, p. 419.


*Chapter 14*

1. SAMUEL, p. 187.

2. BULLOCK, p. 323.

3. *Memoirs of a Conservative*, p. 250

4. BULLOCK, pp. 323–324.

5. CITRINE, p. 186.

6. JONES, pp. 39–40.

7. CITRINE, p. 186.

8. JONES, p. 42.

9. SITWELL, pp. 217–221.

10. WEBB, pp. 3–4.

11. SITWELL, p. 228.

12. CITRINE, p. 194.

13. Quoted in SYMONS, pp. 241–247.

14. HERBERT SMITH : *Report, 1927*, p. 19; A. J. COOK : *Report, 1927*, p. 34.

15. Quoted in CROOK, pp. 390–395.

16. SAMUEL, p. 190.

17. The acount of this meeting is based on HERBERT SMITH : *Report*,

*1927*, p. 19; BULLOCK, p. 329; CITRINE, pp. 198–199; COOK, pp. 20–21.

18. CITRINE, p. 197.
19. BULLOCK, p. 330.
20. BEN TURNER : *About Myself*, pp. 311–312.
21. CITRINE, p. 200.
22. BULLOCK, p. 330.
23. CITRINE, p.200.
24. BULLOCK, p. 330.
25. TURNER, p. 312.
26. SITWELL, p. 232.

*Chapter 15*

Unless otherwise indicated the account of how local Strike Committees reacted to the calling-off of the strike is based on T.U.C. Files and reports in BURNS and POSTGATE *et al.*

1. COOK, p. 22.
2. The Miners' notes of the meeting were read out by Cook at the Conference of Executives in January 1927. *Report, 1927*, p. 21. See also BULLOCK, p. 333; COOK, pp. 22–23.
3. JONES, p. 48.
4. BULLOCK, p. 334.
5. An official report of the meeting was issued from Downing Street on the evening of 12 May 1926. It is reproduced in full in SYMONS, pp. 235–240.
6. CITRINE, p. 202.
7. BULLOCK, p. 334.
8. MIDDLEMAS and BARNES, p. 416.
9. WILLIAM CAMP : *The Glittering Prizes*, p. 194.
10. JONES, p. 38.
11. TURNER, p. 312.
12. BULLOCK, p. 337.
13. SYMONS, p. 222.
14. BULLOCK, p. 337; CITRINE, p. 203.
15. PRO, Lab 27 No 9.
16. BULLOCK, p. 339.
17. POSTGATE *et al*, pp. 85–86.
18. HUTT, pp. 158–159.
19. British Library of Political and Economic Science.
20. BROCKWAY, p. 191.
21. PAUL, pp. 98–100.
22. WEBB, p. 98.

23. *Lansbury's Labour Weekly*, 22 May 1926.
24. JONES, p. 55.
25. ANGELA TUCKETT : *Up With All That's Down: A History of Swindon Trades Council*, p. 68.
26. JONES, pp. 55–56.
27. *British Worker*, 15 May.
28. JONES, p. 46.

Chapter 16

 1. MIDDLEMAS and BARNES, pp. 424–425.
 2. JONES, p. 60.
 3. JONES, pp. 60–61.
 4. NICOLSON, p. 421.
 5. *The Miners: Years of Struggle*, pp. 498 and 520.
 6. J. R. CLYNES : *Memoirs*, p. 91; CHARLES LOCH MOWAT : *Britain Between the Wars*, p. 335.
 7. F. A. IREMONGER : *William Temple*, pp. 337–343.
 8. *The Miners: Years of Struggle*, pp. 473–475.
 9. *The Miners: Years of Struggle*, pp. 475–476.
10. JONES, p. 68.
11. JONES, pp. 71–72.
12. JONES, p. 78.
13. *The Miners: Years of Struggle*, pp. 481–483; JONES, p. 78.
14. *Memoirs of a Conservative*, p. 255.
15. *Memoirs of a Conservative*, pp. 258–259.
16. *Memoirs of a Conservative*, p. 259.
17. *The Miners: Years of Struggle*, pp. 485–486.
18. JONES, pp. 79–80.
19. MIDDLEMAS and BARNES, p. 437.
20. CAMP, p. 194.
21. HUGH DALTON : *Call Back Yesterday*, p. 203.
22. WEBB, p. 93.
23. CAMP, p. 194.
24. MOWAT, p. 410; STEPHEN ROSKILL : *Hankey, Man of Secrets*, p. 569.
25. *Memoirs of a Conservative*, pp. 376–377.
26. *The Times*, 6 November 1931.

# Bibliography

*An Account of the Proceedings of the Northumberland and Durham General Council Joint Strike Committee.* Duplicated on behalf of the Council, May, 1926.

V. L. ALLEN, *Trade Unions and the Government.* Longmans Green, 1960.

L. S. AMERY, *My Political Life, Vol II.* Hutchinson, 1953.

R. PAGE ARNOT, *The General Strike.* Labour Research Department, 1926.

R. PAGE ARNOT, *The Miners: Years of Struggle.* Allen & Unwin, 1953.

R. PAGE ARNOT, *The Impact of the Russian Revolution in Britain.* Lawrence & Wishart, 1967.

LORD BEAVERBROOK, *The Decline and Fall of Lloyd George.* Collins, 1963.

LORD BEAVERBROOK, *Politicians and the War.* Oldbourne, 1959.

G. K. A. BELL, *Randall Davidson, Archbishop of Canterbury.* Oxford University Press, 1935.

ROBERT BENEWICK, *Political Violence and Public Order.* Allen Lane The Penguin Press, 1969.

ARNOLD BENNETT, *Journals, 1921–28.* Cassell, 1933.

ARNOLD BENNETT, *Letters to His Nephew.* Heinemann, 1936.

JOHN W. WHEELER-BENNETT, *John Anderson, Viscount Waverley.* Macmillan, 1962.

LORD BEVERIDGE, *Power and Influence.* Hodder & Stoughton, 1953.

GREGORY BLAXLAND, *J. H. Thomas: A Life for Unity.* Frederick Muller, 1964.

MARGARET BONDFIELD, *A Life's Work.* Hutchinson, 1949.

ROBERT BOOTHBY, *I Fight to Live.* Gollancz, 1947.

JOHN BOWLE, *Viscount Samuel.* Gollancz, 1957.

LORD BRABAZON OF TARA, *The Brabazon Story.* Heinemann, 1956.

ASA BRIGGS, *The History of Broadcasting in the United Kingdom, Vol I: The Birth of Broadcasting.* Oxford University Press, 1961.

FENNER BROCKWAY, *Inside the Left.* Allen & Unwin, 1942.

ALAN BULLOCK, *The Life and Times of Ernest Bevin, Vol I.* Heinemann, 1960.

EMILE BURNS, *The General Strike, May 1926: Trades Councils in Action.* Labour Research Department, 1926.

WILLIAM CAMP, *The Glittering Prizes: A Biographical Study of F. E. Smith, first Earl of Birkenhead.* Macgibbon & Kee, 1960.

LORD CITRINE, *Men and Work.* Hutchinson, 1964.

J. F. CLARKE and J. W. LEONARD, *The General Strike, 1926,* University of Newcastle Upon Tyne, Department of Education, 1971.

J. R. CLYNES, *Memoirs.* Hutchinson, 1937.

MARGARET COLE (editor), *Beatrice Webb's Diaries, 1924–1932.* Longmans Green, 1956.

A. J. COOK, *The Nine Days.* Co-operative Printing Society, 1926.

DUFF COOPER (Viscount Norwich), *Old Men Forget.* Hart-Davis, 1953.

JOHN CORBETT, *The Birmingham Trades Council, 1866–1966.* Lawrence & Wishart, 1966.

W. H. CROOK, *The General Strike.* Chapel Hill University of North Carolina Press, 1931.

COLIN CROSS, *Philip Snowden.* Barrie & Rockliff, 1966.

HUGH DALTON, *Call Back Yesterday.* Muller, 1953.

JANE DEGRAS (editor), *The Communist International: Documents, Vol. II 1923–1928.* Oxford University Press, 1960.

ROY DOUGLAS, *History of the Liberal Party, 1895–1970.* Sidgwick & Jackson, 1971.

G. G. EASTWOOD, *George Isaacs.* Odhams Press, 1952.

KEITH FEILING, *Life of Neville Chamberlain.* Macmillan, 1946.

HAMILTON FYFE, *Behind the Scenes of the Great Strike.* Labour Publishing Co., 1926.

W. GALLACHER, *The Rolling of the Thunder.* Lawrence & Wishart, 1947.

*The General Strike in the North-East.* Pamphlet No 22 issued in the summer of 1961 by the History Group of the British Communist Party.

W. R. GARSIDE, *The Durham Miners, 1919–1960.* Allen and Unwin, 1971.

GRAHAM GREENE, *A Sort of Life.* Bodley Head, 1971.

W. HANNINGTON, *Unemployed Struggles 1919–36.* Lawrence & Wishart, 1936.

LIDDELL HART, *Memoirs, Vol I.* Cassell, 1965.

ARTHUR HORNER, *Incorrigible Rebel.* MacGibbon & Kee, 1960.

ALAN HUTT, *The Post-War History of the British Working Class.* Gollancz, 1937.

F. A. IREMONGER, *William Temple.* Oxford University Press, 1948.

ROBERT RHODES JAMES, *Memoirs of a Conservative. J.C.C. Davidson's Memoirs and Papers, 1910–37.* Weidenfeld & Nicolson, 1969.

ROBERT RHODES JAMES, *Churchill, A Study in Failure, 1900–1939.* Weidenfeld & Nicolson, 1970.

WILLIAM JAMES, *The Eyes of the Navy.* Methuen, 1955.

ROY JENKINS, *Asquith.* Collins, 1964.

WALTER KENDALL, *The Revolutionary Movement in Britain, 1900–1921: The Origin of British Communism.* Weidenfeld & Nicolson, 1969.

J. M. KEYNES, *The Economic Consequences of Mr Churchill.* Hogarth Press, 1925.

JAMES KLUGMANN, *History of the Communist Party of Great Britain, Vol II: The General Strike, 1925–1926.* Lawrence & Wishart, 1969.

JACK LAWSON, *The Man in the Cloth Cap. The Life and Times of Herbert Smith.* Methuen, 1941.

L. J. MACFARLANE, *The British Communist Party. Its Origin and Development until 1929.* MacGibbon & Kee, 1966.

KINGSLEY MARTIN, *The British Public and the General Strike.* Hogarth Press, 1926.

KINGSLEY MARTIN, *Father Figures.* Hutchinson, 1966.

RODERICK MARTIN, *Communism and the British Trade Unions, 1924–1933. A Study of the National Minority Movement.* Clarendon Press, 1969.

A. MASON, *The Local Press and the General Strike: An Example from the North-East, Durham University Journal,* June, 1969.

A. MASON, *The Government and the General Strike, 1926. International Review of Social History,* XIV, 1969.

A. MASON, *The General Strike, Bulletin* of the Society for the Study of Labour History, 20, 1970.

A. MASON, *The General Strike in the North-East,* Hull University Press, 1970.

R. K. MIDDLEMAS (editor), *The Clydesiders, A Left Wing Struggle for Parliamentary Power.* Hutchinson, 1965.

R. K. MIDDLEMAS, *Thomas Jones. Whitehall Diary, Vol II. 1926–1930.* Oxford University Press, 1969.

R. K. MIDDLEMAS AND JOHN BARNES, *Baldwin: A Biography.* Weidenfeld & Nicolson, 1969.

R. J. MINNEY, *Viscount Southwood.* Odhams Press, 1954.

ABE MOFFATT, *My Life with the Miners.* Lawrence & Wishart, 1965.

C. L. MOWAT, *Britain Between the Wars, 1918–1940.* Methuen, 1955.

JOHN MURRAY, *The General Strike.* Lawrence & Wishart, 1951.

HAROLD NICOLSON, *Curzon: The Last Phase.* Constable, 1934.

HAROLD NICOLSON, *King George the Fifth. His Life and Reign.* Constable, 1952.

THE EARL OF OXFORD AND ASQUITH. *Memories and Reflections, Vol II.* Cassell, 1928.

JOHN PATON, *Left Turn.* Secker & Warburg, 1936.

LESLIE PAUL, *Angry Young Man.* Faber & Faber, 1951.

HENRY PELLING, *The British Communist Party. A Historical Profile.* Adam and Charles Black, 1958.

HENRY PELLING, *A History of British Trade Unionism.* Pelican Books, 1971.

RAYMOND POSTGATE AND OTHERS, *A Workers' History of the Great Strike.* Plebs League, 1927.

RAYMOND POSTGATE, *Life of George Lansbury.* Longmans Green, 1951.

J. C. W. REITH, *Into the Wind.* Hodder & Stoughton, 1949.

B. C. ROBERTS, *The Trades Union Congress.* Allen & Unwin, 1958.

STEPHEN ROSKILL, *Hankey, Man of Secrets.* Collins, 1972.

VISCOUNT SAMUEL, *Memoirs.* Cresset Press, 1945.

JOHN SIMON, *Three Speeches on the General Strike.* Macmillan, 1926.

OSBERT SITWELL, *Laughter in the Next Room.* Macmillan, 1949.

HENRY SLESSER, *Judgment Reserved.* Hutchinson, 1941.

PHILIP VISCOUNT SNOWDEN, *An Autobiography, Vol II.* Nicholson & Watson, 1934.

FRANCES STEVENSON (editor), *Lloyd George.* Hutchinson, 1971.

*Strike Nights in Printing House Square.* Privately printed, 1932.

JULIAN SYMONS, *The General Strike.* Cresset Press, 1957.

A. J. P. TAYLOR, *English History, 1914–1945.* Oxford University Press, 1965.

VISCOUNT TEMPLEWOOD, *Nine Troubled Years.* Collins, 1954.

J. H. THOMAS, *My Story.* Hutchinson, 1937.

ANGELA TUCKETT, *Up With All That's Down! A History of Swindon Trades Council.* The Quill Press, 1971.

BEN TURNER, *About Myself.* Cayme Press, 1930.

TREVOR WILSON, *The Downfall of the Liberal Party, 1914–1935.* Collins, 1966.

TREVOR WILSON (editor), *The Political Diaries of C. P. Scott, 1911–1928.* Collins, 1970.

EARL WINTERTON, *Orders of the Day.* Cassell, 1953.

G. M. YOUNG, *Stanley Baldwin.* Hart-Davis, 1952.

## CONTEMPORARY SOURCES

Cabinet papers.

Newspapers and periodicals: for the period of the strike particular use has been made of the *British Worker, Workers' Bulletin, British Gazette,* and Emergency Editions of the *Manchester Guardian.*

Reports of meetings between representatives of the Government, the T.U.C. and the Miners' Federation.

Strike Bulletins.

Reports of Special Trade Union Conferences on the Mining Crisis and the General Strike.

Statements by the Miners' Federation and the General Council on the Mining Crisis and the General Strike.

Report of the Samuel Commission on the Mining Industry, 1926.

Reports of the T.U.C. Intelligence Committee and local strike committees.

# Index

Index

# *Index*

All-Russian Trade Union Council, 172

Amalgamated Engineering Union, 118

Amery, Leopold, 109, 241

Ammon, C. G., 156, 277

Anderson, Sir John (Lord Waverley), 38, 40, 184, 188, 247

Anglo-Soviet Trade Union Conference, 31

Arlington, Dr, 193

Arnot, Robin Page, 173-5, 178; draws up 'Plan of Campaign', 173-4

Asquith, Herbert Henry, *later* 1st Earl of Oxford and Asquith, 2, 4-5, 18, 204-7

Associated Society of Locomotive Engineers and Firemen, 117, 222, 257

Astbury, Mr Justice, 209-11

Astor, Lord, 217n

Asylum Workers' Union, 98

Bailey, Sir Abe, 216

Baldwin, Stanley, 1st Earl of Bewdley, 1, 5-6, 11, 13, 24-7, 41, 45-6, 52, 57, 59-60, 64-9, 71-2, 76, 89, 101-2, 111-13, 129-30, 145, 149, 208, 211-13, 217-18, 221, 223, 231-6, 241, 246, 249, 252, 258, 262; forms Government, 4; tactical objectives, 7; pleads for ending of class bitterness, 17-18; attempts to win over public opinion, 29; capitilatuon of, 31-2; decision to launch political trial of Communists, 37-8; reactions to Samuel Report, 62-3; talks with union leaders regarding Samuel Report and proposed industrial action by miners, 72-88; meeting with Evan Williams and Mining Association, 83; meets Industrial Committee of Trades Union Congress, 83-4; meeting with TUC Negotiating Committee, 89; plot to overthrow, 103-4; recommends Chur-

chill as editor of *British Gazette*, 125; broadcasts on BBC, 150; reaffirms pledges to stand by volunteers, 241

Baldwin, Lady, 78-80

Balfour, Arthur, 1st Earl of, 6, 213

Barnston, Sir Harry, 179

Barrie, Sir J. M., 78

Beard, Jack, 225-6

Beatty, Lord, 191

Beaverbrook, Lord, 1, 126-7, 129-30

Benbow, William, 8

Beveridge, William Henry, 1st Baron, 52-6, 112

Bevin, Ernest, 12, 24, 32, 34-5, 86-7, 91-2, 97-8, 101, 103, 107, 110-11, 122-3, 134-5, 214-16, 223, 225-6, 230-2, 234-5, 242, 248: denounces Communists, 35; strained relations with J. H. Thomas, 35, 122; his contempt for Parliamentary Labour party, 92; plea for settlement by, 110; plans division of strikers, 120-1; his willingness to undertake administration of the General Strike, 121; his determination to impose discipline in TUC, 152-3; assists miners, 248

Birkenhead, Earl of (F. E. Smith), 6, 18, 72, 77, 94, 96, 101-6, 109n., 128, 131, 146, 188, 211, 218-19, 231, 233, 241, 247, 254n., 259, 261; proposed Formula, 106-7, 109, 110n.

Bishop's Memorandum, 252-3

Black Friday, 10, 18, 23, 38, 235

Black and Tans, 20, 195, 277

Bolton, Harry, 174, 179-81

Bondfield, Margaret, 45, 158

Boothby, Lord, 172, 255

Bourne, Cardinal, 147-8

Bowen, J. W., 135

*Bradford Worker*, 160

Bramley, Fred, 15–16, 33, 46
Brentford, William Joynson-Hicks, 1st
    Viscount, 29, 36–7, 40–1, 130, 132,
    145, 188–9, 193–4, 199n., 231, 241;
    his views on OMS, 41–2; grave
    doubts regarding his rationality, 188;
    appeal for special constables, 189
Bridgeman, W. C., 109, 231
*Bristol Bulletin*, 161
British Broadcasting Company (later)
    Corporation, 39, 158–9, 191, 220, 234,
    269; attitude during the General
    Strike, 143
British Empire Union, 26
British Fascists, 43–4
*British Gazette*, 109n., 124, 127, 129–32,
    134–6, 138–9, 141–2, 144, 147–8, 151,
    159, 164, 185, 187, 190–1, 193, 205,
    211, 215n.; production of, 127–9;
    circulation increase of, 129
*British Independent*, 148–9
*British Worker*, 110n., 130, 133, 135–8,
    142, 145, 147, 158, 160–1, 170, 172n.,
    176, 179, 189, 214, 217, 235–7, 244,
    266; increase in circulation of, 135–6
*Brixton Free Press*, 139
Brockway, Fenner, 20, 137, 237, 240, 243
Bromley, John, 44–5, 58, 66, 93, 217–18,
    222, 242, 256–7
Brown, Ernest, 168
Brown, Isobel, 200
Brown, W. J., 32, 92
Burnham, Viscount, 125

Cabinet: plans to employ troops, 90;
    decision to break off negotiations until
    the General Strike instructions with-
    drawn, 108
Cabinet Coal Committee, 61, 253, 255,
    258
Caird, David, 127, 131
*Cambridge Strike Bulletin*, 153
Campbell, J. R., 3; Campbell Case, 3, 11
*Cardiff Strike Bulletin*, 160
Carmichael, Duncan, 171
Cawdor, Lord, 37
Cave, Lord, 211
Cecil, Lord Robert, 6
Chamberlain, Sir Austen, 6–7, 18–20
Chamberlain, Neville, 7, 27, 94, 96, 104,
    212, 223n., 231, 249

Chartists, The, 8
Chesterton, G. K., 195
Churchill, Sir Winston, 6, 18–20, 27,
    29–30, 39, 46, 50, 94, 103–4, 112–13,
    119–20, 123–6, 129–30, 138, 145–7,
    149, 187–8, 211–12, 219, 223n., 239n.,
    241n., 250, 253–5, 257, 271–2; becomes
    Chancellor of the Exchequer, 19;
    announces Britain's return to gold
    standard, 20–1; his 1925 Budget, 21–2
    efforts to falsify effects of the General
    Strike, 130–1; interference in produc-
    tion and distribution of *British Gazette*,
    132; sympathy with strikers, 248
Churchill, Lady, 151
Citrine, Lord Walter, 15, 25, 27, 33, 46–51,
    55, 63, 88, 91, 93–5, 98, 102–3, 105–6,
    108, 110–12, 118–22, 134, 153, 218,
    225–7, 229, 233–4, 260, 263, 266;
    appearance and personality, 46n.,
    47n.; prepares Memorandum, 47–9;
    warns of serious crisis, 55; urges ETU
    to abandon strike plan, 118; offers
    cooperation, 119
Civil Constabulary Reserve, establish-
    ment of, 194
Clydeside Brigade, 11, 18
Clynes, J. R., 34, 68
Coal Merchants' Federation, 58
coal subsidy, renewing of, 54–5
coal trade: boom in, 10; revival in
    exports, 16
Cole, Margaret, 158
Collins, Sir Godfrey, 206
committees formed by TUC during the
    General Strike: Building, 121; Central
    London Strike, 171; Central Strike,
    122, 154, 157; Information, 157;
    Interviewing, 122; Joint Strike, 175–9;
    National Transport, 120–1, 163–4;
    Political, 122; Press and Publicity, 122,
    133, 135; Strike Organisation, 121;
    reaction by, to ending of strike, 236
Communist Party (British), 2–3, 13–14,
    33, 36–7, 43; wooing of Labour
    movement by, 13; reaction to Samuel
    Report, 58; activities of, 167–9;
    domination of councils by, 171;
    increased membership, 260
Connolly, Martin, 179, 182
Cook, Arthur James, 14–16, 24–5, 27,

31–4, 36, 48–50, 53–6, 58–9, 62–3, 66, 68–73, 75, 84, 93, 96, 99–102, 106–7, 111, 201, 217, 221–2, 225, 230–1, 245–6, 248, 252, 254, 257–8, 260, 262; elected Secretary of Miners' Federation, 14–16; appearance and character, 15; power of, 15; refusal to see King George V, 25; makes revolutionary speech, 32; makes misleading statement regarding Co-operative Movement, 48; slanging match with J. H. Thomas, 48; declares opposition to wage cuts, 58; pleads cause in Brussels, 70; his ideas on crisis, 84; makes embarrassing speech, 93; demands inclusion in talks, 217; death, 262; Works, *The Nine Days*, 230q., 245q.

Cooper, Alfred Duff, Viscount Norwich, 141, 187, 193, 205, 209, 241

*Co-operative News*, 137

Co-operative Printing Society, 137–8

Co-operative Publishing Society, 137

Co-operative Societies, 47

Co-operative Union, 48–50

Co-operative Wholesale Society, 138, 164–6, 178; urges retail societies to withhold striker's credits, 164–5

Cope, Sir Alfred, 68, 72

Copock, Richard, 119

Cramp, Charles, 35, 42, 98, 242

Cromer, Evelyn, 1st Earl of, 212–13

Cunliffe-Lister, Sir Philip, *later* Lord Swinton, 191

Curzon, 1st Marquess, 4, 7

*Daily Chronicle*, 142, 207n.

*Daily Express*, 109, 126–7, 129, 140

*Daily Herald*, 30, 32, 41, 43, 48, 80, 96, 98, 114, 129, 133–5, 138, 145

*Daily Mail*, 83–4, 108–9, 118, 125–6, 133; unofficial dispute on, 108–12; Continental, 139

*Daily News*, 19, 142, 207n.

*Daily Telegraph*, 80, 125

Dalton, Hugh, *later* Lord Dalton, 260

Davidson, J. C. C., 7n., 13, 37–40, 42, 45, 59, 90, 104, 117, 126–32, 139, 144–50, 187–8, 208n., 211, 215n., 234, 256, 262; creates nucleus of emergency organisation, 38–9; in charge of Government

publicity, 90, 125–32; brings BBC under his control, 144–5

Davidson, Randall, Archbishop of Canterbury, 131, 145–8, 262

Davies, David, 53

Davies, Selwyn, 226–7

Dawes Plan, 33

Dawson, A. W., 137–8, 176, 180

Dawson, Geoffrey, 130

docks: impact of the General Strike in, 118; reopening of, 190–1

Duckham, Sir Arthur, 17

Duff, Patrick, 256

Dukes, Charles, 152

Dunnico, Rev. Herbert, 208n.

Dutt, R. P., 60

*Economist, The*, 260

Edwards, Ebby, 174

Eight Hours Bill, 248–50, 256

Electrical Power Engineers' Association, 119

Electrical Trades Union, 23, 46, 118

Elias, J. S., 126

Elliott, Walter, 213

Elvin, H. H., 201–2

Emergency Powers Act, 40, 115, 134; prosecutions under, 199–200

*Emergency Strike Bulletin*, 140

Engels, Friedrich, 244; Works, *The Condition of the Working Class in England*, 245q.

*English Review*, 247

essential goods, non-interruption in movement of, 119

*Evening News*, 118

*Evening Standard*, 118

Eyres-Monsell, Bolton, 103, 213, 233

Fascism(ts), 42–3, 195

Fenn, Mrs Anderson, 251

Ferguson, Aitken, 168

financial losses through the General Strike, 259–60

Flynn, Charles, 174–7, 179

food permits, 162–4

food shortages, threatened, 190

Foster, Ferguson, 174

Foundry Workers, 23

Fraser, Sir Malcolm, 127, 132

Fyfe, Hamilton, 96, 133–5, 147, 172n., 183, 194, 223n., 225n., 243

Gainford, Lord, 219
Gaitskell, Hugh, 158
Gardiner, A. G., 19
Garvin, J. L., 82
George V, King, 2–5, 7, 11, 27, 45, 95, 97, 109, 113, 132, 212–13, 231n., 250, 262; his opposition to class warfare, 5; signs Emergency Proclamation, 97
Gibbs, Sir Philip, 143, 183
*Gloucester Strike Bulletin*, 160
Goldbeater's Trade Society, 121
Goodhart, A. L., 210
Government: preparations for the General Strike, 115–16; appeal for volunteers, 116–17; attack on regarding suppression of Anglican and Free Church appeal on BBC, 147; rift with Church, 149; immense prestige gained, 244; presents scheme for settlement, 246; reaction to coal-owners attitude, 247; formula for negotioation presented, 254–5; modification of formula, 256
Gower, Sir Patrick, 103, 226, 256
Granet, Sir Guy, 242n.
Greene, Graham, 130, 140, 194
Greenwood, Arthur, 273
Grey, Sir Edward, *later* Viscount, 151, 204–6
Griffiths, Ben, 37
Grigg, P. C., 132

Hailsham, Douglas, 1st Viscount, 43, 110n., 211
Hall, Admiral Sir Reginald (Blinker), 45, 128
Hankey, Maurice, 1st Baron, 26, 39, 42, 78, 82, 103–4, 114
Hardie, Keir, 15
Hardinge of Penshurst, 1st Baron, 41, 44, 247
Hardinge, Rt. Hon. Sir Arthur, 44
Hayday, Arthur, 45
Hayes, J. H., 208n.
Henderson, Arthur, 11–12, 93–4, 113, 122, 135, 204, 262
Henderson, Hubert, 22

Hendon, *Cricklewood and Golders Green Gazette*, 139
Hicks, George, 34, 36, 44, 59, 236
Hoare, Sir Samuel, *later* Lord Templewood, *see* Templewood, Samuel Gurney Hoare, 1st Viscount
Hodges, Frank, 9–10, 14, 25, 39, 47n., 66, 69–70, 72, 249
Hogg, Sir Douglas, 43, 110n., 211, *see also* Hailsham, Douglas, 1st Viscount
Hopkinson, Austin, 247
Horne, Sir Robert, 112
Horner, Arthur, 71
Horrabin, J. F., 158
House of Commons debate regarding threatened general strike, 111–13

Illegal Strikes Bill: produced, 212; deferment of, 213
Industrial Alliance, 23, 44
Inkpin, Albert, 36
International Federation of Trade Unions, 14, 31
Iron and Steel Trades Confederation, 23, 34
Irwin, Lord, later Edward Frederick Lindley Wood, 1st Earl of Halifax, 144, 233, 259
Isaacs, George, 108

Jackson, Tommy, 169
Jellicoe, John, 1st Earl, 41
Johnstone, 201
Jones, Tom, 53–4, 61, 64–7, 69, 72–4, 76–80, 84, 103–5, 107, 112, 124, 211–14, 217n., 221, 223, 233, 241n., 252, 254–5, 258; appointed secretary of Cabinet Coal Committee, 61; relations with Prime Minister, 78–9
Joynson-Hicks, Sir William, *see* Brentford, William Joynson-Hicks, 1st Viscount

*Kensington Strike Bulletin*, 161
Keynes, John Maynard, 1st Baron, 20–1, 23, 78
Kipling, Rudyard, 7, 66
Kirkwood, David, 199n., 200n.

Labour party, rift in, 30–1
Labour Research Department, 173, 175

300

Lane-Fox, Colonel G. R., 61, 146–7, 231, 250n., 256

Lansbury, George, 3, 31, 33, 36–7, 58–9, 167, 208, 257, 262

*Lansbury's Bulletin*, 160–1, 229

*Lansbury's Labour Weekly*, 244

Laski, Harold J., 206, 241, 246

Law, Andrew Bonar, 4–7, 19

Lawrence, General Sir Herbert, 52, 54, 112

Lawrence, Maud, 78

Lawther, Will, 173, 175, 179–81

Lee, Sir Kenneth, 52, 54

legality of the General Strike questioned, 209–10

Leggett, Frederick, 111

Leon, Daniel de, 8

Lichfield, Bishop of, 252

Lindsay, A. D., 148

Lloyd, Lieutenant-General Sir Francis, 41

Lloyd George of Dwyfor, David, 1st Earl, 5–6, 9–10, 16, 19, 30, 38, 40, 53, 77, 80, 85, 101, 113, 124, 131, 203–9, 248, 250; Coalition premiership of, 6; normalises Anglo-Russian relations, 9; orders immediate return of mines to private ownership, 16; ambitions, 19; blamed for instigating crisis, 77; scathing attack on by Prime Minister, 113; rupture with Lord Oxford and Asquith, 205–8; blames Government for starting the General Strike, 206; refusal to intervene in 1921 coal crisis, 248

Lodge, Sir Oliver, 144

London Haulage Committee, 116

London Society of Compositors, 127, 139

Londonderry, Charles Stewart, 7th Marquess of, 68, 219

Long, Sidney, 127

Loyalists, 44

*Luton News*, 139

Lytton, 2nd Earl of, 1

MacDonald, James Ramsay, 2–5, 11–12, 20, 30, 33–8, 58, 66–8, 92, 94, 99–100, 111–14, 124, 134, 146, 149, 203–4, 208–9, 217, 230, 233n., 249, 254–7, 262; his precipitate handling of Bolsheviks, 2–3; unpopularity of by Labour party, 11; loss of prestige, 31; intense hatred of Ernest Bevin, 32, 35; requests making personal broadcast, 149–50; as leader of National Government, 262

Maintenance of Order Corps, 156

*Manchester Evening Bulletin*, 124

*Manchester Guardian*, 1, 142, 242

*Manchester Guardian Bulletin*, 166, 183, 186, 193, 217

Mann, Tom, 8, 14, 59–60

Marlowe, Thomas, 108–9

Marshall, Rev. H., 214

Martin, Kingsley, 71, 142, 198

Mary, Queen, 25

mass picketing, 163, 185–6

Maude, Colonel, 140

Maxton, James, 3, 31, 33, 260, 262

Meath, Earl of, 193–4

Melchett, Alfred Mond, Baron, 74

Milbanke, Sir John 'Buffles', 193

Military precautions effected, 116

Millar, J. P. M., 155–6, 158–9, 163, 165

Miners' Federation of Great Britain, 9, 14, 23–4, 27–8, 47–9, 56, 58, 61, 64, 73, 75, 77, 90, 100, 227, 230, 249, 251, 259, 261

Miners' International, 66, 69–70, 249

Miners' Minority Movement, 64, 71, 155, 253, 257

Miners' Relief Fund, 250n.

mines, lock-out in, 9

Mining Association of Great Britain, 27–9, 53–4, 58, 63, 65, 72–4, 83, 85, 93, 255, 257

mining industry, progressive decline of, 18

Mitchell-Thompson, Sir William, 39, 42, 104, 215

Moffatt, Abe, 163

Mond, Sir Alfred, *see* Melchett, Alfred Mond, Baron

Montgomery, Sir Kerr, 177

Moon, R. S., 177

Moore, T. F., 140

Moore-Brabazon, Colonel, *later* Lord Brabazon, 191–2

*Morning Post*, 52, 80, 125–8, 131–2, 208n.

Mosley, Sir Oswald, 43

Mountbatten, Lady Louis, 140

Munro, Major, 116
Munro, Captain Gordon, 144
Murphy, J. T., 169–70
Murray, Professor Gilbert, 149
Murray, A. C., 203
Murray, Gladstone, 144

*Nation*, 78
National Appeal Tribunal, 258
National Citizens' Union, 26
National Confederation of Employers' Organisations, 258
National Conference of Action, 59–60
National Congress of Action, 60
National Fascisti, 43, 113
National Federation of Building Trades Operatives, 119
National Fuel and Power Committee, 56
National Hands off Russia Committee, 14
National Industrial Council, establishment of, 261
National Liberal Federation, 207
National Mining Board proposed, 107, 110
National Minority Movement, 14, 33, 36, 59–60, 92, 167–8, 260; Conference of Action, 153, 168
National Union of Railwaymen, 10, 12, 34–5, 42, 44–5, 98, 117, 121, 236, 242, 260
National Wages Board, 56, 77, 216, 224, 246–7, 264
negotiations restarted to end the General Strike, 215–27
*Newcastle Chronicle*, 141
*Newcastle Journal*, 141, 177
*New Republic*, 204
*New Statesman*, 78, 124, 142
New York *Herald-Tribune*, 238
*News of the World*, 126
Newspaper Proprietors' Association, 126
Nimmo, Sir Adam, 58, 65, 76
Norman, Baron Montagu, 212
*Northern Echo*, 141
*Northern Light*, 160, 176, 180–1
Northumberland, Duke of, 52–3, 126
Norwood, Rev. Dr F. W., 148

*Observer, The*, 82
Organisation for the Maintenance of Supplies, 40–2, 44, 95, 116, 118–19,
177, 179, 247–8; Labour reaction to, 42

Palmer, Sir Alfred, 181–2
Partridge, James, 197
Paterson, James, 116
Paton, John, 115; Works, *Left Turn*, 115q.
Paul, Leslie, 237, 239, 243
Paul, William, 185
peace manifesto on BBC and reactions to, 145–8
permits, problem of, 176–8
*Philadelphia Evening Bulletin*, 143, 183
Pole, Sir Felix, 242n.
police; role of in the General Strike, 188–9, 197; methods adopted by, 198–9
Pollitt, Harry, 14, 36, 43, 59, 169
Pollitt, Marjorie, 169, 260
Pollock, Sir Frederick, 210
Postgate, Raymond, 167; Works, *Life of George Lansbury*, 167q.
Poulton, E. L., 135–6
power, non-interference with by TUC General Council, 118–19
*Preston Strike News*, 161
printing unions, calling out of, 127–42
public transport, paralysis of, 117–18
Pugh, Arthur, 34, 44, 74, 79–80, 84–5, 88, 90, 93, 96, 101, 105–6, 108, 110, 134, 221–2, 224, 230, 233, 238–9, 257, 263, 266; announces termination of strike, 231
Purcell, Alf, 13–14, 27, 34, 59, 87, 97, 121–2, 230
Purves, Miss, 251

Quaile, Mary, 25, 101

Radek, Karl, 172–3
*Radio Times*, 143–4
Railway Clerks' Association, 81, 117, 222n., 236
Reading, Rufus Daniel, 1st Marquess of, 123, 219, 221, 223, 227, 262
Red Friday, 29–30, 32, 37, 40, 46, 58, 60, 90, 115, 155, 168, 170
Red International of Labour Unions, 14
Red Letter Election, 1924, 7, 10
Reith, John Charles, 1st Baron, 143–6, 149–51

Relief Committee, 252
Richardson, W. P., 100, 111, 221
Rickett, Cecil, 116
Riddell, George Allardice, 1st Baron, 126
Robson, W. A., 198
Rogers, James, 175
Rothermere, Harold, 1st Viscount, 142
Royal Commission for mining industry, setting-up of, 16–17, 49–50
rumours, spread of, 187
Rutland, 9th Duke of, 193

Saklatvala, Shapurji, 59, 200
Samuel, Herbert Louis, 1st Viscount, 52, 57–8, 215–24, 234, 237, 246, 262–3, 266; Memorandum, 224, 230, 235, 246, 263–5
Samuel Commission, 52–5: Report of, 55–8, 90, 110, 219, 249, 253–4; reactions to and criticisms of, 58–67, 69–70
Sankey, John, 1st Viscount, 15–17
Sankey Commission and Report, 51n., 75, 85
Scarborough, Major-General Lord, 41
Scott, C. P., 142, 203
security forces, expansion of, 189–90, 193–4
Segrave, Major, 215
Seven Hours Act, 76, 84, 107, 246, 249
Shaw, George Bernard, 36, 43
Sheffield Forward, 159
Sheffield Telegraph, 159
Simon, John Allsebrook, Viscount, 203, 206, 208–11, 215, 262, 269
Sitwell, Sir Osbert, 210, 219–20; Works, Triple Fugue, 219q.
Slesser, Sir Henry, 208n., 209–11
Slough Observer, 270
Smillie, Robert, 31, 39, 245
Smith, Sir Allen, 217
Smith, Herbert, 24–5, 28, 30–1, 49–50, 53–6, 62, 68–70, 75, 80, 89, 94–6, 99–100, 102–3, 111, 217–18, 220–2, 224, 230, 246, 248, 253–4, 257; bluntness of, 24; pleads cause in Brussels, 70; obstinate refusal to negotiate over wages, 80; willingness to accept Samuel Report, 99; demands inclusion in talks, 217; obstinacy of, 257
Snowden, Philip, 1st Viscount, 11, 21,

208, 241, 262
Snowden, Viscountess, 114, 208n., 219
Somerville, John, 150
Soviet Trade Delegation, 261
speeches during the General Strike, incautious, 200–1
Spender, J. A., 219
St. Pancras Bulletin, 161–2
Stamfordham, Lord, 2, 4n., 34, 132, 213, 250
Stamp, Sir Josiah, 25
Star, 118, 142
Steel-Maitland, Sir Arthur, 55, 61–2, 65, 69, 72, 77, 81, 85–6, 101–2, 105, 112–13, 218, 231, 233n., 246–7, 256
Stevenson, Frances (Dowager Countess Lloyd George), 203–4
Stewart, Bob, 169
Streatham News, 139
strike bulletins, production of, 158–62
Strike News, (Preston), 160
Strike Organisation Committee, 121
strikers: increasing violence by, 180–2, 185–6, 192–3; relations with police, 183–5, 197; rioting by, 185–7; reaction to strike call, 215n.
Sunday Express, 140
Sunday News, 142
Sunday Times, 139, 141
Sunday Worker, 36
Supply and Transport Committee, 38, 40, 42, 90, 145, 184, 187, 190, 231, 247
Swales, Alonzo, 13–14, 33–5, 44, 81, 93, 101, 105, 223, 273
syndicalism, 8, 12, 14, 186

Talbot, Dame Meriel, 78
Tarbit, James, 176
Tariff Election, 1923, 7, 18, 204
Tawney, R. H., 24n., 53
telegrams, censorship of, 201
Temple, Dr, 252
Templewood, Samuel Gurney Hoare, 1st Viscount, 187–8, 241
Tennyson, Hon. Lionel, 193
Thomas, J. H., 10, 12, 14, 31, 33–5, 42, 44–6, 48–50, 55, 63–4, 66, 71–2, 80–1, 83–9, 91–8, 101–3, 105–7, 109n., 112, 120–2, 150, 203–4, 215–17, 219–20, 223, 225–7, 230–2, 236, 242–3, 261–2; as social climber, 12; bad feelings with

Ernest Bevin, 35, 87; slanging match with Arthur Cook, 48; warns Prime Minister of serious consequences if formula not found, 80–1; opposes Ernest Bevin's strategy, 120–1; urges TUC General Council to negotiate, 215; announces end of the General Strike, 227; loses popularity, 243; bitterness between miners' leaders and, 260

Thomas, Peggy, 261n.

Tillett, Ben, 45, 89, 93

*Times, The*, 41, 80, 114, 124, 130, 139–42, 148, 192, 269, 271; arson attempts at, 140–1

Tinker, Joe, 137

Tomsky, Michael, 33

*Tottenham Strike Bulletin*, 228

Trade Disputes Act, 1906, 67, 209–10

Trade Unions: alienation of leaders, 12; resurgence of militancy in, 18; refusal to co-operate with trades councils, 153–5; slump in membership of, 260

Trades Union Congress, 9, 24, 56–8, 60, 64, 77, 79, 81, 83, 93, 101–9, 116, 121, 136–7, 145, 151, 154, 157, 163–5, 170, 172, 174, 178–9, 195, 198–9, 201–2, 205, 209, 216–18, 221–3, 227, 230–3, 236, 239, 243, 246, 248, 256, 259, 263, 265; decision to call general strike, 98–101; Manifesto, 266

Trades Union Congress General Council, 24–5, 30–1, 33–4, 36, 44–6, 48–50, 60, 64, 86–8, 90, 97–8, 100–12, 117–22, 124, 130, 133–5, 138, 145, 152–3, 155, 162–3, 172–3, 215, 217, 220–7, 229–30, 234–6, 237–41, 243, 246, 249, 250n., 251, 257, 260, 266–7; strike communique, 120–1; boycott of BBC by, 149; calls off strike, 202; adopts Samuel Memorandum, 224; failure to guard against wages and working conditions assault, 238; strike committees anger with, 239–43, 248; refusal to impose embargo on coal-handling, 251; Committees, Industrial (later) Negotiating, 44–51, 55, 60, 63–4, 66, 74, 78–83, 85–8, 92–6, 101, 105, 123; Intelligence, 139, 142, 160, 180, 195, 197, 222n., 230, 240, 268; appraisals, 268–72; report of to

General Council, 273–80; Negotiating, 89, 122, 215–17, 221; Ways and Means, 87, 97

transport, limitation of running of, 117–18

Triple Alliance, 8–10, 14

Trotsky, Lev Davidovitch, 168–9, 172

Turner, Ben, 134, 225n., 230, 234

Tweed, Colonel, 207n.

Typographical Association, 136–8, 159–60, 176

Usher, George, 129

Varley, Frank, 50

Walkden, Arthur, 45, 81–2, 236, 242

Walker, R. B., 273

Wall Street Crash, 262

Warwick, Dowager Countess of, 36

Warwickshire Miners' Association, 166

Webb, Mrs Beatrice, 11, 13, 15, 31, 33, 35–6, 45, 46n., 52, 114, 143, 204–5, 208, 219n., 239, 244, 249, 251, 257, 260

Webb, Sidney, Baron Passfield, 11, 16, 208

Wedgwood, Josiah, 39, 198

Weir, Lord, 77

*Westminster Gazette*, 142, 207n., 219

*Westminster Worker*, 161, 163

Westwood, Joseph, 208n.

Wheatley, John, 33

White, James, 174–6

*Wigan Strike Bulletin*, 159–60

Wigram, Clive, 51

Wilkinson, Ellen, 143–4, 158, 211

Williams, Evan, 27, 53–4, 65, 73–7, 83, 85, 246–7, 253, 255–8

Williams, Robert, 133–4, 208n., 259

Williams-Drummond, Colonel F. Dudley 37

Willingdon, Lady, 78

Wilson, Edward, 181

Wilson, Havelock, 209

Wilson, Sir Horace, 65, 69, 77–9, 86, 102–3, 106, 111, 231, 233n., 256

Wimborne, Lord, 219, 221, 223, 226–7

Wimborne, Lady, 219

Winterton, Edward Turnour, 6th Earl, 1, 190, 194

Wise, E. F., 214

Wood, Sir Kingsley, 176–7, 179, 182
*Workers' Bulletin*, 169–70, 200
*Workers' Chronicle*, 175
*Workers' Daily*, 169, 200
Workers' Defence Corps, 155
*Workers' Record*, 140
*Workers' Searchlight*, 176
Workers' Vigilant Corps, 156
*Workers' Weekly*, 2–3, 28, 36, 60, 169

Worthington-Evans, Sir Laming, 72, 231, 235
Wrexham Committee, 42
Wright, W., 195–6

Young, G. M., 130
Young Communist League, 36, 178

Zinoviev, Gregory, 3, 167–8; Zinoviev Letter, 10–11, 108